PLINY

NATURAL HISTORY

III

LCL 353

PLINY

NATURAL HISTORY

BOOKS VIII–XI

WITH AN ENGLISH TRANSLATION BY

H. RACKHAM

HARVARD UNIVERSITY PRESS

CAMBRIDGE, MASSACHUSETTS

LONDON, ENGLAND

First published 1940
Reprinted 1947, 1955, 1967
Second edition 1983
Reprinted 1997

LOEB CLASSICAL LIBRARY® is a registered trademark
of the President and Fellows of Harvard College

ISBN 0-674-99389-6

Printed in Great Britain by St Edmundsbury Press Ltd,
Bury St Edmunds, Suffolk, on acid-free paper.
Bound by Hunter & Foulis Ltd, Edinburgh, Scotland.

CONTENTS

PREFACE TO SECOND EDITION

THE first edition of this volume prompted the ichthyologist Alfred C. Andrews of the University of Miami to compile and send in a large number of corrections (chiefly of identifications of fishes in Book IX). When therefore in 1963 Professor E. H. Warmington composed the Index of Fishes which occupies pages 585–596 of the eighth volume of the Loeb Pliny, these corrections were duly incorporated, and in this second edition of volume III they now appear in their proper place against the Latin text. The Loeb Classical Library again acknowledges its indebtedness to Professor Andrews.

The volume would be incomplete without a reference to D'Arcy Thompson's splendid *Glossaries*, and these with other books which will provide researchers with bibliographies and other relevant information may here be mentioned.

Editions:
  C. Mayhoff, Bibliotheca Teubneriana, Leipzig 1892–1909.
  The Budé Pliny (1950–1981) is now complete, and includes: *Histoire naturelle, Livre VIII*, ed. A. Ernout, Paris 1952; *Histoire naturelle, Livre IX*, ed. E. de Saint-Denis, Paris 1955; *Histoire naturelle, Livre X*, ed. E. de Saint-Denis, Paris

1961; *Histoire naturelle, Livre XI*, ed. E. de Saint-Denis, Paris 1947.

The Tusculum Pliny (vol. I, 1973) edited by Roderich König with the collaboration of Gerhard Winkler, is still in progress, but Books VIII and IX have already appeared, Heimeran Verlag, Munich, 1976 and 1980.

General:

H. le Bonniec, *Bibliographie de l'Histoire naturelle de Pline l'Ancien*, Paris 1946.

Otto Schneider, *Index*, Hildesheim 1967 (reprint of volumes 7 and 8 of Julius Sillig's edition, 1857 and 1858).

Zoological:

M. J. Cotte, *Poissons et animaux aquatiques au temps de Pline: commentaires sur le Livre IX de l'Histoire naturelle de Pline*, Paris 1945.

O. Keller, *Die antike Tierwelt*, 2 vols, Leipzig 1909, 1913.

Helmut Leitner, *Zoologische Terminologie beim Älteren Plinius*, Hildesheim 1972.

J. Pollard, *Birds in Greek Life and Myth*, London 1977.

E. de Saint-Denis, *Le vocabulaire des animaux marins en latin classique*, Paris 1947.

D'Arcy Wentworth Thompson, *A Glossary of Greek Birds*, London 1936.

D.Arcy Wentworth Thompson, *A Glossary of Greek Fishes*, London 1947.

New Haven, 1983   G. P. G.

NOTE ON NOMENCLATURE

In identifying the zoological species described in this volume I am indebted for aid to my friend and colleague Mr. J. T. Saunders, who has gone through the whole and given me the modern equivalents of the Latin names; although he warns me that in a good many cases the identification is doubtful.

There are consequently some discrepancies between the nomenclature in the translation here and that used in Book I, the Table of Contents. Pliny presumably compiled it after completing the rest of the work; but as editorial exigencies precluded the postponement of Volume I of this translation till the others were finished, I had to be content, for Book I, with the renderings given in Lewis and Short or in Bostock and Riley's translation.

H. R.

INTRODUCTION

THIS volume contains Books VIII–XI of Pliny's
Naturalis Historia; their subject is Zoology.

The detailed contents will be found in Pliny's
own outline of his work, which, with lists of the
authorities used for each Book, constitutes Book I;
for Books VIII–XI see Volume I, pp. 40-64, of this
edition.

Book VIII deals with various mammals, wild and
domesticated; and among them are introduced
snakes, crocodiles and lizards.

Book IX treats aquatic species, including Nereids,
Tritons and the sea-serpent. There are considerable
passages on their economic aspects—the use of fish
as food, pearls, dyes obtained from fish, and on their
physiology, sensory and reproductive.

Book X. Ornithology: hawks trained for fowling;
birds of evil omen; domestication of birds for food;
talking birds; reproduction. Appendix on other
viviparous species, passing on to animals in general
—their methods of reproduction, senses, nutrition,
friendship and hostility between different species,
sleep.

Book XI. Insects, their physiology and habits—
especially bees, silk-worms, spiders. Classification
of animals by varieties of bodily structure—animal
and human physiology.

PLINII: NATURALIS HISTORIA

LIBER VIII

I. Ad reliqua transeamus animalia et primum terrestria.

Maximum est elephans proximumque humanis sensibus, quippe intellectus illis sermonis patrii et imperiorum obedientia, officiorum quae didicere memoria, amoris et gloriae voluptas, immo vero quae etiam in homine rara, probitas, prudentia, aequitas, religio quoque siderum solisque ac lunae
2 veneratio. auctores sunt in Mauretaniae saltibus ad quendam amnem cui nomen est Amilo nitescente luna nova greges eorum descendere ibique se purificantes sollemniter aqua circumspergi atque ita salutato sidere in silvas reverti vitulorum fatigatos
3 prae se ferentes. alienae quoque religionis intellectu creduntur maria transituri non ante naves conscendere quam invitati rectoris iureiurando de reditu. visique sunt fessi aegritudine (quando et illas moles infestant morbi) herbas supini in caelum iacientes,

PLINY: NATURAL HISTORY

BOOK VIII

I. Let us pass to the rest of the animals, and first those that live on land.

The largest land animal is the elephant, and it is the nearest to man in intelligence: it understands the language of its country and obeys orders, remembers duties that it has been taught, is pleased by affection and by marks of honour, nay more it possesses virtues rare even in man, honesty, wisdom, justice, also respect for the stars and reverence for the sun and moon. Authorities state that in the forests of Mauretania, when the new moon is shining, herds of elephants go down to a river named Amilo and there perform a ritual of purification, sprinkling themselves with water, and after thus paying their respects to the moon return to the woods carrying before them those of their calves who are tired. They are also believed to understand the obligations of another's religion in so far as to refuse to embark on board ships when going overseas before they are lured on by the mahout's sworn promise in regard to their return. And they have been seen when exhausted by suffering (as even those vast frames are attacked by diseases) to lie on their backs and throw grass up to the heaven,

3

veluti tellure precibus allegata. nam quod ad docilitatem attinet regem adorant, genua submittunt, coronas porrigunt. Indis arant minores, quos appellant nothos.

4 II. Romae iuncti primum subiere currum Pompei Magni Africano triumpho, quod prius India victa triumphante Libero patre memoratur. Procilius negat potuisse Pompei triumpho iunctos egredi porta. Germanici Caesaris munere gladiatorio quosdam etiam inconditos meatus[1] edidere saltantium 5 modo. vulgare erat per auras arma iacere non auferentibus ventis atque inter se gladiatorios congressus edere aut lascivienti pyrriche conludere. postea et per funes incessere, lecticis etiam ferentes quaterni singulos puerperas imitantes, plenisque homine tricliniis accubitum iere per lectos ita libratis 6 vestigiis ne quis potantium attingeretur. III. Certum est unum tardioris ingenii in accipiendis quae tradebantur saepius castigatum verberibus eadem illa meditantem noctu repertum. mirum et adversis quidem funibus subire, sed maxime[2] regredi,[3] utique pronis. Mucianus iii consul auctor est aliquem ex his et litterarum ductus Graecarum didicisse solitumque perscribere eius linguae verbis:

[1] v.l. motus.
[2] maxime hic Mayhoff: post mirum.
[3] v.l. regredi magis.

as though deputing the earth to support their prayers. Indeed so far as concerns docility, they do homage to their king by kneeling before him and proffering garlands. The Indians employ the smaller breed, *Its domestication in India.* which they call the bastard elephant, for ploughing.

II. At Rome they were first used in harness to *Elephants used at Rome for shows.* draw the chariot of Pompey the Great in his African triumph, as they are recorded to have been used before when Father Liber went in triumph after his conquest of India. Procilius states that at Pompey's triumph the team of elephants were unable to pass out through the gate. At the gladiatorial show given by Germanicus Caesar some even performed clumsy movements in figures, like dancers. It was a common display for them to hurl weapons through the air without the wind making them swerve, and to perform gladiatorial matches with one another or to play together in a sportive war-dance. Subsequently they even walked on tight-ropes, four at a time actually carrying in a litter one that pretended to be a lady lying-in; and walked among the couches in dining-rooms full of people to take their places among the guests, planting their steps carefully so as not to touch any of the drinking party.

III. It is known that one elephant which was rather *Instances of their intelligence.* slow-witted in understanding instructions given to it and had been punished with repeated beatings, was found in the night practising the same. It is surprising that they can even climb up ropes, but especially that they can come down them again, at all events when they are stretched at a slope. Mucianus who was three times consul states that one elephant actually learnt the shapes of the Greek letters, and used to write out in words of that language : ' I myself

'Ipse ego haec scripsi et spolia Celtica dicavi,' item- .
que se vidente Puteolis, cum advecti e nave egredi
cogerentur, territos spatio pontis procul a continente
porrecti, ut sese longinquitatis aestimatione fallerent,
aversos retrorsus isse.

7 IV. Praedam ipsi in se expetendam sciunt solam
esse in armis suis quae Iuba cornua appellat, Herodotus tanto antiquior et consuetudo melius dentes;
quamobrem deciduos casu aliquo vel senecta defodi-
unt. hoc solum ebur est: cetero et in his quoque
quae corpus intexit vilitas ossea; quamquam nuper
ossa etiam in laminas secari coepere paenuria, etenim
rara amplitudo iam dentium praeterquam ex India
reperitur, cetera in nostro orbe cessere luxuriae.
8 dentium candore intellegitur iuventa. circa hos
beluis summa cura: alterius mucroni parcunt ne sit
proeliis hebes, alterius operario usu fodiunt radices,
inpellunt moles; circumventique a venantibus primos
constituunt quibus sint minumi, ne tanti proelium
putetur, postea fessi inpactos arbori frangunt praeda-
que se redimunt.

9 V. Mirum in plerisque animalium scire quare

---

a III. 97.

wrote this and dedicated these spoils won from the Celts;' and also that he personally had seen elephants that, when having been brought by sea to Pozzuoli they were made to walk off the ship, were frightened by the length of the gangway stretching a long way out from the land and turned round and went backwards, so as to cheat themselves in their estimation of the distance.

IV. They themselves know that the only thing in them that makes desirable plunder is in their weapons which Juba calls 'horns,' but which the author so greatly his senior, Herodotus,[a] and also common usage better term 'tusks;' consequently when these fall off owing to some accident or to age they bury them in the ground. The tusk alone is of ivory: otherwise even in these animals too the skeleton forming the framework of the body is common bone; albeit recently owing to our poverty even the bones have begun to be cut into layers, inasmuch as an ample supply of tusks is now rarely obtained except from India, all the rest in our world having succumbed to luxury. A young elephant is known by the whiteness of its tusks. The beasts take the greatest care of them; they spare the point of one so that it may not be blunt for fighting and use the other as an implement for digging roots and thrusting massive objects forward; and when surrounded by a party of hunters they post those with the smallest tusks in front, so that it may be thought not worth while to fight them, and afterwards when exhausted they break their tusks by dashing them against a tree and ransom themselves at the price of the desired booty.

Elephant tusks used for ivory.

V. It is remarkable in the case of most animals

petantur, sed et fere [1] cuncta quid caveant. elephans
homine obvio forte in solitudine et simpliciter
oberrante clemens placidusque etiam demonstrare
viam traditur, idem vestigio hominis animadverso
prius quam homine intremescere insidiarum metu,
subsistere olfactu,[2] circumspectare, iras proflare,
nec calcare sed erutum proxumo tradere, illum
sequenti, simili nuntio usque ad extremum, tunc
agmen circumagi et reverti aciemque dirigi: adeo
omnium odori durare virus illud, maiore ex parte ne
10 nudorum quidem pedum. sic et tigris, etiam feris
ceteris truculenta atque ipsa elephanti quoque
spernens vestigia, hominis viso transferre dicitur protinus catulos—quonam modo agnito, ubi ante conspecto illo quem timet? etenim tales silvas minime
frequentari certum est. sane mirentur ipsam vestigii
raritatem; sed unde sciunt timendum esse? immo
vero cur vel ipsius conspectum paveant tanto
viribus, magnitudine, velocitate praestantiores? nimi-
rum haec est natura rerum, haec potentia eius,
saevissimas ferarum maximasque numquam vidisse
quod debeant timere et statim intellegere cum sit
timendum.

<hr>

[1] *Salm.*: et per.   [2] *v.l.* ab olfactu.

that they know why they are hunted, but also that *Elephant's* almost all know what they must beware of. It is said *fear of hunters.* that when an elephant accidentally meets a human being who is merely wandering across its track in a solitary place it is good-tempered and peaceful and will actually show the way; but that when on the other hand it notices a man's footprint before it sees the man himself it begins to tremble in fear of an ambush, stops to sniff the scent, gazes round, trumpets angrily, and avoids treading on the footprint but digs it up and passes it to the next elephant, and that one to the following, and on to the last of all with a similar message, and then the column wheels round and retires and a battle line is formed: since the smell in question lasts to be scented by them all, though in the majority of cases it is not even the smell of bare feet. Similarly a tigress also, it is said, even though savage to all other animals and herself scorning the footprints even of an elephant, when she sees the track of a human being at once carries her cubs elsewhere—though how has she recognized or where has she seen before the person that she fears? For it is certain that such forests are very little frequented. Granted that no doubt they may be surprised by the mere rarity of the print; but how do they know that it is something to be afraid of? Indeed there is a further point, why should they dread even the sight of a man himself when they excel him so greatly in strength, size and speed? Doubtless it is Nature's law and shows her power, that the fiercest and largest wild beasts may have never seen a thing that they ought to fear and yet understand immediately when they have to fear it.

11   Elephanti gregatim semper ingrediuntur; ducit agmen maximus natu, cogit aetate proximus. amnem transituri minimos praemittunt, ne maiorum ingressu atterente alveum crescat gurgitis altitudo. Antipater auctor est duos Antiocho regi in bellicis usibus celebres etiam cognominibus fuisse; etenim novere ea. certe Cato, cum inperatorum nomina annalibus detraxerit, elephantum[1] qui fortissime proeliatus esset in Punica acie Syrum tradidit vocatum altero dente mutilato.

12 Antiocho vadum fluminis experienti renuit Aiax, alioqui dux agminis semper; tum pronuntiatum eius fore pricipatum qui transisset, ausumque Patroclum ob id phaleris argenteis, quo maxime gaudent, et reliquo omni primatu donavit. ille qui notabatur inedia mortem ignominiae praetulit; mirus namque pudor est, victusque vocem fugit victoris, terram ac

13 verbenas porrigit. pudore numquam nisi in abdito coeunt, mas quinquennis, femina decennis; initur autem biennio quinis, ut ferunt, cuiusque anni diebus nec amplius, sexto perfunduntur amne, non ante reduces ad agmen. nec adulteria novere, nullave propter feminas inter se proelia ceteris animalibus

---

[1] *Rackham*: eum.

---

[a] The term is used of branches of bay, olive and other trees used for ritual purposes.

Elephants always travel in a herd; the oldest *Its intel-* leads the column and the next oldest brings up the *ligence,* rear. When going to ford a river they put the *moral sense and affection.* smallest in front, so that the bottom may not be worn away by the tread of the larger ones, thus increasing the depth of the water. Antipater states that two elephants employed for military purposes by King Antiochus were known to the public even by name; indeed they know their own names. It is a fact that Cato, although he has removed the names of military commanders from his *Annals,* has recorded that the elephant in the Carthaginian army that was the bravest in battle was called the Syrian, and that it had one broken tusk. When Antiochus was trying to ford a river his elephant Ajax refused, though on other occasions it always led the line; thereupon Antiochus issued an announcement that the elephant that crossed should have the leading place and he rewarded Patroclus, who made the venture, with the gift of silver harness, an elephant's greatest delight, and with every other mark of leadership. The one disgraced preferred death by starvation to humiliation; for the elephant has a remarkable sense of shame, and when defeated shrinks from the voice of its conqueror, and offers him earth and foliage.[a] Owing to their modesty, elephants never mate except in secret, the male at the age of five and the female at ten; and mating takes place for two years, on five days, so it is said, of each year and not more; and on the sixth day they give themselves a shower-bath in a river, not returning to the herd before. Adultery is unknown among them, or any of the fighting for females that is so disastrous to the other animals—though not because

pernicialia, nec quia desit illis amoris vis, namque
traditur unus amasse quandam in Aegypto corallas
vendentem ac (ne quis volgariter electam putet)
mire gratam Aristophani celeberrimo in arte gramma-
14 tica, alius Menandrum Syracusanum incipientis
iuventae in exercitu Ptolomaei, desiderium eius, quotiens non videret, inedia testatus. et unguentariam
quandam dilectam Iuba tradit. omnium amoris fuere
argumenta gaudium ad conspectum blanditiaeque
inconditae, stipesque quas populus dedisset servatae
et in sinum effusae. nec mirum esse amorem quibus
15 sit memoria. idem namque tradit agnitum in senecta
multos post annos qui rector in iuventa fuisset; idem
divinationem quandam iustitiae, cum Bocchus rex
triginta elephantis totidem in quos saevire instituerat
stipitibus adligatos obiecisset, procursantibus inter
eos qui lacesserent, nec[1] potuisse effici ut crudelitatis
alienae ministerio fungerentur.
16 VI. Elephantos Italia primum vidit Pyrri regis
bello et boves Lucas appellavit in Lucanis viso anno
urbis CCCCLXXIV,[2] Roma autem in triumpho v[3]
annis ad superiorem numerum additis, eadem pluri-
mos anno DII victoria L. Metelli pontificis in Sicilia

---

[1] v.l. non.   [2] Rackham: CCCCLXXII.
    [3] Rackham: VII.

---

[a] The MS. reading erroneously gives the date of Pyrrhus's
invasion as A.U.C. 472, 282 B.C., and so it puts the triumph
of M'Curius Dentatus after defeating Pyrrhus at Beneventum
(A.U.C. 479, 275 B.C.) seven years later.

they are devoid of strong affection, for it is reported that one elephant in Egypt fell in love with a girl who was selling flowers, and (that nobody may think that it was a vulgar choice) who was a remarkable favourite of the very celebrated scholar Aristophanes; and another elephant is said to have fallen in love with a young soldier in Ptolemy's army, a Syracusan named Menander, and whenever it did not see him to have shown its longing for him by refusing food. Also Juba records a girl selling scent who was loved by an elephant. In all these cases the animals showed their affection by their delight at the sight of the object and their clumsy gestures of endearment, and by keeping the branches given to them by the public and showering them in the loved one's lap. Nor is it surprising that animals possessing memory are also capable of affection. For the same writer records a case of an elephant's recognizing many years later in old age a man who had been its mahout in its youth, and also an instance of a sort of insight into justice, when King Bocchus tied to stakes thirty elephants which he intended to punish and exposed them to a herd of the same number, men running out among them to provoke them to the attack, and it proved impossible to make them perform the service of ministering to another's cruelty.

VI. Italy saw elephants for the first time in the war with King Pyrrhus, and called them Lucan oxen because they were seen in Lucania, 280 *a* B.C.; but Rome first saw them at a date five years later, in a triumph, and also a very large number that were captured from the Carthaginians in Sicily by the victory of the pontiff Lucius Metellus, 252 B.C.

First appearance of elephants in Italy.

13

de Poenis captos. CXLII fuere aut, ut quidam, CXL
travecti ratibus quas doliorum consertis ordinibus
17 inposuerat. Verrius eos pugnasse in circo inter-
fectosque iaculis tradit, paenuria consilii, quoniam
neque ali placuisset neque donari regibus; L. Piso
inductos dumtaxat in circum atque, ut contemptus
eorum incresceret, ab operariis hastas praepilatas
habentibus per circum totum actos. nec quid deinde
iis factum sit auctores explicant qui non putant
interfectos.

18   VII. Clara est unius e Romanis dimicatio adversus elephantum, cum Hannibal captivos nostros
dimicare inter sese coegisset. namque unum qui
supererat obiecit elephanto, et ille, dimitti pactus si
interemisset, solus in harena congressus magno
Poenorum dolore confecit. Hannibal, cum famam
eius dimicationis contemptum adlaturam beluis
intellegeret, equites misit qui abeuntem interficerent.
proboscidem eorum facillime amputari Pyrri proelio-
19 rum experimentis patuit. Romae pugnasse Fenestella
tradit primum omnium in circo Claudi Pulchri
aedilitate curuli M. Antonio A. Postumio coss. anno
urbis DCLV, item post annos viginti Lucullorum
20 aedilitate curuli adversus tauros. Pompei quoque

---

a 55 B.C.

There were 142 of them, or by some accounts 140, and they had been brought over on rafts that Metellus constructed by laying decks on rows of casks lashed together. Verrius records that they fought in the Circus and were killed with javelins, because it was not known what use to make of them, as it had been decided not to keep them nor to present them to native kings; Lucius Piso says that they were merely led into the Circus, and in order to increase the contempt felt for them were driven all round it by attendants carrying spears with a button on the point. The authorities who do not think that they were killed do not explain what was done with them afterwards.

VII. There is a famous story of one of the Romans fighting single-handed against an elephant, on the occasion when Hannibal had compelled his prisoners from our army to fight duels with one another. For he pitted one survivor against an elephant, and this man, having secured a promise of his freedom if he killed the animal, met it single-handed in the arena and much to the chagrin of the Carthaginians dispatched it. Hannibal realized that reports of this encounter would bring the animals into contempt, so he sent horsemen to kill the man as he was departing. Experiences in our battles with Pyrrhus made it clear that it is very easy to lop off an elephant's trunk. Fenestella states that the first elephant fought in the circus at Rome in the curule aedileship of Claudius Pulcher and the consulship of Marcus Antonius and Aulus Postumius, 99 B.C., and also that the first fight of an elephant against bulls was twenty years later in the curule aedileship of the Luculli. Also in Pompey's second consulship,[a] at the dedica-

Fights with elephants in war and in the circus.

15

altero consulatu, dedicatione templi Veneris Victricis,
viginti pugnavere in circo aut, ut quidam tradunt,
XVII, Gaetulis ex adverso iaculantibus, mirabili
unius dimicatione, qui pedibus confossis repsit genibus
in catervas, abrepta scuta iaciens in sublime, quae
decidentia voluptati spectantibus erant in orbem
circumacta, velut arte non furore beluae iacerentur.
magnum et in altero miraculum fuit uno ictu occiso;
pilum etenim[1] sub oculo adactum in vitalia capitis
21 venerat. universi eruptionem temptavere, non sine
vexatione populi, circumdatis claustris ferreis. qua
de causa Caesar dictator postea simile spectaculum
editurus euripis harenam circumdedit, quos Nero
princeps sustulit equiti loca addens. sed Pompeiani
missa fugae spe misericordiam vulgi inenarrabili
habitu quaerentes supplicavere quadam sese lamen-
tatione conplorantes, tanto populi dolore ut obli-
tus imperatoris ac munificentiae honori suo exquisitae
flens universus consurgeret dirasque Pompeio quas
22 ille mox luit[2] inprecaretur. pugnavere et Caesari
dictatori tertio consulatu eius viginti contra pedites
D, iterumque totidem turriti cum sexagenis pro-

---

[1] etenim? *Mayhoff*: autem.
[2] *v.l.* luit poenas.

---

[a] 49 B.C.   [b] 46 B.C.

tion of the Temple of Venus Victrix, twenty, or, as some record, seventeen, fought in the Circus, their opponents being Gaetulians armed with javelins, one of the animals putting up a marvellous fight—its feet being disabled by wounds it crawled against the hordes of the enemy on its knees, snatching their shields from them and throwing them into the air, and these as they fell delighted the spectators by the curves they described, as if they were being thrown by a skilled juggler and not by an infuriated wild animal. There was also a marvellous occurrence in the case of another, which was killed by a single blow, as the javelin striking it under the eye had reached the vital parts of the head. The whole band attempted to burst through the iron palisading by which they were enclosed and caused considerable trouble among the public. Owing to this, when subsequently Caesar in his dictatorship [a] was going to exhibit a similar show he surrounded the arena with channels of water; these the emperor Nero removed when adding special places for the Knighthood. But Pompey's elephants when they had lost all hope of escape tried to gain the compassion of the crowd by indescribable gestures of entreaty, deploring their fate with a sort of wailing, so much to the distress of the public that they forgot the general and his munificence carefully devised for their honour, and bursting into tears rose in a body and invoked curses on the head of Pompey for which he soon afterwards paid the penalty. Elephants also fought for the dictator Caesar in his third consulship,[b] twenty being matched against 500 foot soldiers, and on a second occasion an equal number carrying castles each with a garrison of 60 men, who fought a pitched

pugnatoribus eodem quo priore numero peditum et
pari equitum ex adverso dimicante, postea singuli
principibus Claudio et Neroni in consummatione
gladiatorum.

23   Ipsius animalis tanta narratur clementia contra
minus validos ut in grege pecudum occurrentia manu
dimoveat, ne quod obterat inprudens. nec nisi
lacessiti nocent, idque cum gregatim semper ambulent, minime ex omnibus solivagi. equitatu circum-
venti infirmos aut fessos vulneratosve in medium
agmen recipiunt, aciei[1] velut imperio aut ratione per
vices subeunt.

24   Capti celerrime mitificantur hordei suco. VIII.
capiuntur autem in India unum ex domitis agente
rectore qui deprehensum solitarium abactumve a
grege verberet ferum; quo fatigato transcendit in
eum nec secus ac priorem regit. Africa foveis capit,
in quas deerrante aliquo protinus ceteri congerunt
ramos, moles devolvunt, aggeres construunt, omni-
25 que vi conantur extrahere. ante domitandi gratia
reges equitatu cogebant in convallem manu factam
et longo tractu fallacem, cuius inclusos ripis fossisque
fame domabant: argumentum erat ramus homine

---

[1] *Rackham* (acie *Mueller*): ac.

battle against the same number of infantry as on the former occasion and an equal number of cavalry; and subsequently for the emperors Claudius and Nero elephants *versus* men single-handed, as the crowning exploit of the gladiators' careers.

A story is told that the animal's natural gentleness *Gentleness of* towards those not so strong as itself is so great that *elephants.* if it gets among a flock of sheep it will remove with its trunk those that come in its way, so as not unwittingly to crush one. Also they never do any harm unless provoked, and that although they go about in herds, being of all animals the least solitary in habit. When surrounded by horsemen they withdraw the weak ones or those that are exhausted or wounded into the middle of their column, and advance into the fighting line in relays as if by command or strategy.

When captured they are very quickly tamed by *Elephants* means of barley juice. VIII. The method of cap- *captured for* turing them in India is for a mahout riding one of *tion and* the domesticated elephants to find a wild elephant *for food.* alone or detach it from the herd and to flog it, and when it is tired out he climbs across on to it and manages it as he did his previous mount. Africa captures elephants by means of pit-falls; when an elephant straying from the herd falls into one of these all the rest at once collect branches of trees and roll down rocks and construct ramps, exerting every effort in the attempt to get it out. Previously for the purpose of taming them the kings used to round them up with horsemen into a trench made by hand so as to deceive them by its length, and when they were enclosed within its banks and ditches they were starved into submission; the proof of this

porrigente clementer acceptus. nunc dentium
26 causa pedes eorum iaculantur alioqui mollissimos.
Trogodytae contermini Aethiopiae, qui hoc solo
venatu aluntur, propinquas itineri eorum conscendunt
arbores, inde totius agminis novissimum speculati
extremas in clunes desiliunt; laeva adprehenditur
cauda, pedes stipantur in sinistro femine; ita
pendens alterum poplitem dextra caedit ac [1] praeacuta
bipenni, hoc crure tardato profugienti [2] alterius
poplitis nervos ferit, cuncta praeceleri pernicitate
peragens. alii tutiore genere sed magis fallaci
ingentes arcus intentos defigunt humi longius; hos
praecipui viribus iuvenes continent, alii conixi pari
conatu tendunt ac praetereuntibus sagittarum
vice [3] venabula infigunt, mox sanguinis vestigia
secuntur.

27 IX. Elephantorum generis feminae multo pavidiores. domantur autem rabidi fame et verberibus,
elephantis aliis admotis qui tumultuantem catenis
coerceant. et alias circa coitus maxime efferantur
et stabula Indorum dentibus sternunt. quapropter
arcent eos coitu feminarumque pecuaria separant,
quae haud alio modo quam armentorum habent.
domiti militant et turres armatorum in dorsis ferunt,

---

[1] v.l. om. ac.   [2] Rackham: profugiens.
          [3] vice add. Rackham.

would be if when a man held out a branch to them they gently took it from him. At the present day hunters for the sake of their tusks shoot them with javelins in the foot, which in fact is extremely soft. The Cavemen on the frontier of Ethiopia, whose only food is elephant meat obtained by hunting, climb up trees near the elephants' track and there keep a look out for the last of the whole column and jump down on to the hind part of its haunches; the tail is grasped in the man's left hand and his feet are planted on the animal's left thigh, and so hanging suspended, with his right hand and with a very sharp axe he hamstrings one leg, and as the elephant runs forward with its leg crippled he strikes the sinews of the other leg, performing the whole of these actions with extreme rapidity. Others employing a safer but less reliable method fix great bows rather deep in the ground, unbent; these are held in position by young men of exceptional strength, while others striving with a united effort bend them, and as the elephants pass by they shoot them with hunting-spears instead of arrows and afterwards follow the tracks of blood.

IX. The females of the genus elephant are much more timid than the males. Mad elephants can be tamed by hunger and blows, other elephants being brought up to one that is unmanageable to restrain it with chains. Besides this they get very wild when in heat and overthrow the stables of the Indians with their tusks. Consequently they prevent them from coupling, and keep the herds of females separate, in just the same way as droves of cattle are kept. Male elephants when broken in serve in battle and carry castles manned with armed warriors *Training of elephants.*

21

magnaque ex parte orientis bella conficiunt: pro-
sternunt acies, proterunt armatos. iidem minimo
suis stridore terrentur; vulneratique et territi retro
semper cedunt haut minore partium suarum pernicie.
Indicum Africi pavent nec contueri audent, nam et
maior Indicis magnitudo est.

28   X. Decem annis gestare in utero vulgus existimat,
Aristoteles biennio, nec amplius quam [semel gignere
pluresque quam][1] singulos, vivere ducenis annis
et quosdam ccc. iuventa eorum a sexagesimo
incipit.   Gaudent amnibus maxime et circa fluvios
vagantur, cum alioquin nare propter magnitudinem
corporis non possint, iidem frigoris inpatientes;
maximum hoc malum, inflationemque et profluvium
alvi nec alia morborum genera sentiunt. olei
potu tela quae corpori eorum inhaereant decidere
29 invenio, a sudore autem facilius adhaerescere. et
terram edisse iis tabificum est, nisi saepius mandant;
devorant autem et lapides, truncos quidem gratissimo
in cibatu habent, palmas excelsiores fronte proster-
nunt atque ita iacentium absumunt fructum.   mandunt ore, spirant et bibunt ordoranturque haud
inproprie appellata manu.   animalium maxime odere
murem, et si pabulum in praesepio positum attingi
ab eo videre fastidiunt.   cruciatum in potu maximum

---

[1] *Seclusa om. v.l.*

[a] This is not the case.
[b] Some MSS. give ' never bear more than once or more than
one at a time '; but Aristotle's statement is as above, *Hist.
An.* 546*b* 11.
[c] This mistake, with all the context, is from Aristotle.

on their backs; they are the most important factor
in eastern warfare, scattering the ranks before them
and trampling armed soldiers underfoot. Nevertheless they are scared by the smallest squeal of a pig;
and when wounded and frightened they always give
ground, doing as much damage to their own side as
to the enemy. African elephants are afraid of an
Indian elephant, and do not dare to look at it, as
Indian elephants are indeed of a larger size.[a]

X. Their period of gestation is commonly supposed *Breeding*
to be ten years, but Aristotle puts it at two years, *elephants—*
and says that they never bear more than one at a *their age.*
time,[b] and that they live 200 and in some cases
300 years. Their adult life begins at 60. They take
the greatest pleasure in rivers and roam in the
neighbourhood of streams, although at the same
time they are unable to swim [c] because of the size
of their bodies, and also as they are incapable of
enduring cold: this is their greatest infirmity; they
are also liable to flatulence and diarrhoea, but not
to other kinds of disease. I find it stated that
missiles sticking in their body fall out when they
drink oil, but that perspiration makes it easier for
them to keep their hold. It also causes them disease
to eat earth unless they chew it repeatedly; but
they devour even stones, consider trunks of trees a
great delicacy, and bend down the loftier palm trees
by butting against them with their foreheads and
when thus prostrate consume their fruit. They eat
with the mouth, but they breathe and drink and
smell with the organ not unsuitably called their
hand. They hate the mouse worst of living creatures,
and if they see one merely touch the fodder placed
in their stall they refuse it with disgust. They are

sentiunt hausta hirudine (quam sanguisugam vulgo coepisse appellari adverto): haec ubi in ipso animae canali se fixit, intolerando adficit dolore.

30 Durissimum dorso tergus, ventri molle, saetarum nullum tegimentum, ne in cauda quidem praesidium abigendo taedio muscarum—namque id et tanta vastitas sentit—sed cancellata cutis et invitans id genus animalium odore; ergo cum extentis [1] recepere examina, artatis in rugas repente cancellis conprehensas enecant, hoc iis pro cauda, iuba, villo est.

31 Dentibus ingens pretium et deorum simulacris lautissima ex his materia. invenit luxuria commendationem et aliam expetiti in callo manus saporis haut alia de causa, credo, quam quia ipsum ebur sibi mandere videtur. magnitudo dentium videtur quidem in templis praecipua, sed tamen in extremis Africae, qua confinis Aethiopiae est, postium vicem in domiciliis praebere, saepesque in his et pecorum stabulis pro palis elephantorum dentibus fieri Polybius tradidit auctore Gulusa regulo.

32 XI. Elephantos fert Africa ultra Syrticas solitudines et in Mauretania, ferunt Aethiopes et Trogodytae, ut dictum est, sed maximos India bellantesque

---

[1] *Mueller*: extenti.

---

[a] XXXIX. 1, 2.
[b] Son of the great Massinissa (Livy 42. 23).

liable to extreme torture if in drinking they swallow
a leech (the common name for which I notice has
now begun to be 'blood-sucker'); when this attaches
itself in the actual breathing passage it causes
intolerable pain.

The hide of the back is extremely hard, but that *Their hide.*
of the belly is soft; it has no covering of bristles,
not even on the tail as a guard for driving away the
annoyance of flies—for even that huge bulk is
sensitive to this—but the skin is creased, and is
inviting to this kind of creature owing to its smell;
consequently they stretch the creases open and let
the swarms get in, and then crush them to death by
suddenly contracting the creases into wrinkles.
This serves them instead of tail, mane and fleece.

The tusks fetch a vast price, and supply a very *Ivory.*
elegant material for images of the gods. Luxury
has also discovered another thing that recommends
the elephant, the flavour in the hard skin of the
trunk, sought after, I believe, for no other reason
than because the epicure feels that he is munching
actual ivory. Exceptionally large specimens of
tusks can indeed be seen in the temples, but nevertheless Polybius[a] has recorded on the authority of
the chieftain Gulusa[b] that in the outlying parts of
the province of Africa where it marches with Ethiopia
elephants' tusks serve instead of doorposts in the
houses, and partitions in these buildings and in
stabling for cattle are made by using elephants'
tusks for poles.

XI. Elephants are produced by Africa beyond the *Wild ele-*
deserts of Sidra and by the country of the Moors; *phants,*
also by the land of Ethiopia and the Cave-dwellers, *African and*
as has been said; but the biggest ones by India, as *Indian.*

25

cum his perpetua discordia dracones tantae magnitudinis et ipsos ut circumplexu facili ambiant nexuque
nodi praestringant. conmoriuntur ea dimicatione,[1]
victusque conruens conplexum elidit pondere.

33   XII. Mira animalium pro se cuique sollertia est,
ut his. una est scandendi [2] in tantam altitudinem
difficultas draconi; itaque tritum iter ad pabula
speculatus ab excelsa se arbore inicit. scit ille
inparem sibi luctatum contra nexus, itaque arborum aut rupium attritum quaerit. cavent hoc
dracones, ob idque gressus primum alligant cauda.
resolvunt illi nodos manu. at hi in ipsas nares
caput condunt, pariterque spiritum praecludunt
et mollissimas lancinant partes; idem obvii deprehensi in adversos erigunt se oculosque maxime
petunt : ita fit ut plerumque caeci ac fame et maeroris
tabe confecti reperiantur.

34   Quam quis aliam tantae discordiae causam attulerit
nisi naturam spectaculum sibi ac paria conponentem ?

Est et alia dimicationis huius fama : elephantis
frigidissimum esse sanguinem, ob id aestu torrente
praecipue a draconibus expeti; quamobrem in am-

---

[1] *Detlefsen* : commoritur ea dimicatio.
[2] *Detlefsen* : una exscandendo.

---

a Viz. pythons.

well as serpents [a] that keep up a continual feud and warfare with them, the serpents also being of so large a size that they easily encircle the elephants in their coils and fetter them with a twisted knot. In this duel both combatants die together, and the vanquished elephant in falling crushes with its weight the snake coiled round it.

The Indian elephant's enemy—the snake.

XII. Every species of animal is marvellously cunning for its own interests, as are those which we are considering. One difficulty that the serpent has is in climbing to such a height; consequently it keeps watch on the track worn by the elephant going to pasture and drops on him from a lofty tree. The elephant knows that he is badly handicapped in fighting against the snake's coils, and therefore seeks to rub it against trees or rocks. The snakes are on their guard against this, and consequently begin by shackling the elephants' steps with their tail. The elephants untie the knots with their trunk. But the snakes poke their heads right into the elephants' nostrils, hindering their breathing and at the same time lacerating their tenderest parts; also when caught in the path of the elephants they rear up against them, going specially for their eyes: this is how it comes about that elephants are frequently found blind and exhausted with hunger and wasting misery.

What other cause could anybody adduce for such a quarrel save Nature arranging a match between a pair of combatants to provide herself with a show?

There is also another account of this contest—that elephants are very cold-blooded, and consequently in very hot weather are specially sought after by the snakes; and that for this reason they submerge

27

nes mersos insidiari bibentibus, coortosque[1] inligata
manu in aurem morsum defigere, quoniam is tantum
locus defendi non possit manu; dracones esse tantos
ut totum sanguinem capiant, itaque elephantos ab
his ebibi siccatosque concidere et dracones inebriatos
opprimi conmorique.

35   XIII. Generat eos Aethiopia Indicis pares, vice-
num cubitorum; id modo mirum unde cristatos
Iuba crediderit. Asachaei vocantur Aethiopes apud
quos maxime nascuntur, narrantque in maritimis
eorum quaternos quinosque inter se cratium modo
inplexos erectis capitibus velificantes ad meliora
pabula Arabiae vehi fluctibus.

36   XIV. Megasthenes scribit in India serpentes in
tantam magnitudinem adolescere ut solidos hauriant
cervos taurosque, Metrodorus circa Rhyndacum
amnem in Ponto supervolantes quamvis alte pernici-
37 terque alites haustu raptas absorbeant. nota est in
Punicis bellis ad flumen Bagradam a Regulo impera-
tore ballistis tormentisque ut oppidum aliquod
expugnata serpens cxx pedum longitudinis; pellis
eius maxillaeque usque ad bellum Numantinum
duravere Romae in templo. faciunt his fidem in
Italia appellatae boae[2] in tantam amplitudinem
exeuntes ut divo Claudio principe occisae in Vaticano

---

[1] *Mayhoff:* coartatosque (contortosque *Detlefsen*).
[2] *v.l.* bovae.

---

[a] In Africa near Utica, now the Mejerdah; 256 B.C.
[b] 142–133 B.C., resulting in the acknowledgement of Roman
supremacy in Spain.

themselves in rivers and lie in wait for the elephants when drinking, and rising up coil round the trunk and imprint a bite inside the ear, because that place only cannot be protected by the trunk; and that the snakes are so large that they can hold the whole of an elephant's blood, and so they drink the elephants dry, and these when drained collapse in a heap and the serpents being intoxicated are crushed by them and die with them.

XIII. Ethiopia produces elephants that rival those of India, being 30 ft. high; the only surprising thing is what led Juba to believe them to be crested. The Ethiopian tribe in whose country they are chiefly bred are called the Asachaeans; it is stated that in the coast districts belonging to this tribe the elephants link themselves four or five together into a sort of raft and holding up their heads to serve as sails are carried on the waves to the better pastures of Arabia. *The African elephant.*

XIV. Megasthenes writes that in India snakes grow so large as to be able to swallow stags and bulls whole; and Metrodorus that in the neighbourhood of the river Rhyndacus in Pontus they catch and gulp down birds passing over them even though they are flying high and fast. There is the well-known case of the snake 120 ft. long that was killed during the Punic Wars on the River Bagradas [a] by General Regulus, using ordnance and catapults just as if storming a town; its skin and jaw-bones remained in a temple at Rome down to the Numantine War.[b] Credibility attaches to these stories on account of the serpents in Italy called boas, which reach such dimensions that during the principate of Claudius of blessed memory a whole child was found in the *Snakes of exceptional size.*

solidus in alvo spectatus sit infans.   aluntur primo
bubuli lactis suco, unde nomen traxere.

38   XV. Ceterorum animalium quae modo convecta
undique Italiam [1] contigere [2] saepius formas nihil
attinet scrupulose referre.   paucissima Scythia gignit
inopia fruticum ; pauca contermina illi Germania,
insignia tamen boum ferorum genera, iubatos
bisontes excellentique et vi et velocitate uros,
quibus inperitum volgus bubalorum nomen inponit,
cum id gignat Africa vituli potius cervique quadam
39   similitudine.   XVI. Septentrio fert et equorum greges ferorum, sicut asinorum Asia et Africa, praeterea
alcen, iuvenco similem ni proceritas aurium et cervicis
distingueret ; [3] item natam in Scadinavia insula nec
umquam visam in hac urbe,[4] multist amen narratam
achlin, haud dissimilem illi, sed nullo suffraginum
flexu ideoque non cubantem sed adclinem arbori
in somno, eaque incisa ad insidias capi, alias velocitatis memoratae.   labrum ei superius praegrande ;
ob id retrograditur in pascendo, ne in priora tendens
40   involvatur.   tradunt in Paeonia feram quae bonasus
vocetur equina iuba, cetera tauro similem, cornibus

[1] *Hardouin* : Italiae.
[2] contigit videre ? *Dalecamp.*
[3] *Mayhoff* : distinguat, -ant.
[4] *v.l.* hoc orbe.

[a] *Bos primigenius,* now extinct.
[b] Perhaps the moose or the reindeer, though the statement
about its leg is of course untrue. *Achlis* is presumably a
vernacular name.
[c] Probably Zealand.
[d] So far this startling account of the *achlis* comes from
Caesar, *B.G.* vi. 27, where it is given of the *alces* of the

belly of one that was killed on the Vatican Hill. Their primary food is milk sucked from a cow; from this they derive their name.

XV. It is not our concern to give a meticulous *Other wild* account of all the other species of animals that recently *species in various* have reached Italy more frequently by importation *countries.* from all quarters. Scythia, owing to its lack of vegetation, produces extremely few; its neighbour Germany few, but some remarkable breeds of wild oxen, the maned bison and the exceptionally powerful and swift aurochs,[a] to which the ignorant masses give the name of buffalo, though the buffalo is really a native of Africa and rather bears some resemblance to the calf and the stag. XVI. The North also produces herds of wild horses, as do Asia and Africa of wild asses, and also the elk, which resembles a bullock save that it is distinguished by the length of its ears and neck; also the achlis,[b] born in the island of Scandinavia [c] and never seen in Rome, although many have told stories of it—an animal that is not unlike the elk but has no joint at the hock and consequently is unable to lie down but sleeps leaning against a tree, and is captured by the tree being cut through to serve as a trap,[d] but which nevertheless has a remarkable turn of speed. Its upper lip is exceptionally big; on account of this it walks backward when grazing, so as to avoid getting tripped up by it in moving forward. There are reports of a wild animal in Paeonia called the bonasus,[e] which has the mane of a horse but in all other respects resembles a bull; its horns are curved back

silva Hercynia, which included the Black Forest and the Harz.

[a] The bison, *Bos bonasus*.

ita in se flexis ut non sint utilia pugnae; quapropter
fuga sibi auxiliari reddentem in ea fimum interdum
et trium iugerum longitudine, cuius contactus sequentes ut ignis aliquis amburat.

41 XVII. Mirum pardos, pantheras, leones et similia
condito in corporis vaginas unguium mucrone, ne
refringantur hebetenturve, ingredi, aversisque falculis
currere nec nisi in adpetendo protendere.

42 Leoni praecipua generositas tum[1] cum colla ar-
mosque vestiunt iubae; id enim aetate contingit
e leone conceptis, quos vero pardi generavere semper
insigni hoc carent; simili modo feminae. magna
his libido coitus et ob hoc maribus ira; Africa haec
maxime spectat inopia aquarum ad paucos amnes
congregantibus se feris. ideo multiformes ibi animalium partus varie feminis cuiusque generis mares
aut vi aut voluptate miscente. unde etiam vulgare
Graeciae dictum semper aliquid novi Africam adferre.

43 odore pardi coitum sentit in adultera leo totaque vi
consurgit in poenam; idcirco ea culpa flumine abluitur,
aut longius comitatur. semel autem edi partum
lacerato unguium acie utero in enixu volgum credidisse

---

[1] tum ? *Mayhoff*: tunc.

---

[a] The species so called is really a large Indian leopard.
[b] Ἀεὶ Λιβύη φέρει τι καινόν, Aristotle, *Hist. An.*, 606b 20.

in such a manner as to be of no use for fighting, and
it is said that because of this it saves itself by running
away, meanwhile emitting a trail of dung that sometimes covers a distance of as much as three furlongs,
contact with which scorches pursuers like a sort of
fire.

XVII. It is remarkable that leopards, panthers,[a] *Feline*
lions and similar animals walk with the point of their *species—*
claws sheathed inside the body so that they may not *their gait.*
get broken or blunted, and run with their talons
turned back and do not extend them except when
attempting to catch something.

The lion is specially high-spirited at the time when *The lion—its*
its neck and shoulders are clothed with a mane—for *hybrid-*
this occurs at maturity in the case of those sired by *ization.*
a lion, though those begotten by leopards always
lack this characteristic; and the females likewise.
Sexual passion is strong in this species, with its
consequence of quarrelsomeness in the males; this
is most observed in Africa, where the shortage of
water makes the animals flock to the few rivers.
There are consequently many varieties of hybrids in
that country, either violence or lust mating the males
with the females of each species indiscriminately.
This is indeed the origin of the common saying of
Greece that Africa is always producing some
novelty.[b] A lion detects intercourse with a leopard
in the case of an adulterous mate by scent, and
concentrates his entire strength on her chastisement;
consequently this guilty stain is washed away in a
stream, or else she keeps her distance when accompanying him. But I notice that there used to be
a popular belief that the lioness only bears a cub
once, as her womb is wounded by the points of

33

video. Aristoteles diversa tradit, vir quem in his mag-
44 na secuturus ex parte praefandum reor. Alexandro
Magno rege inflammato cupidine animalium naturas
noscendi delegataque hac commentatione Aristoteli,
summo in omni doctrina viro, aliquot milia hominum
in totius Asiae Graeciaeque tractu parere ei[1] iussa,
omnium quos venatus, aucupia piscatusque alebant
quibusque vivaria, armenta, alvearia, piscinae,
aviaria in cura erant, ne quid usquam genitum
ignoraretur ab eo. quos percunctando quinquaginta
ferme volumina illa praeclara de animalibus condidit.
quae a me collecta in artum cum iis quae ignoraverat
quaeso ut legentes boni consulant, in universis
rerum naturae operibus medioque clarissimi regum
omnium desiderio cura nostra breviter perigrinantes.
45 is ergo tradit leaenam primo fetu parere quinque
catulos, ac per annos singulos uno minus,[2] ab uno
sterilescere; informes minimasque carnes magnitudine mustellarum esse initio, semenstres vix ingredi
posse nec nisi bimenstres moveri; in Europa autem
inter Acheloum tantum Mestumque amnes leones
esse, sed longe viribus praestantiores iis quos Africa
et[3] Syria gignant.
46   XVIII. Leonum duo genera: conpactile et breve
crispioribus iubis—hos pavidiores esse quam longos

----

[1] ei *add. Harduin.*   [2] *v.l.* singulis minus.
       [3] *Rackham:* aut.

----

[a] Herodotus III, 108.   [b] The Aspropotamo.
       [c] Or Nestus, now the Mesto, in Thrace.

its claws in delivery.[a] Aristotle, however, whose *Aristotle's zoological researches.* authority I feel bound to cite first as I am going in great part to follow him on these subjects, gives a different account. King Alexander the Great being fired with a desire to know the natures of animals and having delegated the pursuit of this study to Aristotle as a man of supreme eminence in every branch of science, orders were given to some thousands of persons throughout the whole of Asia and Greece, all those who made their living by hunting, fowling, and fishing and those who were in charge of warrens, herds, apiaries, fishponds and aviaries, to obey his instructions, so that he might not fail to be informed about any creature born anywhere. His enquiries addressed to those persons resulted in the composition of his famous works on zoology, in nearly 50 volumes. To my compendium of these, with the addition of facts unknown to him, I request my readers to give a favourable reception, while making a brief excursion under our direction among the whole of the works of Nature, the central interest of the most glorious of all sovereigns. Aristotle then states that a lioness at the first birth produces five cubs, and each year one fewer, and after bearing a single cub becomes barren; and that the cubs are mere lumps of flesh and very small, at the beginning of the size of weasels, and at six months are scarcely able to walk, not moving at all until they are two months old; also that lions are found in Europe only between the rivers Achelous [b] and Mestus,[c] but that these far exceed in strength those produced by Africa and Syria.

XVIII. He states that there are two kinds of lions, *Varieties of lion; their habits.* one thickset and short, with comparatively curly manes —these being more timid than the long, straight-

35

simplicique villo, eos contemptores vulnerum. urinam mares crure sublato reddere ut canes. gravem
odorem, nec minus halitum. raros in potu, vesci [1]
alternis diebus, a saturitate interim triduo cibis carere;
quae possint in mandendo solida devorare, nec
capiente aviditatem alvo coniectis in fauces unguibus
extrahere, ut, si fugiendum sit, non in satietate [2]
47 abeant. vitam iis longam docet argumento
quod plerique dentibus defecti reperiantur. Polybius
Aemiliani comes in senecta hominem ab his adpeti
refert, quoniam ad persequendas feras vires non
suppetant; tunc obsidere Africae urbes, eaque
de causa cruci fixos vidisse se cum Scipione, quia
ceteri metu poenae similis absterrerentur eadem
noxa.

48   XIX. Leoni tantum ex feris clementia in supplices;
prostratis parcit, et, ubi saevit, in viros potius quam
in feminas fremit, in infantes non nisi magna fame.
credit Iuba [3] pervenire intellectum ad eos precum:
in [4] captivam certe Gaetuliae reducem audivit
multorum in silvis impetum esse [5] mitigatum adlo-
quio ausam dicere se feminam, profugam, infirmam,
supplicem animalis omnium generosissimi ceterisque
imperitantis, indignam eius gloria praedam. Varia
circa hoc opinio ex ingenio cuiusque vel casu, mulceri

---

[1] *v.l.* nec vesci : nec vesci ⟨nisi⟩? *Rackham.*
[2] aut si fugiendum in satietate *codd. plurimi.*
[3] *Pintianus* (*cf.* § 55): Libya.
[4] in *add. Welzhauer.*   [5] *Mayhoff*: a se.

haired kind; the latter despise wounds. The males lift one leg in making water, like dogs. Their smell is disagreeable, and not less their breath. They are infrequent drinkers, and they feed every other day, after a full meal occasionally abstaining from food for three days; when chewing they swallow whole what they can, and when their belly will not contain the result of their gluttony, they insert their clenched claws into their throats and drag it out, so that if they have to run away they may not go in a state of repletion. From the fact that many specimens are found lacking teeth he infers that they are long-lived. Aemilianus's companion Polybius states that in old age their favourite prey is a human being, because their strength is not adequate to hunting wild animals; and that at this period of their lives they beset the cities of Africa, and consequently when he was with Scipio he saw lions crucified, because the others might be deterred from the same mischief by fear of the same penalty.

XIX. The lion alone of wild animals shows mercy to suppliants; it spares persons prostrated in front of it, and when raging it turns its fury on men rather than women, and only attacks children when extremely hungry. Juba believes that the meaning of entreaties gets through to them: at all events he was informed that the onset of a herd of lions in the forests upon a woman of Gaetulia who was captured and got away again had been checked by a speech in which she dared to say that she was a female, a fugitive, a weakling, a suppliant to the most generous of all the animals, the lord of all the rest, a booty unworthy of his glory. Opinion will vary in accordance with each person's

Psychology of the lion.

37

alloquiis feras, quippe ubi etiam serpentes extrahi
cantu cogique in poenam verum falsumne sit non
49 vita decreverit. leonum animi index cauda sicut
et equorum aures: namque et has notas generosissi-
mo cuique natura tribuit. inmota ergo placido, clemens ⟨motus⟩ [1] blandienti, quod rarum est, crebrior
enim iracundia, cuius in principio terra verberatur,
incremento terga ceu quodam incitamento flagellantur.
vis summa in pectore. ex omni vulnere sive ungue
inpresso sive dente ater profluit sanguis. idem
50 satiati innoxii sunt. generositas in periculis maxime
deprehenditur, non illo [2] tantum modo quod spernens
tela diu se terrore solo tuetur ac velut cogi testatur
cooriturque non tamquam periculo coactus sed
tamquam amentia iratus: illa nobilior animi significatio—quamlibet magna canum et venantium urguente vi contemptim restitansque cedit in campis et
ubi spectari potest; idem ubi virgulta silvasque
penetravit acerrimo cursu fertur velut abscondente
turpitudinem loco. dum sequitur insilit saltu, quo
51 in fuga non utitur. vulneratus observatione mira
percussorem novit et in quantalibet multitudine ad-

[1] *Mayhoff?*   [2] *Mayhoff*: in illo.

temperament, or with chance, as to this point—that wild animals are placated by appeals addressed to them, inasmuch as experience has not decided whether it be true or false that even serpents can be enticed out by song and forced to submit to chastisement. Lions indicate their state of mind by means of their tail, as horses do by their ears: for Nature has assigned even these means of expression to all the noblest animals. Consequently the lion's tail is motionless when he is calm, and moves gently when he wishes to cajole—which is seldom, since anger is more usual; at the onset of which the earth is lashed, and as the anger grows, his back is lashed as if for a mode of incitement. A lion's greatest strength is in the chest. Black blood flows from every wound, whether made by claw or tooth. Yet when lions are glutted they are harmless. The lion's nobility of spirit is detected most in dangers, not merely in the way that despising weapons he protects himself for a long time only by intimidation, and protests as it were that he is acting under compulsion, and rises to the encounter not as if forced by danger but as though enraged by madness; but a nobler indication of this spirit is this, that however large a force of hounds and hunters besets him, in level plains and where he can be seen he retires contemptuously and constantly halting, but when he has made his way into brushwood and forest he proceeds at top speed, as if aware that the lie of the land conceals his disgrace. When pursuing he advances by leaps and bounds, but he does not use this gait when in flight. When he has been wounded he marks down his assailant in a marvellous way, and knows him and picks him out in however large a

petit. eum vero qui telum quidem miserit sed non vul-
neraverit correptum rotatumque sternit nec vulnerat.
cum pro catulis feta dimicat, oculorum aciem traditur
52 defigere in terram ne venabula expavescat. cetero
dolis carent et suspicione, nec limis intuentur oculis
aspicique simili modo nolunt. creditum est a moriente humum morderi lacrimamque leto dari.
atque hoc tale tamque saevum animal rotarum
orbes circumacti currusque inanes et gallinaceorum
cristae cantusque etiam magis terrent, sed maxime
ignes. aegritudinem fastidii tantum sentit, in qua
medetur ei contumelia, in rabiem agente adnexarum [1]
lascivia simiarum; gustatus deinde sanguis in remedio
est.

53   XX. Leonum simul plurium pugnam Romae
princeps dedit Q. Scaevola P. f. in curuli aedilitate,
centum autem iubatorum primus omnium L. Sulla,
qui postea dictator fuit, in praetura; post eum
Pompeius Magnus in circo DC, in iis iubatorum
cccxv, Caesar dictator cccc.

54   XXI. Capere eos ardui erat quondam operis,
foveisque maxime. principatu Claudii casus ratio-
nem docuit pudendam paene talis ferae nomine
pastorem [2] Gaetuliae, sago contra ingruentis impetum
obiecto, quod spectaculum in harenam protinus

[1] adversarum *vel* adnixarum *edd.*
[2] *Detlefsen* : pastore (⟨a⟩pastore *Mayhoff*).

---

    a Consul 95 B.C.   *b* 93 B.C.
         c 49, 48, 46, 45 and 44 B.C.

crowd. Yet a person who discharges a weapon at him but fails to wound him he seizes and whirling him round flings him on the ground, but does not wound him. It is said that when a mother lion is fighting in defence of her cubs she fixes the gaze of her eyes upon the ground so as not to flinch from the hunting spears. Otherwise lions are devoid of craft and suspicion, and they do not look at you with eyes askance and dislike being looked at in a similar way. The belief has been held that a dying lion bites the earth and bestows a tear upon death. Yet though of such a nature and of such ferocity this animal is frightened by wheels turning round and by empty chariots, and even more by the crested combs and the crowing of cocks, but most of all by fires. The only malady to which it is liable is that of distaste for food; in this condition it can be cured by insulting treatment, the pranks of monkeys tied to it driving it to fury; and then tasting their blood acts as a remedy.

XX. A fight with several lions at once was first bestowed on Rome by Quintus Scaevola,[a] son of Publius, when consular aedile, but the first of all who exhibited a combat of 100 maned lions was Lucius Sulla, later dictator, in his praetorship.[b] After Sulla Pompey the Great showed in the Circus 600, including 315 with manes, and Caesar when dictator[c] 400. *Lions in the circus.*

XXI. Capturing lions was once a difficult task, chiefly effected by means of pitfalls. In the principate of Claudius accident taught a Gaetulian shepherd a method that was almost one to be ashamed of in the case of a wild animal of this nature: when it charged he flung a cloak against its onset—a feat that was immediately transferred to the arena as a show,—the *The capture and taming of lions.*

translatum est, vix credibili modo torpescente tanta
illa feritate quamvis levi iniectu operto capite, ita
ut devinciatur non repugnans. videlicet omnis vis
constat in oculis, quo minus mirum fit [1] a Lysimacho
Alexandri iussu simul incluso strangulatum leonem.
55 iugo subdidit eos primusque Romae ad currum
iunxit M. Antonius, et quidem civili bello cum
dimicatum esset in Pharsaliis campis, non sine
ostento quodam temporum,[2] generosos spiritus
iugum subire illo prodigio significante. nam quod
ita vectus est cum mima Cytheride, super monstra
etiam illarum calamitatum fuit. primus autem
hominum leonem manu tractare ausus et ostendere
mansuefactum Hanno e clarissimis Poenorum traditur
damnatusque illo argumento, quoniam nihil non
persuasurus vir tam artificis ingenii videbatur, et
male credi libertas ei cui in tantum cessisset etiam
feritas.
56   Sunt vero et fortuitae [3] eorum quoque clementiae
exempla. Mentor Syracusanus in Syria leone
obvio suppliciter volutante attonitus pavore, cum
refugienti undique fera opponeret sese et vestigia
lamberet adulanti similis, animadvertit in pede eius
tumorem vulnusque; extracto surculo liberavit
cruciatu: pictura casum hunc testatur Syracusis.

----

[1] *v.l.* sit.
[2] *Gelen*: tempore (tempore ⟨eo⟩ ? *Mayhoff*).
[3] *Mayhoff*: fortuita.

----

[a] The defeat of Pompey by Caesar, 48 B.C.

creature's great ferocity abating in an almost incredible manner when its head is covered with even a light wrap, with the result that it is vanquished without showing fight. The fact is that all its strength is concentrated in its eyes, which makes it less remarkable that when Lysimachus by order of Alexander was shut up in a lion's cage he succeeded in strangling it. Mark Antony broke lions to the yoke and was the first person at Rome to harness them to a chariot, and this in fact during the civil war, after the decisive battle [a] in the plains of Pharsalia, not without some intention of exhibiting the position of affairs, the portentous feat signifying that generous spirits can bow to a yoke. For his riding in this fashion with the actress Cytheris at his side was a thing that outdid even the portentous occurrences of that disastrous period. It is recorded that Hanno, one of the most distinguished of the Carthaginians, was the first human being who dared to handle a lion and exhibit it as tamed, and that this supplied a reason for his impeachment, because it was felt that a man of such an artful character might persuade the public to anything, and that their liberty was ill entrusted to one to whom even ferocity had so completely submitted.

But there are also instances of occasional mercifulness even in lions. The Syracusan Mentor in Syria met a lion that rolled on the ground in suppliant wise and struck such terror into him that he was running away, when the lion stood in his way wherever he turned, and licked his footsteps as if fawning on him; he noticed a swelling and a wound in its foot, and by pulling out a thorn set the creature free from torment: a picture at Syracuse is evidence

Their mercifulness and gratitude.

57 Simili modo Elpis Samius natione in Africam delatus
nave iuxta litus conspecto leone hiatu minaci arborem fuga petit Libero patre invocato, quoniam tum
praecipuus votorum locus est cum spei nullus est.
neque profugienti, cum potuisset, fera institerat,
et procumbens ad arborem hiatu quo terruerat
miserationem quaerebat. os morsu avidiore in-
haeserat dentibus cruciabatque inedia, non tantum[1]
poena in ipsis eius telis, suspectantem ac velut
mutis precibus orantem, dum[2] fortuitis[3] fides[4]
58 non est contra feram, multoque diutius miraculo
quam metu cessatur. set[5] degressus tandem evellit
praebenti et qua maxime opus esset adcommodanti;
traduntque quamdiu navis ea in litore steterit retulisse gratiam venatus adgerendo. qua de causa
Libero patri templum in Samo Elpis sacravit, quod
ab eo facto Graeci κεχηνότος Διονύσου appellavere.
ne miremur postea vestigia hominum intellegi a
feris, cum etiam auxilia ab uno animalium sperent:
cur enim non ad alia iere, aut unde medicas manus
hominis sciunt? nisi forte vis malorum etiam feras
omnia experiri cogit.

59   Aeque memorandum et de panthera tradit De-

---

[1] *Mayhoff* : ntantum *aut* tantum.
[2] dum—cessatur ? *supra ante* neque profugienti *transponenda*
Warmington.
[3] *Sillig* : fortuita.   [4] *Mayhoff ?* : fidens.
[5] *Mayhoff ?* : cessatum est.

---

a Perhaps 'while chance . . . alarm' should be moved up to
come before 'The beast had not stood in his way.'

of this occurrence. In a similar manner a native of Samos named Elpis on landing from a ship in Africa, saw near the coast a lion opening its jaws in a threatening way, and took refuge up a tree, calling on Father Liber for help, since the chief occasion for praying is an emergency where there is no room for hope. The beast had not stood in his way when he tried to run away although it might have done, and lying down by the tree began to beg for compassion with the gaping jaws by which it had scared the man. Owing to its biting its food too greedily a bone had stuck in its teeth, and was tormenting it with starvation and not merely with the punishment contained in the actual prickles, as it gazed up and looked as if making a silent prayer for aid—while chance events are not to be relied on in face of a wild animal, and much longer hesitation is caused by surprise than by alarm.[a] But finally he came down and pulled out the bone for the lion, which held out its foot to him and adjusted it at the most necessary angle; and they say that as long as that vessel remained on the coast the lion displayed its gratitude by bringing its catches to its benefactor. This led Elpis to consecrate in Samos a temple to Father Liber, to which from that occurrence the Greeks have given the name of Temple of Dionysus with his Mouth Open. After this do not let us be surprised that men's tracks are recognized by wild beasts when they actually hope for assistance from one of the animal race: for why did they not go to other animals, or how do they know of man's healing touch? Unless perchance violent maladies force even wild animals to every expedient.

The natural philosopher Demetrius also records an *Gratitude of a panther.*

45

metrius physicus, iacentem in media via hominis
desiderio repente apparuisse patri cuiusdam Philini
adsectatoris sapientiae. illum pavore coepisse regredi, feram vero circumvolutari non dubie blan-
dientem seseque conflictantem maerore qui etiam
in panthera intellegi possit: feta erat catulis procul
60 in foveam delapsis. primum ergo miserationis fuit
non expavescere, proximum et curam intendere;
secutusque qua trahebat vestem unguium levi
iniectu, ut causam doloris intellexit simulque salutis
suae mercedem, exemit catulos, ea cum his prosequente usque extra solitudines deductus laeta atque
gestiente, ut facile appareret gratiam referre et
nihil in vicem inputare, quod etiam in homine rarum
est.

61   XXII. Haec fidem et Democrito adferunt qui
Thoantem in Arcadia servatum a dracone narrat.
nutrierat eum puer dilectum admodum, parensque
serpentis naturam et magnitudinem metuens in
solitudines tulerat, in quibus circumvento latronum
insidiis agnitoque voce subvenit. nam quae de
infantibus ferarum lacte nutritis cum essent exposti
produntur, sicut de conditoribus nostris a lupa,
magnitudini fatorum accepta referri[1] aequius quam
ferarum naturae arbitror.

---

[1] *Rackham*: ferri *aut* fieri.

equally remarkable story about a panther, which out of desire for human aid lay in the middle of a road, where the father of a certain student of philosophy named Philinus suddenly came in sight of it. The man, so the story goes, began to retreat, but the animal rolled over on its back, obviously trying to cajole him, and tormented by sorrow that was intelligible even in a panther: she had a litter of cubs that had fallen into a pit some distance away. The first result of his compassion therefore was not to be frightened, and the next to give her his attention; and he followed where she drew him by lightly touching his clothes with her claws, and when he understood the cause of her grief and at the same time the recompense due for his own security, he got the cubs out of the pit; and the panther with her young escorted him right to the edge of the desert, guiding him with gestures of delight that made it quite clear that she was expressing gratitude and not reckoning on any recompense, which is rare even in a human being.

XXII. These stories give credibility to Demo- *Gratitude of* critus also, who tells a tale of Thoas in Arcadia *a snake.* being saved by a snake. When a boy he had fed it and made a great pet of it, and his parent being afraid of the snake's nature and size had taken it away into an uninhabited region, where it recognized Thoas's voice and came to his rescue when he was entrapped by an ambush of brigands. For as to the reports about infants when they had been exposed being fed by the milk of wild animals, as well as those about our founders being nursed by a she-wolf, I deem it more reasonable for them to be credited to the grandeur of their destinies than to the nature of the wild animals.

62　XXIII. Panthera et tigris macularum varietate prope solae bestiarum spectantur, ceteris unus ac suus cuique generi color est, leonum tantum in Syria niger. pantheris in candido breves macularum oculi. ferunt odore earum mire sollicitari quadripedes cunctas, sed capitis torvitate terreri; quamobrem occultato eo reliqua dulcedine invitatas corripiunt. sunt qui tradant in armo iis similem lunae esse maculam crescentem in orbem seque [1] cavan-

63　tem [2] pari modo [3] nunc varias, et pardos qui mares sunt, appellant in eo omni genere, creberrimo in Africa Syriaque; quidam ab his pantheras candore solo discernunt, nec adhuc aliam differentiam inveni.

64　XXIV. Senatus consultum fuit vetus ne liceret Africanas in Italiam advehere. contra hoc tulit ad populum Cn. Aufidius tribunus plebis, permisitque circensium gratia inportare. primus autem Scaurus in [4] aedilitate sua varias CL universas misit, dein Pompeius Magnus CCCCX, divus Augustus CCCCXX.

65　XXV. idem Q. Tuberone Paullo Fabio Maxumo coss. IIII. non. Mai. theatri Marcelli dedicatione tigrim primus omnium Romae ostendit in cavea mansuefactam, divus vero Claudius simul IIII.

---

[1] *Mayhoff*: orbem et.　　[2] curvantem *Detlefsen.*
[3] *v.l.* modo cornua.　　[4] in *add.* Frobeen.

---

[a] *I.e.* in the shape of a crescent moon, bounded by a convex and a concave curve.
[b] 114 B.C.　　[c] 58 B.C.　　[d] 11 B.C.

XXIII. The panther and the tiger almost alone of *The panther.* beasts are distinguished by a variety of markings, whereas the rest have a single colour, each kind having its own—black in the case of lions in Syria only. Panthers have small spots like eyes on a light ground. It is said that all four-footed animals are wonderfully attracted by their smell, but frightened by the savage appearance of their head; for which reason they catch them by hiding their head and enticing them to approach by their other attractions. Some authorities report that they have a mark on the shoulder resembling a moon, expanding into a circle and hollowed out in a similar manner.[a] As it is, people use the name 'spotted ladies', and for the males 'pards', in the whole of this genus, which occurs most frequently in Africa and Syria; some persons distinguish panthers from these by their light colour only, nor have I hitherto discovered any other difference.

XXIV. There was an old Resolution of the Senate *Importation* prohibiting the importation of African elephants into *of wild* Italy. Gnaeus Aufidius when Tribune of the Plebs[b] *animals for* carried in the Assembly of the People a resolution *shows.* repealing this and allowing them to be imported for shows in the Circus. But Scaurus in his aedileship[c] first sent in procession 150 female leopards in one flock, then Pompey the Great 410, and the late lamented Augustus 420. XXV. Augustus also, in the consulship[d] of Marcus Tubero and Paullus Fabius, at the dedication of the Theatre of Marcellus, on May 7, was the first of all persons at Rome who exhibited a tamed tiger in a cage, although his late Majesty Claudius exhibited four at one time.

66 Tigrim Hyrcani et Indi ferunt, animal velocitatis tremendae, et maxime cognitae dum capitur totus eius fetus, qui semper numerosus est. ab insidiante rapitur equo quam maxime pernici, atque in recentes subinde transfertur. at ubi vacuum cubile reperit feta (maribus enim subolis cura non est) fertur praeceps odore vestigans. raptor adpropinquante fremitu abicit unum ex catulis. tollit illa morsu et pondere etiam ocior acta remeat iterumque consequitur, ac subinde donec in navem regresso inrita feritas saevit in litore.

67 XXVI. Camelos inter armenta pascit oriens, quarum duo genera, Bactriae et Arabiae, differunt, quod illae bina habent tubera in dorso, hae singula et sub pectore alterum cui incumbant: dentium superiore ordine ut boves carent in utroque genere. omnes autem iumentorum ministeriis dorso funguntur atque etiam equitatus in proeliis; velocitas infra equos.[1]

68 sed cuique mensura sicuti vires; nec ultra adsuetum procedit spatium, nec plus instituto onere recipit. odium adversus equos gerunt naturale. sitim et quadriduo tolerant, implenturque cum bibendi occasio est et in praeteritum et in futurum, obturbata proculcatione prius aqua: aliter potu non gaudent. vivunt quinquagenis annis, quaedam et centenis;

[1] *Detlefsen*: inter equos (ut equos *Mayhoff*).

Hyrcania and India produce the tiger, an animal *Tiger*
of terrific speed, which is most noticeable when the *hunting.*
whole of its litter, which is always numerous, is
being captured. The litter is taken by a man lying
in wait with the swiftest horse obtainable, and is
transferred successively to fresh horses. But when
the mother tiger finds the lair empty (for the males
do not look after their young) she rushes off at headlong speed, tracking them by scent. The captor
when her roar approaches throws away one of the
cubs. She snatches it up in her mouth, and returns
and resumes the pursuit at even a faster pace owing
to her burden, and so on in succession until the hunter
has regained the ship and her ferocity rages vainly
on the shore.

XXVI. The East pastures camels among its flocks *The camel*
of cattle; of these there are two kinds, the Bactrian *and the*
and the Arabian, which differ in that the former have *dromedary.*
two humps on the back and the latter one, with a
second hump beneath the chest on which they can
rest their weight; but both kinds resemble oxen
in having no teeth in the upper jaw. All however
perform the services of beasts of burden, and also of
cavalry in battles; their speed is below that of
horses. But the two kinds differ in dimensions, as
also in strength; and a camel will not travel beyond
its customary march, nor carry more than the regula-
tion load. They possess an innate hatred for horses.
They can endure thirst for as much as four days, and
when they have an opportunity they replenish themselves both for the past interval and for the future,
stirring up the water by trampling with their fore
feet before they drink—otherwise they do not enjoy
the draught. They live for fifty years, some even

utcumque rabiem et ipsae sentiunt. castrandi genus
etiam feminas quae bello praeparantur inventum est:
fortiores ita fiunt coitu negato.

69 XXVII. Harum aliqua similitudo in duo transfertur animalia. nabun Aethiopes vocant collo similem
equo, pedibus et cruribus bovi, camelo capite, albis
maculis, rutilum colorem distinguentibus, unde
appellata camelopardalis, dictatoris Caesaris circensibus ludis primum visa Romae. ex eo subinde
cernitur aspectu magis quam feritate conspicua, quare
etiam ovis ferae nomen invenit.

70 XXVIII. Pompei Magni primum ludi ostenderunt
chama, quem Galli rufium vocabant, effigie lupi,
pardorum maculis, iidem ex Aethiopia quas vocant
cephos,¹ quarum pedes posteriores pedibus humanis
et cruribus, priores manibus fuere similes. hoc
animal postea Roma non vidit.

71 XXIX. Isdem ludis et rhinoceros unius in nare
cornus, qualis saepe visus. alter hic genitus hostis
elephanto cornu ad saxa limato praeparat se pugnae,
in dimicatione alvum maxime petens, quam scit
esse molliorem. longitudo ei par, crura multo
breviora, color buxeus.

72 XXX. Lyncas vulgo frequentes et sphingas fusco
pilo, mammis in pectore geminis, Aethiopia generat,
multaque alia monstris similia, pinnatos equos et
cornibus armatos quos pegasos vocant, crocotas

¹ κήπους *Hardouin e Diodoro.*

ᵃ The giraffe.
ᵇ 55 B.C.
ᶜ Possibly baboons.
ᵈ The Indian species. The African has two horns.
ᵉ Unidentified.

for a hundred; although even camels are liable to rabies. A method has been discovered of gelding even the females intended for war; this by denying them intercourse increases their strength.

XXVII. Some resemblance to these is passed on to two animals. The Ethiopians give the name of *nabun* to one that has a neck like a horse, feet and legs like an ox, and a head like a camel, and is of a ruddy colour picked out with white spots, owing to which it is called a camelopard[a]; it was first seen at Rome at the games in the Circus given by Caesar when dictator. From this it has subsequently been recognized to be more remarkable for appearance than for ferocity, and consequently it has also got the name of ' wild sheep.' *The giraffe.*

XXVIII. The games[b] of Pompey the Great first displayed the *chama*, which the Gauls used to call the lynx, with the shape of a wolf and leopard's spots; the same show exhibited what they call *cephi*[c] from Ethiopia, which have hind feet resembling the feet of a man and legs and fore feet like hands. Rome has not seen this animal subsequently. *The lynx.*

XXIX. At the same games there was also a rhinoceros with one horn[d] on the nose such as has often been seen. Another bred here to fight matches with an elephant gets ready for battle by filing its horns on rocks, and in the encounter goes specially for the belly, which it knows to be softer. It equals an elephant in length, but its legs are much shorter, and it is the colour of box-wood. *The rhinoceros.*

XXX. Ethiopia produces lynxes in great numbers, and sphinxes[e] with brown hair and a pair of udders on the breast, and many other monstrosities—winged horses armed with horns, called *pegasi*, hyenas like a *Fauna of Ethiopia.*

velut ex cane lupoque conceptos, omnia dentibus
frangentes protinusque devorata conficientes ventre,
cercopithecos nigris capitibus, pilo asini et dissimiles
ceteris voce, Indicos boves unicornes tricornesque,
leucrocotam pernicissimam feram asini fere magnitudine, clunibus cervinis, collo, cauda, pectore leonis,
capite melium, bisulca ungula, ore ad aures usque
73 rescisso, dentium locis osse perpetuo—hanc feram
humanas voces tradunt imitari. apud eosdem et
quae vocatur eale, magnitudine equi fluviatilis,
cauda elephanti, colore nigra vel fulva, maxillis apri,
maiora cubitalibus cornua habens mobilia quae
alterna in pugna se[1] sistunt varieque[2] infesta aut
74 obliqua, utcumque ratio monstravit. sed atrocissi-
mos habet[3] tauros silvestres maiores agrestibus,
velocitate ante omnis, colore fulvos, oculis caeruleis,
pilo in contrarium verso, rictu ad aures dehiscente,
iuxta cornua mobilia; tergori duritia silicis omne
respuens vulnus. feras omnis venantur, ipsi non
aliter quam foveis capti feritate semper intereunt.
75 apud eosdem[4] nasci Ctesias scribit quam mantichoran appellat, triplici dentium ordine pectinatim
coeuntium, facie et auriculis hominis, oculis glaucis,
colore sanguineo, corpore leonis, cauda scorpionis
modo spicula infigentem, vocis ut si misceatur fistulae

[1] se ? *add. Mayhoff.*
[2] *Sillig*: variaque *aut* variatque.
[3] habet *add. edd.*
[4] apud Indos dein ? *Mayhoff.*

---

[a] The rhinoceros again.   [b] Another sort of hyena.
[c] This mythical animal is used in heraldry, *e.g.* as the
supporters of the shield of Lady Margaret Beaufort, mother
of King Henry VII.
[d] Or possibly 'with horns equally mobile as the yale's'.

cross between a dog and a wolf, that break everything with their teeth, swallow it at a gulp and
masticate it in the belly; tailed monkeys with black
heads, ass's hair and a voice unlike that of any other
species of ape; Indian oxen [a] with one and with three
horns; the *leucrocota*,[b] swiftest of wild beasts, about
the size of an ass, with a stag's haunches, a lion's
neck, tail and breast, badger's head, cloven hoof,
mouth opening right back to the ears, and ridges of
bone in place of rows of teeth—this animal is
reported to imitate the voices of human beings.
Among the same people is also found the animal
called the yale,[c] the size of a hippopotamus, with an
elephant's tail, of a black or tawny colour, with the
jaws of a boar and movable horns more than a cubit
in length which in a fight are erected alternately,
and presented to the attack or sloped backward in
turn as policy directs. But its fiercest animals are
forest bulls, larger than the bulls of the field, sur-
passing all in speed, of a tawny colour, with blue
eyes, hair turned backward, mouth gaping open to
the ears, along with mobile horns [d]; the hide has the
hardness of flint, rejecting every wound. They
hunt all wild animals, but themselves can only be
caught in pits, and when caught always die game.
Ctesias writes that in the same country [e] is born the
creature that he calls the *mantichora*,[f] which has a
triple row of teeth meeting like the teeth of a comb,
the face and ears of a human being, grey eyes, a
blood-red colour, a lion's body, inflicting stings with
its tail in the manner of a scorpion, with a voice like

[e] Perhaps the text should be altered to give ' next in the
Indians' country.'
[f] Fabulous.

et tubae concentus, velocitatis magnae, humani
76 corporis vel praecipue adpetentem. XXXI. in India
et boves solidis ungulis unicornes, et feram nomine
axin hinnulei pelle, pluribus candidioribusque maculis,
sacrorum [1] Liberi patris (Orsaei Indi simias candentes
toto corpore venantur), asperrimam autem feram
monocerotem, reliquo corpore equo similem, capite
cervo, pedibus elephanto, cauda apro, mugitu gravi,
uno cornu nigro media fronte cubitorum duum
eminente. hanc feram vivam negant capi.

77 XXXII. Apud Hesperios Aethiopas fons est Nigris,
ut plerique existimavere, Nili caput, ut argumenta
quae diximus persuadent. iuxta hunc fera appellatur catoblepas, modica alioqui ceterisque membris
iners, caput tantum praegrave aegre ferens, id [2]
deiectum semper in terram, alias internicio humani
generis, omnibus qui oculos eius videre confestim
expirantibus.

78 XXXIII. Eadem et basilisci serpentis est vis.
Cyrenaica hunc generat provincia, duodecim non
amplius digitorum magnitudine, candida in capite
macula ut quodam diademate insignem. sibilo
omnis fugat serpentes, nec flexu multiplici ut reliquae
corpus inpellit sed celsus et erectus in medio incedens.

[1] sacram *edd.*
[2] ideo ? *Mayhoff.*

---

[a] Again an echo of the rhinoceros, confused with the antelope; and the same hybrid in a more lurid shape recurs below
in the unicorn.

[b] Possibly a spotted deer of India.

[c] Mayhoff notes that this sentence looks as if wrongly
inserted here.

[d] N.W. Africa (nowhere near the Nile).

[e] 'The downward-looker,' perhaps the gnu.

the sound of a pan-pipe blended with a trumpet, of great speed, with a special appetite for human flesh. XXXI. He says that in India there are also *Fauna of India.* oxen with solid hoofs and one horn,[a] and a wild animal named *axis*,[b] with the hide of a fawn but with more spots and whiter ones, belonging to the ritual of Father Liber (the Orsaean Indians hunt monkeys that are a bright white all over the body)[c]; but that the fiercest animal is the unicorn, which in the rest of the body resembles a horse, but in the head a stag, in the feet an elephant, and in the tail a boar, and has a deep bellow, and a single black horn three feet long projecting from the middle of the forehead. They say that it is impossible to capture this animal alive.

XXXII. In Western Ethiopia[d] there is a spring, *Fauna of N.W. Africa.* the Nigris, which most people have supposed to be the source of the Nile, as they try to prove by the arguments that we have stated. In its neighbourhood there is an animal called the *catoblepas*,[e] in other respects of moderate size and inactive with the rest of its limbs, only with a very heavy head which it carries with difficulty—it is always hanging down to the ground; otherwise it is deadly to the human race, as all who see its eyes expire immediately.

XXXIII. The basilisk[f] serpent also has the same *The basilisk.* power. It is a native of the province of Cyrenaica, not more than 12 inches long, and adorned with a bright white marking on the head like a sort of diadem. It routs all snakes with its hiss, and does not move its body forward in manifold coils like the other snakes but advancing with its middle raised high. It kills bushes not only by its touch but also

[f] An imaginary monster.

necat frutices non contactos modo verum et adflatos,
exurit herbas, rumpit saxa. aliis [1] vis malo est:
creditur quondam ex equo occisum hasta et per eam
subeunte vi non equitem modo sed equum quoque
79 absumptum. atqui [2] huic tali monstro—saepe enim
enectum concupivere reges videre—mustellarum
virus exitio est: adeo naturae nihil placuit esse sine
pare. iniciunt [3] hos [4] cavernis facile cognitis soli tabe;
necant illae simul odore moriunturque, et naturae
pugna conficitur.
80 XXXIV. Sed in Italia quoque creditur luporum
visus esse noxius, vocemque homini quem priores
contemplentur adimere ad praesens. inertes hos
parvosque Africa et Aegytus gignunt, asperos
trucesque frigidior plaga. homines in lupos verti
rursusque restitui sibi falsum esse confidenter existimare debemus aut credere omnia quae fabulosa tot
saeculis conperimus; unde tamen ista volgo infixa
sit fama in tantum ut in maledictis versipelles habeat
81 indicabitur. Euanthes inter auctores Graeciae non
spretus scribit Arcadas tradere [5] ex gente Anthi
cuiusdam sorte familiae lectum ad stagnum quoddam regionis eius duci vestituque in quercu suspenso
tranare atque abire in deserta transfigurarique in
lupum et cum ceteris eiusdem generis congregari per

___

[1] *v.l.* talis.
[2] *Rackham*: atque.
[3] *Gelen* (*cf.* 35. 169): interficiunt (inferciunt *Sol.*).
[4] *Rackham*: has *aut* eos.
[5] *Mayhoff*: tradit Arcadas scribere.

___

[a] Imaginary.

by its breath, scorches up grass and bursts rocks. Its effect on other animals is disastrous : it is believed that once one was killed with a spear by a man on horseback and the infection rising through the spear killed not only the rider but also the horse. Yet to a creature so marvellous as this—indeed kings have often wished to see a specimen when safely dead— the venom of weasels is fatal: so fixed is the decree of nature that nothing shall be without its match. They throw the basilisks into weasels' holes, which are easily known by the foulness of the ground, and the weasels kill them by their stench and die themselves at the same time, and nature's battle is accomplished.

XXXIV. But in Italy also it is believed that the sight of wolves is harmful, and that if they look at a man before he sees them, it temporarily deprives him of utterance. The wolves produced in Africa and Egypt are feeble and small, but those of colder regions are cruel and fierce. We are bound to pronounce with confidence that the story of men being turned into wolves and restored to themselves again is false—or else we must believe all the tales that the experience of so many centuries has taught us to be fabulous; nevertheless we will indicate the origin of the popular belief, which is so firmly rooted that it classes werewolves [a] among persons under a curse. Evanthes, who holds no contemptible position among the authors of Greece, writes that the Arcadians have a tradition that someone chosen out of the clan of a certain Anthus by casting lots among the family is taken to a certain marsh in that region, and hanging his clothes on an oak-tree swims across the water and goes away into a desolate place and is transformed into a wolf and herds with the others

The wolf; the were-wolf; the lynx.

59

annos IX; quo in tempore si homine se abstinuerit,
reverti ad idem stagnum et, cum tranaverit, effigiem
recipere, ad pristinum habitum addito novem annorum
senio, addit[1] quoque fabulosius[2] eandem reciperare

82 vestem! mirum est quo procedat Graeca cre-
dulitas: nullum tam inpudens mendacium est ut
teste careat. item Apollas[3] qui Olympionicas
scripsit narrat Demaenetum Parrhasium in sacrificio
quod Arcades Iovi Lycaeo humana etiamtum hostia
faciebant, immolati pueri exta degustasse et in lupum se convertisse, eundem X anno restitutum ath-
letice se exercuisse in pugilatu victoremque Olympia

83 reversum. quin et caudae huius animalis creditur
vulgo inesse amatorium virus exiguo in villo eumque
cum capiatur abici nec idem pollere nisi viventi
direptum; dies quibus coeat toto anno non amplius
duodecim; eundem in fame vesci terra inter auguria:
ad dexteram commeantium praeciso itinere si pleno

84 id ore fecerit, nullum omnium ominum[4] praestantius.
sunt in eo genere qui cervarii vocantur, qualem e
Gallia in Pompei Magni harena spectatum diximus.
huic quamvis in fame mandenti, si respexerit,
oblivionem cibi subrepere aiunt digressumque
quaerere aliud.

[1] *Edd.*: id.   [2] *Pellicerius*: Fabius.
[3] *Kalkmann*: Acopas (Scopas *Jan*).
[4] *Rackham*: nullum hominum (n. ominum *aut* omnium *aut* omnino *edd.*).

---

[a] The lynx.   [b] See § 70.

of the same kind for nine years; and that if in that period he has refrained from touching a human being, he returns to the same marsh, swims across it and recovers his shape, with nine years' age added to his former appearance; Evanthes also adds the more fabulous detail that he gets back the same clothes! It is astounding to what lengths Greek credulity will go; there is no lie so shameless as to lack a supporter. Similarly Apollas the author of *Olympic Victors* relates that at the sacrifice which even at that date the Arcadians used to perform in honour of Lycaean Jove with a human victim, Daemenetus of Parrhasia tasted the vitals of a boy who had been offered as a victim and turned himself into a wolf, and furthermore that he was restored ten years later and trained himself in athletics for boxing and returned a winner from Olympia. Moreover it is popularly believed that even the tail of this animal contains a love-poison in a small tuft of hair, and when it is caught it sheds the tuft, which has not the same potency unless plucked from the animal while it is alive; that the days on which it breeds are not more than twelve in a whole year; also that for it to feed on earth when it is hungry counts as an augury: if it does this in large mouthfuls when barring the path of travellers who come upon it on their right hand side, this is the finest of all omens. Some members of the genus are called stag-wolves[a]; a specimen from Gaul was seen in the arena of Pompey the Great, as we have stated.[b] They say that if this animal while devouring its food looks behind it, however hungry it is, forgetfulness of what it is eating creeps over it and it goes off to look for something else.

85 XXXV. Quod ad serpentis attinet, vulgatum est colorem eius plerasque terrae habere in qua occultentur; innumera esse genera; cerastis corpore eminere cornicula saepe quadrigemina, quorum motu reliquo corpore occulto sollicitent ad se aves; geminum caput amphisbaenae, hoc est et a cauda, tamquam parum esset uno ore fundi venenum; aliis squamas esse, aliis picturas, omnibus exitiale virus; iaculum ex arborum ramis vibrari, nec pedibus tantum pavendas serpentes sed ut missile[1] volare tormento; colla aspidum intumescere nullo ictus remedio praeterquam si confestim partes contactae 86 amputentur. unus huic tam pestifero animali sensus vel potius affectus est: coniugia ferme vagantur, nec nisi cum pari vita est. itaque alterutra interempta incredibilis ultionis alteri cura: persequitur interfectorem unumque eum in quantolibet populi agmine notitia quadam infestat, perrumpit omnes difficultates, permeat spatia omnia,[2] nec nisi amnibus arcetur aut praeceleri fuga.

87 Non est fateri rerum natura largius mala an remedia genuerit. iam primum hebetes oculos huic malo dedit, eosque non in fronte ut ex adverso cerneret,[3] sed in temporibus,—itaque excitatur celerius[4] auditu quam visu,—deinde internecivum bellum

---

[1] *Mayhoff*: et missili.
[2] omnia *add. ? Mayhoff.*
[3] *v.l.* aut adversa cernere *et alia.*
[4] *Mayhoff*: saepius.

---

[a] Mythical; but the name is now used of an American snake.

[b] The name is now given to the mongoose.

XXXV. As concerning serpents, it is generally *The snake.*
stated that most of them have the colour of the earth
that they usually lurk in; that there are innumerable
kinds of them; that horned snakes have little horns,
often a cluster of four, projecting from the body, by
moving which so as to hide the rest of the body they
lure birds to them; that the amphisbaena *ᵃ* has a twin
head, that is one at the tail-end as well, as though
it were not enough for poison to be poured out of one
mouth; that some have scales, others coloured
markings, and all a deadly venom; that the javelin-
snake hurls itself from the branches of trees, and
that serpents are not only formidable to the feet but
fly like a missile from a catapult; that when asps'
necks swell up there is no remedy for their sting
except the immediate amputation of the parts
stung. Although so pestilential, this animal has one
emotion or rather affection: they usually roam in
couples, male and female, and only live with their
consort. Accordingly when either of the pair has
been destroyed the other is incredibly anxious for
revenge: it pursues the murderer and by means
of some mark of recognition attacks him and him
only in however large a throng of people, bursting
through all obstacles and traversing all distances, and
it is only debarred by rivers or by very rapid flight.

It is impossible to declare whether Nature has
engendered evils or remedies more bountifully. In
the first place she has bestowed on this accursed
creature dim eyes, and those not in the forehead for
it to look straight in front of it, but in the temples
— and consequently it is more quickly excited by
hearing than by sight; and in the next place she has
given it war to the death with the ichneumon *ᵇ*.

88 cum ichneumone. XXXVI. notum est animal hac
gloria maxime in eadem natum Aegypto. mergit se
limo saepius siccatque sole, mox ubi pluribus eodem
modo se coriis loricavit, in dimicationem pergit.
in ea caudam attollens ictus inritos aversus excipit,
donec obliquo capite speculatus invadat in fauces.
nec hoc contentus aliud haud mitius debellat animal.

89 XXXVII. Crocodilum habet Nilus, quadripes malum et terra pariter ac flumine infestum. unum hoc
animal terrestre linguae usu caret, unum superiore
mobili maxilla inprimit morsum, alias terribile
pectinatim stipante se dentium serie. magnitudine
excedit plerumque duodeviginti cubita. parit ova
quanta anseres, eaque extra eum locum semper
incubat praedivinatione quadam ad quem summo
auctu eo anno egressurus est Nilus. nec aliud
animal ex minore origine in maiorem crescit magnitudinem; et unguibus autem armatus est, contra
omnes ictus cute invicta. dies in terra agit, noctes
90 in aqua, teporis utrumque ratione. hunc saturum
cibo piscium et semper esculento ore in litore
somno datum parva avis, quae trochilos ibi vocatur,
rex avium in Italia, invitat ad hiandum pabuli sui
gratia, os primum eius adsultim repurgans, mox
dentes et intus fauces quoque ad hanc scabendi

---

a Probably the Pluvianus Aegyptius. The story is a fable.

XXXVI. That animal, which is also a native of *The ichneumon.* Egypt, is specially known because of this exploit. The asp repeatedly plunges into mud and dries itself in the sun, and then when it has equipped itself with a cuirass of several coatings by the same method, it proceeds to the encounter. In this it raises its tail and renders the blows it receives ineffectual by turning away from them, till after watching for its opportunity, with head held sideways it attacks its adversary's throat. And not content with this victim it vanquishes another animal no less ferocious, the crocodile.

XXXVII. This belongs to the Nile; it is a curse *The crocodile.* on four legs, and equally pernicious on land and in the river. It is the only land animal not furnished with a tongue and the only one that bites by pressing down the mobile upper jaw, and it is also formidable because of its row of teeth set close together like a comb. In size it usually exceeds 18 ells. It lays as many eggs as a goose, and by a kind of prophetic instinct incubates them always outside the line to which the Nile in that year is going to rise at full flood. Nor does any other animal grow to greater dimensions from a smaller original size; however, it is armed with talons as well, and its hide is invincible against all blows. It passes its days on land and its nights in the water, in both cases for reasons of warmth. This creature when sated with a meal of fish and sunk in sleep on the shore with its mouth always full of food, is tempted by a small bird (called there the trochilus,[a] but in Italy the king-bird) to open its mouth wide to enable the bird to feed; and first it hops in and cleans out the mouth, and then the teeth and inner throat also,

dulcedinem quam maxime hiantes, in qua voluptate somno pressum conspicatus ichneumon per easdem fauces ut telum aliquod inmissus erodit alvom.

91   XXXVIII. Similis crocodilo, sed minor etiam ichneumone, est in Nilo natus scincos, contra venena praecipuus antidotis, item ad inflammandam virorum venerem.

Verum in crocodilo maior erat pestis quam ut uno esset eius hoste natura contenta. itaque et delphini inmeantes Nilo, quorum dorso tamquam ad hunc usum cultellata inest pinna, abigentes eos praeda ac velut in suo tantum amne regnantes, alioquin inpares viribus ipsi astu interimunt. callent enim in hoc cuncta animalia, sciuntque non sua modo commoda verum et hostium adversa, norunt sua tela, norunt occasiones partesque dissidentium inbellis. in ventre mollis est tenuisque cutis crocodilo; ideo se ut territi mergunt delphini subeuntesque alvum illa secant

92 spina. quin et gens hominum est huic beluae adversa in ipso Nilo a Tentyri insula in qua habitat appellata. mensura eorum parva, sed praesentia animi in hoc tantum usu mira. terribilis haec contra

93 fugaces belua est, fugax contra sequentes.[1] sed adversum ire soli hi audent, qui et flumini innatant,

---

[1] *Dalecampius* : serpentes (resistentes *Solinus*).

---

[a] The name is now given to a very small South European lizard; but Pliny probably refers to some large species of lizard.
[b] *Sc.* Tentyritae.   [c] Now Denderah.

which yawns open as wide as possible for the pleasure of this scratching; and the ichneumon watches for it to be overcome by sleep in the middle of this gratification and darts like a javelin through the throat so opened and gnaws out the belly.

XXXVIII. A native of the Nile resembling the crocodile but smaller even than the ichneumon is the skink,*a* which is an outstanding antidote against poisons, and also an aphrodisiac for males. *The scincos.*

But the crocodile constituted too great a plague for Nature to be content with a single enemy for it. Accordingly dolphins also, which have on their backs a sharp fin shaped like a knife as if for this purpose, enter the mouth of the Nile, and when the crocodiles drive them away from their prey and lord it in the river as merely their own domain, kill them by craft, as they are otherwise in themselves no match for them in strength. For all animals are skilful in this, and know not only the things advantageous for themselves but also those detrimental for their enemies, and are acquainted with their own weapons and recognize their opportunities and the unwarlike parts of their adversaries. The crocodile's hide is soft and thin over the belly; consequently the dolphins pretending to be frightened dive and going under them rip the belly with the spine described. Moreover there is also a tribe of human beings right on the Nile, named*b* after the Island of Tentyrus*c* on which it dwells, that is hostile to this monster. They are of small stature but have a readiness of mind in this employment only that is remarkable. The creature in question is terrible against those who run away but runs away from those who pursue it. But these men alone dare to go against them; they actually dive

Enemies of the crocodile: the dolphin and the Tentyrus islanders.

dorsoque equitantium modo inpositi hiantibus resu-
pino capite ad morsum addita in os clava, dextra
ac laeva tenentes extrema eius utrimque, ut frenis
in terram agunt captivos, ac voce etiam sola territos
cogunt evomere recentia corpora ad sepulturam.
itaque uni ei insulae crocodili non adnatant, olfactu-
que eius generis hominum, ut Psyllorum serpentes,

94 fugantur. hebetes oculos hoc animal dicitur habere
in aqua, extra acerrimi visus, quattuorque menses
hiemis semper inedia transmittere in specu. quidam
hoc unum quamdiu vivat crescere arbitrantur; vivit
autem longo tempore.

95 XXXIX. Maior altitudine in eodem Nilo belua
hippopotamus editur, ungulis binis quales bubus,
dorso equi et iuba et hinnitu, rostro resimo, cauda et
dentibus aprorum aduncis sed minus noxiis, tergoris
ad scuta galeasque inpenetrabilis, praeterquam si
umore madeant. depascitur segetes destinatione
ante, ut ferunt, determinatas in diem et ex agro
ferentibus vestigiis, ne quae revertenti insidiae
comparentur.

96 XL. Primus eum et quinque crocodilos Romae
aedilitatis suae ludis M. Scaurus temporario euripo
ostendit. hippopotamus in quadam medendi parte
etiam magister existit; adsidua namque satietate

---

a See VII § 14.
b Apparently by entering the field walking backward.
c 58 B.C.

into the river and mounting on their back as if riding
a horse, when they yawn with the head thrown backward to bite, insert a staff into the mouth, and holding
the staff at both ends with their right and left hands,
drive their prisoners to the land as if with bridles,
and by terrifying them even merely with their shouts
compel them to disgorge the recently swallowed bodies
for burial. Consequently this island only is not visited
by crocodiles, and the scent of this race of men
drives them away, as that of the Psylli[a] does snakes.
This animal is said to have dim sight in the water,
but to be very keen-sighted when out of it; and to
pass four months of the winter in a cave continuously
without food. Some persons think that this alone
of animals goes on growing in size as long as it lives;
but it lives a long time.

XXXIX. A monster of still greater height is also *The hippo-*
produced in the Nile, the hippopotamus, which has *potamus:*
cloven hoofs like those of oxen, a horse's back, mane
and neigh, a snub snout, a boar's tail and curved
tusks, though these are less formidable, and with a
hide that supplies an impenetrable material for
shields and helmets, except if they are soaked in
moisture. It feeds on the crops, marking out a
definite portion beforehand for each day, so it is said,
and making its footprints lead out of the field,[b] so
that no traps may be laid for it when it returns.

XL. A hippopotamus was exhibited at Rome for
the first time, together with five crocodiles, by
Marcus Scaurus at the games which he gave when
aedile[c]; a temporary channel was made to hold
them. The hippopotamus stands out as an actual *its blood-*
master in one department of medicine; for when its *letting.*
unceasing voracity has caused it to overeat itself it

69

obesus exit in litus recentis harundinum caesuras
speculatum atque ubi acutissimam vidit stirpem
inprimens corpus venam quandam in crure vulnerat
atque ita profluvio sanguinis morbidum alias corpus
exonerat et plagam limo rursus obducit.

97   XLI. Simile quiddam et volucris in eadem Aegypto
monstravit quae vocatur ibis, rostri aduncitate per
eam partem se perluens qua reddi ciborum onera
maxime salubre est. nec haec sola: a[1] multis
animalibus reperta sunt usui futura et homini.
dictamnum herbam extrahendis sagittis cervi monstravere percussi eo telo pastuque herbae eius eiecto;
iidem percussi a phalangio, quod est aranei genus,
aut aliquo simili cancros edendo sibi medentur.
est et ad serpentium ictus praecipua herba,[2] qua se
lacerti quotiens cum his conseruere pugnam vulnerati
98 refovent.   chelidoniam visui saluberrimam hirundines
monstravere vexatis pullorum oculis illa medentes.
testudo cunilae quam bubulam vocant pastu vires
contra serpentes refovet, mustella ruta in murium
venatu cum iis dimicatione conserta. ciconia ori-
gano, hedera apri in morbis sibi medentur et cancros
99 vescendo maxime mari eiectos.   anguis, hiberno situ
membrana corpori[3] obducta feniculi suco inpedi-

---

[1] a *om. v.l.*   [2] herba *add.? Mayhoff.*
[3] *Rackham* : corporis.

---

a Perhaps pennyroyal.

comes ashore to reconnoitre places where rushes have recently been cut, and where it sees an extremely sharp stalk it squeezes its body down on to it and makes a wound in a certain vein in its leg, and by thus letting blood unburdens its body, which would otherwise be liable to disease, and plasters up the wound again with mud.

XLI. A somewhat similar display has also been made in the same country of Egypt by the bird called the ibis, which makes use of the curve of its beak to purge itself through the part by which it is most conducive to health for the heavy residue of foodstuffs to be excreted. Nor is the ibis alone, but many animals have made discoveries destined to be useful for man as well. The value of the herb dittany for extracting arrows was shown by stags when wounded by that weapon and ejecting it by grazing on that herb; likewise stags when bitten by the *phalangium*, a kind of spider, or any similar animal cure themselves by eating crabs. There is also a herb that is particularly good for snake-bites, with which lizards heal themselves whenever they fight a battle with snakes and are wounded. Celandine was shown to be very healthy for the sight by swallows using it as a medicine for their chicks' sore eyes. The tortoise eats *cunila*ᵃ, called ox-grass, to restore its strength against the effect of snake-bites; the weasel cures itself with rue when it has had a fight with mice in hunting them. The stork drugs itself with marjoram in sickness, and goats use ivy and a diet consisting mostly of crabs thrown up from the sea. When a snake's body gets covered with a skin owing to its winter inactivity it sloughs this hindrance to its movement by means of fennel-sap and comes

Other species that practise cures.

mentum illud exuit nitidusque vernat; exuit autem
a capite primum, nec celerius quam uno die et nocte,
replicans ut extra fiat membranae quod fuerit intus.
idem hiberna latebra visu obscurato marathro
herbae se adfricans oculos inunguit ac refovet, si
vero squamae obtorpuere spinis iuniperi se scabit.
draco vernam nausiam silvestris lactucae suco res-
100 tinguit. pantheras perfricata carne[1] aconito [vene-
num id est][2] barbari venantur; occupat ilico fauces
earum angor (quare pardalianches id venenum
appellavere quidam), at fera contra hoc excrementis
hominis sibi medetur, et alias tam avida eorum ut a
pastoribus ex industria in aliquo vase suspensa altius
quam ut queat saltu attingere iaculando se ap-
petendoque[3] deficiat et postremo expiret, alioqui
vivacitatis adeo lentae ut eiectis interaneis diu pu-
101 gnet. elephans chamaeleone concolori[4] frondi[5]
devorato occurrit oleastro huic veneno suo. ursi
cum mandragorae malum gustavere formicas lambunt. cervus herba cinare venenatis pabulis
resistit. palumbes, graculi, merulae, perdices lauri
folio annuum fastidium purgant, columbae, turtures
et gallinacei herba quae vocatur helxine, anates,
anseres ceteraeque aquaticae herba siderite, grues
et similes iunco palustri. corvus occiso chamae-

---

[1] v.l. per fricatas carnes.
[2] om. Urlichs.
[3] v.l. iaculando ea petendoque: iaculando se appetens
vel appetat ideoque? Mayhoff.
[4] cum concolori? Mayhoff.
[5] edd.: fronde.

---

[a] The wall-pellitory.

out all glossy for spring; but it begins the process at its head, and takes at least 24 hours to do it, folding the skin backward so that what was the inner side of it becomes the outside. Moreover as its sight is obscured by its hibernation it anoints and revives its eyes by rubbing itself against a fennel plant, but if its scales have become numbed it scratches itself on the spiny leaves of a juniper. A large snake quenches its spring nausea with the juice of wild lettuce. Barbarian hunters catch leopards by means of meat rubbed over with wolf's-bane; their throats are at once attacked by violent pain (in consequence of which some people have given this poison a Greek name meaning choke-leopard), but to cure this the creature doses itself with human excrement, and in general it is so greedy for this that shepherds have a plan of hanging up some of it in a vessel too high for the leopard to be able to reach it by jumping up, and the animal keeps springing up and trying to get it till it is exhausted and finally dies, although otherwise its vitality is so persistent that it will go on fighting for a long time after its entrails have been torn out. When an elephant swallows a chameleon (which is poisonous to it) because it is of the same colour as a leaf, it uses the wild olive as a remedy. When bears have swallowed the fruit of the mandrake they lick up ants. A stag uses wild artichoke as an antidote to poisoned fodder. Pigeons, jays, blackbirds and partridges cure their yearly distaste for food with bay-leaves; doves, turtle-doves and domestic fowls use the plant called *helxine*[a], ducks, geese and other water-fowl water-starwort, cranes and the like marsh-rushes. When a raven has killed a chameleon lizard, which is noxious even to

73

leone, qui etiam victor-suo nocet, lauro infectum virus
extinguit.

102 XLII. Milia [1] praeterea, utpote cum plurimis animalibus eadem natura rerum caeli quoque observa-
tionem et ventorum, imbrium, tempestatum praesa-
gia alia alio modo dederit, quod persequi inmensum
est, aeque scilicet quam reliquam cum singulis
hominum societatem. siquidem et pericula prae-
monent non fibris modo extisque, circa quod magna
mortalium portio haeret, sed et [2] alia quadam signi-
103 ficatione. ruinis inminentibus musculi praemigrant,
aranei cum telis primi cadunt. auguria quidem
artem fecere apud Romanos et sacerdotum collegium
vel maxime sollemne. est inter ea [3] locis rigentibus
et volpes, animal alioqui sollertia dirum [4]; amnes
gelatos lacusque nonnisi ad eius itum reditumque
transeunt: observatum eam aure ad glaciem adposita
104 coniectare crassitudinem gelus. XLIII. Nec minus
clara exitii documenta sunt etiam in [5] contemnendis
animalibus. M. Varro auctor est a cuniculis suf-
fossum in Hispania oppidum, a talpis in Thessalia,
ab ranis civitatem in Gallia pulsam, ab locustis in
Africa, ex Gyara Cycladum insula incolas a muribus
fugatos, in Italia Amynclas a serpentibus deletas.

---

[1] Multa? (cf. § 106) *Mayhoff.*   [2] et add.? *Mayhoff.*
[3] est in Thracia *edd.*   [4] *v.l.* sollerti auditu.

its conqueror, it stanches the poisonous infection with bay-leaves.

XLII. There are thousands of points besides, inasmuch as Nature has likewise also bestowed upon very many animals the faculty of observing the sky, and a variety of different modes of prognosticating winds, rain and storms, a subject which it would be an immense task to pursue, just as much so no doubt as the other points of alliance between particular animals and human beings. For in fact animals even give warning of dangers in advance, not only by means of their entrails and internal organs, a thing that much intrigues a great part of mankind, but also by another mode of indication. When the collapse of a building is imminent, the mice migrate in advance, and spiders with their webs are the first things to fall. Indeed auguries have constituted a science at Rome and have given rise to a priestly college of the greatest dignity. In frostbound countries the fox also is among the creatures believed to give omens, being an animal of formidable sagacity in other respects; people only cross frozen rivers and lakes at points where it goes or returns: it has been observed to put its ear to the frozen surface and to guess the thickness of the ice. XLIII. Nor are there less remarkable instances of destructiveness even in the case of contemptible animals. Marcus Varro states that a town in Spain was undermined by rabbits and one in Thessaly by moles, and that a tribe in Gaul was put to flight by frogs and one in Africa by locusts, and the inhabitants were banished from the island of Gyara in the Cyclades by mice, and Amynclae in Italy was completely destroyed

Animals that prognosticate weather and danger.

Destructive species.

---

⁵ in *add. Sillig.*

citra Cynamolgos Aethiopas late deserta regio est a
scorpionibus et solipugis gente sublata, et a scolopendris abactos Rhoetienses auctor est Theophrastus.

Sed ad reliqua ferarum genera redeamus.

105 XLIV. Hyaenis utramque esse naturam et alternis
annis maris alternis feminas fieri, parere sine mare
vulgus credit, Aristoteles negat. collum ut [1] iuba
in continuitatem [2] spinae porrigitur flectique nisi cir-
106 cumactu totius corporis nequit. multa praeterea mira
traduntur, sed maxime sermonem humanum inter
pastorum stabula adsimulare nomenque alicuius addiscere quem evocatum foris laceret, item vomitionem
hominis imitari ad sollicitandos canes quos invadat;
ab uno animali sepulchra erui inquisitione corporum;
feminam raro capi; oculis mille esse varietates
colorumque mutationes; praeterea umbrae eius
contactu canes obmutescere; et quibusdam magicis
artibus omne animal quod ter lustraverit in vestigio
107 haerere. XLV. Huius generis coitu leaena Aethio-
pica parit corocottam, similiter voces imitantem
hominum pecorumque; acies ei perpetua in utraque
parte oris nullis gingivis, dente continuo, ne contrario
occursu hebetetur capsarum modo includitur. ho-

---

[1] *Mayhoff*: et.
[2] *Mayhoff*: iuba et unitate.

---

a An unknown animal.

by snakes. North of the Ethiopic tribe of the Bitch-milkers there is a wide belt of desert where a tribe was wiped out by scorpions and poisonous spiders, and Theophrastus states that the Rhoetienses were driven away by a kind of centipede.

But let us return to the remaining kinds of wild animals.

XLIV. The hyena is popularly believed to be *The hyena.* bi-sexual and to become male and female in alternate years, the female bearing offspring without a male; but this is denied by Aristotle. Its neck stretches right along the backbone like a mane, and cannot bend without the whole body turning round. A number of other remarkable facts about it are reported, but the most remarkable are that among the shepherds' homesteads it simulates human speech, and picks up the name of one of them so as to call him to come out of doors and tear him in pieces, and also that it imitates a person being sick, to attract the dogs so that it may attack them; that this animal alone digs up graves in search of corpses; that a female is seldom caught; that its eyes have a thousand variations and alterations of colour; moreover that when its shadow falls on dogs they are struck dumb; and that it has certain magic arts by which it causes every animal at which it gazes three times to stand rooted to the spot. XLV. When crossed with this race of animals the *Hyena* Ethiopian lioness gives birth to the corocotta,ᵃ that *hybrids* mimics the voices of men and cattle in a similar way. It has an unbroken ridge of bone in each jaw, forming a continuous tooth without any gum, which to prevent its being blunted by contact with the opposite jaw is shut up in a sort of case. Juba states

minum sermones imitari et mantichoran in Aethiopia
auctor est Iuba.

108   XLVI. Hyaenae plurimae gignuntur in Africa,
quae et asinorum silvestrium multitudinem fundit.
mares in eo genere singuli feminarum gregibus
imperitant. timent libidinis aemulos et ideo gravidas
custodiunt morsuque natos mares castrant; contra
gravidae latebras petunt et parere furto cupiunt.
gaudentque copia libidinis.

109   XLVII. Easdem partes sibi ipsi Pontici amputant
fibri periculo urguente, ob hoc se peti gnari:
castoreum id vocant medici. alias animal horrendi
morsus arbores iuxta flumina ut ferro caedit; hominis parte conprehensa non ante quam fracta
concrepuerint ossa morsus resolvit. cauda piscium
his, cetera species lutrae: utrumque aquaticum,
utrique mollior pluma pilus.

110   XLVIII. Ranae quoque rubetae, quarum et in
terra et in umore vita, plurimis refertae medicaminibus deponere ea cotidie[1] ac resumere pastu
dicuntur, venena tantum semper sibi reservantes.

111   XLIX. Similis et vitulo marino victus in mari ac
terra, simile fibris et ingenium. evomit fel suum ad
multa medicamenta utile, item coagulum ad comi-

---

[1] *v.l.* assidue.

[a] See § 75.
[b] The Latin name has been transferred to a vegetable oil.
[c] *I.e.* the toad.

that in Ethiopia the mantichora [a] also mimics human speech.

XLVI. Hyenas occur most numerously in Africa, *The wild ass.* which also produces a multitude of wild asses. In that species each male is lord of a separate herd of females. They are afraid of rivals in their affections, and consequently they keep a watch on their females when in foal, and geld their male offspring with a bite; to guard against this the females when in foal seek hiding-places and are anxious to give birth by stealth. Also they are fond of a great deal of sexual indulgence.

XLVII. The beavers of the Black Sea region prac- *The beaver.* tise self-amputation of the same organ when beset by danger, as they know that they are hunted for the sake of its secretion, the medical name for which is beaver-oil.[b] Apart from this the beaver is an animal with a formidable bite, cutting down trees on the river banks as if with steel; if it gets hold of part of a man's body it does not relax its bite before the fractured bones are heard grinding together. The beaver has a fish's tail, while the rest of its con-formation resembles an otter's; both species are aquatic, and both have fur that is softer than down.

XLVIII. Also the bramble-frog,[c] which is amphi- *The bramble-* bious in its habit, is replete with a great number of *frog.* drugs, which it is said to evacuate daily and to re-place by the food that it eats, always keeping back only the poisons for itself.

XLIX. The seal also resembles the beaver both *The seal.* in its amphibious habits and in its nature. It gets rid of its gall, which is useful for many drugs, by vomiting it up, and also its rennet, a cure for epileptic

tiales morbos, ob ea se peti prudens. Theophrastus auctor est anguis [1] modo et stelliones senectutem exuere itaque protinus devorare praeripientis comitiali morbo remedium.[2] eosdem innocui ferunt [3] in Graecia morsus, noxios [4] esse in Sicilia.

112 L. Cervis quoque est sua malignitas, quamquam placidissimo animalium. urguente vi canum ultro confugiunt ad hominem, et in pariendo semitas minus cavent humanis vestigiis tritas quam secreta ac feris opportuna. conceptus earum post arcturi sidus. octonis mensibus ferunt partus, interim et geminos. a conceptu separant se, at mares relicti rabie libidinis saeviunt, fodiunt scrobes; tunc rostra eorum nigrescunt donec aliqui abluant imbres. feminae autem ante partum purgantur herba quadam quae seselis dicitur, faciliore ita utentes utero. a partu duas herbas quae tamnus et seselis appellantur pastae redeunt ad fetum: illis imbui lactis primos volunt sucos quacumque de causa.

113 editos partus exercent cursu et fugam meditari docent, ad praerupta ducunt saltumque demonstrant. iam mares soluti desiderio libidinis avide petunt pabula; ubi se praepingues sensere, latebras quaerunt fatentes incommodum pondus. et alias semper in fuga adquiescunt stantesque respiciunt, cum prope

[1] *Gelen (cf.* **xxx.** 89): angues.
[2] *Rackham:* remedii *aut* remedia.
[3] *Mayhoff:* ponti ferunt *aut* mortiferi.
[4] *Mayhoff:* Graecia mortuos.

---

[a] As well as the animals in § 111: they grudge mankind their horns, § 115.

attacks; it does this because it knows that it is hunted for the sake of these products. Theophrastus states that geckoes also slough off their old skin as a snake does, and similarly swallow the slough at once, it being a cure for epilepsy if one snatches it from them. It is also said that their bite is harmless in Greece but that they are noxious in Sicily.

L. Deer also [a] have their own form of stinginess, although the stag is the gentlest of animals. When beset by a pack of hounds they fly for refuge of their own accord to a human being, and when giving birth to young are less careful to avoid paths worn by human footprints than secluded places that are advantageous for wild beasts. The mating season is after the rising of Arcturus. Pregnancy lasts eight months, and occasionally they bear twins. After mating the hinds withdraw, but the deserted males rage in a fury of desire, and score the ground with their horns; afterwards their snouts are black till a considerable rainfall washes off the dirt. The females before giving birth use a certain plant called hartwort as a purge, so having an easier delivery. After giving birth they browse on the two plants named dittany and seseli before they return to the young: for some reason or other they desire the sucklings' first draughts of milk to be flavoured with those herbs. When the fawns are born they exercise them in running and teach them to practise escaping, and take them to cliffs and show them how to jump. The males when at last freed from lustful desire greedily seek pasture; when they feel they are too fat, they look for lairs to hide in, showing that they are conscious of inconvenient weight. And on other occasions when running away from pursuit they always stop and stand gazing backward, when

Habits of deer.

81

ventum est rursus fugae praesidia repetentes: hoc
fit intestini dolore tam infirmi ut ictu levi rumpatur
114 intus. fugiunt autem latratu canum audito secunda
semper aura, ut vestigia cum ipsis abeant. mulcentur fistula pastorali et cantu. cum erexere aures,
acerrimi sunt auditus, cum remisere, surdi. cetero
animal simplex et omnium rerum miraculo stupens
in tantum ut equo aut bucula accedente propius
hominem iuxta venantem non cernant aut, si cernant,
arcum ipsum sagittasque mirentur. maria trameant
gregatim nantes porrecto ordine et capita inponentes
praecedentium clunibus vicibusque ad terga redeuntes: hoc maxime notatur a Cilicia Cyprum
traicientibus; nec vident terras, sed in odorem[1]
115 earum natant. cornua mares habent, solique
animalium omnibus annis stato veris tempore amittunt; ideo sub ista die quam maxime invia petunt.
latent amissis velut inermes, sed et hi bono suo
invidentes: dextrum cornu negant inveniri ceu
medicamento aliquo praeditum; idque mirabilius
fatendum est cum et in vivariis mutent omnibus
annis; defodi ab iis putant. accensi autem utrius
libeat odore comitiales morbi deprehenduntur.
116 indicia quoque aetatis in illis gerunt, singulos annis
adicientibus ramos usque ad sexennes; ab eo

[1] *Gelen*: odore.

the hunters draw near again seeking refuge in flight: this is done owing to pain in the gut, which is so weak that a light blow causes internal rupture. But when they hear the baying of hounds they always run away down wind, so that their scent may go away with them. They can be charmed by a shepherd's pipe and by song. Their hearing is very keen when they raise their ears, but dull when they drop them. In other respects the deer is a simple animal and stupefied by surprise at everything—so much so that when a horse or a heifer is approaching they do not notice a huntsman close to them, or if they see him merely gaze in wonder at his bow and arrows. They cross seas swimming in a herd strung out in line with their heads resting on the haunches of the ones in front of them, and taking turns to drop to the rear: this is most noticed when they are crossing from Cilicia to Cyprus; and they do not keep land in sight but swim towards its scent. The males have horns, and alone of animals shed them every year at a fixed time in spring; consequently when the day in question approaches they resort as much as possible to unfrequented places. When they have lost their horns they keep in hiding as if disarmed—although these animals also are grudging of their special good: people say that a stag's right horn, which is endowed with some sort of healing drug, is never found; and this must be confessed to be the more surprising in view of the fact that even stags kept in warrens change their horns every year: it is thought that they bury them. The smell of either horn when burnt arrests attacks of epilepsy. They also bear marks of their age in their horns, each year till they are six years old adding one tine;

tempore similia revivescunt nec potest aetas discerni,
sed dentibus senecta declaratur; aut enim paucos
aut nullos habent, nec in cornibus imis ramos alioqui
117 ante frontem prominere solitos iunioribus. non
decidunt castratis cornua nec nascuntur, erumpunt
autem renascentibus tuberibus primo aridae cuti
similia, dein[1] teneris increscunt ferulis harundineas
in paniculas molli plumatas[2] lanugine. quamdiu
carent iis, noctibus procedunt ad pabula. incres-
centia solis vapore durant ad arbores subinde ex-
perientes: ubi placuit robur, in aperta prodeunt;
captique iam sunt hedera in cornibus viridante, ex
attritu arborum ut in aliquo ligno teneris dum
experiuntur innata. sunt[3] aliquando et candido
colore, qualem fuisse tradunt Q. Sertorii cervam
quam esse fatidicam Hispaniae gentibus persuaserat
118 et his cum serpente pugna: vestigant cavernas
nariumque spiritu extrahunt renitentes. ideo singulare abigendis serpentibus odor adusto cervino cornu,
contra morsus vero praecipuum remedium ex
119 coagulo hinnulei matris in utero occisi. vita cervis
in confesso longa, post c annos aliquibus denuo[4]
captis cum torquibus aureis quos Alexander Magnus
addiderat adopertis iam cute in magna obesitate.
febrium morbos non sentit hoc animal, quin et

---

[1] *Mayhoff*: eadem.
[2] *Rackham*: plumata.
[3] *Pintianus*: fuit.
[4] *Mayhoff*: annos a quibusdam *aut* annos aliquibus.

though thenceforward the horns grow again like the old ones and the age cannot be told by them. But old age is indicated by the teeth, for the old have either few or none, nor have they tines at the bottom of the horns, though otherwise these usually jut out in front of the brow when they are younger. When stags have been gelt the horns do not fall off nor grow again, but burst out with excrescences that keep springing again, at first resembling dry skin, and then grow up with tender shoots into reedy tufts feathered with soft down. As long as the stags are without them, they go out to graze in the nights. When they are growing again they harden them with the heat of the sun, subsequently testing them on trees, and only go out into the open when satisfied with their strength; and before now they have been caught with green ivy on their antlers, that has been grafted on the tender horns as on a log of wood as a result of rubbing them against trees while testing them. Stags are sometimes even of a white colour, as Quintus Sertorius's hind is said to have been, which he had persuaded the tribes of Spain to believe prophetic. Even stags are at war with a snake; they track out their holes and draw them out by means of the breath of their nostrils in spite of their resistance. Consequently the smell made by burning stag's horn is an outstanding thing for driving away serpents, while a sovereign cure against bites is obtained from the rennet of a fawn killed in its mother's womb. Stags admittedly have a long life, some having been caught a hundred years later with the gold necklaces that Alexander the Great had put on them already covered up by the hide in great folds of fat. This animal is not liable to feverish dis-

medetur huic timori: quasdam modo principes
feminas scimus omnibus diebus matutinis carnem
eam degustare solitas et longo aevo caruisse febribus;
quod ita demum existimant ratum si vulnere uno
interierit.

120   Est eadem specie, barba tantum et armorum villo
distans, quem tragelaphon vocant, non alibi quam
iuxta Phasim amnem nascens.[a]

LI. Cervos Africa propemodum sola non gignit,
at chamaeleonem et ipsa, quamquam frequentiorem
India.[1] figura et magnitudo erant[2] lacerti, nisi
crura essent recta et excelsiora. latera ventri
iunguntur ut piscibus, et spina simili modo eminet.
121 rostrum, ut in parvo, haut absimile suillo, cauda
praelonga in tenuitatem desinens et implicans se
viperinis orbibus, ungues adunci, motus tardior ut
testudini, corpus asperum ceu crocodilo, oculi in
recessu cavo, tenui discrimine praegrandes et corpori concolores. numquam eos operit, nec pupillae
122 motu sed totius oculi versatione circumspicit.[b] ipse
celsus hianti semper ore solus animalium nec cibo nec
potu alitur nec alio quam aeris alimento, rictu
terrifico[3] fere, innoxius alioqui. et coloris natura
mirabilior; mutat namque eum subinde et oculis et
cauda et toto corpore, redditque semper quemcumque
proxime   attingit   praeter   rubrum   candidumque.

---

[1] *Mayhoff*: Indiae (frequentior est in India? *Rackham*).
[2] *Rackham*: erat.
[3] *Mayhoff*: circa caprificos.

---

[a] The Rion, running into the Black Sea.
[b] In point of fact it lives on insects, which it catches by
shooting out the tongue and drawing it back so quickly that
the ancients did not notice it.
[c] The MSS. give ' it is usually about wild fig-trees.'

eases—indeed it even supplies a prophylactic against their attack; we know that recently certain ladies of the imperial house have made a practice of eating venison every day in the morning and have been free from fevers throughout a long lifetime; though it is thought that this only holds good if the stag has been killed by a single wound.

The animal called the goat-stag, occurring only near the river Phasis,[a] is of the same appearance, differing only in having a beard, and a fleece on the shoulders. *The goat-stag.*

LI. Africa almost alone does not produce stags, but Africa also has the chamaeleon, although India produces it in greater numbers. Its shape and size were those of a lizard, were not the legs straight and longer. The flanks are joined on to the belly as in fishes, and the spine projects in a similar manner. It has a snout not unlike a pig's, considering its small size, a very long tail that tapers towards the end and curls in coils like a viper, and crooked talons; it moves rather slowly like a tortoise and has a rough body like a crocodile's, and eyes in a hollow recess, close together and very large and of the same colours as its body. It never shuts its eyes, and looks round not by moving the pupil but by turning the whole eye. It holds itself erect with its mouth always wide open, and it is the only animal that does not live on food or drink or anything else but the nutriment that it derives from the air,[b] with a gape that is almost terrifying,[c] but otherwise it is harmless. And it is more remarkable for the nature of its colouring, since it constantly changes the hue of its eyes and tail and whole body and always makes it the colour with which it is in closest contact, except *The chamaeleon.*

defuncto pallor est. caro in capite et maxillis et ad commissuram caudae admodum exigua, nec aliubi toto corpore; sanguis in corde et circa oculos tantum; viscera sine splene. hibernis mensibus latet ut lacerta.

123   LII. Mutat colores et Scytharum tarandrus, nec aliud ex iis quae pilo vestiuntur nisi in Indis lycaon, cui iubata traditur cervix. nam thoes, — luporum id genus est procerius longitudine, brevitate crurum dissimile, velox saltu, venatu vivens, innocuum homini, — habitum, non colorem, mutant, per hiemes
124 hirti, aestate nudi. tarandro magnitudo quae bovi est, caput maius cervino nec absimile, cornua ramosa, ungulae bifidae, villus magnitudine ursorum sed, cum libuit sui coloris esse, asini similis. tergori tanta duritia ut thoraces ex eo faciant. colorem omnium arborum, fruticum, florum locorumque reddit metuens in quibus latet, ideoque raro capitur. mirum esset habitum corpori tam multiplicem dari, mirabilius est et villo.

125   LIII. Hystrices generat India et Africa spinea[1] contectas cute[2] irenaceorum genere, sed hystrici longiores aculei et, cum intendit cutem, missiles: ora urguentium figit canum et paulo longius iaculatur. hibernis autem se mensibus condit, quae natura multis et ante omnia ursis.

---

[1] v.l. spina.   [2] *Mayhoff*: contecta acu.

---

[a] This is not true.

red and white. When dead it is of a pallid colour. It has flesh on the head and jaws and at the junction of the tail in a rather scanty amount, and nowhere else in the whole body; blood in the heart and around the eyes only; its vital parts contain no spleen. It hibernates like a lizard in the winter months.

LII. The reindeer of Scythia also changes its colours, but none other of the fur-clad animals does so except the Indian wolf, which is reported to have a mane on the neck. For the jackal—which is a kind of wolf, longer in the body and differing in the shortness of the legs, quick in its spring, living by hunting, harmless to man—changes its raiment though not its colour, being shaggy through the winter but naked in summer. The reindeer is the size of an ox; its head is larger than that of a stag but not unlike it; it has branching horns, cloven hooves, and a fleece as shaggy as a bear's but, when it happens to be self-coloured, resembling an ass's coat. The hide is so hard that they use it for making cuirasses. When alarmed it imitates the colours of all the trees, bushes and flowers and places where it lurks,[a] and consequently is rarely caught. It would be surprising that its body has such variety of character, but it is more surprising that even its fleece has. *The reindeer: seasonal changes of colour.*

LIII. The porcupine is a native of India and Africa. It is covered with a prickly skin of the hedgehogs' kind, but the spines of the porcupine are longer and they dart out when it draws the skin tight: it pierces the mouths of hounds when they close with it, and shoots out at them when further off. In the winter months it hibernates, as is the nature of many animals and before all of bears. *The porcupine.*

126 LIV. Eorum coitus hiemis initio, nec vulgari quadripedum more sed ambobus cubantibus conplexisque; deinde secessus in specus separatim, in quibus pariunt xxx die plurimum quinos. hi sunt candida informisque caro, paulo muribus maior, sine oculis, sine pilo; ungues tantum prominent. hanc lambendo paulatim figurant. nec quicquam rarius quam parientem videre ursam. ideo mares quadragenis diebus latent, feminae quaternis mensibus.

127 specus si non habuere, ramorum fruticumque congerie aedificant impenetrabiles imbribus mollique fronde constratos. primis diebus bis septenis tam gravi somno premuntur ut ne vulneribus quidem excitari queant; tunc mirum in modum veterno pinguescunt (illi sunt adipes medicaminibus apti contraque defluvium capilli tenaces). ab his diebus residunt ac priorum pedum suctu vivunt. fetus rigentes adprimendo pectori fovent non alio incubitu

128 quam ad ova volucres. mirum dictu, credit Theophrastus per id tempus coctas quoque ursorum carnes, si adserventur, increscere, cibi nulla tunc argumenta nec nisi umoris minimum in alvo inveniri, sanguinis exiguas circa corda tantum guttas, reliquo

129 corpori nihil inesse. procedunt vere, sed mares praepingues, cuius rei causa non prompta est, quippe ne somno quidem saginatis, praeter quattuordecim dies ut diximus. exeuntes herbam quandam arum

LIV. Bears couple at the beginning of winter, *The bear.* and not in the usual manner of quadrupeds but both lying down and hugging each other; afterwards they retire apart into caves, in which they give birth on the thirtieth day to a litter of five cubs at most. These are a white and shapeless lump of flesh, little larger than mice, without eyes or hair and only the claws projecting. This lump the mother bears slowly lick into shape. Nor is anything more unusual than to see a she-bear giving birth to cubs. Consequently the males lie in hiding for periods of forty days, and the females four months. If they have not got caves, they build rainproof dens by heaping up branches and brushwood, with a carpet of soft foliage on the floor. For the first fortnight they sleep so soundly that they cannot be aroused even by wounds; at this period they get fat with sloth to a remarkable degree (the bear's grease is useful for medicines and a prophylactic against baldness). As a result of these days of sleep they shrink in bulk and they live by sucking their fore paws. They cherish their freezing offspring by pressing them to their breast, lying on them just like birds hatching eggs. Strange to say, Theophrastus believes that even boiled bear's flesh, if kept, goes on growing in size for that period; that no evidence of food and only the smallest amount of water is found in the belly at this stage, and that there are only a few drops of blood in the neighbourhood of the heart and none in the rest of the body. In the spring they come out, but the males are very fat, a fact the cause of which is not evident, as they have not been fattened up even by sleep, except for a fortnight as we have said. On coming out they devour a plant

nomine laxandis intestinis alioquin concretis devorant friantque [1] surculos dentibus [2] praedomantes
ora. oculi eorum hebetantur, qua maxime causa
favos expetunt, ut convulneratum ab apibus os levet
130 sanguine gravedinem illam. invalidissimum urso
caput, quod leoni firmissimum; ideo urguente vi
praecipitaturi se ex aliqua rupe manibus cooperto
iaciuntur, ac saepe in harena colapho infracto
exanimantur. cerebro veneficium inesse Hispaniae
credunt, occisorumque in spectaculis capita cremant
testato, quoniam potum in ursinam rabiem agat.
131 ingrediuntur et bipedes; arborem aversi derepunt.
tauros ex ore cornibusque eorum omnibus pedibus
suspensi pondere fatigant; nec alteri animalium in
maleficio stultitia sollertior. annalibus notatum est
M. Pisone M. Messala coss. a. d. XIV kal. Oct.
Domitium Ahenobarbum aedilem curulem ursos
Numidicos centum et totidem venatores Aethiopas
in circo dedisse. miror adiectum Numidicos fuisse,
cum in Africa ursum non gigni constet.
132   LV. Conduntur hieme et Pontici mures, dumtaxat
albi, quorum palatum in gustu sagacissimum auctores
quonam modo intellexerint miror. conduntur et
Alpini, quibus magnitudo melium est, sed hi pabulo

---

[1] *Mayhoff*: circaque.   [2] *Mayhoff*: dentium.

---

[a] 61 B.C.   [b] Marmots.

called wake-robin to loosen the bowels, which are otherwise constipated, and they rub their teeth on tree-stumps to get their mouths into training. Their eyes have got dim, which is the chief reason why they seek for hives, so that their face may be stung by the bees to relieve that trouble with blood. A bear's weakest part is the head, which is the lion's strongest; consequently if when hard pressed by an attack they are going to fling themselves down from a rock they make the jump with their head covered with their fore paws, and in the arena are often killed by their head being broken by a buffet. The Spanish provinces believe that a bear's brain contains poison, and when bears are killed in shows their heads are burnt in the presence of a witness, on the ground that to drink the poison drives a man bear-mad. Bears even walk on two feet, and they crawl down trees backward. They tire out bulls with their weight by hanging by all four feet from their mouth and horns; and no other animal's stupidity is more cunning in doing harm. It is noted in the Annals that on 19 September in the consulship [a] of Marcus Piso and Marcus Messala, Domitius Ahenobarbus as curule aedile provided in the circus a hundred Numidian bears and the same number of Ethiopian huntsmen. I am surprised at the description of the bears as Numidian, since it is known that the bear does not occur in Africa.

LV. The mice of the Black Sea region also hibernate, at all events the white ones, which are stated to have a very discriminating palate, though I am curious to know how the authorities detected this. Alpine mice,[b] which are the size of badgers, also hibernate, but these carry a supply of fodder into their caves

Hibernation of field-mice

PLINY: NATURAL HISTORY

ante in specus convecto.[1] quidam narrant alternos
marem ac feminam subrosae conplexos fascem herbae
supinos cauda mordicus adprehensa invicem detrahi
ad specum, ideoque illo tempore detrito esse dorso.
sunt his pares et in Aegypto, similiterque resident
in clunes et in binis pedibus gradiuntur prioribusque
ut manibus utuntur.

133 LVI. Praeparant hiemi et irenacei cibos ac
volutati supra iacentia poma adfixa spinis, unum
amplius tenentes ore, portant in cavas arbores.
iidem mutationem aquilonis in austrum condentes
se in cubile praesagiunt. ubi vero sensere venantem,
contracto ore pedibusque ac parte omni inferiore,
qua raram et innocuam habent lanuginem, convol-
vuntur in formam pilae, ne quid conprehendi possit
134 praeter aculeos. in desperatione vero urinam in se
reddunt tabificam tergori suo spinisque noxiam,
propter hoc se capi gnari. quamobrem exinanita
prius urina venari ars est. et tum praecipua dos
tergori, alias corrupto, fragili, putribus spinis atque
deciduis, etiam si vivat subtractus fuga. ob id non
nisi in novissima spe maleficio eo perfunditur,
quippe et ipsi odere suum veneficium, ita parcentes
sibi terminumque supremum opperientes ut ferme
ante captivitas occupet. calidae postea aquae

---

[1] *Detlefsen* : cum quidam *aut* cum quidem.

---

[a] Possibly jerboas.

beforehand. Some people say that they let themselves down into their cave in a string, male and female alternately holding the next one's tail in their teeth, and lying on their backs, embracing a bundle of grass that they have bitten off at the roots, and that consequently at this season their backs show marks of rubbing. There are also mice [a] resembling these in Egypt, and they sit back on their haunches in a similar way, and walk on two feet and use their forepaws as hands.

LVI. Hedgehogs also prepare food for winter, and fixing fallen apples on their spines by rolling on them and holding one more in their mouth carry them to hollow trees. The same animals foretell a change of wind from North to South by retiring to their lair. But when they perceive someone hunting them they draw together their mouth and feet and all their lower part, which has thin and harmless down on it, and roll up into the shape of a ball, so that it may not be possible to take hold of any part of them except the prickles. But when desperate they make water over themselves, which corrodes their hide and damages their spines, for the sake of which they know that people catch them. Hence the scientific way is to hunt them just after they have discharged their water. And then the hide is of particular value, whereas otherwise it is spoiled and fragile, with the spines rotting and falling out, even if the animal escapes by flight and lives. On this account it does not drench itself with this damaging stuff except as a last resort, since even the creatures themselves hate this self-poisoning, sparing themselves and waiting for the final limit so long that usually capture overtakes them beforehand. After-

95

adspersu resolvitur pila, adprehensusque pes alter e
posterioribus suspendiosa fame necat: aliter non
135 est occidere et tergori parcere. ipsum animal non,
ut remur plerique, vitae hominum supervacuum est,
si non sint[1] illi aculei, frustra vellerum mollitia in
pecude mortalibus data: hac cute expoliuntur vestes.
magnum fraus et ibi lucrum monopolio invenit, de
nulla re crebrioribus senatus consultis nulloque non
principe adito querimoniis provincialibus.

136 LVII. Urinae et duobus aliis animalibus ratio
mira. leontophonon accipimus vocari parvom nec
aliubi nascens quam ubi leo gignitur, quo gustato
tanta illa vis et[2] ceteris quadripedum imperitans
ilico expiret. ergo corpus eius exustum aspergunt
aliis carnibus polentae modo insidiantes ferae,
necantque etiam cinere: tam contraria est pestis.
haut inmerito igitur odit leo visumque frangit et
citra morsum exanimat; ille contra urinam spargit,
prudens hanc quoque leoni exitialem.

137 Lyncum umor ita redditus[3] ubi gignuntur glaciatur
arescitve in gemmas carbunculis similes et igneo
colore fulgentes, lyncurium vocatas atque ob id
sucino a plerisque ita generari prodito. novere hoc

---

[1] essent? *Rackham.* [2] *Mayhoff* (cf. § 48): ut.
[3] Lyncum urina reddita? *Mayhoff.*

---

[a] Fabulous.

wards the ball into which they roll up can be made to
unroll by a sprinkle of hot water, and to fasten them
up by one of the hind feet kills them through starvation when hanging: it is not possible to kill them in
any other way and avoid damaging the hide. The
animal itself is not, as most of us think, superfluous
for the life of mankind, since, if it had not spines,
the softness of the hides in cattle would have been
bestowed on mortals to no purpose: hedgehog skin
is used in dressing cloth for garments. Even here
fraud has discovered a great source of profit by
monopoly, nothing having been the subject of more
frequent legislation by the senate, and every emperor
without exception having been approached by complaints from the provinces.

LVII. The urine of two other animals also has
remarkable properties. We are told that there is a
small animal called ' lion's-bane '[a] that only occurs
in regions where the lion is found, to taste of which
causes that mighty creature, the lord of all the other
four-footed animals, to expire immediately. Consequently men burn this creature's body and sprinkle
it like pearl barley on the flesh of other animals as a
bait for a lion, and even kill their prey with its
ashes: so noisome a bane it is. Therefore the lion
naturally hates it, and when he sees it crushes it
and does all he can short of biting it to kill it; while
it meets the attack by spraying urine, knowing already
that this also is deadly to a lion.

The water of lynxes, voided in this way when
they are born, solidifies or dries up into drops like
carbuncles and of a brilliant flame-colour, called lynx-
water—which is the origin of the common story that
this is the way in which amber is formed. The

The lion's-bane.

Other cases of self-protection—the lynx, the badger.

sciuntque lynces, et invidentes urinam terra operiunt eoque celerius solidatur illa.

138 Alia sollertia in metu melibus: sufflatae cutis distentu ictus hominum et morsus canum arcent.

LVIII. Provident tempestatem et sciuri obturatisque qua spiraturus est ventus cavernis ex alia parte aperiunt fores; de cetero ipsis villosior cauda pro tegumento est. ergo in hiemes aliis provisum pabulum, aliis pro cibo somnus.

139 LIX. Serpentium vipera sola terra dicitur condi, ceterae arborum aut saxorum cavis. et alias vel annua fame durant algore modo dempto. omnia secessus tempore veneno orba dormiunt. simili modo et cocleae, illae quidem iterum et aestatibus, adhaerentes maxime saxis, aut etiam iniuria resu-
140 pinatae avolsaeque non tamen exeuntes. in Baliaribus vero insulis cavaticae appellatae non prorepunt e cavis terrae neque herba vivunt, sed uvae modo inter se cohaerent. est et aliud genus minus vulgare adhaerente operculo eiusdem testae se operiens. obrutae terra semper hae et circa maritimas tantum Alpes quondam effossae coepere iam erui et in Veliterno; omnium tamen laudatissimae in Astypalaea insula.

141 LX. Lacertae, inimicissimum genus cocleis, ne-

a Velletri in Latium.
b One of the Sporades near Crete.

lynxes have learnt this and know it, and they jealously cover up their urine with earth, thereby causing it to solidify more quickly.

Another case of ingenuity in alarm is that of the badgers: they ward off men's blows and the bites of dogs by inflating and distending their skin.

LVIII. Squirrels also foresee a storm, and stop up their holes to windward in advance, opening doorways on the other side; moreover their own exceptionally bushy tail serves them as a covering. Consequently some have a store of food ready for the winter and others use sleep as a substitute for food. *The squirrel.*

LIX. It is said that the viper is the only snake that hides in the ground, all the others using holes in trees or rocks. And for the rest they can last out a year's starvation if only they are protected against cold. All kinds sleep at the period of retirement and are not poisonous. Snails also hibernate in the same way, these indeed retiring again in the summers also, mostly clinging to rocks, or even when violently bent back and torn away, nevertheless not going out. But those in the Balearic Islands called cave-snails do not crawl out of their holes in the ground and do not live on grass, but cling together in a cluster like a bunch of grapes. There is also another kind, which is not so common, that shuts itself in with a tightly fitting lid formed of the same material as its shell. These are always buried in the earth, and formerly were only dug up in the neighbourhood of the Maritime Alps, but they have now begun to be pulled up in the Velitrae *a* district also; however the most highly commended kind of all is on the island of Astypalaea.*b* *Hibernation of snakes and snails.*

LX. The greatest enemy of the snail is the lizard; *The lizard.*

99

gantur semenstrem vitam excedere. lacertae [1] Arabiae cubitales, in Indiae vero Nyso monte xxiv in longitudinem pedum, coloris [2] fulvi aut punicei aut caerulei.

142 LXI. Ex his quoque animalibus quae nobiscum degunt multa sunt cognitu digna, fidelissimumque ante omnia homini canis atque equus. pugnasse adversus latrones canem pro domino accepimus confectumque plagis a corpore non recessisse, volucres ac feras abigentem; ab alio in Epiro agnitum in conventu percussorem domini laniatuque et latratu coactum fateri scelus. Garamantum regem canes CC ab exilio reduxere proeliati contra resistentes.

143 propter bella Colophonii itemque Castabalenses cohortes canum habuere; hae primae dimicabant in acie numquam detrectantes, haec erant fidissima auxilia nec stipendiorum indiga. canes defendere Cimbris caesis domus eorum plaustris inpositas. canis Iasone Lycio interfecto cibum capere noluit inediaque consumptus est. is vero cui nomen Hyrcani reddit Duris accenso regis Lysimachi rogo iniecit se flammae, similiterque Hieronis regis.

144 memorat et Pyrrhum Gelonis tyranni canem Philistus; memoratur et Nicomedis Bithyniae regis uxore eius Consingi lacerata propter lasciviorem cum marito iocum. apud nos Vulcatium nobilem qui Cascellium ius civile docuit asturcone e suburbano redeuntem, cum advesperavisset, canis a grassatore

---

[1] lacertae ? *Mayhoff* : lacesti.
[2] coloris ? *Mayhoff* : colore.

---

[a] An African tribe.
[b] Cf. § 166.

this genus is said not to live more than six months. The lizard of Arabia is 18 inches long, but those on Mount Nysus in India reach a length of 24 feet, and are coloured yellow or scarlet or blue.

LXI. Many also of the domestic animals are *Domestic* worth studying, and before all the one most faithful *animals.* to man, the dog, and the horse. We are told of *Fidelity of dogs.* a dog that fought against brigands in defence of his master and although covered with wounds would not leave his corpse, driving away birds and beasts of prey; and of another dog in Epirus which recognized his master's murderer in a gathering and by snapping and barking made him confess the crime. The King of the Garamantes *a* was escorted back from exile by 200 dogs who did battle with those that offered resistance. The people of Colophon and also those of Castabulum had troops of dogs for their wars; these fought fiercely in the front rank, never refusing battle, and were their most loyal supporters, never requiring pay. When some Cimbrians were killed their hounds defended their houses placed on waggons. When Jason of Lycia had been murdered his dog refused to take food and starved to death. But a dog the name of which Duris gives as Hyrcanus when king Lysimachus's pyre was set alight threw itself into the flame, and similarly at the funeral of King Hiero. Philistus also records the tyrant Gelo's dog Pyrrhus; also the dog of Nicomedes king of Bithynia is recorded to have bitten the King's wife Consingis because she played a rather loose joke with her husband. Among ourselves the famous Vulcatius, Cascellius's tutor in civil law, when returning on his cob *b* from his place near Rome after nightfall was defended by his dog

defendit, item Caelium senatorem aegrum Placentiae
ab armatis oppressum, nec prius ille vulneratus est
145 quam cane interempto. sed super omnia in nostro
aevo actis p. R. testatum Appio Iunio et P. Silio
coss., cum animadverteretur ex causa Neronis
Germanici fili in Titium Sabinum et servitia eius,
unius ex his canem nec in carcere abigi potuisse nec
a corpore recessisse abiecti in gradibus gemitoriis
maestos edentem ululatus magnae p. R. coronae,[1]
ex qua cum quidam ei cibum obiecisset, ad os de-
functi tulisse; innatavit idem cadaver [2] in Tiberim
abiecti [3] sustentare conatus, effusa multitudine ad
spectandam animalis fidem.

146 Soli dominum novere, et ignotum quoque si
repente veniat intellegunt; soli nomina sua, soli
vocem domesticam agnoscunt; itinera quamvis
longa meminere, nec ulli praeter hominem memoria
maior. impetus eorum et saevitia mitigatur ab
147 homine considente humi. plurima alia in his cotidie
vita invenit, sed in venatu sollertia et sagacitas
praecipua est. scrutatur vestigia atque persequitur,
comitantem ad feram inquisitorem loro trahens, qua
visa quam silens et occulta set quam significans demon-
stratio est cauda primum, deinde rostro. ergo etiam
senecta fessos caecosque ac debiles sinu ferunt

---

[1] *Rackham*: magna p. R. corona.
[2] *v.l.* cadavere: cadaveri? *Mayhoff.*
[3] *Brotier*: abiecto.

---

[a] A.D. 28.

from a highwayman; and so was the senator Caelius, an invalid, when set upon by armed men at Piacenza, and he did not receive a wound till the dog had been despatched. But above all cases, in our own generation it is attested by the National Records that in the consulship *a* of Appius Julius and Publius Silius when as a result of the case of Germanicus's son Nero punishment was visited on Titius Sabinus and his slaves, a dog belonging to one of them could not be driven away from him in prison and when he had been flung out on the Steps of Lamentation would not leave his body, uttering sorrowful howls to the vast concourse of the Roman public around, and when one of them threw it food it carried it to the mouth of its dead master; also when his corpse had been thrown into the Tiber it swam to it and tried to keep it afloat, a great crowd streaming out to view the animal's loyalty.

Dogs alone know their master, and also recognize *Intelligence of dogs.* a sudden arrival as a stranger; they alone recognize their own names, and the voice of a member of the household; they remember the way to places however distant, and no creature save man has a longer memory. Their onset and rage can be mollified by a person sitting down on the ground. Experience daily discovers very many other qualities in these animals, but it is in hunting that their skill and sagacity is most outstanding. A hound traces and follows footprints, dragging by its leash the tracker that accompanies it towards his quarry; and on sighting it how silent and secret but how significant an indication is given first by the tail and then by the muzzle! Consequently even when they are exhausted with old age and blind and weak, men

ventos et odorem captantes protendentesque rostra
ad cubilia.

148 E tigribus eos Indi volunt concipi, et ob id in silvis
coitus tempore alligant feminas. primo et secundo
fetu nimis feroces putant gigni, tertio demum educant. hoc idem e lupis Galli, quorum greges suum
quisque ductorem e canibus[1] et ducem habent:
illum in venatu comitantur, illi parent; namque inter
se exercent etiam magisteria. certum est iuxta
Nilum amnem currentes lambere, ne crocodilorum
149 aviditati occasionem praebeant. Indiam petenti
Alexandro Magno rex Albaniae dono dederat
inusitatae magnitudinis unum, cuius specie delec-
tatus iussit ursos, mox apros et deinde damas emitti,
contemptu inmobili iacente eo; qua segnitia tanti
corporis offensus imperator generosi spiritus interimi
eum iussit. nuntiavit hoc fama regi; itaque alterum
mittens addidit mandata ne in parvis experiri vellet
sed in leone elephantove; duos sibi fuisse, hoc
150 interempto praeterea nullum fore. nec distulit
Alexander, leonemque fractum protinus vidit. postea
elephantum iussit induci, haud alio magis spectaculo
laetatus: horrentibus quippe villis per totum corpus
ingenti primum latratu intonuit, mox ingruit[2]

---

[1] [e canibus]? *Rackham.*
[2] *Gronovius:* increvit *aut* in cervicem.

carry them in their arms sniffing at the breezes
and scents and pointing their muzzles towards
cover.

The Indians want hounds to be sired by tigers, *Dogs crossed*
and at the breeding season they tie up bitches in the *with wild*
woods for this purpose. They think that the first *animals.*
and second litters are too fierce and they only rear
the third one. Similarly the Gauls breed hounds
from wolves; each of their packs has one of the
dogs as leader and guide; the pack accompanies
this leader in the hunt and pays it obedience; for
dogs actually exercise authority among themselves.
It is known that the dogs by the Nile lap up water
from the river as they run, so as not to give the
greed of the crocodiles its chance. When Alexander *A famous*
the Great was on his way to India, the king of Albania *hound.*
had presented him with one dog of unusually large
size; Alexander was delighted by its appearance,
and gave orders for bears and then boars and finally
hinds to be let slip—the hound lying contemptuously
motionless. This slackness on the part of so vast an
animal annoyed the generous spirit of the Emperor,
who ordered it to be destroyed. Report carried
news of this to the king; and accordingly sending
a second hound he added a message that Alexander
should not desire to test it on small game but on a
lion or an elephant; he had only possessed two of
the breed and if this one was destroyed there would
be none left. Alexander did not put off the trial,
and forthwith saw a lion crushed. Afterwards he
ordered an elephant to be brought in, and no other
show ever gave him more delight: for the dog's
hair bristled all over his body and it first gave a
vast thunderous bark, then kept leaping up and

adsultans contraque membra[1] exurgens hinc et illinc
artifici dimicatione, qua maxume opus esset infestans
atque evitans, donec adsidua rotatum vertigine
adflixit ad casum eius tellure concussa.

151 LXII. Canum generi bis anno partus. iusta ad
pariendum annua aetas. gerunt uterum sexagenis
diebus. gignunt caecos, et quo largiore aluntur
lacte eo tardiorem visum accipiunt, non tamen
umquam ultra xxi diem nec ante septimum.
quidam tradunt, si unus gignatur, nono die cernere,
si gemini, decumo, itemque in singulos adici totidem
tarditatis ad lucem dies, et ab ea quae sit femina ex
primipara genita citius[2] cerni. optumus in fetu qui
novissimus cernere incipit, aut quem primum fert in
cubile feta.

152 LXIII. Rabies canum sirio ardente homini pestifera, ut diximus, ita morsis letali aquae metu.
quapropter obviam itur per xxx eos dies gallinaceo
maxime fimo inmixto canum cibis aut, si praevenerit
morbus, veratro. a morsu vero unicum remedium
oraculo quodam nuper repertum radix silvestris
153 rosae quae cynorrhoda appellatur. Columella auctor
est, si xl die quam sit natus castretur morsu cauda
summusque eius articulus auferatur, spinae[3] nervo
exempto nec caudam crescere nec canes rabidos
fieri. canem locutum in prodigiis, quod equidem

---

[1] *v.l.* contraque beluam.   [2] *Edd.*: clunos *aut* faunos.
[3] *Mayhoff e Columella*: sequi.

---

[a] Cf. II 107.

rearing against the creature's limbs on this side and that, in scientific combat, attacking and retiring at the most necessary points, until the elephant turning round and round in an unceasing whirl was brought to the ground with an earth-shaking crash.

LXII. The genus dog breeds twice a year. Ma- *Dog breeding.* turity for reproduction begins at the age of one. They carry their young for sixty days. Puppies are born blind, and acquire sight the more slowly the more copious the milk with which they are suckled; though the blind period never lasts more than three weeks or less than one. Some people report that a puppy born singly sees on the 9th day, twins on the 10th, and so on, a corresponding number of days' delay in seeing light being added for each extra puppy; and that a bitch of a first litter begins to see sooner. The best in a litter is the one that begins to see last, or else the one that the mother carries into the kennel first after delivery.

LXIII. Rabies in dogs, as we have said, is dangerous *Precautions against rabies.* to human beings in periods when the dog-star is shining,[a] as it causes fatal hydrophobia to those bitten in those circumstances. Consequently a precautionary measure during the 30 days in question is to mix dung—mostly chicken's droppings, in the dog's food, or, if the disease has come already, hellebore. But after a bite the only cure is one which was lately discovered from an oracle, the root of the wild-rose called in Greek dog-rose. Columella states that if a dog's tail is docked by being bitten off and the end joint amputated 40 days after birth, the spinal marrow having been removed the tail does not grow again and the dog is not liable to rabies. The only cases that have come down to us among portents, so far

adnotaverim, accepimus et serpentem latrasse cum
pulsus est regno Tarquinius.

154 LXIV. Eidem Alexandro et equi magna raritas
contigit. Bucephalan eum vocarunt sive ab aspectu
torvo sive ab insigni taurini capitis armo inpressi.
XVI talentis ferunt ex Philonici Pharsalii grege
emptum etiam tum puero capto eius decore. neminem hic alium quam Alexandrum regio instratu
ornatus recepit in sedem, alias passim recipiens.
idem in proeliis memoratae cuiusdam perhibetur
operae, Thebarum oppugnatione vulneratus in
alium transire Alexandrum non passus; multa
praeterea eiusdem modi, propter quae rex defuncto
ei duxit exequias urbemque tumulo circumdedit
155 nomine eius. nec Caesaris dictatoris quemquam
alium recepisse dorso equus traditur, idemque similis
humanis pedes priores habuisse, hac effigie locatus
ante Veneris Genetricis aedem. fecit et divus
Augustus equo tumulum, de quo Germanici Caesaris
carmen est. Agrigenti conplurium equorum tumuli
pyramides habent. equum adamatum a Samiramide
156 usque in coitum[1] Iuba auctor est. Scythici quidem
equitatus equorum gloria strepunt: occiso regulo ex
provocatione dimicantem hostem, cum ad spoliandum

---

[1] usque ad rogum ? *Brotier.*

[a] Say nearly £4000 gold.
[b] Bucephala, see VI 77.
[c] *I.e.* with toes not united into a hoof: if true, a throw-
back to the prehistoric horse.
[d] Hyginus *Fab.* 243: equo amisso in pyram se coniecit.

as I have noted, of a dog talking and a snake barking were when Tarquin was driven from his kingdom.

LXIV. Alexander also had the good fortune to own a great rarity in horseflesh. They called the animal Bucephalus, either because of its fierce appearance or from the mark of a bull's head branded on its shoulder. It is said that it was bought for sixteen talents [a] from the herd of Philonicus of Pharsalus while Alexander was still a boy, as he was taken by its beauty. This horse when adorned with the royal saddle would not allow itself to be mounted by anybody except Alexander, though on other occasions it allowed anybody to mount. It is also celebrated for a memorable feat in battle, not having allowed Alexander during the attack on Thebes to change to another mount when it had been wounded; and a number of occurrences of the same kind are also reported, on account of which when it died the king headed its funeral procession, and built a city round its tomb which he named after it.[b] Also the horse that belonged to Caesar the Dictator is said to have refused to let anyone else mount it; and it is also recorded that its fore feet were like those of a man,[c] as it is represented in the statue that stands in front of the Temple of Venus Genetrix. The late lamented Augustus also made a funeral mound for a horse, which is the subject of a poem by Germanicus Caesar. At Girgenti a great number of horses' tombs have pyramids over them. Juba attests that Semiramis fell so deeply in love with a horse that she married it.[d] The Scythian cavalry regiments indeed resound with famous stories of horses: a chieftain was challenged to a duel by an enemy and killed, and when his adversary came to strip

venisset, ab equo eius ictibus morsuque confectum,
alium detracto oculorum operimento et cognito cum
matre coitu petisse praerupta atque exanimatum.
eadem [1] ex causa in Reatino agro laceratum prorigam
invenimus. namque et cognationum intellectus his
est, atque in grege prioris anni sororem libentius
157 etiam quam matrem equa comitatur. docilitas
tanta est ut universus Sybaritani exercitus equitatus
ad symphoniae cantum saltatione quadam moveri
solitus inveniatur. idem praesagiunt pugnam, et
amissos lugent dominos: lacrimas [2] interdum desiderio fundunt. interfecto Nicomede rege equos
158 eius inedia vitam finivit. Phylarchus refert Cen-
taretum e Galatis in proelio occiso Antiocho potitum
equo eius conscendisse ovantem, at illum indignatione
accensum domitis frenis ne regi posset praecipitem
in abrupta isse exanimatumque una; Philistus a
Dionysio relictum in caeno haerentem, ut se evellisset,
secutum vestigia domini examine apium iubae
inhaerente, eoque ostento tyrannidem a Dionysio
occupatam.

159   LXV. Ingenia eorum inenarrabilia. iaculantes
obsequia experiuntur difficiles conatus corpore ipso
nisuque iuvantium [3]; item [4] tela humi collecta equiti
porrigunt. nam in circo ad currus iuncti non dubie

---

[1] v.ll. aequa eadem, equa eadem.
[2] v.l. lacrimasque.
[3] *Hardouin* : invitantium.
[4] *Mayhoff* : iam.

his body of its armour, his horse kicked him and bit
him till he died; another horse, when its blinkers
were removed and it found out that a mare it had
covered was its dam, made for a precipice and com-
mitted suicide. We read that an ostler in the Reate
district was savaged by a horse for the same reason.
For horses actually understand the ties of relationship, and a filly in a herd is even fonder of going
with a sister a year older than with their dam.
Their docility is so great that we learn that the entire
cavalry of the army of Sybaris used to perform a sort
of ballet to the music of a band. The Sybarite
horses also know beforehand when there is going to
be a battle, and when they lose their masters mourn
for them: sometimes they shed tears at the bereave-
ment. When King Nicomedes was killed his horse
ended its life by refusing food. Phylarchus records
that when Antiochus fell in battle one of the Galatians
Centaretus caught his horse and mounted it in
triumph, but it was fired with indignation and taking
the bit between its teeth so as to become unmanageable, galloped headlong to a precipice where it
perished with its rider. Philistus records that
Dionysius left his horse stuck in a bog, and when
it extricated itself it followed its master's tracks
with a swarm of bees clinging to its mane; and that
in consequence of this portent Dionysius seized the
tyranny.

LXV. The cleverness of horses is beyond descrip- *Other proofs*
tion. Mounted javelinmen experience their docility *of intelligence*
in assisting difficult attempts with the actual swaying *in horses.*
of their body; also they gather up the weapons
lying on the ground and pass them to their rider.
Horses harnessed to chariots in the circus un-

160 intellectum adhortationis et gloriae fatentur. Claudi
Caesaris saecularium ludorum circensibus excusso
in carceribus auriga albati Corace occupavere
primatum, optinuere, opponentes effundentes omniaque contra aemulos quae debuissent peritissimo
auriga insistente facientes, et [1] cum puderet hominum
artem ab equis vinci, peracto legitimo cursu ad
161 cretam stetere. maius augurium apud priscos plebeis
circensibus excusso auriga ita ut si staret in Capitol-
ium cucurrisse equos aedemque ter lustrasse; maximum vero eodem pervenisse a Veis cum palma et
corona effuso Ratumenna qui ibi vicerat: unde
162 postea nomen portae est. Sarmatae longinquo
itineri [2] inedia pridie praeparant eos, potum tantum
exiguum inpertientes, atque ita per centena milia et
quinquaginta continuo cursu euntibus insident.

Vivunt annis quidam quinquagenis, feminae
minore spatio; eaedem quinquennio finem crescendi
capiunt, mares anno addito. forma equorum qualis
maxime elegi [3] oporteat pulcherrime quidem Ver-
gilio vate absoluta est, sed et nos diximus in libro
de iaculatione equestri condito, et fere inter
omnes constare video. diversa autem circo ratio

---

[1] et add. ? Mayhoff.   [2] Mayhoff: acturi.
[3] Rackham: legi.

---

[a] A.D. 47.
[b] The Porta Ratumenna at Rome.
[c] About 138 English miles.
[d] Georgics III 72.

questionably show that they understand the shouts
of encouragement and applause. At the races in
the circus forming part of the Secular Games[a] of
Claudius Caesar a charioteer of the Whites named
Raven was thrown at the start, and his team took the
lead and kept it by getting in the way of their rivals
and jostling them aside and doing everything against
them that they would have had to do with a most
skilful charioteer in control, and as they were
ashamed for human science to be beaten by horses,
when they had completed the proper course they
stopped dead at the chalk line. A greater portent
was when in early days a charioteer was thrown
at the plebeian circus races and the horses galloped
on to the Capitol and raced round the temple three
times just the same as if he still stood at the reins;
but the greatest was when a chariot-team reached
the same place from Veii with the palm-branch and
wreath after Ratumenna who had won at Veii
had been thrown: an event which subsequently
gave its name to the gate.[b] The Sarmatians get
their horses into training for a long journey by giving
them no fodder the day before and only allowing
them a small amount of water, and by these means
they ride them on a journey of 150 miles[c] without
drawing rein.

Some horses live fifty years, but mares live a shorter *Age of horses.*
time; mares stop growing when five years old, the *Varieties of build.*
males a year later. The appearance of the horse
that ought to be most preferred has been very
beautifully described in the poetry of Virgil,[d] but we
also have dealt with it in our book on the Use of
the Javelin by Cavalry, and I observe that there is
almost universal agreement about it. But a different

quaeritur; itaque cum bimi[1] alio subiungantur imperio, non ante quinquennes ibi certamen accipit.

163 LXVI. Partum in eo genere undenis mensibus ferunt, duodecimo gignunt. coitus verno aequinoctio bimo utrimque vulgaris, sed a trimatu firmior partus. generat mas ad annos XXXIII, utpote cum a circo post vicesimum annum mittantur ad subolem. Opunte et ad quadraginta durasse tradunt adiutum

164 modo in attollenda priore parte corporis. sed ad generandum paucis animalium minor fertilitas; qua de causa intervalla admissurae dantur, nec tamen quindecim initus eiusdem anni valet tolerare. equarum libido extinguitur iuba tonsa; gignunt annis omnibus ad quadragesimum. vixisse equam[2] LXXV annos proditur.

165 In hoc genere gravida stans parit; praeterque ceteras fetum diligit. et sane equis amoris innascitur[3] veneficium hippomanes appellatum in fronte, caricae magnitudine, colore nigro, quod statim edito partu devorat feta aut partum ad ubera non admittit. si quis praereptum habeat, olfactu in rabiem id genus agitur. amissa parente in grege armenti reliquae fetae educant orbum. terram attingere ore triduo proximo quam sit genitus negant posse.

---

[1] *Rackham* : bimi in.
[2] *Rackham* : equum.
[3] *Rackham* : innasci.

build is required for the Circus; and consequently though horses may be broken as two-year-olds to other service, racing in the Circus does not claim them before five.

LXVI. Gestation in this genus lasts eleven months *Horse-breeding.* and the foal is born in the twelfth month. Breeding takes place as a rule in the spring equinox when both animals are two-year-olds, but the progeny is stronger if breeding begins at three. A stallion goes on serving to the age of 33, as they are sent from the race-course to the stud at 20. It is recorded that a stallion at Opus even continued to 40, only he needed assistance in lifting his fore-quarters. But few animals are such unfertile sires as the horse; consequently intervals are allowed in breeding, and nevertheless a stallion cannot stand serving fifteen times in the same year. Mares in heat are cooled down by having their manes shorn; they foal yearly up to 40. It is stated that a mare has lived to 75.

In the equine genus the pregnant female is delivered standing up; and she loves her offspring more than all other female animals. And in fact a love-poison called horse-frenzy is found in the forehead of horses at birth, the size of a dried fig, black in colour, which a brood mare as soon as she has dropped her foal eats up, or else she refuses to suckle the foal. If anybody takes it before she gets it, and keeps it, the scent drives him into madness of the kind specified. If a foal loses its dam the other brood mares in the same herd rear the orphan. It is said that a foal is unable to reach the ground with its mouth within the first three days after birth. The greedier it is in drinking the deeper

quo quis acrior in bibendo profundius nares mergit. Scythae per bella feminis uti malunt, quoniam urinam cursu non inpedito reddant.

166 LXVII. Constat in Lusitania circa Olisiponem oppidum et Tagum amnem equas favonio flante obversas animalem concipere spiritum, idque partum fieri et gigni pernicissimum ita, sed triennium vitae non excedere. in eadem Hispania Gallaica gens et Asturica equini generis,[1] quos theldones vocamus, minore forma appellatos asturcones, gignunt quibus non vulgaris in cursu gradus sed mollis alterno crurum explicatu glomeratio, unde equis tolutim capere incursum traditur arte.

Equo fere qui homini morbi, praeterque vesicae conversio, sicut omnibus in genere veterino.

167 LXVIII. Asinum cccc nummum emptum Q. Axio senatori auctor est M. Varro, haut scio an omnium pretio animalium victo. opera sine dubio generi munifica arando quoque, sed mularum maxime progeneratione. patria etiam spectatur in his, Arcadicis in Achaia, in Italia Reatinis. ipsum animal frigoris maxime impatiens: ideo non generatur in Ponto, nec aequinoctio verno ut cetera pecua

168 admittitur sed solstitio. mares in remissione operis deteriores. partus a tricensimo mense ocissimus

---

[1] *Barbarus*: generis hi sunt.

---

[a] Aristotle, *H.A.* VI 572a 13, places this occurrence in Crete.
[b] About £3200 gold.

it dips its nostrils into the water. The Scythians prefer mares as chargers, because they can make water without checking their gallop.

LXVII. It is known that in Lusitania *a* in the neighbourhood of the town of Lisbon and the river Tagus mares when a west wind is blowing stand facing towards it and conceive the breath of life and that this produces a foal, and this is the way to breed a very swift colt, but it does not live more than three years. Also in Spain the Gallaic and Asturian tribes breed those of the horse kind that we call 'theldones,' though when more of a pony type they are designated 'cobs', which have not the usual paces in running but a smooth trot, straightening the near and off-side legs alternately, from which the horses are taught by training to adopt an ambling pace. *Horse-breeding in Spain.*

The horse has nearly the same diseases as mankind, and is also liable to shifting of the bladder, as are all beasts of the draft class. *Diseases of the horse.*

LXVIII. Marcus Varro states that an ass was bought for the senator Quintus Axius at 400,000 sesterces,*b* which perhaps beats the price paid for any other animal. The services of the ass kind are undoubtedly bountiful in ploughing as well, but especially in breeding mules. In mules also regard is paid to locality of origin—in Greece the Arcadian breed is esteemed and in Italy the Reatine. The ass itself is very bad at enduring cold, and consequently is not bred in the Black Sea district; and it is not allowed to breed at the spring equinox like all other cattle, but at midsummer. The males make worse sires when not in work. The females breed at two and a half years old at earliest, but *Ass-breeding.*

sed a trimatu legitimus: totidem quot equae et
isdem mensibus et simili modo. sed incontinens
uterus urinam genitalem reddit ni cogatur in cursum
verberibus a coitu. raro geminos parit. paritura
lucem fugit et tenebras quaerit, ne conspiciatur ab
homine. gignit tota vita, quae est ei ad tricensimum
169 annum. partus caritas summa, sed aquarum taedium maius: per ignes ad fetus tendunt, eaedem
si rivus minimus intersit horrent imos[1] pedes
omnino tinguere. nec nisi adsuetos potant fontes
quae sunt in pecuariis atque ita ut sicco tramite ad
potum eant; nec pontes transeunt pro raritate
eorum tralucentibus fluviis; mirumque dictu,
sitiunt et, si mutentur aquae, ut bibant cogendae
exorandaeve sunt. nec nisi spatiosa in cubitu
laxitas tuta; varia namque somno visa concipiunt
ictu pedum crebro, qui nisi per inane emicuit, repulsu durioris materiae clauditatem ilico adfert.
170 quaestus ex his opima praedia exuperat: notum
est in Celtiberia singulas quadringentena milia
nummum enixas, mularum maxume partu. aurium
referre in his et palpebrarum pilos aiunt; quamvis
enim unicolor reliquo corpore, totidem tamen
colores quot ibi fuere reddit. pullos earum epulari
Maecenas instituit multum eo tempore praelatos

---

[1] *Detlefsen*: horrentia ut (horrent etiam) *Mayhoff*.

[a] See note on § 167.

regularly from three; they can breed as many times as mares, and in the same months and in a similar way. But the womb cannot retain the genital fluid but discharges it, unless the animal is whipped into a gallop after coupling. It seldom bears twins. When about to bear a foal it shuns the sunlight and seeks the shadow, so as not to be seen by a human being. It breeds through all its lifetime, which is thirty years. It has a very great affection for its young, but a greater dislike for water: she-asses will go through fire to their foals, but yet if the smallest stream intervenes they are afraid of merely wetting their hooves. Those kept in pastures will only drink at springs they are used to, and where they can get to drink by a dry track; and they will not go across bridges with interstices in their structure allowing the gleam of the river to be seen through them; and, surprising to say, they may be thirsty and have to be forced or coaxed to drink, if the stream is not the one they are used to. Only a wide allowance of stall-room is safe for them to lie down in, for when asleep they have a variety of dreams and frequently let out with their hooves, which at once causes lameness by hitting timber that is too hard unless they have plenty of room to kick in. The profit made out of she-asses surpasses the richest spoils of war. It is known that in Celtiberia their foals have made 400,000 sesterces[a] per dam, especially when mules are bred. They say that in she-asses the hair of the ears and the eye-lids is an important point, for although the rest of the dam's body is all one colour, the foal reproduces all the colours that were in those places. Maecenas set the fashion of eating donkey foals at banquets, and they were

onagris; post eum interiit auctoritas saporis asino. moriente visu [1] celerrime id genus deficit.

171 LXIX. Ex asino et equa mula gignitur mense XIII, animal viribus in labores eximium. ad tales partus equas neque quadrimis minores neque decennibus maiores legunt. arcerique utrumque genus ab altero narrant nisi in infantia eius generis quod ineat lacte hausto; quapropter subreptos pullos in tenebris equarum uberi asinarumve eculeos admovent. gignitur autem mula et [2] ex equo et asina, sed effrenis et tarditatis indomitae.lenta omnia et [3] e

172 vetulis. conceptum ex equo secutus asini coitus abortu perimit, non item ex asino equi. feminas a partu optime septimo die impleri observatum, mares fatigatos melius implere. quae non prius quam dentes quos pullinos appellant iaciat conceperit sterilis esse [4] intellegitur, et quae non primo initu generare coeperit. equo et asina genitos mares hinnulos antiqui vocabant, contraque mulos quos

173 asini et equae generarent. observatum ex duobus diversis generibus nata tertii generis fieri et neutri parentium esse similia, eaque ipsa quae sunt ita nata non gignere in omni animalium genere; idcirco mulas non parere. est in annalibus nostris peperisse

---

[1] v.l. viso.   [2] et add. Detlefsen.
   [3] Mayhoff: omnia esse.   [4] esse add. Rackham.

---

[a] A variant text gives ' but after his time this delicacy went out of favour. Animals of this genus very quickly flag when they have seen a dying donkey.'

much preferred to wild asses at that period; but after his time the ass lost favour as a delicacy. Animals of this genus very quickly flag when their sight begins to go.[a]

LXIX. A mare coupled with an ass after twelve *Mule-breeding.* months bears a mule, an animal of exceptional strength for agricultural operations. To breed mules they choose mares not less than four or more than ten years old. Also breeders say that females of either genus refuse stallions of the other one unless as foals they were suckled by females of the same genus as the stallions; for this reason they stealthily remove the foals in the dark and put them to mares' or she-asses' udders respectively. But a mule is also got by a horse out of an ass, though it is unmanageable, slow and obstinate. Also all the foals from old mares are sluggish. It causes miscarriage for a mare in foal by a horse to be put to an ass, but not *vice versa.* It has been observed that female asses are best coupled six days after they have borne a foal, and that males couple better when tired. It is noticed that a female that does not conceive before she casts what are called her milk-teeth is barren, as is one that does not begin to produce foals from the first coupling. Male foals of an ass by a horse were in old days called hinnies, while the term mules was used for the foals of a mare by an ass. It has been noticed that the offspring of two different races of animals belong to a third kind and resemble neither parent; and that such hybrids are not themselves fertile: this is the case with all kinds of animals, and is the reason why mules are barren. A number of cases of reproduction by *Cases of* mules are recorded in our Annals, but these were *fertility in mules.*

saepe, verum prodigii loco habitum. Theophrastus vulgo parere in Cappadocia tradit, sed esse id animal ibi sui generis. mulae calcitratus inhibetur vini

174 crebriore potu. in plurium Graecorum est monumentis cum equa muli coitu natum quod vocaverint ginnum, id est parvum mulum. generantur ex equa et onagris mansuefactis mulae veloces in cursu, duritia eximia pedum, verum strigoso corpore, indomito animo. sed generator onagro et asina genitus omnes antecellit. onagri in Phrygia et Lycaonia praecipui. pullis eorum ceu praestantibus sapore Africa gloriatur, quos lalisiones appellat.

175 mulum LXXX annis vixisse Atheniensium monimentis apparet; gavisi namque, cum templum in arce facerent, quod derelictus senecta scandentia iumenta comitatu nisuque exhortaretur, decretum fecere ne frumentarii negotiatores ab incerniculis eum arcerent.

176 LXX. Bubus Indicis camelorum altitudo traditur, cornua in latitudinem quaternorum pedum. in nostro orbe Epiroticis laus maxima a Pyrrhi, ut ferunt, iam inde regis cura. id consecutus est non ante quadrimatum ad partus vocando; praegrandes itaque fuere et hodieque reliquiae stirpium durant. at nunc anniculae fecunditatem poscuntur, tolerantius tamen bimae, tauri generationem quadrimi. inplent

---

^a The Arni-buffalo.

considered portentous. Theophrastus states that mules breed commonly in Cappadocia, but that the Cappadocian mule is a peculiar species. A mule can be checked from kicking by rather frequent drinks of wine. It is stated in the records of a good many Greeks that a foal has been got from a mare coupled with a mule, called a *ginnus*, which means a small mule. She-mules bred from a mare and tamed wild-asses are swift in pace and have extremely hard hooves, but a lean body and an indomitable spirit. But as a sire the foal of a wild-ass and a domestic she-ass excels all others. The wild-asses in Phrygia and Lycaonia are pre-eminent. Africa boasts of their foals as an outstanding table delicacy; the vernacular word for them is *lalisio*. Records at Athens attest a mule's having lived 80 years; for the citizens were so delighted because after it had been put aside owing to old age it encouraged the teams by its company and assistance in their uphill work during the construction of a temple on the citadel, that they made a decree that the corn-dealers were not to keep it away from their stands.

LXX. Indian oxen[a] are reported to be as tall as camels and to have horns with a span of four feet. *Oxen, varieties of:* In our part of the world the most famous are those of Epirus, having been so, it is said, ever since the attention given to them by King Pyrrhus. Pyrrhus achieved this result by not requisitioning them for breeding before the age of four; consequently his oxen were very large, and the remains of his breeds continue even to-day. But now yearling heifers *breeding and* are called upon for breeding, though they can *breaking of.* stand it better at two years, while bulls are made to serve at four. Each bull serves ten cows in the

singuli denas eodem anno. tradunt, si a coitu in
dexteram partem abeant tauri, generatos mares
177 esse, si in laevam, feminas. conceptio uno initu
peragitur, quae si forte pererravit, xx post diem
marem femina repetit. pariunt mense x; quicquid
ante genitum inutile est. sunt auctores ipso com-
plente decumum mensem die parere. gignunt
raro geminos. coitus a delphini exortu a. d. pr.
non. Ianuarias diebus triginta, aliquis et autumno,
gentibus quidem quae lacte vivunt ita dispensatus
ut omni tempore anni supersit id alimentum.
178 tauri non saepius quam bis die ineunt. boves
animalium soli et retro ambulantes pascuntur, apud
Garamantas quidem haut aliter. vita feminis xv
annis longissima, maribus xx; robur in quinquen-
natu. lavatione calidae aquae traduntur pinguescere,
et si quis incisa cute spiritum harundine in viscera
179 adigat. non degeneres existimandi etiam minus
laudato aspectu: plurimum lactis Alpinis quibus
minimum corporis, plurimum laboris capite non
cervice iunctis. Syriacis non sunt palearia sed
gibber in dorso. Carici quoque in parte Asiae foedi
visu tubere super armos a cervicibus eminente,
luxatis cornibus, excellentes in opere narrantur,
cetero nigri coloris candidive ad laborem damnantur;
tauris minora quam bubus cornua tenuioraque.
180 domitura boum in trimatu, postea sera, ante prae-

same year. It is said that if the bulls after coupling go away towards the right hand side the offspring will be males, and if towards the left, females. Conception is effected by one coupling, and if this happens to miss, the female goes to a male again twenty days after. They bear the calf in the tenth month; one produced before is of no use. Some authorities say that they bear on the actual last day of the tenth month. They rarely produce twins. Coupling takes place in the thirty days following the rise of the Dolphin on January 4, and occasionally in the autumn also, though nations that live on milk spread it out so that there may be a supply of this nutriment at every season of the year. Bulls do not couple more than twice in one day. Oxen are the only animals that graze even while walking backward; indeed among the Garamantes that is their only way of grazing. The longest life of a cow is 15 years and of a bull 20; they grow to full strength at 5. Washing in hot water is said to fatten them, and also cutting a hole in the hide and blowing air into the flesh with a reed. Even the breeds less praised for their appearance are not to be deemed inferior: the Alpine cows which are the smallest in size give most milk, and do most work, although they are yoked by the head and not the neck. Syrian oxen have no dewlaps, but a hump on the back. Also the Carian breed in a district of Asia is said to be ugly in appearance, with a swelling that projects from the neck over the shoulders and with the horns displaced, but excellent in work—although when black and white in colour they are said to be no good for ploughing; the bulls have smaller and thinner horns than the cows. Oxen should be broken when three

matura; optume cum domito iuvencus inbuitur.
socium enim laboris agrique culturae habemus hoc
animal, tantae apud priores curae ut sit inter exempla
damnatus a p. R. die dicta qui concubino procaci
rure omassum edisse se negante occiderat bovem,
actusque in exilium tamquam colono suo interempto.

181   Tauris in aspectu generositas, torva fronte, auribus
saetosis, cornibus in procinctu dimicationem po-
scentibus; sed tota comminatio prioribus in pedibus:
stat ira gliscente alternos replicans spargensque
in alvum harenam, et solus animalium eo stimulo
182 ardescens. vidimus ex imperio dimicantes et ideo
monstratos [1] rotari, cornibus cadentes excipi iterumque resurgere,[2] modo iacentes ex humo tolli, bigarum-
que etiam cursu [3] citato velut aurigas insistere.
Thessalorum gentis inventum est equo iuxta quad-
ripedante cornu intorta cervice tauros necare;
primus id spectaculum dedit Romae Caesar dictator.
183 hinc victimae opimae et lautissima deorum placatio.
huic tantum animali omnium quibus procerior cauda
non statim nato consummatae ut ceteris mensurae;
crescit uni donec ad vestigia ima perveniat. quamobrem victimarum probatio in vitulo ut articulum

---

[1] *v.l.* demonstratos (et iocose demonstratos *Mayhoff*).
[2] *Vulg.* regere.
[3] *Gronovius*: curru.

---

years old; after that is too late and before too early;
the best way to train a young bullock is to yoke it
with one already broken in. For we possess in
this animal a partner in labour and in husbandry,
held in such esteem with our predecessors that
among our records of punishments there is a case of
a man who was indicted for having killed an ox
because a wanton young companion said he had
never eaten bullock's tripe, and was convicted by
the public court and sent into exile just as though
he had murdered his farm-labourer.

Bulls have a noble appearance, a grim brow, bristly *Bull-fights.*
ears, and horns bared for action and asking for a
fight; but their chief threat is in their fore feet: a
bull stands glowing with wrath, bending back either
fore foot in turn and splashing up the sand against
his belly—it is the only animal that goads itself into
a passion by these means. We have seen bulls,
when fighting a duel under orders and on show for
the purpose, being whirled round and caught on
the horns as they fall and afterwards rise again,
and then when lying down be lifted off the ground,
and even stand in a car like charioteers with a pair
of horses racing at full speed. It is a device of
the Thessalian race to kill bulls by galloping a horse
beside them and twisting back the neck by the horn;
the dictator Caesar first gave *a* this show at Rome.
The bull supplies costly victims and the most sump- *Bulls for*
tuous appeasement of the gods. In this animal *sacrifice.*
only of all that have a comparatively long tail, the
tail is not of the proper size from birth, as it is in
the others; and with it alone the tail grows till it
reaches right down to the feet. Consequently the
test of victims for sacrifice in the case of a calf is

suffraginis contingat: breviore non litant. hoc
quoque notatum, vitulos ad aras umeris hominis
adlatos non fere litari,[1] sicut nec claudicante nec
aliena hostia deos placari nec trahente se ab aris.
est frequens in prodigiis priscorum bovem locutum,
quo nuntiato senatum sub diu haberi solitum.

184   LXXI. Bos in Aegypto etiam numinis vice colitur;
Apin vocant. insigne ei in dextro latere candicans
macula cornibus lunae crescere incipientis, nodus
sub lingua quem cantharum appellant. non est fas
eum certos vitae excedere annos, mersumque in
sacerdotum fonte necant quaesituri luctu alium quem
substituant, et donec invenerint maerent derasis
etiam capitibus. nec tamen umquam diu quaeritur.
185 inventus deducitur Memphim a sacerdotibus c.
delubra ei gemina, quae vocant thalamos, auguria
populorum: alterum intrasse laetum est, in altero
dira portendit. responsa privatis dat e manu
consulentium cibum capiendo; Germanici Caesaris
manum aversatus est haut multo postea extincti.
cetero secretus, cum se proripuit in coetus, incedit
submotu lictorum, gregesque puerorum comitantur
carmen honori eius canentium; intellegere videtur

----

[1] litari ? *Brotier* : litare.

----

[a] A.D. 49, in Egypt. His murder was attributed to Piso,
legate of Syria.

that the tail must reach the joint of the hock; if it is shorter the offering is not acceptable. It has also been noted that calves are not usually acceptable if carried to the altars on a man's shoulders, and also that the gods are not propitiated if the victim is lame or is not of the appropriate sort, or if it drags itself away from the altar. It frequently occurs among the prodigies of old times that an ox spoke, and when this was reported it was customary for a meeting of the senate to be held in the open air.

LXXI. In Egypt an ox is even worshipped in place of a god; its name is Apis. Its distinguishing mark is a bright white spot in the shape of a crescent on the right flank, and it has a knob under the tongue which they call a beetle. It is not lawful for it to exceed a certain number of years of life, and they kill it by drowning it in the fountain of the priests, proceeding with lamentation to look for another to put in its place, and they go on mourning till they have found one, actually shaving the hair off their heads. Nevertheless the search never continues long. When the successor is found it is led by 100 priests to Memphis. It has a pair of shrines, which they call its bedchambers, that supply the nations with auguries: when it enters one this is a joyful sign, but in the other one it portends terrible events. It gives answers to private individuals by taking food out of the hand of those who consult it; it turned away from the hand of Germanicus Caesar, who was made away with not long after.[a] Usually living in retirement, when it sallies forth into assemblies it proceeds with lictors to clear the way, and companies of boys escort it singing a song in its honour; it seems to understand, and to desire to be

Worship of an ox in Egypt.

et adorari velle. hi greges repente lymphati futura
186 praecinunt. femina bos ei semel anno ostenditur,
suis et ipsa insignibus, quamquam aliis; semperque
eodem die et inveniri eam et extingui tradunt.
Memphi est locus in Nilo quem a figura vocant
Phialam; omnibus annis ibi auream pateram argen-
teamque mergunt iis [1] diebus quos habent natales
Apis. septem hi sunt; mirumque neminem per
eos a crocodilis attingi, octavo post horam diei
sextam redire beluae feritatem.

187 LXXII. Magna et pecori gratia vel in placamentis
deorum vel in usu vellerum. ut boves victum hominum excolunt ita corporum tutela pecori debetur.
generatio bimis utrimque ad novenos annos, quibusdam et ad x. primiparis minores fetus. coitus
omnibus ab arcturi occasu, id est a. d. iii idus Maias
ad aquilae occasum x kal. Aug.; gerunt partum
diebus cl. postea concepti invalidi; cordos vocabant antiqui post id tempus natos. multi hibernos
agnos praeferunt vernis, quoniam magis intersit
ante solstitium quam ante brumam firmos esse
188 solumque hoc animal utiliter bruma nasci. arieti
naturale agnas fastidire, senectam ovium consectari;
et ipse melior senecta, mutilus quoque utilior.

[1] *Brotier* : mergentes.

worshipped. These companies are suddenly seized with frenzy and chant prophecies of future events. Once a year a cow is displayed to it, she too with her decorations, although they are not the same as his; and it is traditional for her always to be found and put to death on the same day. At Memphis there is a place in the Nile which from its shape they call the Goblet; every year they throw into the river there a gold and a silver cup on the days which they keep as the birthdays of Apis. These are seven; and it is a remarkable fact that during these days nobody is attacked by crocodiles, but that after midday on the eighth day the creature's savagery returns.

LXXII. Sheep are also of great service either *Sheep-breeding.* in respect of propitiatory offerings to the gods or in the use of their fleeces. As oxen improve men's diet, so the protection of their bodies is owed to sheep. They breed when two years old on both sides, till the age of nine, and in some cases even till ten. The lambs at the first birth are smaller. They all couple from the setting of Arcturus, that is May 13th, to the setting of Aquila, July 23rd; they carry their lambs 150 days. Lambs conceived after the date mentioned are weak; in old days those born later were called *cordi.* Many people prefer winter lambs to spring ones, holding that it is more important for them to be well-established before midsummer than before midwinter, and that this animal alone is advantageously born in winter. It is inbred in the ram to despise lambs as mates and to desire maturity in sheep; and the ram himself is better in old age, and also more serviceable when polled. His wildness is restrained by boring a hole

ferocia eius cohibetur cornu iuxta aurem terebrata.
dextro teste praeligato feminas generat, laevo
mares. tonitrua solitariis ovibus abortus inferunt;
remedium est congregare eas, ut coetu iuventur.
189 aquilonis flatu mares concipi dicunt, austri feminas;
atque in eo genere arietum maxime spectantur ora,
quia cuius coloris sub lingua habuere venas eius et
lanicium in fetu est, variumque, si plures fuere. et
mutatio aquarum potusque variat.

Ovium summa genera duo, tectum et colonicum,
illud mollius, hoc in pascuo delicatius, quippe cum
tectum[1] rubis vescatur.[2] operimenta eis ex Arabicis
praecipue.

190 LXXIII. Lana autem laudatissima Apula et
quae in Italia Graeci pecoris appellatur, alibi Italica.
tertium locum Milesiae oves optinent. Apulae
breves villo nec nisi paenulis celebres; circa Tarentum
Canusiumque summam nobilitatem habent, in
Asia vero eodem genere Laudiceae. alba Circum-
padanis nulla praefertur, nec libra centenos nummos
191 ad hoc aevi excessit ulla. oves non ubique tondentur,
durat quibusdam in locis vellendi mos. colorum
plura genera, quippe cum desint etiam nomina
eis quas nativas appellant aliquot modis: Hispania

---

[1] *Brotier*: quippe contectum.
[2] quippe non tectum rubis vexatur *Mayhoff*.

---

[a] A conjectural reading gives 'in fact not being jacketed
they are troubled by brambles.'
[b] Say 12 shillings.

in the horn close to the ear. If a ligature is put on the right testicle he gets females and if on the left males. Claps of thunder cause sheep to miscarry when solitary; the remedy is to herd them in flocks, so as to be cheered by company. They say that male lambs are got when a north wind is blowing and female when a south; and in this breed the greatest attention is given to the mouths of the rams, as the wool in the case of the progeny is of the colour of the veins under the tongue of the parent ram, and if these were of several colours the lamb is vari-coloured. Also changing the water they drink varies their colour.

There are two principal breeds of sheep, jacketed sheep and farm sheep; the former are softer and the latter more delicate in their pasture, inasmuch as the jacketed sheep feeds on brambles.[a] The best jackets for them are made of Arabian sheep's wool.

LXXIII. The most highly esteemed wool is the Apulian and the kind that is called in Italy wool of the Greek breed and elsewhere Italian wool. The third place is held by the sheep of Miletus. The Apulian fleeces are short in the hair, and not of great repute except for cloaks; they have a very high reputation in the districts of Taranto and Canossa, as have the Laodicean fleeces of the same breed in Asia. No white fleece is valued above that from the district of the Po, and none has hitherto gone beyond the price of 100 sesterces [b] a pound. Sheep are not shorn everywhere—in some places the practice survives of plucking off the wool. There are several sorts of colour, in fact even names are lacking for the wools which are variously designated after their places of origin: Spain has the principal

Varieties and uses of sheep's wool.

133

nigri velleris praecipuas habet, Pollentia iuxta
Alpes cani, Asia rutili quas Erythraeas vocant,
item Baetica, Canusium fulvi, Tarentum et suae
pulliginis. sucidis omnibus medicata vis. Histriae
Liburniaque pilo propior quam lanae, pexis aliena
vestibus, et quam Salacia scutulato textu commendat
in Lusitania. similis circa Piscinas provinciae Narbonensis, similis et in Aegypto, ex qua vestis de-
trita usu pingitur rursusque aevo durat. est et
hirtae pilo crasso in tapetis antiquissima gratia:
iam certe priscos[1] iis usos Homerus auctor est.
aliter haec Galli pingunt, aliter Parthorum gentes.

192 lanae et per se coactae vestem faciunt et, si addatur
acetum, etiam ferro resistunt, immo vero etiam
ignibus novissimo sui purgamento. quippe aenis
polientium extracta in tomenti usum veniunt,
Galliarum, ut arbitror, invento: certe Gallicis

193 hodie nominibus discernitur. nec facile dixerim
qua id aetate coeperit; antiquis enim torus e stramento erat, qualiter etiam nunc in castris. gausapae patris mei memoria coepere, amphimallia
nostra, sicut villosa etiam ventralia; nam tunica
lati clavi in modum gausapae texi nunc primum
incipit. lanarum nigrae nullum colorem bibunt;
de reliquarum infectu suis locis dicemus in conchyliis
maris aut herbarum natura.

[1] priscos *om. v.l.*

---

[a] *Odyssey* 4. 298 'Αλκίππη δὲ τάπητα φέρεν μαλακοῦ ἐρίοιο,
et passim.
[b] IX c. 62.   [c] XXI c. 12.

black wool fleeces, Pollentia near the Alps white, Asia the red fleeces that they call Erythrean, Baetica the same, Canossa tawny, Taranto also a dark colour of its own. All fresh fleeces have a medicinal property. Istrian and Liburnian fleece is nearer to hair than wool, and not suitable for garments with a soft nap; and the same applies to the fleece that Salacia in Lusitania advertises by its check pattern. There is a similar wool in the district of the Fishponds in the province of Narbonne, and also in Egypt, which is used for darning clothes worn by use and making them last again for a long period. Also the coarse hair of a shaggy fleece has a very ancient popularity in carpets: Homer [a] is evidence that they were undoubtedly in use even in very early times. Different methods of dyeing these fleeces are practised by the Gauls and by the Parthian races. Self-felted fleeces make clothing, and also if vinegar is added withstand even steel, nay more even fire, the latest method of cleaning them. In fact fleeces drawn from the coppers of the polishers serve as stuffing for cushions, I believe by a French invention: at all events at the present day it is classified under Gallic names. And I could not easily say at what period this began: for people in old times had bedding of straw, in the same way as in camp now. Frieze cloaks began within my father's memory and cloaks with hair on both sides within my own, as also shaggy body-belts; moreover weaving a broad-striped tunic after the manner of a frieze cloak is coming in for the first time now. Black fleeces will not take dye of any colour; we will discuss the dyeing of the other sorts in their proper places under the head of marine shellfish [b] or the nature of various plants.[c]

194　LXXIV. Lanam in colo et fuso Tanaquilis, quae
eadem Gaia Caecilia vocata est, in templo Sanci
durasse prodente se auctor est M. Varro, factamque
ab ea togam regiam undulatam in aede Fortunae,
qua Ser. Tullius fuerat usus. inde factum ut
nubentes virgines comitaretur colus compta et fusus
cum stamine. ea prima texuit rectam tunicam,
qualis cum toga pura tirones induuntur novaeque
195　nuptae. undulata vestis prima e laudatissimis
fuit; inde sororiculata defluxit. togas rasas Phryxia-
nasque divi Augusti novissimis temporibus coepisse
scribit Fenestella. crebrae papaveratae antiquiorem
habent originem iam ab Lucilio poeta in Torquato
notatae. praetextae apud Etruscos originem inve-
nere. trabeis usos accipio reges; pictae vestes iam
apud Homerum sunt iis, et inde [1] triumphales natae.
196　acu facere id Phryges invenerunt, ideoque Phrygio-
niae appellatae sunt. aurum intexere in eadem
Asia invenit Attalus rex, unde nomen Attalicis.
colores diversos picturae intexere Babylon maxume
celebravit et nomen inposuit. plurimis vero liciis
texere quae polymita appellant Alexandria instituit,
scutulis dividere Gallia. Metellus Scipio tricliniaria
Babylonica sestertium octingentis milibus venisse
iam tunc ponit in Capitonis [2] criminibus, quae

[1] *Mayhoff*: Homerum fuisse unde.
[2] *Caesareus*: Catonis.

---

[a] For the use of poppy-stem fibre mixed with flax in weaving, to give gloss, see XIX 21.
[b] Helen embroiders one with battle scenes, *Od.* 3. 125.

LXXIV. Marcus Varro informs us, on his own *Woollen* authority, that the wool on the distaff and spindle of *cloth;* Tanaquil (who was also called Gaia Caecilia) was still *dyeing.* preserved in the temple of Sancus; and also in the shrine of Fortune a pleated royal robe made by her, which had been worn by Servius Tullius. Hence arose the practice that maidens at their marriage were accompanied by a decorated distaff and a spindle with thread. Tanaquil first wove a straight tunic of the kind that novices wear with the plain white toga, and newly married brides. The pleated robe was the first among those most in favour; consequently the spotted robe went out of fashion. Fenestella writes that togas of smooth cloth and of Phryxian wool began in the latest times of the late lamented Augustus. Togas of closely woven poppy-cloth have [a] an older source, being noticed as far back as the poet Lucilius in the case of Torquatus. Bordered robes found their origin with the Etruscans. I find it recorded that striped robes were worn by the kings, and they had embroidered robes as far back as Homer,[b] these being the origin of those worn in triumphs. Embroidering with the needle was discovered by the Phrygians, and consequently embroidered robes are called Phrygian. Gold embroidery was also invented in Asia, by King Attalus, from whom Attalic robes got their name. Weaving different colours into a pattern was chiefly brought into vogue by Babylon, which gave its name to this process. But the fabric called damask woven with a number of threads was introduced by Alexandria, and check patterns by Gaul. Metellus Scipio counts it among the charges against Capito that Babylonian coverlets were already then sold for

Neroni principi quadragiens sestertio nuper stetere.
197 Servi Tulli praetextae quibus signum Fortunae ab
eo dicatae coopertum erat, duravere ad Seiani
exitum, mirumque fuit neque diffluxisse eas neque
teredinum iniurias sensisse annis quingentis sexaginta. vidimus iam et viventium [1] vellera purpura,
cocco, conchylio, sesquipedalibus libris [2] infecta, velut
illa sic nasci cogente luxuria.

198   LXXV. In ipsa ove satis generositatis ostenditur
brevitate crurum, ventris vestitu.[3] quibus nudus
esset apicas vocabant damnabantque. Syriae cubitales ovium caudae, plurimumque in ea parte
lanicii. castrari agnos nisi quinquemenstres prae-
maturum existimatur.

199   Est in Hispania, sed maxime Corsica, non absimile
pecori genus musmonum caprino villo quam pecoris
velleri propius, quorum e genere et ovibus natos
prisci Umbros vocaverunt. infirmissimum pecori
caput, quamobrem aversum a sole pasci cogendum.
quam stultissima animalium lanata: qua timuere
ingredi, unum cornu raptum sequuntur. vita longissima anni x, in Aethiopia xiii; capris eodem loco xi,
in reliquo orbe plurimum octoni. utrumque genus
intra quartum coitum impletur.

200   LXXVI. Caprae pariunt et quaternos, sed raro
admodum; ferunt v mensibus, ut oves. capri

----

[1] *v.l.* bidentum.
[2] *v.l.* s. labris (sesquilibris *Gronovius*).
[3] *v.l.* vestitus.

----

a Over £7000 gold.   *b* A.D. 31.
c A variant gives ' even of sheep.'
d The words omitted, ' with eighteen inch scales ' or
' pounds,' have not been satisfactorily explained or emended.

800,000 sesterces,[a] which lately cost the Emperor Nero 4,000,000. The state robes of Servius Tullius, with which the statue of Fortune dedicated by him was draped, lasted till the death [b] of Sejanus, and it was remarkable that they had not rotted away or suffered damage from moths in 560 years. We have before now seen the fleeces even of living animals [c] dyed with purple, scarlet, crimson . . .,[d] as though luxury forced them to be born like that.

LXXV. In the sheep itself breed is sufficiently *Sheep-* shown by shortness of the legs and a well-clothed *breeding.* belly. Sheep with the belly bare used to be called ' misfits '[e] and turned down. The sheep of Syria have tails 18 inches long, and a great deal of wool on that part. It is considered too soon for lambs to be gelt unless five months old.

In Spain, but particularly in Corsica, there is an animal not unlike the sheep, the moufflon, with hair nearer the goat's than the sheep's; these when crossed with sheep produce what in old days were called Umbrians. Sheep are very weak in the head, and consequently must be made to graze with their backs to the sun. The fleecy sheep is the stupidest of animals; if afraid to go into a place they will follow one of the flock that is taken by the horn. Their longest term of life is 10 years, in Ethiopia 13; goats in Ethiopia live 11 years, but in other parts of the world at most eight. In breeding with either kind to couple three times at most is sufficient.

LXXVI. Goats bear as many as four kids at once, *Goat-* but rather seldom; they carry their young for *breeding.* 5 months, like sheep. He-goats are made sterile by *goats.*

Habits of

---

[e] From ἀπεικώς, Lewis and Short; or perhaps more probably ' apĭcas ' (πόκος, πέκω) ' without fleece.'

pinguitudine sterilescunt. ante trimos [1] minus utiliter generant et in senecta, nec ultra quadriennium.
incipiunt septimo mense et adhuc lactantes. mu-
tilum in utroque sexu utilius. primus in die coitus
non implet, sequens efficacior ac deinde. concipiunt Novembri mense ut Martio pariant turgescen-
tibus virgultis, aliquando anniculae, semper bimae,
nisi trimae vix utiles.[2] pariunt octonis annis.
201 abortus frigori obnoxius. oculos suffusos capra
iunci punctu sanguine exonerat, caper rubi. sollertiam eius animalis Mucianus visam sibi prodidit,
in ponte praetenui duabus obviis e diverso cum
circumactum angustiae non caperent nec reciproca-
tionem longitudo in exilitate caeca,[3] torrente rapido
minaciter subterfluente, alteram decubuisse atque
202 ita alteram proculcatae supergressam. mares quam
maxime simos, longis auribus infractisque, armis
quam villosissimis probant. feminarum generositatis
insigne laciniae corporibus e cervice binae dependentes; non omnibus cornua, sed quibus sunt, in his
et indicia annorum per incrementa nodorum;
mutilis lactis maior ubertas; auribus eas spirare,
non naribus, nec umquam febri carere Archelaus
auctor est; ideo fortassis anima his quam ovibus
203 ardentior calidioresque concubitus. tradunt et
noctu non minus cernere quam interdiu, et ideo,

---

[1] ante trinos annos? *Mayhoff.*
[2] *Mayhoff?*: bimae, in trimatu inutiles.
[3] caecam? *Rackham.*

over-fattening. They are not very useful as sires till three years old, nor in old age, and they do not serve for more than four years. They begin when six months old and before they are weaned. Both sexes breed better with the horns removed. The first coupling in the day has no result, but the following and subsequent ones are more effectual. She-goats conceive in November so as to bear kids in March when the bushes are budding—yearlings sometimes and two-year-olds always, but they are not of much use for breeding unless three years old. They go on bearing for eight years. They are liable to miscarriage from cold. A she-goat cures its eyes when bloodshot by pricking them on a rush, he-goats on a bramble. Mucianus has described a case of this animal's cleverness seen by himself—two goats coming in opposite directions met on a very narrow bridge, and as the narrow space did not permit them to turn round and the length did not allow of backing blindly on the scanty passageway with a rushing torrent flowing threateningly below, one of them lay down and so the other one passed over, treading on top of it. People admire he-goats that are as snub-nosed as possible, with long drooping ears and extremely shaggy flanks. It is a mark of good breeding in she-goats to have two dewlaps hanging down from the neck; not all have horns, but in those that have there are also indications of their years furnished by the growths of the knobs; they give more milk when without horns; according to Archelaus they breathe through the ears, not the nostrils, and are never free from fever: this is perhaps the reason why they are more high-spirited than sheep and hotter in coupling. It is said that goats can see by night as well as they

si caprinum iecur vescantur, restitui vespertinam
aciem iis quos nyctalopas vocant. in Cilicia circaque
Syrtes villo tonsili vestiuntur. capras in occasum
declini sole in pascuis negant contueri inter sese sed
aversas iacere, reliquis autem horis adversas et inter
se cognationes. dependet omnium mento villus
204 quem aruncum vocant. hoc si quis adprehensam ex
grege unam trahat, ceterae stupentes spectant;
id etiam evenit et[1] cum quandam herbam aliqua
ex eis momorderit. morsus earum arbori est
exitialis; olivam lambendo quoque sterilem faciunt,
eaque ex causa Minervae non immolantur.

205 LXXVII. Suilli pecoris admissura a favonio ad
aequinoctium vernum, aetas octavo mense, quibusdam in locis etiam quarto, usque ad octavum annum.
partus bis in anno, tempus utero quattuor mensum,
numerus fecunditati ad vicenos, sed educare neque-
unt tam multos. diebus x circa brumam statim
dentatos nasci Nigidius tradit. implentur uno coitu,
qui et geminatur propter facilitatem aboriendi;
remedium ne prima subatione neque ante flaccidas
206 aures coitus fiat. mares non ultra trimatum generant. feminae senectute fessae cubantes coeunt;
comesse fetus in[2] his non est prodigium. suis fetus
sacrificio die quinto purus est, pecoris die vii,
bovis xxx. Coruncanius ruminalis hostias donec

---

[1] *Mayhoff*: evenire.
[2] in *add. Mueller.*

can in the daytime, and that consequently a diet of goat's liver restores twilight sight to persons suffering from what is called night-blindness. In Cilicia and the Syrtes region people wear clothes made of hair shorn from goats. They say that she-goats in the pastures when the sun is setting do not look at one another but lie down with their backs to each other, though at other times of the day they lie facing each other and take notice of one another. From the chin of all goats hangs a tuft of hair called their beard. If you grasp a she-goat by this and drag her out of the herd the others look on in amazement; this also happens as well when one of them nibbles a particular plant. Their bite kills a tree; they make an olive tree barren even by licking it, and for this reason they are not offered in sacrifice to Minerva.

LXXVII. Swine are allowed to breed from the beginning of spring to the vernal equinox, beginning at seven months old and in some places even at three months, and continuing to their eighth year. Sows bear twice a year, carrying their pigs four months: litters number up to 20, but sows cannot rear so many. Nigidius states that for ten days at midwinter pigs are born with the teeth already grown. Sows are impregnated by one coupling, which is also repeated because they are so liable to abortion; the remedy is not to allow coupling at the first heat or before the ears are pendulous. Hogs cannot serve when over three years old. Sows exhausted by age couple lying down; it is nothing out of the way for them to eat their litter. A pig is suitable for sacrifice four days after birth, a lamb in a week and a calf in a month. Coruncanius asserted that ruminant animals are not acceptable as victims before they grow

Swine-breeding: pig-keeping. Intelligence in pigs. Dressing of pork.

bidentes fierent puras negavit. suem oculo amisso
putant cito extingui, alioqui vita ad xv annos, quibusdam et vicenos; verum efferantur, et alias obno-
xium genus morbis, anginae maxime et strumae.
207 index suis invalidae cruor in radice saetae dorso
evolsae, caput obliquom in incessu. paenuriam lactis praepingues sentiunt; et primo fetu minus sunt
numerosae. in luto volutatio generi grata. intorta
cauda; id etiam notatum, facilius litare in dexterum
quam in laevum detorta. pinguescunt LX diebus,
sed magis tridui inedia saginatione orsa. animalium
hoc maxime brutum, animamque ei pro sale datam
208 non inlepide existimabatur. conpertum agnitam
vocem suarii furto abactis, mersoque navigio inclina-
tione lateris unius renasse.[1] quin et duces in urbe
forum nundinarium domosque petere discunt; et
feri sapiunt vestigia palude confundere, urina fugam
209 levare. castrantur feminae sic quoque uti et cameli
post bidui inediam suspensae pernis prioribus vulva
recisa; celerius ita pinguescunt. adhibetur et ars
iecori feminarum sicut anserum, inventum M.
Apici, fico arida saginatis, a satie necatis repente

---

[1] *Rackham*: remeasse.

---

[a] The two projecting teeth in the lower jaw which give their
name to the species.
[b] To keep it from putrefaction: Cicero *N.D.* II 160 attributes this to Chrysippus.

their front teeth.[a] It is thought that a sow that loses an eye soon dies, but that otherwise sows live to fifteen and in some cases even twenty years; but they become savage, and in any case the breed is liable to diseases, especially quinsy and scrofula. Symptoms of bad health in a sow are when blood is found on the root of a bristle pulled out of its back and when it holds its head on one side in walking. If too fat they experience lack of milk; and they have a smaller number of pigs in their first litter. The breed likes wallowing in mud. The tail is curly; also it has been noticed that it is easier to kill them for sacrifice when the tail curls to the right than when to the left. They take 60 days to fatten, but fatten better if feeding up is preceded by three days' fast. The pig is the most brutish of animals, and there used to be a not unattractive idea that its soul was given it to serve as salt.[b] It is a known fact that some pigs carried off by thieves recognized the voice of their swineherd, crowded to one side of the ship till it capsized and sank, and swam back to shore. Moreover the leaders of a herd in the city learn to go to the market place and to find their way home; and wild hogs know how to obliterate their tracks by crossing marshy ground, and to relieve themselves when running away by making water. Sows are spayed in the same way as also camels are, by being hung up by the fore legs after two days without food and having the matrix cut out; this makes them fatten quicker. There is also a method of treating the liver of sows as of geese, a discovery of Marcus Apicius—they are stuffed with dried fig, and when full killed directly after having been

mulsi potu dato. neque alio ex animali numerosior
materia ganeae: quinquaginta prope sapores, cum
ceteris singuli. hinc censoriarum legum paginae,
interdictaque cenis abdomina, glandia, testiculi,
vulvae, sincipita verrina, ut tamen Publi mimorum
poetae cena postquam servitutem exuerat nulla
memoretur sine abdomine, etiam vocabulo suminis
ab eo inposito.

210 LXXVIII. Placuere autem et feri sues. iam
Catonis censoris orationes aprunum exprobrant
callum. in tres tamen partes diviso media pone-
batur, lumbus aprunus appellata. solidum aprum
Romanorum primus in epulis adposuit P. Servilius
Rullus, pater eius Rulli qui Ciceronis in consulatu
legem agrariam promulgavit: tam propinqua origo
nunc cotidianae rei est; et hoc annales notarunt,
horum scilicet ad emendationem morum, quibus
non tota quidem cena sed in principio bini ternique
pariter manduntur apri.

211 Vivaria eorum ceterarumque silvestrium primus
togati generis invenit Fulvius Lippinus: is[1] in
Tarquiniensi feras pascere instituit; nec diu imi-
tatores defuere L. Lucullus et Q. Hortensius.

212 Sues ferae semel anno gignunt. maribus in coitu
plurima asperitas; tunc inter se dimicant indurantes

---

[1] is add. ? Mayhoff.

---

^a 184 B.C.   ^b 63 B.C.

given a drink of mead. Nor does any animal supply a larger number of materials for an eating-house: they have almost fifty flavours, whereas all other meats have one each. Hence pages of sumptuary laws, and the prohibition of hog's paunches, sweet-breads, testicles, matrix and cheeks for banquets, although nevertheless no dinner of the pantomime writer Publius after he had obtained his freedom is recorded that did not include paunch—he actually got from this the nickname of Pig's Paunch.

LXXVIII. But also wild boar has been a popular *Boar's meat.* luxury. As far back as Cato the Censor[a] we find his speeches denouncing boar's meat bacon. Neverthe-less a boar used to be cut up into three parts and the middle part served at table, under the name of boar's loin. Publius Servilius Rullus, father of the Rullus who brought in the land settlement act during Cicero's consulship,[b] first served a boar whole at his banquets—so recent is the origin of what is now an everyday affair; and this occurrence has been noted by historians, presumably for the improvement of the manners of the present day, when it is the fashion for two or three boars to be devoured at one time not even as a whole dinner but as the first course.

Fulvius Lippinus was the first person of Roman *Game-* nationality who invented preserves for wild pigs and *preserves.* the other kinds of game: he introduced keeping wild animals in the district of Tarquinii; and he did not long lack imitators, Lucius Lucullus and Quintus Hortensius.

Wild pigs breed once a year. The boars are very rough when mating; at this period they fight each other, hardening their flanks by rubbing against

147

PLINY: NATURAL HISTORY

adtritu arborum costas lutoque se a tergo stercor-
antes.[1] feminae in partu asperiores, et fere similiter
in omni genere bestiarum. apris maribus nonnisi
anniculis generatio. in India cubitales dentium
flexus; gemini ita[2] ex rostro, totidem a fronte ceu
vituli cornua exeunt. pilus aereo similis agrestibus,
ceteris niger. at in Arabia suillum genus non vivit.

213 LXXIX. In nullo alio[3] genere aeque facilis
mixtura cum fero, qualiter natos antiqui hybridas
vocabant ceu semiferos, ad homines quoque ut C.
Antonium Ciceronis in consulatu collegam appella-
tione tralata. non in suibus autem tantum sed in
omnibus quoque animalibus cuiuscumque generis
ullum est placidum eiusdem invenitur et ferum,
utpote cum hominum etiam silvestrium tot genera
214 praedicta sint. caprae tamen in plurimas simili-
tudines transfigurantur: sunt caprae, sunt rupi-
caprae, sunt ibices pernicitatis mirandae, quamquam
onerato capite vastis cornibus gladiorum ceu vaginis;
in haec se librat ut tormento aliquo rotatus, in
petris[4] potissimum e monte alio[5] in alium transilire
quaerens, atque recusu[6] pernicius quo libuerit
exultat. sunt et oryges, soli a[7] quibusdam dicti
contrario pilo vestiri et ad caput verso, sunt et
dammae et pygargi et strepsicerotes multaque alia

[1] *Mayhoff*: se tergorantes. [2] *Mayhoff*: gemina.
[3] alio *add. Rackham*. [4] *Rackham*: petras.
[5] *Rackham*: aliquo. [6] *v.l.* recussu.
[7] a *add. Rackham*.

---

[a] 63 B.C.
[b] The allusion of his surname Hybrida is uncertain; perhaps his mother was of foreign descent.
[c] *I.e.* the goat, chamois and ibex above.

148

trees and plastering their behinds with mud. The females are fiercer when with young, and this is more or less the same in every kind of wild animal. Male boars do not mate till one year old. In India they have curved tusks 18 in. long: two project from the jaw, and two from the forehead like a calf's horns. The wild boar's hair is a sort of copper colour; that of the other species is black. But the hog genus does not occur in Arabia.

LXXIX. In the case of no other kind of animal is it so easy to cross with the wild variety; the offspring of such unions in old days were called ' hybrids,' meaning half-wild, a term also applied as a nickname to human beings, for instance, to Cicero's colleague in the consulship,[a] Gaius Antonius.[b] But not only in pigs but in all animals as well whenever there is any tame variety of a genus there is also found a wild one of the same genus, inasmuch as even in the case of man an equal number of savage races have been predicted to exist. Nevertheless the formation of the goat is transferred to a very large number of similar species: there are the goat, the chamois and the ibex—an animal of marvellous speed, although its head is burdened with enormous horns resembling the sheaths of swords, towards which it sways itself as though whirled with a sort of catapult, chiefly when on rocks and seeking to leap from one crag to another, and by means of the recoil leaps out more nimbly to the point to which it wants to get. There are also the oryx, the only species according to certain authorities clothed with hair lying the wrong way, towards the head, and the antelope, the white-rumped antelope, the twisted-horn antelope and a great many other not dissimilar species. But the former[c]

Wild varieties of domestic species.

haut dissimilia. sed illa Alpes, haec transmarini situs mittunt.

215 LXXX. Simiarum quoque genera[1] hominis figurae proxima caudis inter se distinguntur. mira sollertia: visco inungui, laqueisque calciari imitatione venantium tradunt, Mucianus et latrunculis lusisse, fictas cera nuces visu distinguere, luna cava tristes esse quibus in eo genere cauda sit, novam exultatione adorari: nam defectum siderum et 216 ceterae pavent quadripedes. simiarum generi praecipua erga fetum adfectio. gestant catulos quae mansuefactae intra domos peperere. omnibus demonstrant tractarique gaudent, gratulationem intellegentibus similes; itaque magna ex parte conplectendo necant. efferatior cynocephalis natura sicut mitissima[2] satyris. callitriches toto paene aspectu differunt: barba est in facie, cauda late fusa primori parte. hoc animal negatur vivere in alio quam Aethiopiae quo gignitur caelo.

217 LXXXI. Et leporum plura sunt genera. in Alpibus candidi quos[3] hibernis mensibus pro cibatu nivem credunt esse—certe liquescente ea rutilescunt annis omnibus—et est alioqui animal intolerandi rigoris alumnum. leporum generis sunt et quos

[1] genera ⟨plura⟩ *Mayhoff.*
[2] *Edd.* : miarsima (*v.l. om.*).
[3] *Rackham* : quibus.

---

[a] Perhaps the ourang-outang, which comes from Borneo.
[b] The semnopithecus, or perhaps the cercopithecus.

we receive from the Alps, the latter from places across the sea.

LXXX. The kinds of apes also which are closest to the human shape are distinguished from each other by the tails. They are marvellously cunning: people say that they use bird-lime as ointment, and that they put on the nooses set to snare them as if they were shoes, in imitation of the hunters; according to Mucianus the tailed species have even been known to play at draughts, are able to distinguish at a glance sham nuts made of wax, and are depressed by the moon waning and worship the new moon with delight: and it is a fact that the other four-footed animals also are frightened by eclipses. The genus ape has a remarkable affection for its young. Tame monkeys kept in the house who bear young ones carry them about and show them to everybody, and delight in having them stroked, looking as if they understood that they are being congratulated; and as a consequence in a considerable number of cases they kill their babies by hugging them. The baboon is of a fiercer nature, just as the satyrus [a] is extremely gentle. The pretty-haired ape [b] is almost entirely different in appearance: it has a bearded face and a tail flattened out wide at the base. This animal is said to be unable to live in any other climate but that of its native country, Ethiopia.

Varieties of the ape.

LXXXI. There are also several kinds of hare. In the Alps there are white hares, which are believed to eat snow for their fodder in the winter months—at all events they turn a reddish colour every year when the snow melts—and in other ways the animal is a nurseling of the intolerable cold. The animals in

The hare and the rabbit.

Hispania cuniculos appellat, fecunditatis innumerae
famemque Baliarum insulis populatis messibus
adferentes. fetus ventri exectos vel uberibus abla-
tos non repurgatis interaneis gratissimo in cibatu
218 habent: laurices vocant. certum est Baliaricos
adversus proventum eorum auxilium militare a divo
Augusto petisse. magna propter venatum eum
viverris gratia est: iniciunt eas in specus qui sunt
multifores in terra (unde et nomen animali) atque
ita eiectos superne capiunt. Archelaus auctor est
quot sint corporis cavernae ad excrementa lepori
totidem annos esse aetatis: varius certe numerus
reperitur. idem utramque vim singulis inesse ac sine
219 mare aeque gignere. benigna circa hoc natura
innocua et esculenta animalia fecunda generavit.
lepus omnium praedae nascens solus praeter dasypo-
dem superfetat, aliud educans, aliud in utero pilis
vestitum, aliud inplume, aliud inchoatum gerens
pariter. nec non et vestes leporino pilo facere
temptatum est, tactu non perinde molli ut in cute,
220 propter brevitatem pili dilabidas.[1]

LXXXII. Hi mansuescunt raro, cum feri dici
iure non possint: conplura namque sunt nec placida

---

[1] *v.l.* dilabidam.

---

[a] Actually the word *cuniculus* ' rabbit ' is of Iberian origin,
but the relationship to it of *cuniculus* ' tunnel ' is obscure (cf.
Walde, *LEW* [3] I, 308).

[b] A variant reading gives ' as it is when on the animal's
skin owing to the yielding nature of the short-haired fur.'

Spain called rabbits also belong to the genus hare;
their fertility is beyond counting, and they bring
famine to the Balearic Islands by ravaging the crops.
Their young cut out from the mother before birth or
taken from the teat are considered a very great
delicacy, served without being gutted; the name for
them is *laurex*. It is an established fact that the
peoples of the Balearics petitioned the late lamented
Augustus for military assistance against the spread
of these animals. The ferret is extremely popular
for rabbit-hunting; they throw ferrets into the
burrows with a number of exits that the rabbits
tunnel in the ground (this is the derivation of their
name ' cony '[a]) and so catch the rabbits when they
are driven out to the surface. Archelaus states that
a hare is as many years old as it has folds in the bowel:
these are certainly found to vary in number. The
same authority says that the hare is a hermaphrodite
and reproduces equally well without a male. Nature
has shown her benevolence in making harmless and
edible breeds of animals prolific. The hare which is
born to be all creatures' prey is the only animal
beside the shaggy-footed rabbit that practises superfetation, rearing one leveret while at the same time
carrying in the womb another clothed with hair and
another bald and another still an embryo. Also the
experiment has been made of using the fur of the
hare for making clothes, although it is not so soft to
the touch as it is when on the animal's skin, and the
garments soon come to pieces because of the shortness of the hair.[b]

LXXXII. Hares rarely grow tame, although they
cannot properly be termed wild animals—for in
fact there are a good many creatures that are

*Half-
domestic
species.
The mouse*

nec fera, sed mediae inter utrumque naturae, ut
in volucribus hirundines, apes,[1] in mari delphini.
221 quo in genere multi et hos incolas domuum
posuere mures, haut spernendum in ostentis etiam
publicis animal: adrosis Lanuvi clipeis argenteis
Marsicum portendere bellum, Carboni imperatori
apud Clusium fasceis quibus in calciatu utebatur exitium. plura eorum genera in Cyrenaica regione,
alii lata fronte, alii acuta, alii irenaceorum genere
222 pungentibus pilis. Theophrastus auctor est in
Gyara insula cum incolas fugassent,[2] ferrum quoque
rosisse eos, id quod natura quadam et ad Chalybas
facere in ferrariis officinis; aurariis quidem in metallis
ob hoc alvos eorum excidi semperque furtum id
deprehendi, tantam esse dulcedinem furandi. venisse murem cc denariis[3] Casilinum obsidente
Hannibale, eumque qui vendidisset[4] fame interisse,
223 emptorem vixisse, annales tradunt. cum candidi
provenere, laetum faciunt ostentum. nam sauricum
occentu dirimi auspicia annales refertos habemus.
saurices et ipsos hieme condi auctor est Nigidius,
sicut glires, quos censoriae leges principesque M.
Scaurus in consulatu non alio modo cenis ademere

---

[1] v.l. aper (apri ? Rackham) in campo.
[2] incolae fugissent ? Rackham.
[3] denariis add. Budæus e Val. Max.
[4] Rackham: vendiderat.

---

[a] A variant gives 'swallows, on the plain the boar.'
[b] The Social War, 91–88 B.C.
[c] Carbo was defeated by Sulla at Clusium in Etruria, 82 B.C.
Later in the same year he had to fly to Africa, and was killed
there.
[d] One of the Cyclades.
[e] Perhaps to be emended 'when the inhabitants had fled.'
[f] On the Black Sea.

neither wild nor tame but of a character intermediate between each, for instance among winged things swallows and bees,ᵃ in the sea dolphins. Many people have also placed in this class these denizens of our homes the mice, a creature not to be ignored among portents even in regard to public affairs; they foretold the warᵇ with the Marsians by gnawing the silver shields at Lanuvium, and the death of General Carbo by gnawing at Chiusiᶜ the puttees that he wore inside his sandals. There are more varieties of mice in the district of Cyrene, some with broad and others with pointed heads, and others like hedgehogs with prickly bristles. Theophrastus states that on the island of Chiuraᵈ when they had banished the inhabitantsᵉ they even gnawed iron, and that they also do this by a sort of instinct in the iron foundries in the country of the Chalybesᶠ: indeed, he says, in gold mines because of this their bellies get cut away and their theft of gold is always detected,ᵍ so fond are they of thieving. The Public Records relate that during the siegeʰ of Casilinum by Hannibal a mouse was sold for 200 francs, and that the man who sold it died of hunger while the buyer lived. The appearance of white mice constitutes a joyful omen. For we have our Records full of instances of the auspices being interruptedⁱ by the squeaking of shrews. Nigidius states that shrews themselves also hibernate as do dormice, which sumptuary legislation and Marcus Scaurus the Head of the State during his consulshipᵏ ruled out

ᵍ Or perhaps 'their bellies are cut open and some stolen gold is always found.'

ʰ 216 B.C., after the battle of Cannae.

ⁱ *I.e.* the squeaking during the taking of auspices was a bad omen.   ᵏ 115 B.C.

224 ac [1] conchylia aut ex alio orbe convectas aves. semi-
ferum et ipsum animal, cui vivaria in doliis idem qui
apris instituit. qua in re notatum non congregare
nisi populares eiusdem silvae et, si misceantur alie-
nigenae amne vel monte discreti, interire dimicando.
genitores suos fessos senecta alunt insigni pietate.
senium finitur hiberna quiete: conditi enim et hi
cubant, rursus aestate iuvenescunt. similis et nitelis
quies est hieme.[2]

225 LXXXIII. Hic mirum rerum naturam non solum
alia aliis dedisse terris animalia sed in eodem quoque
situ quaedam aliquis locis negasse. in Maesia silva
Italiae non nisi in parte reperiuntur hi glires. in
Lycia dorcades non transeunt montes Sexis vicinos,
onagri limitem qui Cappadociam a Cilicia dividit.
in Hellesponto in alienos fines non commeant cervi,
et circa Arginusam Elaphum montem non excedunt,
auribus etiam in monte fissis. in Pordoselene insula
226 viam mustelae non transeunt. item [3] Boeotiae
Lebadeae inlatae solum ipsum fugiunt quae iuxta in
Orchomeno tota arva subruunt talpae. quarum e
pellibus cubicularia vidimus stragula: adeo ne religio
quidem a portentis submovet delicias. in Ithaca
lepores inlati moriuntur extremis quidem in litori-

---

[1] ac *add. Detlefsen.*
[2] *Mayhoff*: simili (*aut* similis) et nitelis quiete.
[3] *Mayhoff*: in.

---

[a] See § 211.
[b] *I.e.* the old mice die off during hibernation.
[c] In Etruria.
[d] Aristotle *Hist. An.* 278b 26 ἐν δὲ τῷ ὄρει τῷ Ἐλαφώεντι
καλουμένῳ . . . ἔλαφοι πᾶσαι τὸ οὖς ἐσχισμέναι εἰσίν.
[e] Between Lesbos and the Asiatic coast.

from banquets just as they did shell-fish or birds imported from other parts of the world. The shrew-mouse itself also is a half-wild animal, and keeping it alive in jars was originated by the same person as started keeping wild pigs.[a] In this connexion it has been noticed that shrew-mice do not associate unless they are natives of the same forest, and if foreigners separated by a river or mountain are introduced they die fighting one another. They feed their parents when exhausted by old age with remarkable affection. Their old age comes to its end during the winter repose [b]—for these creatures also hibernate, and renew their youth at the coming of summer. Dormice hibernate similarly.

LXXXIII. In this connexion it is surprising that Nature has not only assigned different animals to different countries, but has also denied certain animals to some places in the same region. In the Mesian forest [c] in Italy dormice of which we are now speaking are only found in one part. In Lycia the gazelles do not cross the mountains near the Sexi, nor the wild asses the boundary dividing Cappadocia from Cilicia. The stags on the Hellespont do not migrate into unfamiliar districts, and those in the neighbourhood of Arginusa do not go beyond Mount Elaphus, even those on the mountain having cleft ears.[d] In the island of Pordoselene [e] weasels do not cross a road. Similarly in Boeotia moles that under-mine the whole of the fields in Orchomenus near by, when imported into Lebadea are shy of the very soil. We have seen counterpanes for beds made out of their skins: so powerless is even superstition to protect the miraculous against luxury. In Ithaca imported hares die on the very edge of the shore, as

Local distribution of species.

bus, in Ebuso cuniculi, scatentibus[1] iuxta Hispania
227 Baliaribusque. Cyrenis mutae fuere ranae, inlatis e
continente vocalibus durat genus earum. mutae
sunt etiamnum in Seripho insula, eaedem alio tra-
latae canunt, quod accidere et in lacu Thessaliae
Siccaneo[2] tradunt. in Italia muribus araneis vene-
natus est morsus; eosdem ulterior Apennino regio non
habet. iidem ubicumque sunt, orbitam si transiere,
moriuntur. in Olympo Macedoniae monte non sunt
228 lupi nec in Creta insula. ibi quidem nec vulpes ursive
atque omnino nullum maleficum animal praeter
phalangium: in[3] araneis id genus dicemus suo loco.
mirabilius in eadem insula cervos praeterquam in
Cydoneatarum regione non esse, item apros,[4] atta-
genas, irenaceos, in Africa autem nec apros nec
cervos nec capreas nec ursos.

229   LXXXIV. Iam quaedam animalia indigenis in-
noxia advenas interimunt, sicut serpentes parvi in
Tirynthe quos terra nasci proditur. item in Syria
angues circa Euphratis maxime ripas dormientes
Syros non adtingunt aut, etiamsi calcati momordere,
non sentiuntur malefici,[5] aliis cuiuscumque gentis
infesti, avide et cum cruciatu exanimantes, quamo-

---

[1] *Mayhoff*: scatent.
[2] *Mayhoff* (*Aelian* οὐκ ἀέναος) ?: Sicandro.
[3] in *add. Mayhoff*.
[4] *Rackham*: apros et.

do rabbits in Iviza, although Spain and the Balearic Islands close by are teeming with them. At Cyrene the frogs were silent, and though croaking frogs have been imported from the mainland the silent breed goes on. Frogs are also silent in the island of Seriphus, but the same frogs croak when removed to some other place, which is also said to happen in the Siccanean Lake in Thessaly. The bite of the shrew-mouse in Italy is venomous, but the venomous species is not found in the district beyond the Apennines. Also wherever it occurs it dies if it crosses the track of a wheel. There are no wolves on Mount Olympus in Macedon, nor in the island of Crete. In fact in Crete there are no wolves or bears either, and no noxious animal at all except a poisonous spider: we shall speak of this species in its place,[a] under the head of spiders. It is more remarkable that in the same island there are no stags except in the district of Cydonea, and the same is the case with wild boars and francolins and hedgehogs, while in Africa there are neither wild boars nor stags nor wild goats nor bears.

LXXXIV. Again, some animals harmless to natives *Species* of the country are deadly to foreigners, for instance *noxious only* some small snakes at Tiryns that are said to be born *to foreigners.* from the earth. Similarly serpents in Syria specially found about the banks of the Euphrates do not touch Syrians when asleep, or even if they bite them when trodden on are not felt to cause any evil effect, but they are maleficent to other people of whatever race, killing them voraciously and with torturing pain, on

[a] XI 79, XVIII 156.

[b] *Mayhoff*: maleficia.

brem et Syri non necant eos. contra in Latmo
Cariae monte Aristoteles tradit a scorpionibus hospites non laedi, indigenas interimi.

Sed reliquorum quoque animalium [et praeterea [1]]
terrestrium dicemus genera.

[1] *Secl. Jan.*

account of which the Syrians also do not kill them. On the other hand Aristotle[a] relates that the scorpions on Mount Latmos in Caria do not wound strangers but kill natives.

But we will also speak of the remaining kinds of land animals.

[a] Fr. 605 Rose.

BOOK IX

LIBER IX

1 I. ANIMALIUM quae terrestria appellavimus hominum quadam consortione degentia indicata natura est. ex reliquis minimas esse volucres convenit. quamobrem prius aequorum amnium stagnorumque dicentur.

2 Sunt autem complura in his maiora etiam terrestribus. causa evidens umoris luxuria. alia sors alitum quibus vita pendentibus. in mari autem tam late supino mollique ac fertili nutrimento, accipiente causas genitales e sublimi semperque pariente natura, pleraque etiam monstrifica reperiuntur perplexis et in semet aliter atque aliter nunc flatu nunc fluctu convolutis seminibus atque principiis, vera ut fiat vulgi opinio quicquid nascatur in parte naturae ulla et in mari esse, praeterque multa quae nusquam
3 alibi. rerum quidem, non solum animalium, simulacra inesse licet intellegere intuentibus uvam, gladium, serram,[1] cucumin vero et colore et odore similem; quo minus miremur equorum capita in tam parvis eminere cocleis.

---

[1] *Rackham* : serras.

BOOK IX

I. WE have indicated the nature of the species that we have designated land animals, as living in some kind of association with men. Of the remaining kinds it is agreed that birds are the smallest. We will therefore first speak of the creatures of the seas, rivers and ponds.

There are however a considerable number of these that are larger even than land animals. The obvious cause of this is the lavish nature of liquid. Birds, which live hovering in the air, are in a different condition. But in the sea, lying so widely outspread and so yielding and productive of nutriment, because the element receives generative causes from above and is always producing offspring, a great many actual monstrosities are found, the seeds and first principles intertwining and interfolding with each other now in one way and now in another, now by the action of the wind and now by that of the waves, so ratifying the common opinion that everything born in any department of nature exists also in the sea, as well as a number of things never found elsewhere. Indeed we may realize that it contains likenesses of things and not of animals only, when we examine the 'sea-grape', the sword-fish, the saw-fish, and the cucumber-fish, the last resembling a real cucumber both in colour and scent; which makes it less surprising that in marine snails that are so tiny there are horses' heads projecting.

4 II. Plurima autem et maxima animalia in Indico mari, ex quibus ballaenae quaternum iugerum, pristes ducenum cubitorum, quippe ubi locustae quaterna cubita impleant, anguillae quoque in Gange amne 5 tricenos pedes. sed in mari beluae circa solstitia maxime visuntur. tunc illic ruunt turbines, tunc imbres, tunc deiectae montium iugis procellae ab imo vertunt maria pulsatasque ex profundo beluas cum fluctibus volvunt tanta, ut[1] alias thynnorum, multitudine, ut Magni Alexandri classis haut alio modo quam hostium acie obvia contrarium agmen adversa fronte direxerit: aliter [sparsis][2] non erat evadere. non voce, non sonitu non fragore sed 6 ictu[3] terrentur, nec nisi ruina turbantur. Cadara appellatur Rubri Maris paeninsula ingens; huius obiectu vastus efficitur sinus xii dierum et noctium remigio enavigatus Ptolomaeo regi, quando nullius aurae recipit afflatum. huius loci quiete praecipue[4] ad immobilem magnitudinem beluae adolescunt. 7 Gedrosos qui Arabim amnem accolunt Alexandri Magni classium praefecti prodiderunt in domibus fores maxillis beluarum facere, ossibus tecta contignare, ex quibus multa quadragenum cubitorum longitudinis reperta. exeunt et pecori similes

---

[1] *Mueller*: volvunt et alias tanta.
[2] sparsis *an delendum ? Mueller.*
[3] *sic ? Mueller*: non ictu sed fragore.
[4] *v.l.* praecipua.

---

[a] The *iuger* was about two-thirds of an English acre, the *cubitus* or ell about 1½ ft.
[b] This sailed from the Indus to the Euphrates, as recorded, with all the details given above, by Arrian, *Indica* 21–42.
[c] The MS. text inserts an explanatory gloss ' by dispersing.'

II. But the largest number of animals and those *Whales,* of the largest size are in the Indian sea, among them *sharks and other very* whales covering three acres each, and sharks 100 ells *large species.* long[a]: in fact in those regions lobsters grow to 6 ft. long, and also eels in the river Ganges to 300 ft. The monsters in the sea are mostly to be seen about the solstices. At those periods in that part of the world there are rushing whirlwinds and rain-storms and tempests hurtling down from the mountain ridges that upturn the seas from their bottom, and roll with their waves monsters forced up from the depths in such a multitude, like the shoals of tunnies in other places, that the fleet[b] of Alexander the Great deployed its column in line of battle to encounter them, in the same way as if an enemy force were meeting it: it was not possible to escape them in any other manner.[c] They are not scared by shouts or noises or uproar, but only by impact, and they are only routed by a violent collision. There is an enormous peninsula in the Red Sea called Cadara, the projection of which forms a vast bay which took King Ptolemy twelve days and nights of rowing to cross, as it does not admit a breath of wind from any quarter. In this tranquil retreat particularly the creatures grow to a huge motionless bulk. The admirals[d] of the fleets of Alexander the Great have stated that the Gedrosi[e] who live by the river Arabis[f] make the doorways in their houses out of the monsters' jaws and use their bones for roof-beams, many of them having been found that were 60 ft. long. Also great creatures resembling sheep come

[d] Nearchus and Onesicritus.
[e] The inhabitants of the modern Makran.
[f] Either the Purali or the Habb.

beluae ibi in terram pastaeque radices fruticum remeant; et quaedam equorum, asinorum, taurorum capitibus quae depascuntur sata.

8 III. Maximum animal in Indico mari pristis et ballaena est, in Gallico oceano physeter ingentis columnae modo se attollens altiorque navium velis diluviem quandam eructans, in Gaditano oceano arbor in tantum vastis dispansa ramis ut ex ea causa fretum numquam intrasse credatur. apparent et rotae appellatae a similitudine, quaternis distinctae hae radiis, modiolos earum oculis duobus utrimque claudentibus.

9 IV. Tiberio principi nuntiavit Olisiponensium legatio ob id missa visum auditumque in quodam specu concha canentem Tritonem qua noscitur forma. et Nereidum falsa non est, squamis modo hispido corpore etiam qua humanam effigiem habent; namque haec in eodem spectata litore est, cuius morientis etiam cantum tristem accolae audivere longe; et divo Augusto legatus Galliae complures in litore apparere exanimes Nereidas

10 scripsit. Auctores habeo in equestri ordine splendentes visum ab his in Gaditano oceano marinum hominem toto corpore absoluta similitudine; ascendere eum navigia nocturnis temporibus statimque degra-

out on to the land in that country and after grazing
on the roots of bushes return; and there are some with
the heads of horses, asses and bulls that eat up the
crops.

III. The largest animals in the Indian Ocean are
the shark and the whale; the largest in the Bay of
Biscay is the sperm-whale, which rears up like a
vast pillar higher than a ship's rigging and belches
out a sort of deluge; the largest in the Gulf of Cadiz
is the giant octopus, which spreads out such vast
branches that it is believed never to have entered the
Straits of Gibraltar because of this. The creatures
called Wheels from their resemblance to cart-wheels
are also observed: they are marked with four
radiating rays, with the two eyes located on either
side of the nave.

IV. An embassy from Lisbon sent for the purpose *Tritons,*
reported to the Emperor Tiberius that a Triton had *Nereids and*
been seen and heard playing on a shell in a certain *aquatic*
cave, and that he had the well-known shape. The *monsters.*
description of the Nereids also is not incorrect, except
that their body is bristling with hair even in the
parts where they have human shape; for a Nereid
has been seen on the same coast, whose mournful
song moreover when dying has been heard a long
way off by the coast-dwellers; also the Governor of
Gaul wrote to the late lamented Augustus that a large
number of dead Nereids were to be seen on the shore.
I have distinguished members of the Order of Knighthood as authorities for the statement that a man of the
sea has been seen by them in the Gulf of Cadiz, with
complete resemblance to a human being in every
part of his body, and that he climbs on board ships
during the hours of the night and the side of the

vari quas insederit partes et, si diutius permaneat,
etiam mergi. Tiberio principe contra Lugdunensis
provinciae litus in insula simul trecentas amplius
beluas reciprocans destituit oceanus mirae varietatis
et magnitudinis, nec pauciores in Santonum litore
interque reliquas elephantos et arietes candore [1]
tantum cornibus adsimulatis, Nereidas vero multas.

11 Turranius prodidit expulsam beluam in Gaditano
litore cuius inter duas pinnas ultimae caudae cubita
sedecim fuissent, dentes eiusdem CXX, maximi
dodrantium mensura, minimi semipedum. beluae
cui dicebatur exposita fuisse Andromeda ossa
Romae apportata ex oppido Iudaeae Ioppe ostendit
inter reliqua miracula in aedilitate sua M. Scaurus
longitudine pedum XL, altitudine costarum Indicos
elephantos excedente, spinae crassitudine sesqui-
pedali.

12 V. Balaenae et in nostra maria penetrant. in
Gaditano oceano non ante brumam conspici eas
tradunt, condi autem aestatis temporibus in quodam
sinu placido et capaci, mire gaudentes ibi parere;
hoc scire orcas, infestam iis beluam et cuius imago
nulla repraesentatione exprimi possit alia quam
13 carnis immensae dentibus truculentae. inrumpunt
ergo in secreta ac vitulos earum aut fetas vel etiamnum gravidas lancinant morsu, incursuque ceu
Liburnicarum rostris fodiunt. illae ad flexum immobiles, ad repugnandum inertes et pondere suo
oneratae, tunc quidem et utero graves pariendive

---

[1] *v.l.* tumore.

---

[a] Emperor A.D. 14–37.
[b] Aedile 58 B.C., son of M. Scaurus mentioned VIII 223.

vessel that he sits on is at once weighed down, and if he stays there longer actually goes below the water. During the rule of Tiberius,[a] in an island off the coast of the province of Lyons the receding ocean tide left more than 300 monsters at the same time, of marvellous variety and size, and an equal number on the coast of Saintes, and among the rest elephants, and rams with only a white streak to resemble horns, and also many Nereids. Turranius has stated that a monster was cast ashore on the coast at Cadiz that had 24 feet of tail-end between its two fins, and also 120 teeth, the biggest 9 inches and the smallest 6 inches long. The skeleton of the monster to which Andromeda in the story was exposed was brought by Marcus Scaurus[b] from the town of Jaffa in Judaea and shown at Rome among the rest of the marvels during his aedileship; it was 40 ft. long, the height of the ribs exceeding the elephants of India, and the spine being 1 ft. 6 inches thick.

V. Whales even penetrate into our seas. It is said that they are not seen in the Gulf of Cadiz before midwinter, but during the summer periods hide in a certain calm and spacious inlet, and take marvellous delight in breeding there; and that this is known to the killer whale, a creature that is the enemy of the other species and the appearance of which can be represented by no other description except that of an enormous mass of flesh with savage teeth. The killer whales therefore burst into their retreats and bite and mangle their calves or the females that have calved or are still in calf, and charge and pierce them like warships ramming. The whales being sluggish in bending and slow in retaliating, and burdened by their weight, and at this season also heavy with young

Whales attacked by grampuses.

poenis invalidae, solum auxilium novere in altum
profugere et se tuto[1] defendere oceano.   contra
occurrere laborant seseque opponere et caveatas
angustiis trucidare, in vada urguere, saxis inlidere.
spectantur ea proelia ceu mari ipsi sibi irato, nullis in
sinu ventis, fluctibus vero ad anhelitus ictusque
14 quantos nulli turbines volvant.   orca et in portu
Ostiensi visa est oppugnata a Claudio principe;
venerat tum exaedificante eo portum invitata nau-
fragiis tergorum advectorum e Gallia, satiansque se
per complures dies alveum in vado sulcaverat attumu-
lata fluctibus in tantum ut circumagi nullo modo
posset et, dum saginam persequitur in litus fluctibus
propulsam, emineret dorso multum supra aquas
15 carinae vice inversae.   praetendi iussit Caesar plagas
multiplices inter ora portus, profectusque ipse cum
praetorianis cohortibus populo Romano spectaculum
praebuit lanceas congerente milite e navigiis adsultantibus, quorum unum mergi vidimus reflatu beluae
oppletum unda.
16 VI. Ora ballaenae habent in frontibus, ideoque
summa aqua natantes in sublime nimbos efflant.
spirant autem confessione omnium et paucissima alia

[1] *Mayhoff*: tute *aut* toto.

---

[a] This is unlikely; it was probably a cachalot.
[b] Emperor A.D. 41–54.

or weakened by travail in giving birth, know only one refuge, to retreat to the deep sea and defend their safety by means of the ocean. Against this the killer whales use every effort to confront them and get in their way, and to slaughter them when cooped up in narrow straits or drive them into shallows and make them dash themselves upon rocks. To spectators these battles look as if the sea were raging against itself, as no winds are blowing in the gulf, but there are waves caused by the whales blowing and thrashing that are larger than those aroused by any whirlwinds. A killer whale was actually seen *Grampus in* in the harbour of Ostia *a* in battle with the Emperor *Italian waters.* Claudius *b*; it had come at the time when he was engaged in completing the structure of the harbour, being tempted by the wreck of a cargo of hides imported from Gaul, and in glutting itself for a number of days had furrowed a hollow in the shallow bottom and had been banked up with sand by the waves so high that it was quite unable to turn round, and while it was pursuing its food which was driven forward to the shore by the waves its back projected far above the water like a capsized boat. Caesar gave orders for a barrier of nets to be stretched between the mouths of the harbour and setting out in person with the praetorian cohorts afforded a show to the Roman public, the soldiery hurling lances from the vessels against the creatures when they leapt up alongside, and we saw one of the boats sunk from being filled with water owing to a beast's snorting.

VI. Whales have their mouths in their foreheads, *The breathing of* and consequently when swimming on the surface of *aquatic* the water they blow clouds of spray into the air. *species.* It is universally admitted that a very few other

in mari quae internorum viscerum pulmonem
habent, quoniam sine eo spirare animal nullum
putatur. nec piscium branchias habentes anhelitum
reddere ac per vices recipere existimant quorum haec
opinio est, nec multa alia genera etiam branchiis
carentia, in qua sententia fuisse Aristotelem video et

17 multis persuasisse doctrinae indaginibus.[1] nec me
protinus huic opinioni eorum accedere haut dissimulo,
quoniam et pulmonum vice alia possint spirabilia
inesse viscera ita volente natura, sicut et pro sanguine est multis alius umor. in aquas quidem penetrare vitalem hunc halitum quis miretur qui etiam
reddi ab his eum cernat et is terras quoque tanto
spissiorem naturae partem penetrare argumento
animalium quae semper defossa vivunt, ceu talpae?

18 accedunt apud me certe efficacia ut credam etiam
omnia in aquis spirare naturae suae sorte, primum
adnotata piscium aestivo calore quaedam anhelatio
et alia tranquillo velut oscitatio, ipsorum quoque qui
sunt in adversa opinione de somno piscium confessio,
—quis enim sine respiratione somno locus?—
praeterea bullantium aquarum sufflatio lunaeque
effectu concharum quoque corpora augescentia.
super omnia est quod esse auditum et odoratum
piscibus non erit dubium, ex aeris utrumque materia:

---

[1] doctrina insignibus *Urlichs.*

---

[a] *Hist. An.* VIII 2 *init.*
[b] A conjectural variant gives ' and caused to be accepted by
many distinguished *savants.*'
[c] Pliny's judgement is confirmed by modern science.

creatures in the sea also breathe, those whose internal organs include a lung, since it is thought that no animal is able to breathe without one. Those who hold this opinion believe that the fishes possessing gills do not alternately expire and inspire air, and that many other classes even lacking gills do not —an opinion which I notice that Aristotle[a] held and supported by many learned researches.[b] Nor do I pretend that I do not myself immediately accept this view of theirs,[c] since it is possible that animals may also possess other respiratory organs in place of lungs, if nature so wills, just as also many possess another fluid instead of blood. At all events who can be surprised that this life-giving breath penetrates into water if he observes that it is also given back again from the water, and that it also penetrates into the earth, that much denser element, as is proved by animals that live always in underground burrows, like moles? Undoubtedly to my mind there are additional facts that make me believe that in fact all creatures in the water breathe, owing to the condition of their own nature—in the first place a sort of panting that has often been noticed in fishes during the summer heat, and another form of gasping, so to speak, in calm weather, and also the admission in regard to fishes sleeping made even by those persons who are of the opposite opinion—for how can sleep occur without breathing?—and moreover the bubbles caused on the surface of the water by air rising from below, and the effect of the moon in causing the bodies even of shellfish to increase in size. Above all there is the fact that it will not be doubted that fish have the sense of hearing and smell, both of which are derived from the substance of air:

odorem quidem non aliud quam infectum aera
intellegi possit. quamobrem de his opinetur ut
19 cuique libitum erit. branchiae non sunt ballaenis,
nec delphinis. haec duo genera fistula spirant quae
ad pulmonem pertineat [1], ballaenis a fronte, delphinis
a dorso. et vituli marini, quos vocant phocas,
spirant ac dormiunt in terra. item testudines, de
quibus mox plura.

20 VII. Velocissimum omnium animalium, non solum
marinorum, est delphinus ocior volucre, acrior telo,
ac nisi multum infra rostrum os illi foret medio
paene in ventre, nullus piscium celeritatem eius
evaderet. sed adfert moram providentia naturae,
quia nisi resupini atque conversi non corripiunt.
quae causa praecipue velocitatem eorum ostendit:
nam cum fame conciti fugientem in vada ima perse-
cuti piscem diutius spiritum continuere ut arcu
missi ad respirandum emicant, tantaque vi exsiliunt
21 ut plerumque vela navium transvolent. vagantur
fere coniugia, pariunt catulos decimo mense aestivo
tempore, interim et binos. nutriunt uberibus, sicut
ballaena, atque etiam gestant fetus infantia infirmos;
quin et adultos diu comitantur magna erga partum
22 caritate. adolescunt celeriter, x annis putantur
ad summam magnitudinem pervenire. vivunt et
tricenis, quod cognitum praecisa cauda in experimentum. abduntur tricenis diebus circa canis

---

[1] *Mayhoff*: fistulae (-is *edd.*) . . . spirant.

---

scent indeed could not possibly be interpreted as anything else than an infection of the air. Consequently it is open to every person to form whatever opinion about these matters he pleases. Whales do not possess gills, nor do dolphins. These two genera breathe with a tube that passes to the lung, in the case of whales from the forehead and in the case of dolphins from the back. Also sea-calves, called seals, breathe and sleep on land, as also do tortoises, about whom more shortly.

VII. The swiftest of all animals, not only those of *The dolphin.* the sea, is the dolphin; it is swifter than a bird and darts faster than a javelin, and were not its mouth much below its snout, almost in the middle of its belly, not a single fish would escape its speed. But nature's foresight contributes delay, because they cannot seize their prey except by turning over on their backs. This fact especially shows their speed; for when spurred by hunger they have chased a fleeing fish into the lowest depths and have held their breath too long, they shoot up like arrows from a bow in order to breathe again, and leap out of the water with such force that they often fly over a ship's sails. They usually roam about in couples, husband and wife; [a] they bear cubs after nine months, in the summer season, occasionally even twins. They suckle their young, as do whales, and even carry them about while weak from infancy; indeed they accompany them for a long time even when grown up, so great is their affection for their offspring. They grow up quickly, and are believed to reach their full size in 10 years. They live as much as 30 years, as has been ascertained by amputating the tail of a specimen for an experiment. They are in retirement

ortum occultanturque incognito modo, quod eo
magis mirum est si spirare in aqua non queunt.
solent in terram erumpere incerta de causa, nec
statim tellure tacta moriuntur, multoque ocius
23 fistula clausa. lingua est is contra naturam aquatilium mobilis, brevis atque lata, haut differens
suillae. pro voce gemitus humano similis, dorsum
repandum, rostrum simum: qua de causa nomen
simonis omnes miro modo agnoscunt maluntque ita
appellari.

24 VIII. Delphinus non homini tantum amicum
animal verum et musicae arti, mulcetur symphoniae
cantu set praecipue hydrauli sono. hominem non
expavescit ut alienum, obviam navigiis venit, adludit
exultans, certat etiam et quamvis plena praeterit
25 vela. divo Augusto principe Lucrinum lacum
invectus pauperis cuiusdam puerum ex Baiano
Puteolos in ludum litterarium itantem, cum meridiano
immorans appellatum eum simonis nomine saepius
fragmentis panis quem ob iter ferebat adlexisset,
miro amore dilexit—pigeret referre ni res Maecenatis
et Fabiani et Flavi Alfii multorumque esset litteris
mandata,—quocumque diei tempore inclamatus a
puero quamvis occultus atque abditus ex imo advola-

for 30 days about the rising of the dog-star and hide themselves in an unknown manner, which is the more surprising in view of the fact that they cannot breathe under water. They have a habit of sallying out on to the land for an unascertained reason, and they do not die at once after touching earth—in fact they die much more quickly if the gullet is closed up. The dolphin's tongue, unlike the usual structure of aquatic animals, is mobile, and is short and broad, not unlike a pig's tongue. For a voice they have a moan like that of a human being; their back is arched, and their snout turned up, owing to which all of them in a surprising manner answer to the name of ' Snubnose ' and like it better than any other.

VIII. The dolphin is an animal that is not only *The dolphin* friendly to mankind but is also a lover of music, *susceptible* and it can be charmed by singing in harmony, but *to music.* particularly by the sound of the water-organ. It is not afraid of a human being as something strange to it, but comes to meet vessels at sea and sports and gambols round them, actually trying to race them and passing them even when under full sail. In the reign *Cases of tame* of the late lamented Augustus a dolphin that had been *dolphins.* brought into the Lucrine Lake fell marvellously in love with a certain boy, a poor man's son, who used to go from the Baiae district to school at Pozzuoli, because fairly often the lad when loitering about the place at noon called him to him by the name of Snubnose and coaxed him with bits of the bread he had with him for the journey,—I should be ashamed to tell the story were it not that it has been written about by Maecenas and Fabianus and Flavius Alfius and many others,—and when the boy called to it at what-ever time of day, although it was concealed in hiding

bat pastusque e manu praebebat ascensuro dorsum,
pinnae aculeos velut vagina condens, receptumque
Puteolos per magnum aequor in ludum ferebat simili
modo revehens pluribus annis, donec morbo extincto
puero subinde ad consuetum locum ventitans tristis
et maerenti similis ipse quoque, quod nemo dubitaret,
26 desiderio expiravit. alius intra hos annos Africo litore
Hipponis Diarruti simili modo ex hominum manu
vescens praebensque se tractandum et adludens
nantibus impositosque portans unguento perunctus
a Flaviano proconsule Africae et sopitus, ut apparuit,
odoris novitate fluctuatusque similis exanimi caruit
hominum conversatione ut iniuria fugatus per aliquot
menses; mox reversus in eodem miraculo fuit.
iniuriae potestatum in hospitales ad visendum venie-
tium Hipponenses in necem eius compulerunt.
27 ante haec similia de puero in Iaso urbe memorantur,
cuius amore spectatus longo tempore, dum abeuntem
in litus avide sequitur, in harenam invectus expiravit;
puerum Alexander Magnus Babylone Neptunio
sacerdotio praefecit, amorem illum numinis propitii
fuisse interpretatus. in eadem urbe Iaso Hegesidemus scribit et alium puerum Hermian nomine similiter
maria perequitantem, cum repentinae procellae
fluctibus exanimatus esset, relatum, delphinumque

it used to fly to him out of the depth, eat out of his hand, and let him mount on its back, sheathing as it were the prickles of its fin, and used to carry him when mounted right across the bay to Pozzuoli to school, bringing him back in similar manner, for several years, until the boy died of disease, and then it used to keep coming sorrowfully and like a mourner to the customary place, and itself also expired, quite undoubtedly from longing. Another dolphin in recent years at Hippo Diarrhytus on the coast of Africa similarly used to feed out of people's hands and allow itself to be stroked, and play with swimmers and carry them on its back. The Governor of Africa, Flavianus, smeared it all over with perfume, and the novelty of the scent apparently put it to sleep: it floated lifelessly about, holding aloof from human intercourse for some months as if it had been driven away by the insult; but afterwards it returned and was an object of wonder as before. The expense caused to their hosts by persons of official position who came to see it forced the people of Hippo to destroy it. Before these occurrences a similar story is told about a boy in the city of Iasus, with whom a dolphin was observed for a long time to be in love, and while eagerly following him to the shore when he was going away it grounded on the sand and expired; Alexander the Great made the boy head of the priesthood of Poseidon at Babylon, interpreting the dolphin's affection as a sign of the deity's favour. Hegesidemus writes that in the same city of Iasus another boy also, named Hermias, while riding across the sea in the same manner lost his life in the waves of a sudden storm, but was brought back to the shore, and the dolphin confessing itself the

causam se[1] leti fatentem non reversum in maria
atque in sicco expirasse. hoc idem et Naupacti
28 accidisse Theophrastus tradit. nec modus exem-
plorum: eadem Amphilochi et Tarentini de pueris
delphinisque narrant; quae faciunt ut credatur
Arionem quoque citharoedicae artis, interficere
nautis in mari parantibus ad intercipiendos eius
quaestus, eblanditum uti prius caneret cithara.
congregatis cantu delphinis, cum se iecisset in mare
exceptum ab uno Taenarum in litus pervectum.

29   IX. Est provinciae Narbonensis et in Nemausiensi
agro stagnum Latera appellatum ubi cum homine
delphini societate piscantur. innumera vis mugilum
stato tempore angustis faucibus stagni in mare
erumpit observata aestus reciprocatione, qua de
causa praetendi non queunt retia, aeque molem
ponderis nullo modo toleratura[2] etiamsi non sollertia
insidiaretur[3] tempori. simili ratione in altum
protinus tendunt quod vicino gurgite efficitur,
locumque solum pandendis retibus habilem effugere
30 festinant. quod ubi animadvertere piscantes,—
concurrit autem multitudo temporis gnara et magis
etiam voluptatis huius avida,—totusque populus e
litore quanto potest clamore conciet simonem in
spectaculi eventum, celeriter delphini exaudiunt
desideria aquilonum flatu vocem prosequente, austro

------

[1] causam se ? *Mayhoff*: causa.
[2] *v.ll.* tolleretur, tolletur.
[3] *Rackham*: insidietur.

cause of his death did not return out to sea and expired on dry land. Theophrastus records that exactly the same thing occurred at Naupactus too. Indeed there are unlimited instances: the people of Amphilochus and Taranto tell the same stories about boys and dolphins; and these make it credible that also the skilled harper Arion, when at sea the sailors were getting ready to kill him with the intention of stealing the money he had made, succeeded in coaxing them to let him first play a tune on his harp, and the music attracted a school of dolphins, whereupon he dived into the sea and was taken up by one of them and carried ashore at Cape Matapan.

IX. In the region of Nismes in the Province of Narbonne there is a marsh named Latera where dolphins catch fish in partnership with a human fisherman. At a regular season a countless shoal of mullet rushes out of the narrow mouth of the marsh into the sea, after watching for the turn of the tide, which makes it impossible for nets to be spread across the channel—indeed the nets would be equally incapable of standing the mass of the weight even if the craft of the fish did not watch for the opportunity. For a similar reason they make straight out into the deep water produced by the neighbouring eddies, and hasten to escape from the only place suitable for setting nets. When this is observed by the fishermen—and a crowd collects at the place, as they know the time, and even more because of their keenness for this sport—and when the entire population from the shore shouts as loud as it can, calling for 'Snubnose' for the dénouement of the show, the dolphins quickly hear their wishes if a northerly breeze carries the shout out to sea, though if the wind is in the

Dolphins that assist fishermen.

vero tardius ex adverso referente; sed tum quoque
31 inproviso in auxilium advolare properant.[1] apparet
acies quae protinus disponitur in loco ubi coniectus
est pugnae; opponunt sese ab alto trepidosque in
vada urguent. tum piscatores circumdant retia
furcisque sublevant. mugilum nihilominus velocitas
transilit; at illos excipiunt delphini et occidisse ad
32 praesens contenti cibos in victoriam differunt. opere
proelium fervet includique retibus se fortissime
urguentes gaudent ac, ne id ipsum fugam hostium
stimulet, inter navigia et retia nantesve homines ita
sensim elabuntur ut exitus non aperiant; saltu,
quod est alias blandissimumi is, nullus conatur
evadere, ni summittantur sibi retia. egressus
protinus ante vallum proeliatur. ita peracta captura
quos interemere diripiunt. sed enixioris operae
quam in unius diei praemium conscii sibi opperiuntur
in posterum, nec piscibus tantum sed et intrita panis
e vino satiantur.
33 X. Quae de eodem genere piscandi in Iasio sinu
Mucianus tradit hoc differunt, quod ultro neque
inclamati praesto sint partesque e manibus accipiant
et suum quaeque cumba e delphinis socium habeat

---

[1] *Mueller*: aduolant properare *aut* aduolant propere.

south, against the sound, it carries it more slowly;
but then too they suddenly hasten to the spot, in
order to give their aid. Their line of battle comes
into view, and at once deploys in the place where
they are to join battle; they bar the passage on the
side of the sea and drive the scared mullet into the
shallows. Then the fishermen put their nets round
them and lift them out of the water with forks.
None the less the pace of some mullets leaps
over the obstacles; but these are caught by the
dolphins, which are satisfied for the time being with
merely having killed them, postponing a meal till
victory is won. The action is hotly contested, and
the dolphins pressing on with the greatest bravery are
delighted to be caught in the nets, and for fear that
this itself may hasten the enemy's flight, they glide
out between the boats and the nets or the swimming
fishermen so gradually as not to open ways of escape;
none of them try to get away by leaping out of
the water, which otherwise they are very fond of
doing, unless the nets are put below them. One that
gets out thereupon carries on the battle in front
of the rampart. When in this way the catch has
been completed they tear in pieces the fish that
they have killed. But as they are aware that they
have had too strenuous a task for only a single day's
pay they wait there till the following day, and are
given a feed of bread mash dipped in wine, in addition
to the fish.

X. Mucianus's account of the same kind of fishing *Other cases*
in the Iasian Gulf differs in this—the dolphins stand *of dolphins' intelligence.*
by of their own accord and without being summoned
by a shout, and receive their share from the fishermen's hands, and each boat has one of the dolphins

quamvis noctu et ad faces. ipsis quoque inter se
publica est societas: capto a rege Cariae alligatoque
in portu ingens reliquorum convenit multitudo
maestitia quadam quae posset intellegi miserationem
petens, donec dimitti rex eum iussit. quin et parvos
semper aliquis grandior comitatur ut custos; con-
spectique iam sunt defunctum portantes, ne lacerare-
tur a beluis.

34   XI. Delphinorum similitudinem habent qui vocantur thursiones (distant et tristitia quadam aspectus,
abest enim illa lascivia), maxime tamen rostris
canicularum maleficentiae adsimulati.

35   XII. Testudines tantae magnitudinis Indicum
mare emittit uti singularum superficie habitabiles
casas integant atque inter insulas Rubri praecipue
maris his navigent cumbis. capiuntur multis quidem
modis, sed maxime evectae in summa pelagi anteme-
ridiano tempore blandito, eminente toto dorso per
tranquilla fluitantes, quae voluptas libere spirandi in
tantum fallit oblitas sui ut solis vapore siccato
cortice non queant mergi invitaeque fluitent oppor-
36 tunae venantium praedae. ferunt et pastum egressas
noctu avideque saturatas lassari atque, ut remea-
verint matutino, summa in aqua obdormiscere; id

ᵃ The Indian sea-tortoise (*Chelonia cephalo*) and the real
tortoiseshell-turtle (*C. imbricata*).

as its ally although it is in the night and by torchlight.
The dolphins also have a form of public alliance of
their own: when one was caught by the King of
Caria and kept tied up in the harbour a great multitude of the remainder assembled, suing for compassion with an unmistakable display of grief, until
the king ordered it to be released. Moreover small
dolphins are always accompanied by a larger one
as escort; and before now dolphins have been seen
carrying a dead comrade, to prevent its body being
torn in pieces by sea-monsters.

XI. The creatures called porpoises have a resem- *The*
blance to dolphins (at the same time they are dis- *porpoise.*
tinguished from them by a certain gloomy air, as
they lack the sportive nature of the dolphin), but
in their snouts they have a close resemblance to the
maleficence of dogfish.

XII. The Indian Ocean produces turtles *a* of *Turtle-*
such size that the natives roof dwelling-houses *fishing.*
with the expanse of a single shell, and use them as
boats in sailing, especially among the islands of the
Red Sea. They are caught in a number of ways, but
chiefly as they rise to the surface of the sea when
the weather in the morning attracts them, and float
across the calm waters with the whole of their backs
projecting, and this pleasure of breathing freely
cheats them into self-forgetfulness so much that their
hide gets dried up by the heat and they are unable
to dive, and go on floating against their will, an
opportune prey for their hunters. They also say that
turtles come ashore at night to graze and after
gorging greedily grow languid and when they have
gone back in the morning doze off to sleep on the
surface of the water; that this is disclosed by the

prodi stertentium sonitu; tum adnatare leniter singulis ternos, a duobus in dorsum verti, a tertio laqueum inici supinae atque ita e terra a pluribus trahi. in Phoenicio mari haud ulla difficultate capiuntur; ultroque veniunt stato tempore anni in amnem Eleutherum effusa multitudine.

37 Dentes non sunt testudini, set rostri margines acuti superna parte, interiorem claudente pyxidum modo tanta oris duritia ut lapides comminuant. in mari conchyliis vivunt, in terram egressae herbis. pariunt ova avium ovis similia ad centena numero, eaque defossa extra aquas et cooperta terra ac pavita [1] pectore et complanata incubant noctibus. educunt fetus annuo spatio. quidam oculis spectandoque ova foveri ab iis putant, feminas coitum fugere donec mas festucam aliquam inponat aversae.

38 Trogodytae cornigeras habent ut in lyra adnexis cornibus latis sed mobilibus, quorum in natando remigio se adiuvant; chelium [2] id vocatur, eximiae testudinis sed rarae; namque scopuli praeacuti Chelonophagos terrent, Trogodytae autem, ad quos adnatant, ut sacras adorant. sunt et terrestres, quae ob id in operibus chersinae vocantur, in Africae desertis qua parte maxime sitientibus harenis

---

[1] terra pavita hac *Mayhoff.*
[2] *C. Müller*: celtium.

---

[a] *Testudo marginata,* the land-tortoise.

noise of their snoring; and that then the natives swim quietly up to them, three men to one turtle, and two turn it over on its back while the third throws a noose over it as it lies, and so it is dragged ashore by more men hauling from the beach. Turtles are caught without any difficulty in the Phoenician Sea; and at a regular period of the year they come of their own accord into the river Eleutherus in a straggling multitude.

The turtle has no teeth, but the edges of the beak *Structure and* are sharp on the upper side, and the mouth closing *habits of the* the lower jaw like a box is so hard that they can crush stones. They live on shell-fish in the sea and on plants when they come ashore. They bear eggs like birds' eggs numbering up to 100 at a time; these they bury in the ground somewhere ashore, cover them with earth rammed down and levelled with their chests, and sleep on them at night. They hatch the young in the space of a year. Some people think that they cherish their eggs by gazing at them with their eyes; and that the females refuse to couple till the male places a wisp of straw on one as she turns away from him. The Cavemen have horned turtles with broad horns twisted inward like those of a lyre but movable, which they use as oars to aid themselves in swimming; the name for this horn is *chelium*; it is of tortoise shell of exceptional quality, but it is seldom seen, as the very sharp rocks frighten the Turtle-eater tribe, while the Cavemen, on whose coasts the turtles swim, worship them as sacred. There are also turtles living on land,[a] and *The land-* consequently called in works on the subject the *tortoise.* Terrestrial species; these are found in the deserts of Africa in the region of the dryest and most arid

squalent, roscido, ut creditur, umore viventes.
39 neque aliud ibi animal provenit. XIII. testudinum
putamina secare in laminas lectosque et repositoria
his vestire Carvilius Pollio instituit, prodigi et sagacis
ad luxuriae instrumenta ingenii.

40 XIV. Aquatilium tegumenta plura sunt. alia
corio et pilo integuntur ut vituli et hippopotami, alia
corio tantum ut delphini, cortice ut testudines, silicum
duritia ut ostreae et conchae, crustis ut locustae,
crustis et spinis ut echini, squamis ut pisces, aspera
cute ut squatina, qua lignum et ebora poliuntur,
molli ut murenae, alia nulla ut polypi.

41 XV. Quae pilo vestiuntur animal pariunt ut
pristis, ballaena, vitulus. hic parit in terra, pecudum
more secundas partus reddit, in coitu canum modo
cohaeret, parit nonnumquam geminis plures, educat
mammis fetum, non ante duodecimum diem deducit
in mare, ex eo subinde assuefaciens. interficiuntur
difficulter nisi capite eliso. ipsis in sono mugitus,
unde nomen vituli; accipiunt tamen disciplinam,
voceque [1] pariter et nisu [2] populum salutant, incon-
42 dito fremitu nomine vocati respondent. nullum
animal graviore somno premitur. pinnis quibus in
mari utuntur humi quoque vice pedum serpunt.
pelles eorum etiam detractas corpori sensum aequor-

[1] v.l. vocemque.   [2] Mueller : visu aut iussu.

sands, and it is believed that they live on the moisture of dew. No other animal occurs there. XIII. The practice of cutting tortoiseshell into plates and using it to decorate bedsteads and cabinets was introduced by Carvilius Pollio, a man of lavish talent and skill in producing the utensils of luxury. *Tortoise-shell.*

XIV. The aquatic animals have a variety of coverings. Some are covered with hide and hair, for instance seals and hippopotamuses; others with hide only, as dolphins, or with shell, as turtles, or a hard flinty exterior, as oysters and mussels, with rind, as lobsters, with rind and spines, as sea-urchins, with scales. as fishes, with rough skin which can be used for polishing wood and ivory, as angel-fish, with soft skin, as morays; others with no skin at all, as octopuses. *Various coverings of aquatic species.*

XV. The aquatic animals clad with hair are viviparous—for instance the saw-fish, the whale and the seal. The last bears its young on land; it produces after-birth like cattle; in coupling it clings together as dogs do; it sometimes gives birth to more than two in a litter; it rears its young at the breast; it does not lead them down into the sea before the twelfth day, thereafter continually accustoming them to it. Seals are with difficulty killed unless the head is shattered. Of themselves they make a noise like lowing, whence their name ' sea-calves '; yet they are capable of training, and can be taught to salute the public with their voice and at the same time with bowing, and when called by name to reply with a harsh roar. No animal sleeps more heavily. The fins that they use in the sea also serve them on land as feet to crawl with. Their hides even when flayed from the body are said to retain a sense *Viviparous aquatic species.*

um retinere tradunt semperque aestu maris recedente inhorrescere; praeterea dextrae pennae vim soporiferam inesse somnosque allicere subditam capiti.

43 Pilo carentium duo omnino animal pariunt, delphinus ac vipera.

XVI. Piscium species sunt LXXIV praeter crustis intectas [1] quae sunt XXX de singulis alias dicemus, nunc enim naturae tractantur insignium.

44 XVII. Praecipua magnitudine thynni; invenimus talenta XV pependisse, eiusdem caudae latitudinem duo cubita et palmum. fiunt et in quibusdam amnibus haut minores, silurus in Nilo, isox in Rheno, attilus in Pado inertia pinguescens ad mille aliquando libras, catenato captus hamo nec nisi boum iugis extractus. atque hunc minimus appellatus clupea venam quandam eius in faucibus mira cupidine appe-
45 tens morsu exanimat. silurus grassatur ubicumque est omne animal appetens, equos innatantes saepe demergens. praecipue in Moeno Germaniae amne protelis boum et in Danuvio marris extrahitur porculo marino simillimus; et in Borysthene memoratur praecipua magnitudo nullis ossibus spinisve
46 intersitis, carne praedulci. in Gange Indiae platanistas vocant rostro delphini et cauda, magnitudine autem XVI cubitorum. in eodem esse Statius Sebosus haut modico miraculo affert vermes branchiis

---

[1] *Rackham* : intecta.

---

[a] The catfish also occurs in Europe, where it is the largest freshwater fish, in the Danube running to 400 lb. in weight and 10 ft. or more in length.

of the tides, and always to bristle when the tide is going out; and it is also said that the right fin possesses a soporific influence, and when placed under the head attracts sleep.

Two only of the hairless animals are viviparous, the dolphin and the viper.

XVI. There are 74 species of fishes, not including *Varieties of fish.* those that have a hard covering, of which there are thirty. We will speak of them severally in another place, for now we are dealing with the natures of specially remarkable species.

XVII. The tunny is of exceptional size; we are *Exceptionally large species of fish.* told of a specimen weighing a third of a ton and having a tail 3 ft. 4 in. broad. Fish of no less size also occur in certain rivers, the catfish in the Nile,[a] the salmon in the Rhine, the sturgeon in the Po, a fish that grows so fat from sloth that it sometimes reaches a thousand pounds; it is caught with a hook on a chain and only drawn out of the water by teams of oxen. And this monster is killed by the bite of a very small fish called the lamprey which goes for a particular vein in its throat with remarkable voracity. The wels ranges about and goes for every living creature wherever it is, often dragging down horses when swimming. A fish very like a sea-pig is drawn out with teams of oxen, especially in the river Main in Germany, and in the Danube with weeding-hooks; an exceptionally large species with no internal framework of bones or vertebrae and very sweet flesh is recorded in the Dnieper. In the Ganges in India there is a fish called the platanista[b] with a dolphin's beak and tail, but 24 ft. long. Statius Sebosus gives an extremely marvellous account of worms in the

[b] So called to-day; a variety of dolphin.

binis sexaginta cubitorum, caeruleos, qui nomen a facie traxerunt; his tantas esse vires ut elephantos ad potus venientis mordicus comprehensa manu eorum abstrahant.

47 XVIII. Thynni mares sub ventre non habent pinnam. intrant e magno mari Pontum verno tempore gregatim, nec alibi fetificant. cordyla appellatur partus, qui fetas redeuntes in mare autumno comitatur, limosae vere [1] aut e luto pelamydes incipiunt vocari et, cum annuum excessere tempus, thynni.

48 hi membratim caesi cervice et abdomine commendantur atque clidio, recenti dumtaxat, et tum quoque gravi ructu; cetera parte plenis pulpamentis sale adservantur: melandrya vocantur, quercus assulis similia. vilissima ex his quae caudae proxima, quia pingui carent, probatissima quae faucibus; at in alio pisce circa caudam exercitatissima.[2] pelamydes in apolectos particulatimque consectae in genera cybiorum dispertiuntur.

49 XIX. Piscium genus omne praecipua celeritate adolescit, maxime in Ponto; causa multitudo amnium dulces inferentium aquas. amiam vocant cuius incrementum singulus diebus intellegitur. cum thynnis haec et pelamydes in Pontum ad dulciora pabula intrant gregatim suis quaeque ducibus, et

---

[1] *Hardouin*: vero.   [2] exquisitissima *Gronovius*.

---

[a] *I.e. caeruleus,* ' blue-worm.'   [b] πηλός.
[c] Or, emending the text, ' most in demand.'

same river that have a pair of gills measuring 90 ft.; they are deep blue in colour, and named [a] from their appearance; he says that they are so strong that they carry off elephants coming to drink by gripping the trunk in their teeth.

XVIII. Male tunnies have no fin under the belly. *The tunny.* In spring time they enter the Black Sea from the Mediterranean in shoals, and they do not spawn anywhere else. The name of *cordyla* is given to the fry, which accompany the fish when they return to the sea in autumn after spawning; in the spring they begin to be called mudfish or *pelamydes* (from the Greek [b] for 'mud'), and when they have exceeded the period of one year they are called tunny. These fish are cut up into parts, and the neck and belly are counted a delicacy, and also the throat provided it is fresh, and even then it causes severe flatulence; all the rest of the tunny, with the flesh entire, is preserved in salt: these pieces are called *melandrya*, as resembling slabs of oak-wood. The cheapest of them are the parts next the tail, because they lack fat, and the parts most favoured are those next the throat; whereas in other fish the parts round the tail are most in use.[c] At the *pelamys* stage they are divided into choice slices and cut up small into a sort of little cube.

XIX. Fishes of all kinds grow up exceptionally *Rapid growth* fast, especially in the Black Sea; this is due to the *of fish.* fresh water carried into it by a large number of rivers. The name of mackerel is given to a fish whose growth in size can be noticed daily. This fish and the bonito in company with the tunny enter the Black Sea in shoals in search of less brackish feeding-grounds, each kind with its own leaders, and first of all the mackerel,

primi omnium scombri, quibus est in aqua sulpureus
color, extra qui ceteris.   Hispaniae cetarias hi replent
thynnis non commeantibus.

50   XX. Sed in Pontum nulla intrat bestia piscibus
malefica praeter vitulos et parvos delphinos. thynni
dextera ripa intrant, exeunt laeva; id accidere existimatur quia dextro oculo plus cernant, utroque natura
hebeti.   est in euripo Thracii Bospori quo Propontis
Euxino iungitur in ipsis Europam Asiamque sepa-
rantis freti angustiis saxum miri candoris a vado
ad summa perlucens, iuxta Chalcedonem in latere
51 Asiae.   huius aspectu repente territi semper adversum Byzantii promunturium ex ea causa appellatum
Aurei Cornus praecipiti petunt agmine. itaque
omnis captura Byzantii est magna Chalcedonis
paenuria, м passibus medii interfluentis euripi.
opperiuntur autem aquilonis flatum, ut secundo fluctu
exeant e Ponto, nec nisi [1] intrantes portum Byzan-
tium capiuntur. bruma non vagantur: ubicumque
deprehensi, usque ad aequinoctium ibi hibernant.   idem saepe navigia velis euntia comitantes
mira quadam dulcedine per aliquot horarum
spatia et passuum milia a gubernaculis spectantur
ne tridente quidem in eos saepius iacto territi.
quidam eos qui hoc e thynnis faciant pompilos
52 vocant.   multi in Propontide aestivant, Pontum non

---

[1] *Edd.* nisi ⟨infantes⟩ *vel* ⟨parvi⟩ vel ⟨pusilli⟩.

---

[a] Probably the text is to be altered to give ' only the young
fry are taken,' to conform with Arist. *Hist. An.* VIII 13, p.
598a 26.

which when in the water is sulphur-coloured, though out of water it is the same colour as the other kinds. These fill the fish-ponds of Spain, the tunny not going with them.

XX. But no creature harmful to fish enters the *Habits of the Black* Black Sea besides seals and small dolphins. The *Sea tunny.* tunny enter it by the right bank and go out of it by the left; this is believed to occur because they can see better with the right eye, being by nature dim of sight in both eyes. In the channel of the Thracian Bosphorus joining the Sea of Marmora with the Black Sea, in the actual narrows of the channel separating Europe and Asia, there is a rock of marvellous whiteness that shines through the water from the bottom to the surface, near Chalcedon on the Asiatic side. The sudden sight of this always frightens them, and they make for the opposite promontory of Istambul in a headlong shoal; this is the reason why that promontory has the name of the Golden Horn. Consequently all the catch is at Istambul, and there is a great shortage at Chalcedon, owing to the 1000 yards of channel flowing in between. But they wait for a north wind to blow so as to go out of the Black Sea with the current, and are only taken *a* when entering the harbour of Istambul. In winter they do not wander; wherever winter catches them, there they hibernate till the equinox. They are also frequently seen from the stern of vessels proceeding under sail, accompanying them in a remarkably charming manner for periods of several hours and for a distance of some miles, not being scared even by having a harpoon repeatedly thrown at them. Some people give the name of pilot-fish to the tunny that do this. Many pass the summer in the Sea of Marmora without entering the

intrant; item soleae, cum rhombi intrent. nec
sepia adest,[1] cum lolligo reperiatur. saxatilium
turdus et merula desunt, sicut conchylia, cum
ostreae abundent; omnia autem hibernant in Aegaeo.
intrantium Pontum soli non remeant trichiae—
Graecis enim in plerisque nominibus uti par erit,
quando aliis atque aliis eosdem diversi appellavere
53 tractus—, sed hi soli in Histrum[2] subeunt et ex
eo subterraneis eius venis in Hadriaticum mare
defluunt, itaque et illic descendentes nec umquam
subeuntes e mari visuntur. thynnorum captura est
a vergiliarum exortu ad arcturi occasum; reliquo
tempore hiberno latent in gurgitibus imis nisi tepore
aliquo evocati aut pleniluniis. pinguescunt et in
tantum ut dehiscant. vita longissima his bienni.

54 XXI. Animal est parvum scorpionis effigie, aranei
magnitudine. hoc se et thynno et ei qui gladius
vocatur, crebro delphini magnitudinem excedenti,
sub pinna adfigit aculeo, tantoque infestat dolore
ut in naves saepenumero exiliant. quod et alias
faciunt aliorum vim timentes mugiles maxime, tam
praecipuae velocitatis ut transversa navigia interim
superiaciant.[3]

55 XXII. Sunt et in hac parte naturae auguria, sunt et
piscibus praescita. Siculo bello ambulante in litore

---

[1] *Rackham*: est.
[2] *Mayhoff*: Histrum mare *aut* H. amnem.
[3] *Mayhoff* (*cf.* vii. 81): superiactant, -ent.

---

[a] The beginning of summer, the 48th day after the vernal
equinox.
[b] The evening setting, early in November.
[c] Probably a parasitic copepod.
[d] 38–36 B.C.

Black Sea; the same is the case with the sole, though the turbot does enter it. Nor does the sepia occur there, though the cuttle-fish is found. Of rock-fish the thrush-wrasse and merle-wrasse are lacking, as are some purple-fish, though oysters are plentiful; but they all winter in the Aegean. Of those entering the Black Sea the only kind that never returns is the *trichia* or pilchard—it will be convenient to use the Greek names in most cases, as different districts have called the same species by a great variety of names—, but these alone enter the Danube and float down from it by its underground channels into the Adriatic, and consequently there also they are regularly seen going down stream and never coming up from the sea. The season for catching tunny is from the rise [a] of the Pleiads to the setting [b] of Arcturus; during the rest of the winter time they lurk at the bottom of the water unless tempted out by a mild spell or at full moon. They get fat even to the point of bursting. The tunny's longest life is two years.

XXI. There is a small animal [c] shaped like a scorpion, of the size of a spider. This attaches itself with a spike under the fin of both the tunny and the fish called sword-fish, which often exceeds the size of a dolphin, and torments them so painfully that they frequently jump out of the water into ships. This is also done on other occasions from fear of the violence of other fish, especially by mullet, which are so exceptionally swift that they sometimes leap right over ships that lie across their path. *Parasite of the tunny.*

XXII. In this department of nature also there are cases of augury; even fish have fore-knowledge of events. During the Sicilian War [d] when Augustus *Portents given by fish.*

Augusto piscis e mari ad pedes eius exilivit, quo argumento vates respondere Neptunum patrem adoptante tum sibi Sexto Pompeio—tanta erat navalis rei gloria—sub pedibus Caesaris futuros qui maria tempore illo tenerent.

56   XXIII. Piscium feminae maiores quam mares. in quodam genere omnino non sunt mares, sicut erythinus et channis, omnes enim ovis gravidae capiuntur. vagantur gregatim fere cuiusque generis squamosi. capiuntur ante solis ortum: tum maxime piscium fallitur visus. noctibus quies, set inlustribus aeque quam die cernunt. aiunt et si teratur gurges interesse capturae, itaque plures secundo tractu capi quam primo. gustu olei maxime, dein modicis imbribus gaudent alunturque: quippe et harundines quamvis in palude prognatae non tamen sine imbre adolescunt; et alias ubicumque pisces in eadem aqua adsidui, si non affluat, exanimantur.

57   XXIV. Praegelidam hiemem omnes sentiunt, sed maxime qui lapidem in capite habere existimantur, ut lupi, chromes, sciaenae, phagri. cum asperae hiemes fuere, multi caeci capiuntur. itaque his mensibus iacent speluncis conditi (sicut in genere terrestrium retulimus), maxime hippurus et coracini, hieme non capti praeterquam statis diebus paucis et isdem semper, item murena et orphus, conger, percae et saxatiles omnes. terra quidem, hoc est

---

ᵃ VIII 126 ff.
ᵇ Not in this context *Coryphaeus hippurus*.

was walking on the shore a fish leapt out of the sea at his feet, a sign which the priests interpreted as meaning that although Sextus Pompeius was then adopting Neptune as his father—so glorious were his naval exploits,—yet those who at that time held the seas would later be beneath the feet of Caesar.

XXIII. Female fish are larger than the males. In one kind there are no males at all, as is the case with red perch and sea-perch, for all those caught are heavy with eggs. Almost every kind with scales is gregarious. Fish are caught before sunrise ; at that *Modes of* hour their sight is most fallible. In the night they *catching fish.* repose, but on bright nights they can see as well as by day. People also say that scraping the bottom helps the catch, and that consequently more are caught at the second haul than at the first. Fish are fondest of the taste of oil, but next to that they enjoy and derive nourishment from moderate falls of rain : in fact even reeds although growing in a marsh nevertheless do not grow up without rain ; and besides, fishes everywhere die when kept continually in the same water, if there is no inflow.

XXIV. All fish feel a very cold winter, but most of *Hibernating* all those that are believed to have a stone in their *species.* head, for instance the bass, the *chromis,* the ombre and the braize. When the winter has been severe a great many are caught blind. Consequently in the winter months they lie hidden in caves (like cases that we have recorded in the class of land-animals[a]), particularly the gilthead[b] and blackfish, which are not caught in winter except on a few regular days that are always the same, and also the moray and the *orphus,* the conger and perch and all rockfish. It is indeed reported that the electric ray, the plaice and

vado maris excavato, condi per hiemes torpedinem, psettam, soleam tradunt.

58 XXV. Quidam rursus aestus inpatientia mediis fervoribus sexagenis diebus latent, ut glaucus, aselli, auratae. fluviatilium silurus caniculae exortu sideratur, et alias semper fulgure sopitur. hoc et in mari accidere cyprino putant. et alioqui totum mare sentit exortum eius sideris, quod maxime in Bosporo apparet, alga enim et pisces superferuntur, omniaque ab imo versa.

59 XXVI. Mugilum natura ridetur in metu capite abscondito totos se occultari credentium. isdem tam incauta salacitas ut in Phoenice et in Narbonensi provincia coitus tempore e vivariis marem linea longinqua per os ad branchias religata emissum in mare eademque linea retractum feminae sequantur ad litus, rursusque feminam mares partus tempore.

60 XXVII. Apud antiquos piscium nobilissimus habitus accipenser, unus omnium squamis ad os versis, contra quam in nando meat,[1] nullo nunc in honore est, quod equidem[2] miror, cum sit rarus inventu quidam eum elopem vocant.

61 XXVIII. Postea praecipuam auctoritatem fuisse lupo et asellis Nepos Cornelius et Laberius poeta mimorum tradidere. luporum laudatissimi qui appellantur

---

[1] *Rackham*: meant.   [2] *Mayhoff*: quidem.

the sole hide through the winters in the ground, that is, in a hole scraped out at the bottom of the sea.

XXV. Some fish again being unable to endure heat hide for 8 or 9 weeks during the heats of midsummer, for instance the 'gray-fish', the haddock and the gilt-head. Of river fish the catfish has a stroke at the rise of the dogstar, and at other times is always made drowsy by lightning. This is thought to happen to the carp even in the sea. And beside this the whole sea is conscious of the rise of that star, as is most clearly seen in the Dardanelles, for sea-weed and fishes float on the surface, and everything is turned up from the bottom. *Species susceptible to heat and liable to stroke.*

XXVI. It is an amusing trait in the mullet that when frightened it hides its head and thinks it is entirely concealed. The same fish is so incautious in its wantonness that in Phoenicia and in the Province of Narbonne at the breeding season a male mullet from the fish-ponds is sent out into the sea with a long line tied to its gills through its mouth and when it is drawn back by the same line the females follow it to the shore, and again the males follow a female at the laying season. *Catching mullet.*

XXVII. In old days the sturgeon was held to be the noblest of the fishes, being the only one with its scales turned towards the mouth, in the opposite direction to the one in which it swims; but now it is held in no esteem, which for my part I think surprising, as it is a fish seldom to be found. One name for it is the *elops*. *Grades of fish for the table: the sturgeon.*

XXVIII. Cornelius Nepos and the mime-writer Laberius have recorded that at a later period the chief rank belonged to the bass and the hake. The kind of bass most praised is the one called the *Changes of taste: the bass and the hake.*

lanati a candore mollitiaque carnis. asellorum duo
genera, collyri [1] minores et bacchi qui non nisi in
alto capiuntur, ideo praelati prioribus. at in lupis in
amne capti praeferuntur.

62 XXIX. Nunc principatus scaro datur, qui solus
piscium dicitur ruminare herbisque vesci atque non
aliis piscibus, Carpathio maxime mari frequens;
promunturium Troadis Lectum numquam sponte
transit. inde advectos Tiberio Claudio principe
Optatus e libertis eius praefectus classis inter
Ostiensem et Campaniae oram sparsos disseminavit,
63 quinquennio fere cura adhibita ut capti redderentur
mari. postea frequentes inveniuntur Italiae litore,
non antea ibi capti; admovitque sibi gula sapores
piscibus satis et novum incolam mari dedit, ne quis
peregrinas aves Romae parere miretur. proxima
est mensa iecori dumtaxat mustelarum quas, mirum
dictu, inter Alpes quoque lacus Raetiae Brigantinus
aemulas marinis generat.

64 XXX. Ex reliqua nobilitate et gratia maximo
est et copia mullis, sicut magnitudo modica, binasque
libras ponderis raro admodum exuperant, nec in
vivariis piscinisque crescunt. septentrionalis tantum
hos et proxima occidentis parte gignit oceanus.

---

[1] callariae *Hermolaus ex Athen.* vii. 315.

fleecy bass, from the whiteness and softness of its flesh. There are two kinds of hake—the *collyrus*, which is the smaller, and the *bacchus*, which is only caught in deep water, and consequently is preferred to the former. But among bass those caught in a river are preferred.

XXIX. Nowadays the first place is given to the wrasse, which is the only fish that is said to chew the cud and to feed on grasses and not on other fish. It is especially common in the Carpathian Sea; it never of its own accord passes Cape Lectum in the Troad. Some wrasse were imported from there in the principate of Tiberius Claudius by one of his freedmen, Optatus, Commander of the Fleet, and were distributed and scattered about between the mouth of the Tiber and the coast of Campania, care being taken for about five years that when caught they should be put back into the sea. Subsequently they have been frequently found on the coast of Italy, though not caught there before; and thus greed has provided itself with additional dainties by cultivating fish, and has bestowed on the sea a new denizen— so that nobody must be surprised that foreign birds breed at Rome. The next place belongs[a] at all events to the liver of the burbot that strange to say the Lake of Constance in Raetia in the Central Alps also produces to rival the marine variety.

XXX. Of other fish of a good class the surmullet stands first in popularity and also in plentifulness, though its size is moderate and it but rarely exceeds 2 lbs. in weight, nor does it grow larger when kept in preserves and fishponds. This size is only produced by the northern ocean and in its westernmost

The parrot-wrasse.

Varieties of mullet.

---

[a] *Cf.* XIV 16 ante eum Raeticis prior mensa erat avis.

cetero genera eorum plura. nam et alga vescuntur
et ostreis et limo et aliorum piscium carne; et barba
65 gemina insigniuntur inferiore labro. lutarium ex iis
vilissimi generis appellant. hunc semper comitatur
sargus nomine alius piscis, et caenum fodiente
eo excitatum devorat pabulum. nec litoralibus
gratia. laudatissimi conchylium sapiunt. nomen
his Fenestella a colore mulleorum calciamentorum
datum putat. pariunt ter annis: certe totiens fetura
66 apparet. mullum expirantem versicolori quadam
et numerosa varietate spectari proceres gulae narrant, rubentium squamarum multiplici mutatione
pallescentem, utique si vitro spectetur inclusus. M.
Apicius ad omne luxus ingenium natus[1] in sociorum
garo—nam ea quoque res cognomen invenit—
necari[2] eos praecellens putavit, atque e iecore eorum
67 alecem excogitari.[3] XXXI. provocavit—id enim
est facilius dixisse quam quis vicerit—Asinius Celer
e consularibus hoc pisce prodigos[4] omnes, Gaio
principe unum mercatus HS. VIII mullum. quae
reputatio aufert traversum animum ad contempla-
tionem eorum qui in conquestione luxus cocos emi
singulos pluris quam equos queritabant; at nunc
coci trium horum[5] pretiis parantur et cocorum
pisces, nullusque prope iam mortalis aestimatur

---

[1] *Hardouin*: maius.   [2] necare? *Mueller.*
[3] *Rackham*: excogitare.   [4] *Mueller*: prodigus.
[5] *Reinesius (vel* trium equorum): triumphorum.

---

[a] Or perhaps 'Fenestella thinks that this fish (the red mullet)
has received its name from the colour of the shoes called
mullei.'
[b] For this fish-sauce see XXXI 93.
[c] Say £70 gold.

part. For the rest, there are several kinds of mullet. For it feeds on seaweed, bivalves, mud and the flesh of other fish; and it is distinguished by a double beard on the lower lip. The mullet of cheapest kind is called the mud-mullet. This variety is always accompanied by another fish named sea-bream, and it swallows down as fodder mire stirred up by the sea-bream digging. The coast mullet also is not in favour. The most approved kind have the flavour of an oyster. This variety has the name of shoe-mullet, which Fenestella thinks was given it from its colour.[a] It spawns three times a year—at all events that is the number of times that its fry is seen. The leaders in gastronomy say that a dying mullet shows a large variety of changing colours, turning pale with a complicated modification of blushing scales, at all events if it is looked at when contained in a glass bowl. Marcus Apicius, who had a natural gift for every ingenuity of luxury, thought it specially desirable for mullets to be killed in a sauce made of their companions, *garum*[b]—for this thing also has procured a designation—and for fish-paste to be devised out of their liver. XXXI. With a fish of this kind one of the proconsular body, Asinius Celer, in the Gaius' principate, issued a challenge—it is not so easy to say who won the match—to all the spendthrifts by giving 8000 sesterces[c] for a surmullet. The thought of this side-tracks the mind to the consideration of the people who in their complaints about luxury used to protest that cooks were being bought at a higher price per man than a horse; but now the price of three horses is given for a cook, and the price of three cooks for a fish, and almost no human being has come to be more valued than

Prices paid for luxuries

pluris quam qui peritissime censum domini mergit.
68 mullum lxxx librarum in mari Rubro captum Licinius
Mucianus prodidit quanti mercatura eum luxuria
suburbanis litoribus inventum?

XXXII. Est et haec natura ut alii alibi pisces
principatum optineant, coracinus in Aegypto, zaeus,
idem faber appellatus, Gadibus, circa Ebusum salpa,
obscenus alibi et qui nusquam percoqui possit nisi
ferula verberatus; in Aquitania salmo fluviatilis
marinis omnibus praefertur.

69 XXXIII. Piscium alii branchias multiplices habent, alii simplices, alii duplices. his aquam emittunt
acceptam ore. senectutis indicium squamarum
duritia, quae non sunt omnibus similes. duo lacus
Italiae in radicibus Alpium Larius et Verbannus
appellantur, in quibus pisces omnibus annis vergiliarum ortu existunt squamis conspicui crebris atque
praeacutis, clavorum caligarium effigie, nec amplius
circa eum mensem visuntur.

70 XXXIV. Miratur et Arcadia suum exocoetum
appellatum ab eo quod in siccum somni causa exeat.
circa Clitorium vocalis hic traditur et sine branchiis,
idem ab[1] aliquis Adonis dictus.

71 XXXV. Exeunt in terram et qui marini mures
vocantur et polypi et murenae; quin et in Indiae
fluminibus certum genus piscium, ac deinde resilit—
nam in stagna et amnes transeundi plerisque evidens

---

[1] ab *add. Rackham.*

[a] See note on § 53.   [b] Blennius Montagui.

one that is most skilful in making his master bank-rupt. Licinius Mucianus has recorded the capture in the Red Sea of a mullet weighing 80 lbs.; what price would our epicures have paid for it if it had been found on the coasts near the city?

XXXII. It is also a fact of nature that different *Local varieties of* fishes hold the first rank in different places—the *taste.* blackfish in Egypt, the John Dory (called *faber* in Latin) at Cadiz, the saupe in the neighbourhood of Iviza, though elsewhere it is a disgusting fish, and everywhere it is unable to be cooked thoroughly unless it has been beaten with a rod; in Aquitaine the river salmon is preferred to all sea-fish.

XXXIII. Some fish have numerous gills, others *Varieties of* single ones, others double. With the gills they *gills and scales.* discharge the water taken in by the mouth. Hardening of the scales, which are not alike in all fishes, is a sign of age. There are two lakes in Italy at the foot of the Alps, named Como and Maggiore, in which every year at the rising of the Pleiads [a] fish are found that are remarkable for close-set and very sharp scales, shaped like shoe-nails, but they are not commonly seen for a longer period than about a month from then.

XXXIV. Arcadia also has a marvel in its blenny,[b] so called because it climbs out on to the land to sleep. In the district of the river Clitorius this fish is said to have a voice and no gills; the same variety is by some people called the Adonis fish.

XXXV. The fish called the sea-mouse also comes out *Fish that* on to the land, as do the polypus and the moray; *come to land.* so also does a certain kind of fish in the rivers of India, and then jumps back again—for in most cases there is an obvious purpose in getting across into

ratio est ut tutos fetus edant, quia non sint ibi qui devorent partus fluctusque minus saeviant. has intellegi ab iis causas servarique temporum vices magis miretur si quis reputet quoto cuique hominum nosci uberrimam esse capturam sole transeunte piscium signum.

72 XXXVI. Marinorum alii sunt plani, ut rhombi, soleae ac passeres, qui ab rhombis situ tantum corporum differunt—dexter hic resupinatus est illis, passeri laevos; alii longi, ut murena, conger.

73 XXXVII. Ideo pinnarum quoque fiunt discrimina, quae pedum vice sunt datae piscibus, nullis supra quattuor, quibusdam ternae, quibusdam binae, aliquis nullae. in Fucino tantum lacu piscis est qui octonis pinnis natat. binae omnino longis et lubricis, ut anguillis et congris, aliis[1] nullae, ut murenis, quibus nec branchiae. haec omnia flexuoso corporum inpulsu ita mari utuntur ut serpentes terra, et in sicco quoque repunt; ideo etiam vivaciora talia. et e planis aliqua non habent pinnas, ut pastinacae— ipsa enim latitudine natant—et quae mollia appellantur, ut polypi, quoniam pedes illis pinnarum vicem praestant

74 XXXVIII. Anguillae octonis vivunt annis. durant et sine aqua quinis et[2] senis diebus aquilone spirante, austro paucioribus. at hiemem eaedem in exigua

---

[1] aliis *add. Mueller ex Aristotele.*
[2] *Mueller ex Ar.* : sine aquis et.

---

[a] Or flounder; the identification is doubtful.

marshes and lakes so as to produce their offspring safe, as in those waters there are no creatures to devour their young and the waves are less fierce. Their understanding these reasons and their observing the changes of the seasons would seem more surprising to anybody who considers what fraction of mankind is aware that the biggest catch is made when the sun is passing through the sign of the Fishes.

XXXVI. Some sea-fish are flat, for instance the turbot, the sole and the plaice,[a] which differs from the turbot only in the posture of its body—the turbot lies with the right side uppermost and the flounder with the left; while other sea-fish are long, as the moray and the conger. XXXVII. Consequently differences also occur in the fins, which are bestowed on fish instead of feet; none have more than four, some have three, some two, certain kinds none. In the Lago di Celano, but nowhere else, there is a fish that has eight fins to swim with. Long slippery fish like eels and congers generally have two fins, others have none, for instance, the moray which also has no gills. All this class use the sea as snakes do the land, propelling themselves by twisting their bodies, and they also crawl on dry land; consequently this class are also longer-lived. Some of the flat-fish too have not got fins, for example, the prickly ray—for these swim merely by means of their breadth—and the kinds called soft fish, such as polyps, since their feet serve them instead of fins.

XXXVIII. Eels live eight years. They can even last five or six days at a time out of water if a north wind is blowing, but not so long with a south wind. But the same fish cannot endure winter in shallow

Flatfish.

Varieties of fins.

Habits of the eel.

aqua non tolerant, neque in turbida; ideo circa ver-
gilias maxime capiuntur fluminibus tum praecipue
turbidis. pascuntur noctibus. exanimes piscium solae
75 non fluitant. lacus est Italiae Benacus in Veronensi
agro Mincium amnem tramittens, ad cuius emersum [1]
annuo tempore, Octobri fere mense, autumnalj
sidere, ut palam est, hiemato lacu, fluctibus glomer-
atae volvuntur in tantum mirabili multitudine ut in
excipulis eius fluminis ob hoc ipsum fabricatis
singulorum milium reperiantur globi.

76 XXXIX. Murena quocumque mense parit, cum
ceteri pisces stato pariant. ova eius citissime
crescunt. in sicca litora elapsas vulgus coitu
serpentium impleri putat. Aristoteles zmyrum vocat
marem qui generet; discrimen esse quod murena
varia et infirma sit, zmyrus unicolor et robustus
dentesque et [2] extra os habeat. in Gallia septentrionali murenis omnibus dextera in maxilla septenae
maculae ad formam septentrionis aureo colore
fulgent dumtaxat viventibus, pariterque cum anima
77 extinguuntur. invenit in hoc animali documenta
saevitiae Vedius Pollio eques Romanus ex amicis
divi Augusti vivariis earum immergens damnata
mancipia, non tamquam ad hoc feris terrarum non
sufficientibus, sed quia in alio genere totum pariter

[1] *Rackham* : emersus.
[2] et *add. ex Aristotele Mayhoff.*

[a] See on § 53.   [b] *Murena unicolor*

nor in rough water; consequently they are chiefly caught at the rising of the Pleiads,[a] as the rivers are then specially rough. They feed at night. They are the only fish that do not float on the surface when dead. There is a lake called Garda in the territory of Verona through which flows the river Mincio, at the outflow of which on a yearly occasion, about the month of October, when the lake is made rough evidently by the autumn star, they are massed together by the waves and rolled in such a marvellous shoal that masses of fish, a thousand in each, are found in the receptacles constructed in the river for the purpose.

XXXIX. The moray spawns in any month, although all other fish have fixed breeding seasons. *Habits of the moray.* Its eggs grow very quickly. Morays are commonly believed to crawl out on to dry land and to be impregnated by copulating with snakes. Aristotle gives the name of *zmyrus*[b] to the male fish which generates, and says that the difference is that the moray is spotted and feeble whereas the zmyrus is self-coloured and hardy, and has teeth projecting outside the mouth. In Northern Gaul all morays have seven spots on the right jaw arranged like the constellation of the Great Bear, which are of a bright golden colour as long as the fish are alive, and are extinguished when they are deprived of life. Vedius Pollio, Knight of Rome, a member of the Privy Council under the late lamented Augustus, found in this animal a means of displaying his cruelty when he threw slaves sentenced to death into ponds of morays—not that the wild animals on land were not sufficient for this purpose, but because with any other kind of creature he was

hominem distrahi spectare non poterat. ferunt
aceti gustatu [1] praecipue eas in rabiem agi. tenuissimum his tergus, contra anguillis crassius, eoque
verberari solitos tradit Verrius praetextatos, et ob
id multam iis dici non institutum.

78   XL. Planorum piscium alterum est genus quod
pro spina cartilaginem habet, ut raiae, pastinacae,
squatinae, torpedo, et quos bovis, lamiae, aquilae,
ranae nominibus Graeci appellant. quo in numero
sunt squali quoque, quamvis non plani. haec
Graece in universum σελάχη appellavit Aristoteles
primo hoc nomine eis inposito: nos distinguere non
possumus nisi si cartilaginea appellare libeat. omnia
autem carnivora sunt talia, et supina vescuntur, ut
in delphinis diximus, et cum ceteri pisces ova pariant,
hoc genus solum ut ea quae cete appellant animal
parit excepta quam ranam vocant.

79   XLI. Est parvus admodum piscis adsuetus petris
echeneis appellatus. hoc carinis adhaerente naves
tardius ire creduntur inde nomine inposito, quam
ob causam amatoriis quoque veneficiis infamis est et
iudiciorum ac litium mora, quae crimina una laude
pensat fluxus gravidarum utero sistens partusque
continens ad puerperium. in cibos tamen non ad-

----

[1] *Mayhoff*? (*cf.* **x.** 185 &c.): gustu.

----

[a] *Echeneis remora.*

not able to have the spectacle of a man being torn entirely to pieces at one moment. It is stated that tasting vinegar particularly drives them mad. Their skin is very thin, whereas that of eels is rather thick, and Verrius records that it used to be used for flogging boys who were sons of citizens, and that consequently it was not the practice for them to be punished with a fine.

XL. There is a second class of flatfish that has *Boneless* gristle instead of a backbone, for instance rays, *varieties of* prickly rays, angel-sharks, the electric ray, and those *flatfish.* the Greek names for which mean 'ox,' 'sorceress,' 'eagle' and 'frog.' This group includes the *squalus* also, although that is not a flatfish. These Aristotle designated in Greek by the common name of selachians, giving them that name for the first time; but we cannot distinguish them as a class unless we like to call them the cartilaginea. But all such fish are carnivorous, and they feed lying on their backs, as we said in the case of dolphins; and whereas all other fish are oviparous, this kind alone with the exception of the species called the fishing-frog is viviparous, like the creatures termed cetaceans.

XLI. There is a quite small fish that frequents *The remora* rocks, called the sucking-fish.[a] This is believed to make ships go more slowly by sticking to their hulls, from which it has received its name; and for this reason it also has an evil reputation for supplying a love-charm and for acting as a spell to hinder litigation in the courts, which accusations it counterbalances only by its laudable property of stopping fluxes of the womb in pregnant women and holding back the offspring till the time of birth. It is not included however among articles of diet. It is

80 mittitur.   pedes eum habere arbitrantur; Aristoteles
infitias[1] it apposita pinnarum similitudine.

Mucianus muricem esse latiorem purpura, neque
aspero neque rotundo ore neque in angulos prodeunte
rostro sed sicut[2] concha utroque latere sese colligente;
quibus inhaerentibus plenam venti[3] stetisse navem
portantem nuntios a Periandro ut castrarentur
nobiles pueri[4]; conchasque quae id praestiterint
apud Cnidiorum Venerem coli.   Trebius Niger
pedalem esse et crassitudine quinque digitorum,
naves morari; praeterea hanc esse vim eius adservati
in sale ut aurum quod deciderit in altissimos puteos
admotus extrahat.

81   XLII. Mutant colorem candidum maenae et fiunt
aestate nigriores.   mutat et phycis, reliquo tempore
candida, vere varia.   eadem piscium sola nidificat
ex alga atque in nido parit.

82   XLIII. Volat sane perquam similis volucri hirundo[5]
item milvus.   subit in summa maria piscis ex argumento appellatus lucerna, linguaque ignea per os
exerta tranquillis noctibus relucet.   attollit   e
mari sesquipedanea fere cornua quae ab his nomen
traxit.   rursus draco marinus captus atque immissus
in harenam cavernam sibi rostro mira celeritate
excavat.

83   XLIV. Piscium sanguine carent de quibus dicemus.   sunt autem tria genera: primum quae mollia

    [1] infitias *add. Mayhoff.*
    [2] *Mayhoff:* sic *aut* simplici.
    [3] *Mayhoff:* ventis.
    [4] navem Periandri portantem, ut castrarentur, nobiles
pueros *Mayhoff.*
    [5] *Mayhoff:* hirundini (*v.l.* volat his unda sane).

---

        [a] The Romans reckoned 16 *digiti* to the *pes.*

thought by some to have feet, but Aristotle denies this, adding that its limbs resemble wings.

Mucianus states that the murex is broader than *Varieties of* the purple, and has a mouth that is not rough nor *purple-fish.* round and a beak that does not stick out into corners but shuts together on either side like a bivalve shell; and that owing to murexes clinging to the sides a ship was brought to a standstill when in full sail before the wind, carrying despatches from Periander ordering some noble youths to be castrated, and that the shell-fish that rendered this service are worshipped in the shrine of Venus at Cnidus. Trebius Niger says that it is a foot long and four inches *a* wide, and hinders ships, and moreover that when preserved in salt it has the power of drawing out gold that has fallen into the deepest wells when it is brought near them.

XLII. The mendole changes its white colour and *The mendole.* becomes blacker in summer. The *phycis* *b* also *The lamprey.* changes colour, being white all the rest of the time but variegated in spring. Also it is the only fish that lays its eggs in a nest, which it builds of seaweed.

XLIII. The swallow-fish flies just exactly like a *Other* bird, and so does the kite-fish. The fish on this *species.* account called the lamp-fish rises to the surface of the sea, and on calm nights gives a light with its fiery tongue which it puts out from its mouth. The fish that has got its name from its horns raises these up about 18 inches out of the sea. The sea-snake, again, when caught and placed on the sand, with marvellous rapidity digs itself a hole with its beak.

XLIV. We will now speak of the bloodless fishes. *Bloodless* Of these there are three kinds: first those which are *fishes, their varieties and structures.*

b A wrasse, probably *Crenilabrus pavo.*

appellantur, dein contecta crustis tenuibus, postremo testis conclusa duris. mollia sunt lolligo, saepia, polypus et cetera generis eius. his caput inter pedes et ventrem, pediculi octoni omnibus. saepiae et lolligini pedes duo ex his longissimi et asperi quibus ad ora admovent cibos et in fluctibus se velut anchoris stabiliunt, ceteri [1] cirri quibus venantur.

84   XLV. Lolligo etiam volitat extra aquam se efferens, quod et pectunculi faciunt, sagittae modo. saepiarum generis mares varii et nigriores constantiaeque maioris: percussae tridente feminae auxiliantur, at femina icto mare fugit. ambo autem, ubi sensere se adprehendi, effuso atramento quod pro sanguine his est infuscata aqua absconduntur.

85   XLVI. Polyporum multa genera. terreni maiores quam pelagici. omnibus bracchiis ut pedibus ac manibus utuntur, cauda vero, quae est bisulca et acuta, in coitu. est polypis fistula in dorso qua tramittunt mare, eamque modo in dexteram partem, modo in sinistram transferunt. natant obliqui in caput, quod praedurum est ut [2] sufflatione viventibus. cetero per bracchia velut acetabulis dispersis haustu quodam adhaerescunt: tenent supini ut avelli non queant. vada non adprehendunt; et grandibus

---

[1] *Rackham* : cetera (circa *Mayhoff cf. Ar.* περὶ τὸ κύτος).
[2] ut *add. Hardouin coll. Aristotele.*

---

[a] Aristotle *H.A.* 524a 13 νεῖ δὲ πλάγιος ἐπὶ τὴν καλουμένην κεφαλὴν ἐκτείνων τοὺς πύδας.

called soft fish, then those covered with thin rinds, and lastly those enclosed in hard shells. The soft are the cuttle-fish, the sepia, the polyp and the others of that kind. They have the head between the feet and the belly, and all of them have eight little feet. In the sepia and cuttle-fish two of these feet are extremely long and rough, and by means of these they carry food to their mouths, and steady themselves as with anchors in a rough sea; but all the rest are feelers which they use for catching their prey.

XLV. The cuttle-fish even flies, raising itself out of the water, as also do the small scallops, like an arrow. The males of the genus sepia are variegated and darker in colour, and they are more resolute: when a female is struck with a trident they come to her assistance, whereas a female flees when a male is struck. But both sexes on perceiving they are being caught hold of pour out a dark fluid which these animals have instead of blood, so darkening the water and concealing themselves. *The cuttle-fish. The sepia.*

XLVI. There are many sorts of polyp. The land kinds are larger than the marine. They use all their arms as feet and hands, but employ the tail, which is forked and pointed, in sexual intercourse. The polyps have a tube in their back through which they pass the sea-water, and they shift this now to the right side and now to the left. They swim with their head on one side,[a] this while they are alive being hard as though blown out. Otherwise they remain adhering with a kind of suction, by means of a sort of suckers spread over their arms: throwing themselves backward they hold on so that they cannot be torn away. They do not cling to the bottom of the sea, and have less holding-power when *The polyp: its varieties and habits.*

minor tenacitas. soli mollium in siccum exeunt,
86 dumtaxat asperum: levitatem odere. vescuntur
conchyliorum carne, quorum conchas conplexu
crinium frangunt; itaque praeiacentibus testis
cubile eorum deprehenditur. et cum alioqui brutum
habeatur animal, ut quod ad manum hominis adnatet,
in re quodammodo familiari callet: omnia in domum
comportat, dein putamina erosa carne egerit adna-
87 tantesque pisciculos ad ea venatur. colorem mutat
ad similitudinem loci, et maxime in metu. ipsum
bracchia sua rodere falsa opinio est, id enim a congris
evenit ei; sed renasci sicut colotis et lacertis caudas
haut falsum.

88   XLVII. Inter praecipua autem miracula est qui
vocatur nautilos, ab aliis pompilos.[1] supinus in
summa aequorum pervenit, ita se paulatim absubri-
gens ut emissa omni per fistulam aqua velut exonera-
tus sentina facile naviget. postea prima duo
bracchia retorquens membranam inter illa mirae
tenuitatis extendit, qua velificante in aura ceteris
subremigans bracchiis media se cauda ut gubernaculo
regit. ita vadit alto Liburnicarum ludens imagine,[2]
si quid pavoris interveniat, hausta se mergens aqua.
89   XLVIII. Polyporum generis est ozaena dicta a

[1] Pliny misread *pontilos* in Aristot. *H.A.* 525a 21.
[2] imaginem ? *Rackham.*

full-grown. They alone of the soft creatures go out of the water on to dry land, provided it has a rough surface: they hate smooth surfaces. They feed on the flesh of shellfish, the shells of which they break by enfolding them with their tentacles; and consequently their lair can be detected by the shells lying in front of it. And though the polyp is in other respects deemed a stupid animal, inasmuch as it swims towards a man's hand, it has a certain kind of sense in its domestic economy: it collects everything into its home, and then after it has eaten the flesh puts out the refuse and catches the little fishes that swim up to it. It changes its colour to match its environment, and particularly when it is frightened. The notion that it gnaws its own arms is a mistake, for this is done to it by the congers; but the belief that its tails grow again, as is the case with the gecko and the lizard, is correct.

XLVII. But among outstanding marvels is the *The* creature called the nautilus, and by others the pilot- *nautilus.* fish. Lying on its back it comes to the surface of the sea, gradually raising itself up in such a way that by sending out all the water through a tube it so to speak unloads itself of bilge and sails easily. Afterwards it twists back its two foremost arms and spreads out between them a marvellously thin membrane, and with this serving as a sail in the breeze while it uses its other arms underneath it as oars, it steers itself with its tail between them as a rudder. So it proceeds across the deep mimicking the likeness of a fast cutter, if any alarm interrupts its voyage submerging itself by sucking in water.

XLVIII. One variety of the polypus kind is the *The ozaena.* stink-polyp, named from the disagreeable smell of its

gravi capitis odore, ob hoc maxime murenis eam
consectantibus.

Polypi binis mensibus conduntur. ultra bimatum
non vivunt; pereunt autem tabe semper, feminae
celerius et fere a partu.

Non sunt praetereunda et L. Lucullo proconsule
90 Baeticae comperta de polypis quae Trebius Niger e
comitibus eius prodidit: avidissimos esse concharum,
illas ad tactum comprimi praecidentes bracchia
eorum ultroque escam ex praedante capere. carent
conchae visu omnique sensu alio quam cibi et periculi.
insidiantur ergo polypi apertis, impositoque lapillo
extra corpus, ne palpitatu eiciantur; ita securi
grassantur extrahuntque carnes; illae se contra
hunt, sed frustra, discuneatae: tanta sollertia
91 animalium hebetissimis quoque est. praeterea negat
ullum atrocius esse animal ad conficiendum hominem
in aqua; luctatur enim complexu et sorbet acetabulis
ac numeroso suctu distrahit,[1] cum in naufragos
urinantisve impetum cepit. sed si invertatur,
elanguescit vis; exporrigunt enim se resupinati.
cetera quae idem retulit monstro propiora possunt
92 videri. Carteiae in cetariis assuetus exire e mari in

---

[1] *sic (cf. § 27)? Mayhoff*: trahit.

---

[a] Now Rocadillo, in Spain.

head, which causes it to be the special prey of the moray.

Polyps go into hiding for periods of two months. *The polyp's life-period.* They do not live more than two years; but they always die of consumption, the females more quickly and usually as a result of bearing offspring.

We must also not pass over the facts as to the *Its diet shell-fish.* polyp ascertained when Lucius Lucullus was governor of Baetica, and published by one of his staff, Trebius Niger; he says that they are extremely greedy for shell-fish, and that these close their shells at a touch and cut off the polyp's tentacles, so retaliating by obtaining food from their would-be robber. Shell-fish do not possess sight or any other sense except consciousness of food and danger. Consequently the polyps lie in wait for the shell-fish to open, and placing a stone between the shells, not on the fish's body so that it may not be ejected by its throbbing, thus go to work at their ease, and drag out the flesh, while the shell-fish try to shut up, but in vain, as they are wedged open : so clever are even the most stupid of animals. Moreover Niger asserts *The polyp a* that no animal is more savage in causing the death *danger to bathers.* of a man in the water; for it struggles with him by coiling round him and swallows him with its suckercups and drags him asunder by its multiple suction, when it attacks men that have been shipwrecked or are diving. But should it be turned over, its strength gets feebler; for when polyps are lying on their backs they stretch themselves out. The rest of the facts reported by the same authority may possibly be thought to approximate to the miraculous. In *A giant* the fishponds at Carteia *a* a polyp was in the habit of *specimen.*

lacus eorum apertos atque ibi salsamenta populari,
—mire omnibus marinis expetentibus ordorem
quoque eorum, qua de causa et nassis inlinuntur,—
convertit in se custodum indignationem assiduitate
furti immodicam.[1] saepes erant obiectae, sed has
transcendebat per arborem, nec deprehendi potuit
nisi canum sagacitate. hi redeuntem circumvasere
noctu, concitique custodes expavere novitatem:
primum omnium magnitudo inaudita erat, deinde
colos, muria obliti, odore diri; quis ibi polypum
exspectasset aut ita cognosceret? cum monstro
dimicare sibi videbantur, namque et afflatu terribili
canes angebat, nunc extremis crinibus flagellatos,
nunc robustioribus bracchiis clavarum modo incussos;
93 aegreque multis tridentibus confici potuit. ostendere
Lucullo caput eius dolii magnitudine amphorarum
xv capax atque, ut ipsius Trebi verbis utar, ' barbas
quas vix utroque bracchio conplecti esset, clavarum
modo torosas, longas pedum xxx, acetabulis sive
caliculis urnalibus pelvium modo, dentes magnitudini
respondentes.' reliquiae adservatae miraculo pepen-
dere pondo DCC. saepias quoque et lolligines
eiusdem magnitudinis expulsas in litus illud idem
auctor est. in nostro mari lolligines quinum cubitorum capiuntur, saepiae binum. neque his bimatu
longior vita.

1 *Mayhoff*: immodicant *aut* -ca.

getting into their uncovered tanks from the open sea and there foraging for salted fish—even the smell of which attracts all sea creatures in a surprising way, owing to which even fish-traps are smeared with them—and so it brought on itself the wrath of the keepers, which owing to the persistence of the theft was beyond all bounds Fences were erected in its way, but it used to scale these by making use of a tree, and it was only possible to catch it by means of the keen scent of hounds. These surrounded it when it was going back at night, and aroused the guards, who were astounded by its strangeness: in the first place its size was unheard of and so was its colour as well, and it was smeared with brine and had a terrible smell; who would have expected to find a polyp there, or who would recognize it in such circumstances? They felt they were pitted against something uncanny, for by its awful breath it also tormented the dogs, which it now scourged with the ends of its tentacles and now struck with its longer arms, which it used as clubs; and with difficulty they succeeded in despatching it with a number of three-pronged harpoons. They showed its head to Lucullus—it was as big as a cask and held 90 gallons, —and (to use the words of Trebius himself) 'its beards which one could hardly clasp round with both one's arms, knotted like clubs, 30 ft. long, with suckers or cups like basins holding three gallons, and teeth corresponding to its size.' Its remains, kept as a curiosity, were found to weigh 700 lbs. Trebius also states that cuttle-fish of both species of the same size have been driven ashore on that coast. In our own seas one kind is taken that measures 7½ ft. in length and the other kind 3 ft. These fish also do not live more than two years.

Large cuttle-fish.

94 XLIX. Navigeram similitudinem et aliam in Propontide visam sibi prodidit Mucianus: concham esse acati modo carinatam, inflexa puppe, prora rostrata. in hanc condi nauplium, animal saepiae simile, ludendi societate sola. duobus hoc fieri generibus: tranquillo enim vectorem demissis palmulis ferire ut remis, si vero flatus invitent, easdem in usum gubernaculi porrigi pandique concharum sinus aurae. huius voluptatem esse ut ferat, illius ut regat, simulque eam descendere in duo sensu carentia, nisi forte—tristi id enim constat omini navigantium—humana calamitas in causa est.

95 L. Locustae crusta fragili muniuntur in eo genere quod caret sanguine. latent mensibus quinis; similiter cancri qui eodem tempore occultantur; et ambo veris principio senectutem anguium more exuunt renovatione tergorum. cetera in undis natant, locustae reptantium modo fluitant; si nullus ingruat metus, recto meatu cornibus quae sunt propria rotunditate praepilata ad latera porrectis, isdem erectis in pavore oblique in latera procedunt. cornibus inter se dimicant. unum hoc animalium, nisi vivum ferventi aqua incoquatur, fluida carne non 96 habet callum. vivunt petrosis locis, cancri mollibus.

---

^a *I.e.* the imitation of a boat; cf. § 88.

XLIX. Mucianus has stated that he has also seen *The* in the Dardanelles another creature resembling a *nauplius and* ship under sail: it is a shell with a keel like a boat, *its carrier.* and a curved stern and beaked bow. In this (he says) the nauplius, a creature like the cuttle-fish, secretes itself, merely by way of sharing the game.[a] The manner in which this takes place is two-fold: in calm weather the carrier shell strikes the water by dipping its flappers like oars, but if the breezes invite, the same flappers are stretched out to serve as a rudder and the curves of the shells are spread to the breeze. The former creature delights (he continues) to carry and the latter to steer, and this pleasure penetrates two senseless things at once— unless perhaps human calamity forms part of the motive, for it is an established fact that this is a disastrous omen for mariners.

L. In the bloodless class, the langouste is protected *The* by a fragile rind. Langoustes stay in retirement for *langouste.* five months in each year; and likewise crabs, which go into hiding at the same season; and both species discard their old age at the beginning of spring in the same way as snakes do, by renewing their skins. All other aquatic species swim, but langoustes float about in the manner of reptiles; if no danger threatens they go forward in a straight course with their horns, which are buttoned by their own rounded ends, stretched out at their sides, but at a moment of alarm they advance slanting sideways with their horns held erect. They use their horns in fighting one another. The langouste is the only animal whose flesh is of a yielding texture with no hardness, unless it is boiled alive in hot water. Langoustes live in rocky places, whereas crabs live on

hieme aprica litora sectantur, aestate in opaca gurgitum recedunt. omnia eius generis hieme laeduntur, autumno et vere pinguescunt, et plenilunio magis, quia nocte sidus tepido fulgore mitificat.

97 LI. Cancrorum genera carabi, astaci, maeae, paguri, Heracleotici, leones et alia ignobiliora. carabi cauda a ceteris cancris distant; in Phoenice hippoe vocantur, tantae velocitatis ut consequi non sit. cancris vita longa. pedes octoni, omnes in obliquom flexi; feminae primus pes duplex, mari simplex. praeterea bina bracchia denticulatis forficibus; superior pars in primoribus his movetur inferiore immobili. dexterum bracchium omnibus 98 maius. universi aliquando congregantur. os Ponti evincere non valent, quamobrem egressi circumeunt apparetque tritum iter. pinoteres vocatur minumus ex omni genere, ideo opportunus iniuriae. huic sollertia est inanium ostrearum testis se condere et cum adcreverit migrare in capaci-99 ores. cancri in pavore et retrorsi pari velocitate redeunt. dimicant inter se ut arietes, adversis cornibus incursantes. contra serpentium ictus medentur. sole cancri signum transeunte et ipsorum, cum exanimati sint, corpus transfigurari in scorpiones narratur in sicoo.

---

^a *Cf.* II 109.
^b The common crab; the identifications of the varieties that follow are dubious.

soft mud. In winter they haunt sunny shores, but in summer they retire into the dim depths of the sea. All creatures of this class suffer in winter, but get fat in autumn and spring, and more so at full moon, because the moon mellows them with its warm glow by night.[a]

LI. The kinds of crab are the *carabus*,[b] the crayfish, the spider-crab, the hermit-crab, the Heraclean crab, the lion-crab and other inferior species. The carabus differs from the other crabs by its tail; in Phoenicia it is called the horse-crab, being so swift that it is impossible to overtake it. Crabs are long-lived. They have eight feet, all curved crooked; the front foot is double in the female and single in the male. They also have two claws with denticulated nippers; the upper half of the forepart of these moves and the lower half is fixed. The right claw is the larger in every specimen. Sometimes crabs all collect together in a flock. They cannot make the mouth of the Black Sea against the current, and consequently when they are going out of it they travel round in a circle and appear to be following a beaten track. The one called the pea-crab is the smallest of the whole tribe, and consequently very liable to injury. It has the cunning to stow itself in empty bivalve shells and to shift into roomier ones as it grows bigger. When alarmed crabs can retreat backwards with equal speed. They fight duels with one another like rams, charging with horns opposed. They afford a remedy against snake-bite. It is related that when the sun is passing through the sign of Cancer the bodies of crabs also when they expire are transformed into scorpions during the drought.

Varieties of crab.

100 Ex eodem genere sunt echini quibus spinae pro
pedibus. ingredi est his in orbem volvi, itaque
detritis saepe aculeis inveniuntur. ex his echino-
metrae appellantur quorum spinae longissimae, calyces minimi. nec omnibus idem vitreus colos: circa
Toronem candidi nascuntur spina parva. ova omnium amara, quina numero. ora in medio corpore
in terram versa. tradunt saevitiam maris praesagire
eos correptisque opperiri lapillis mobilitatem pondere
stabilientes: nolunt volutatione spinas atterere;
quod ubi videre nautici, statim pluribus anchoris
navigia infrenant.

101 In eodem genere cocleae aquatiles terrestresque
exerentes se domicilio binaque ceu cornua protend-
entes contrahentesque. oculis carent, itaque corniculis praetemptant iter.

Pectines in mari ex eodem genere habentur,
reconditi et ipsi magnis frigoribus ac magnis aestibus,
unguesque velut igne lucentes in tenebris, etiam in
ore mandentium.

102 LII. Firmioris iam testae murices et concharum
genera, in quibus magna ludentis naturae varietas:
tot colorum differentiae, tot figurae, planis, concavis,
longis, lunatis, in orbem circumactis, dimidio orbe
caesis, in dorsum elatis, levibus, rugatis, denticulatis,
striatis; vertice muricatim intorto, margine in mucro-

---

a In point of fact they have black eyes unfolded with the
horns.

The sea-urchin, which has spines instead of feet, *The echinus.*
belongs to the same genus. These creatures can
only go forward by rolling over and over,
and consequently they are often found with their
prickles worn off. Those of them with the longest
spines are called *echinus cidaris*, and the smallest
are called cups. They have not all the same
transparent colour: in the district of Torone some
are born white, with a small spine. The eggs of all
have a bitter taste; they are laid in clutches of five.
Their mouths are in the middle of their body, on the
under side. It is said that they can forecast a rough
sea and that they take the precaution of clutching
stones and steadying their mobility by the weight:
they do not want to wear away their spines by rolling
about. When sailors see them doing this they at
once secure their vessels with more anchors.

In the same family are water and land snails, that *The snail*
protrude out of their abode and shoot out and draw *class.*
in two horns as it were. They have no eyes,[a] and
consequently explore the way in front of them with
their little horns.

Sea-scallops are held to belong to the same class,
which also retire into hiding at seasons of extreme
cold and extreme heat; and piddocks, which shine
as if with fire in dark places, even in the mouth of
persons eating them.

LII. We now come to the purples and the *Purples and*
varieties of shell-fish, which have a stronger shell. *other shell-*
The latter display in great variety nature's love of *fish :*
sport: they show so many differences of colour, and
also of shape—being flat, hollow, long, crescent-
shaped, circular, semi-circular, humped, smooth,
wrinkled, serrated, furrowed; with the crest bent

103 nem emisso, foris effuso, intus replicato; iam dis-
tinctione virgulata, crinita, crispa, canaliculatim,
pectinatim divisa, imbricatim undata, cancellatim
reticulata, in obliquum, in rectum expansa, densata,
porrecta, sinuata; brevi nodo ligatis, toto latere
conexis, ad plausum apertis, ad bucinam [1] recurvis.
navigant ex his Veneriae, praebentesque concavam
sui partem et aurae opponentes per summa aequorum
velificant. saliunt pectines et extra volitant, seque
et ipsi carinant.

104   LIII. Sed quid haec tam parva commemoro,
cum populatio morum atque luxuria non aliunde
maior quam e concharum genere proveniat? iam
quidem ex tota rerum natura damnosissimum
ventri mare est tot modis, tot mensis, tot piscium
105 saporibus quis pretia capientium periculo fiunt. sed
quota haec portio est reputantibus purpuras, conchylia, margaritas! parum scilicet fuerat in gulas
condi maria, nisi manibus, auribus, capite totoque
corpore a feminis iuxta virisque gestarentur. quid
mari cum vestibus, quid undis fluctibusque cum
vellere? non recte recipit haec nos rerum natura
nisi nudos! esto, sit tanta ventri cum eo societas:

[1] *Edd.*: bucinum.

into the shape of a purple, the edge projecting
into a sharp point, or spread outwards, or folded
inwards; and again picked out with stripes or with
flowing locks or with curls, or parted in little channels
or like the teeth of a comb, or corrugated like tiles,
or reticulated into lattice-work, or spread out slantwise or straight, close-packed, diffused, curled;
tied up in a short knot, or linked up all down the side,
or opened so as to shut with a snap, or curved so as
to make a trumpet. Of this species the Venus-shell
sails like a ship, and projecting its hollow portion and
setting it to catch the wind goes voyaging over the
surface of the water. The scallop gives a leap and
soars out of the water, and it also uses its own shell as
a boat.

LIII. But why do I mention these trifles when *their*
moral corruption and luxury spring from no other *contributions*
source in greater abundance than from the genus *to luxury and*
shell-fish? It is true that of the whole of nature *corruption.*
the sea is most detrimental to the stomach in a
multitude of ways, with its multitude of dishes
and of appetizing kinds of fish to which the profits
made by those who catch them spell danger. But
what proportion do these form when we consider purple and scarlet robes and pearls! It had
been insufficient, forsooth, for the seas to be
stowed into our gullets, were they not carried on
the hands and in the ears and on the head and all
over the body of women and men alike. What
connexion is there between the sea and our clothing,
between the waves and waters and woollen fabric?
We only enter that element in a proper manner
when we are naked! Granted that there is so
close an alliance between it and our stomach, but

quid tergori! parum est nisi qui vescimur periculis
etiam vestiamur? adeo per totum corpus anima
hominis quaesita maxime placent?

106 LIV. Principium ergo columenque omnium rerum
preti margaritae tenent. Indicus maxime has mittit
oceanus inter illas beluas tales tantasque quas
diximus per tot maria venientes tam longo terrarum
tractu e tantis solis ardoribus. atque Indis quoque
in insulas petuntur et admodum paucas: fertilissima
est Taprobane et Stoidis, ut diximus in circuitu
mundi, item Perimula promunturium Indiae; praecipue autem laudantur circa Arabiam in Persico
sinu maris Rubri.

107 Origo atque genitura conchae sunt [1] haut multum
ostrearum conchis differentes.[2] has ubi genitalis
anni stimulavit hora, pandentes se quadam oscitatione
impleri roscido conceptu tradunt, gravidas postea
eniti, partumque concharum esse margaritas, pro
qualitate roris accepti: si purus influxerit, candorem
conspici, si vero turbidus, et fetum sordescere.
eundem pallere caelo minante: conceptum ex eo
quippe constare, caelique eis maiorem societatem
esse quam maris, inde nubilum trahi colorem aut pro
108 claritate matutina serenum. si tempestive satientur
grandescere et partus. si fulguret, comprimi con-

---

[1] *Mayhoff*: est.   [2] *Mayhoff*: different.

---

[a] See §§ 4 f. above.   [b] VI 81 and 110.
[c] The story is of course imaginary.

what has it to do with our backs? Are we not
content to feed on dangers without also being clothed
with them? Is it that the rule that we get most
satisfaction from luxuries costing a human life to
procure holds good for the whole of our anatomy?

LIV. The first place therefore and the topmost *Pearls.*
rank among all things of price is held by pearls.
These are sent chiefly by the Indian Ocean, among
the huge and curious animals that we have described [a]
as coming across all those seas over that wide
expanse of lands from those burning heats of the
sun. And to procure them for the Indians as well,
men go to the islands—and those quite few in
number: the most productive is Ceylon, and also
Stoidis, as we said [b] in our circuit of the world, and also
the Indian promontory of Perimula; but those round
Arabia on the Persian Gulf of the Red Sea are
specially praised.

The source and breeding-ground of pearls are *The pearl-*
shells not much differing from oyster-shells. These, *oyster.*
we are told,[c] when stimulated by the generative season
of the year gape open as it were and are filled with
dewy pregnancy, and subsequently when heavy are
delivered, and the offspring of the shells are pearls
that correspond to the quality of the dew received:
if it was a pure inflow, their brilliance is conspicuous
but if it was turbid, the product also becomes dirty in
colour. Also if the sky is lowering (they say) the pearl
is pale in colour: for it is certain that it was conceived
from the sky, and that pearls have more connexion
with the sky than with the sea, and derive from it a
cloudy hue, or a clear one corresponding with a
brilliant morning. If they are well fed in due season,
the offspring also grows in size. If there is lightning,

chas ac pro ieiunii modo minui; si vero etiam tonue-
rit, pavidas ac repente compressas quae vocant physe-
mata efficere, specie modo inani inflatas sine corpore;
hos esse concharum abortus. sani quidem partus
multiplici constant cute, non improprie callum ut
existimari corporis possit; itaque expurgantur a
109 peritis. miror ipso tantum eas caelo gaudere, sole
rubescere candoremque perdere ut corpus humanum;
quare praecipuum custodiunt pelagiae, altius mersae
quam ut penetrent radii; flavescunt tamen et illae
senecta rugisque torpescunt, nec nisi in iuventa
constat ille qui quaeritur vigor.[1] crassescunt etiam
in senecta conchisque adhaerescunt, nec his evelli
queunt nisi lima. quibus una tantum est facies et ab
ea rotunditas, aversis planities, ob id tympania
nominantur; cohaerentes vidimus[2] in conchis, hac
dote unguenta circumferentibus. cetero in aqua
mollis unio, exemptus protinus durescit.

110   LV. Concha ipsa cum manum vidit comprimit sese
operitque opes suas gnara propter illas se peti,
manumque, si praeveniat, acie sua abscidat nulla
iustiore poena, et aliis munita suppliciis, quippe inter
scopulos maior pars invenitur, sed in alto quoque
comitantibus[3] marinis canibus; nec tamen aures
111 feminarum arcentur. quidam tradunt sicut apibus

---

[1] An nitor? *Mayhoff.*   [2] *Hardouin*: videmus.
[3] *Mayhoff*: comitantur.

---

a I.e. sharks.

the shells shut up, and diminish in size in proportion to their abstinence from food; but if it also thunders they are frightened and shut up suddenly, producing what are called ' wind-pearls,' which are only inflated with an empty, unsubstantial show: these are the pearls' miscarriages. Indeed a healthy offspring is formed with a skin of many thicknesses, so that it may not improperly be considered as a hardening of the body; and consequently experts subject them to a cleansing process. I am surprised that though pearls rejoice so much in the actual sky, they redden and lose their whiteness in the sun, like the human body; consequently sea-pearls preserve a special brilliance, being too deeply immersed for the rays to penetrate; nevertheless even they get yellow from age and doze off with wrinkles, and the vigour that is sought after is only found in youth. Also in old age they get thick and stick to the shells, and cannot be torn out of these except by using a file. Pearls with only one surface, and round on that side but flat at the back, are consequently termed tambourine pearls; we have seen them clustering together in shells that owing to this enrichment were used for carrying round perfumes. For the rest, a large pearl is soft when in the water but gets hard as soon as it is taken out.

LV. When a shell sees a hand it shuts itself up and conceals its treasures, as it knows that it is sought for on their account; and if the hand is inserted first it cuts it off with its sharp edge, the most just penalty possible—for it is armed with other penalties also, as for the most part it is found among rocks, while even in deep water it has sea-dogs[a] in attendance—yet nevertheless these do not protect it against women's ears! Some accounts

Diving for pearls.

ita concharum examinibus singulas magnitudine et vetustate praecipuas esse veluti duces mirae ad cavendum sollertiae; has urinantium cura peti, illis captis facile ceteras palantes retibus includi, multo deinde obrutas sale in vasis fictilibus; rosa carne omni nucleos quosdam corporum, hoc est uniones, decidere in ima.

112 LVI. Usu atteri non dubium est, coloremque indiligentia mutare. dos omnis in candore, magnitudine, orbe, levore, pondere, haut promptis rebus in tantum ut nulli duo reperiantur indiscreti: unde nomen unionum Romanae scilicet imposuere deliciae, nam id apud Graecos non est, nec apud barbaros quidem, inventores rei [1] eius, aliud quam

113 margaritae. et in candore ipso magna differentia; clarior in Rubro mari repertis, in [2] Indico specularium lapidum squamas adsimulant,[3] alias magnitudine praecellentes. summa laus coloris est exaluminatos vocari. et procerioribus sua gratia est. elenchos appellant fastigata longitudine alabastrorum

114 figura in pleniorem orbem desinentes. hos digitis suspendere et binos ac ternos auribus feminarum gloria est, subeuntque luxuriae eius nomina externa,[4] exquisita perdito nepotatu, siquidem, cum id fecere, crotalia appellant, ceu sono quoque gaudeant et

---

[1] rei *add. Mayhoff.*   [2] in *add. Mayhoff.*
[3] *Mayhoff:* adsimulat.   [4] *Mayhoff:* nomina et taedia.

---

[a] The Persian Gulf is meant; *cf.* § 106.

say that clusters of shells like bees have one of their number, a specially large and old shell, as their leader, one marvellously skilful in taking precautions; and that these leader-shells are diligently sought for by pearl-divers, as when they are caught all the rest stray about and easily get shut up in the nets, subsequently a quantity of salt being poured over them in earthenware jars; this eats away all the flesh, and a sort of kernels in their bodies, which are pearls, fall to the bottom.

LVI. There is no doubt that pearls are worn away by use, and that lack of care makes them change their colour. Their whole value lies in their brilliance, size, roundness, smoothness and weight, qualities of such rarity that no two pearls are found that are exactly alike: this is doubtless the reason why Roman luxury has given them the name of 'unique gems,' the word *unio* not existing in Greece, and indeed among foreign races, who discovered this fact, the only name for them is *margarita*. There is also a great variety in their actual brilliance; it is brighter with those found in the Red Sea,[a] whereas those found in the Indian Ocean resemble flakes of mica, though they excel others in size. The highest praise given to their colour is for them to be called alum-coloured. The longer ones also have a charm of their own. Those that end in a wider circle, tapering lengthwise in the shape of perfume-caskets, are termed 'probes.' Women glory in hanging these on their fingers and using two or three for a single-earring, and foreign names for this luxury occur, names invented by abandoned extravagance, inasmuch as when they have done this they call them 'castanets,' as if they enjoyed even the sound and

Varieties in pearls; their value.

239

collisu ipso margaritarum; cupiuntque iam et pauperes, lictorem feminae in publico unionem esse dictitantes. quin et pedibus, nec crepidarum tantum obstragulis set totis socculis addunt. neque enim gestare iam margaritas nisi calcent ac per uniones etiam ambulent, satis est.

115 In nostro mari reperiri solebant, crebrius circa Bosporum Thracium, rufi ac parvi in conchis quas myas appellant. at in Acarnania quae vocatur pina [1] gignit; quo apparet non in [2] uno conchae genere nasci, namque et Iuba tradit Arabicis concham esse similem pectini insecto, hirsutam echinorum modo, ipsum unionem in carne grandini similem; conchae non tales ad nos afferuntur. nec in Acarnania ante [3] laudati reperiuntur, enormes et fere [4] coloris [5] marmorei. meliores circa Actium, sed et hi parvi, et in Mauretaniae maritimis. Alexander polyhistor et Sudines senescere eos putant coloremque expirare.

116 LVII. Firmum [6] corpus esse manifestum est, quod nullo lapsu franguntur. non autem semper in media carne reperiuntur sed aliis atque aliis locis, vidimusque iam in extremis etiam marginibus velut e concha exeuntes, et in quibusdam quaternos quinosque. pondus ad hoc aevi semunciae pauci

[1] *Sillig* : pinna.
[2] in *add. Rackham.*
[3] ante *edd.* : autem.
[4] fere *edd.* : feri.
[5] coloris ? *Brotier* : colorisque.
[6] *Mayhoff* : eorum.

the mere rattling together of the pearls; and now-a-days even poor people covet them—it is a common saying that a pearl is as good as a lackey for a lady when she walks abroad! And they even use them on their feet, and fix them not only to the laces of their sandals but all over their slippers. In fact, by this time they are not content with wearing pearls unless they tread on them, and actually walk on these unique gems!

There used to be commonly found in our own sea, *Provenance* and more frequently on the coasts of the Thracian *of pearls.* Bosphorus, small red gems contained in the shells called mussels. But in Acarnania there grows what is termed the sea-pen; which shows that pearls are not born in only one kind of shell, for Juba also records that the Arabs have a shell resembling a toothed comb, that bristles like a hedgehog, and has an actual pearl, resembling a hailstone, in the fleshy part; this kind of shell is not imported to Rome. And there are not found in Acarnania the formerly celebrated pearls of an exceptional size and almost a marble colour. Better ones are found round Actium, but these too are small, and in sea-board Mauretania. Alexander the Encyclopaedist and Sudines think that they grow old and let their colour evaporate.

LVII. It is clear that they are of a firm substance, *Position in* because no fall can break them. Also they are not *the shell.* always found in the middle of the flesh, but in a variety of places, and before now we have seen them even at the extreme edges, as though in the act of passing out of the shell; and in some cases we have seen four or five pearls in one shell. In weight few specimens have hitherto exceeded half an ounce by

singulis scripulis excessere. in Britannia parvos
atque decolores nasci certum est, quoniam divus
Iulius thoracem quem Veneri Genetrici in templo
eius dicavit ex Britannicis margaritis factum voluerit
intellegi.

117   LVIII. Lolliam Paulinam, quae fuit Gai principis
matrona, ne serio quidem aut sollemni caerimoniarum
aliquo apparatu sed mediocrium etiam sponsalium
cena vidi smaragdis margaritisque opertam alterno
textu fulgentibus toto capite, crinibus, [spira]¹
auribus, collo, [monilibus]² digitis, quae³ summa
quadringenties sestertium colligebat, ipsa confestim
parata mancupationem tabulis probare; nec dona
prodigi principis fuerant, sed avitae opes, provinci-
118   arum scilicet spoliis partae. hic est rapinarum
exitus, hoc fuit quare M. Lollius infamatus regum
muneribus in toto oriente interdicta amicitia a C.
Caesare Augusti filio venenum biberet, ut neptis
eius quadringenties HS operta spectaretur ad lucer-
nas! computet nunc aliquis ex altera parte quantum
Curius aut Fabricius in triumphis tulerint, imaginetur
illorum fercula, et ex altera parte Lolliam unam
imperatori⁴ mulierculam accubantem: non illos
119   curru detractos quam in hoc vicisse malit? nec haec
summa luxuriae exempla sunt. duo fuere maximi
uniones per omne aevum; utrumque possedit
Cleopatra Aegypti reginarum novissima per manus

¹ *Friedlaender.*   ² *Friedlaender.*
³ *Mayhoff*: que.   ⁴ *Dalecamp*: imperii.

ᵃ They are found occasionally in the ordinary mussel,
oyster and pinna, but especially in the common fresh-water
mussel.

ᵇ Say a third of a million pounds gold.

more than one scruple. It is established that small pearls of poor colour grow in Britain,[a] since the late lamented Julius desired it to be known that the breastplate which he dedicated to Venus Genetrix in her temple was made of British pearls.

LVIII. I have seen Lollia Paulina, who became the consort of Gaius, not at some considerable or solemn ceremonial celebration but actually at an ordinary betrothal banquet, covered with emeralds and pearls interlaced alternately and shining all over her head, hair, ears, neck and fingers, the sum total amounting to the value of 40,000,000 sesterces,[b] she herself being ready at a moment's notice to give documentary proof of her title to them; nor had they been presents from an extravagant emperor, but ancestral possessions, acquired in fact with the spoil of the provinces. This is the final outcome of plunder, it was for this that Marcus Lollius disgraced himself by taking gifts from kings in the whole of the East, and was cut out of his list of friends by Gaius Caesar son of Augustus and drank poison —that his granddaughter should be on show in the lamplight covered with 40,000,000 sesterces! Now let some one reckon up on one side of the account how much Curius or Fabricius carried in their triumphs, and picture to himself the spoils they displayed, and on the other side Lollia, a single little lady reclining at the Emperor's side—and would he not think it better that they should have been dragged from their chariots than have won their victories with this result? Nor are these the topmost instances of luxury. There have been two pearls that were the largest in the whole of history; both were owned by Cleopatra, the last of the Queens of Egypt—they

Pearls of exceptional value.

Cleopatra's pearls.

243

orientis regum sibi traditos. haec, cum exquisitis
cotidie Antonius saginaretur epulis, superbo simul
ac procaci fastu, ut regina meretrix, lautitiam eius
apparatumque omnem [1] obtrectans, quaerente eo
quid adstrui magnificentiae posset respondit una se
120 cena centiens HS [2] absumpturam. cupiebat discere
Antonius, sed fieri posse non arbitrabatur. ergo
sponsionibus factis postero die, quo iudicium age-
batur, magnificam alias cenam, ne dies periret, sed
cotidianam, Antonio apposuit inridenti computa-
tionemque expostulanti. at illa corollarium id
esse, et consummaturam [3] eam cenam [4] taxationem
confirmans solamque se centiens HS cenaturam,
inferri mensam secundam iussit. ex praecepto
ministri unum tantum vas ante eam posuere aceti,
cuius asperitas visque in tabem margaritas resolvit.
121 gerebat auribus cum maxime singulare illud et vere
unicum naturae opus. itaque expectante Antonio
quidnam esset actura detractum alterum mersit ac
liquefactum obsorbuit. iniecit alteri manum L.
Plancus, iudex sponsionis eius, eum quoque parante
simili modo absumere, victumque Antonium pro-
nuntiavit omine rato. comitatur fama unionis eius
parem, capta illa tantae quaestionis victrice regina,

[1] omnem *hic ? Mayhoff*: *ante* apparatumque.
[2] centiens HS *add. edd.*
[3] *Mayhoff* (*cf.* viii. 183): consumpturam.
[4] se in ea cena *edd.*

---

[a] *Cf.* XI 14 nullus perit otio dies.
[b] No such vinegar exists; Cleopatra no doubt swallowed the
pearl in vinegar knowing that it could be recovered later on.

had come down to her through the hands of the
Kings of the East. When Antony was gorging daily at
recherché banquets, she with a pride at once lofty and
insolent, queenly wanton as she was, poured contempt
on all his pomp and splendour, and when he asked
what additional magnificence could be contrived,
replied that she would spend 10,000,000 sesterces on
a single banquet. Antony was eager to learn how
it could be done, although he thought it was impossible. Consequently bets were made, and on the
next day, when the matter was to be decided, she set
before Antony a banquet that was indeed splendid,
so that the day might not be wasted,[a] but of the kind
served every day—Antony laughing and expostu-
lating at its niggardliness. But she vowed it was a
mere additional douceur, and that the banquet would
round off the account and her own dinner alone would
cost 10,000,000 sesterces, and she ordered the second
course to be served. In accordance with previous
instructions the servants placed in front of her only a
single vessel containing vinegar, the strong rough
quality of which can melt pearls.[b] She was at the
moment wearing in her ears that remarkable and
truly unique work of nature. Antony was full of
curiosity to see what in the world she was going to
do. She took one earring off and dropped the pearl
in the vinegar, and when it was melted swallowed it.
Lucius Plancus, who was umpiring the wager, placed
his hand on the other pearl when she was preparing
to destroy it also in a similar way, and declared that
Antony had lost the battle—an ominous remark that
came true. With this goes the story that, when that
queen who had won on this important issue was
captured, the second of this pair of pearls was

dissectum, ut esset in utrisque Veneris auribus Romae
122 in Pantheo dimidia eorum cena. LIX. non ferent hanc
palmam, spoliabunturque etiam luxuriae gloria.
prior id fecerat Romae in unionibus magnae taxationis
Clodius tragoedi Aesopi filis, relictus ab eo in amplis
opibus heres, ne triumviratu suo nimis superbiat
Antonius paene histrioni comparatus, et quidem
nulla sponsione ad hoc producto, quo magis regium
fiat, sed ut experiretur in gloriam[1] palati quidnam
saperent margaritae; atque ut mire placuere, ne
solus hoc sciret, singulos uniones convivis quoque
absorbendos dedit.

123 Romae in promiscuum ac frequentem usum venisse
Alexandria in dicionem redacta, primum autem
coepisse circa Sullana tempora minutas et viles
Fenestella tradit manifesto errore, cum Aelius Stilo
circa[2] Jugurthinum bellum unionum nomen imponi-
cum maxime grandibus margaritis prodat.

124 LX. Et hoc tamen aeternae prope possessionis est
—sequitur heredem, in mancipatum venit ut praedi-
um aliquod: conchylia et purpuras omnis hora atterit,
quibus eadem mater luxuria paria paene ac[3]
margaritis pretia fecit.

125 Purpurae vivunt annis plurimum septenis. latent
sicut murices circa canis ortum tricenis diebus.
congregantur verno tempore, mutuoque attritu

---

[1] *Mayhoff*: gloria.   [2] circa *add. Mayhoff.*
[3] ac? *Mayhoff*: et.

[a] *I.e.* Antony and Cleopatra.   [b] 47 B.C.
[c] Dictator 81–79 B.C.   [d] 112–106 B.C.

cut in two pieces, so that half a helping of the jewel might be in each of the ears of Venus in the Pantheon at Rome. LIX. They[a] will not carry off this trophy, *An earlier pearl-story.* and will be robbed even of the record for luxury! A predecessor had done this at Rome in the case of pearls of great value, Clodius, the son of the tragic actor Aesopus, who had left him his heir in a vast estate; so that Antony cannot take too much pride in his triumvirate when compared with one who was virtually an actor, and who had indeed been led on to this display not by any wager—which would make it more royal—but to discover by experiment, for the honour of his palate, what is the exact flavour of pearls; and when they proved marvellously acceptable, in order not to keep the knowledge to himself he gave his guests also a choice pearl apiece to swallow.

Fenestella records that they came into common *When introduced at Rome.* use at Rome after the reduction of Alexandria under our sway,[b] but that small and cheap pearls first came in about the period of Sulla[c]—which is clearly a mistake, as Aelius Stilo states that the distinctive name was given to large pearls just at the time of the wars[d] of Jugurtha.

LX. And nevertheless this article is an almost everlasting piece of property—it passes to its owner's heir, it is offered for public sale like some landed estate; whereas every hour of use wears away robes of scarlet and purple, which the same mother, luxury, has made almost as costly as pearls.

Purples live seven years at most. They stay *Habits of the purple and the murex.* in hiding like the murex for 30 days at the time of the rising of the dog-star. They collect into shoals in spring-time, and their rubbing together causes

lentorem cuiusdam cerae salivant. simili modo et
murices, sed purpurae florem illum tinguendis
expetitum vestibus in mediis habent faucibus:
126 liquoris hic minimi est[1] candida vena unde pretiosus
ille bibitur, nigrantis rosae colore sublucens; reliquum corpus sterile. vivas capere contendunt,
quia cum vita sucum eum evomunt; et maioribus
quidem purpuris detracta concha auferunt, minores
cum testa vivas frangunt, ita demum eum exspuentes.
127 Tyri praecipuus hic Asiae, Meninge Africae et
Gaetulo litore oceani, in Laconica Europae. fasces
huic securesque Romanae viam faciunt, idemque
pro maiestate pueritiae est; distinguit ab equite
curiam, dis advocatur placandis, omnemque vestem
inluminat, in triumphali miscetur auro. quapropter
excusata et purpurae sit insania; sed unde conchyliis
pretia, quis virus grave in fuco, color austerus in
glauco et irascenti similis mari?
128   Lingua purpurae longitudine digitali, qua pascitur
perforando reliqua conchylia: tanta duritia aculeo
est. aquae dulcedine necantur et sicubi flumen
inmergitur, alioqui captae et diebus quinquagenis
vivunt saliva sua. conchae omnes celerrime crescunt, praecipue purpurae; anno magnitudinem
implent.

[1] *Mayhoff*: est in.

---

[a] The references are to the purple stripes on the togas of
consuls, boys of noble family, senators (who had the broad
stripe), *equites*, and priests performing sacrifices.

248

them to discharge a sort of waxy viscous slime. The
murex also does this in a similar manner, but it has
the famous flower of purple, sought after for dyeing
robes, in the middle of its throat: here there is a
white vein of very scanty fluid from which that
precious dye, suffused with a dark rose colour, is
drained, but the rest of the body produces nothing.
People strive to catch this fish alive, because it
discharges this juice with its life; and from the
larger purples they get the juice by stripping off
the shell, but they crush the smaller ones alive with
the shell, as that is the only way to make them disgorge the juice. The best Asiatic purple is at Tyre,
the best African is at Meninx and on the Gaetulian
coast of the Ocean, the best European in the district
of Sparta. The official rods and axes of Rome clear *Purple robes*
it a path, and it also marks the honourable estate of *of state.*
boyhood; it distinguishes the senate from the knighthood, it is called in to secure the favour of the gods [a];
and it adds radiance to every garment, while in a
triumphal robe it is blended with gold. Consequently
even the mad lust for the purple may be excused;
but what is the cause of the prices paid for purple-
shells, which have an unhealthy odour when used for
dye and a gloomy tinge in their radiance resembling
an angry sea?

The purple's tongue is an inch long; when *More details*
feeding it uses it for piercing a hole in the other *as to the*
kinds of shell-fish, so hard is its point. These fish *purple-fish.*
die in fresh water and wherever a river discharges
into the sea, but otherwise when caught they live as
much as seven weeks on their own slime. All shell-
fish grow with extreme rapidity, especially the
purple-fish; they reach their full size in a year.

129   LXI. Quod si hactenus transcurrat expositio fraudatam profecto se luxuria credat nosque indiligentiae damnet. quamobrem persequemur etiam officinas, ut tamquam in victu frugum noscitur ratio sic omnes qui istis gaudent in [1] praemio [2] vitae suae

130   calleant. concharum ad purpuras et conchylia— eadem enim est materia, sed distat temperamento— duo sunt genera: bucinum minor concha ad similitudinem eius qua bucinae [3] sonus editur, unde et causa nominis,[4] rotunditate oris in margine incisa; alterum purpura vocatur canaliculato procurrente rostro et canaliculi latere introrsus tubulato, qua proferatur lingua; praeterea clavatum est ad turbinem usque aculeis in orbem septenis fere, qui non sunt bucino, sed utrisque orbes totidem quot habeant annos. bucinum nonnisi petris adhaeret circaque scopulos legitur.

131   Purpurae nomine alio pelagiae vocantur. earum genera plura pabulo et solo discreta: lutense putre limo et algense nutritum [5] alga, vilissimum utrumque. melius taeniense in taeniis maris collectum, hoc quoque tamen etiamnum levius atque dilutius. calculense appellatur a calculo in [6] mari mire aptum conchyliis; et longe optimum purpuris dialutense,

---

[1] in add. *Mayhoff.*   [2] *v.l.* praemia.
[3] *Rackham* : bucini.   [4] *Mayhoff* : nomini.

LXI. But if having come to this point our exposi- *Kinds of shell-fish supplying purple and scarlet dyes.* tion were to pass over elsewhere, luxury would undoubtedly believe itself defrauded and would find us guilty of remissness. For this reason we will pursue the subject of manufactures as well, so that just as the principle of foodstuffs is learnt in food, so everybody who takes pleasure in the class of things in question may be well-informed on the subject of that which is the prize of their mode of life. Shell-fish supplying purple dyes and scarlets—the material of these is the same but it is differently blended— are of two kinds: the whelk is a smaller shell resembling the one that gives out the sound of a trumpet, whence the reason of its name, by means of the round mouth incised in its edge; the other is called the purple, with a channelled beak jutting out and the side of the channel tube-shaped inwards, through which the tongue can shoot out; moreover it is prickly all round, with about seven spikes forming a ring, which are not found in the whelk, though both shells have as many rings as they are years old. The trumpet-shell clings only to rocks and can be gathered round crags.

Another name used for the purple is ' pelagia.' *Their varieties and habits.* There are several kinds, distinguished by their food and the ground they live on. The mud-purple feeds on rotting slime and the seaweed-purple on seaweed, both being of a very common quality. A better kind is the reef-purple, collected on the reefs of the sea, though this also is lighter and softer as well. The pebble-purple is named after a pebble in the sea, and is remarkably suitable for purple dyes; and far the best for these is the

---

132 id est vario soli genere pastum. capiuntur autem purpurae parvulis rarisque textu veluti nassis in alto iactis. inest his esca, clusiles mordacesque conchae, ceu mitulos videmus. has semineces sed redditas mari avido hiatu reviviscentes appetunt purpurae porrectisque linguis infestant. at illae aculeo extimulatae claudunt sese comprimuntque mordentia. its pendentes aviditate sua purpurae tolluntur.

133 LXII. Capi eas post canis ortum aut ante vernum tempus utilissimum, quoniam, cum cerificavere, fluxos habent sucos. sed id tinguentium officinae ignorant, cum summa vertatur in eo. eximitur postea vena quam diximus, cui addi salem necessarium, sextarios ferme centenas in libras; macerari triduo iustum, quippe tanto maior vis quanto recentior, fervere in plumbo, singulasque amphoras aquae,[1] quinqua-genas[2] medicaminis libras aequali[3] ac modico vapore torreri adducto [4] longinquae fornacis cuniculo. ita despumatis subinde carnibus quas adhaesisse venis necesse est, decimo ferme die liquata cortina vellus elutriatum mergitur in experimentum et, donec spei satis fiat, uritur liquor. rubens color nigrante

134 deterior. quinis lana potat horis rursusque mergitur

---

[1] *Detlefsen* : amphoras centenas atque.
[2] *edd. nonnulli* : quingentenas.
[3] *Jan* : aequari.
[4] adducto (*an* ex aeneo ?) *Mayhoff* : et ideo.

melting-purple, that is, one fed on a varying kind *How caught.* of mud. Purples are taken in a sort of little lobster-pot of fine ply thrown into deep water. These contain bait, cockles that close with a snap, as we observe that mussels do. These when half-killed but put back into the sea gape greedily as they revive and attract the purples, which go for them with outstretched tongues. But the cockles when pricked by their spike shut up and nip the creatures nibbling them. So the purples hang suspended because of their greed and are lifted out of the water.

LXII. It is most profitable for them to be taken *Preparation* after the rising of the dog-star or before spring-time, *of the dye;* since when they have waxed themselves over with *varieties.* slime, they have their juices fluid. But this fact is not known to the dyers' factories, although it is of primary importance. Subsequently the vein of which we spoke [a] is removed, and to this salt has to be added, about a pint for every hundred pounds; three days is the proper time for it to be steeped (as the fresher the salt the stronger it is), and it should be heated in a leaden pot, and with 50 lbs. of dye to every six gallons of water kept at a uniform and moderate temperature by a pipe brought from a furnace some way off. This will cause it gradually to deposit the portions of flesh which are bound to have adhered to the veins, and after about nine days the cauldron is strained and a fleece that has been washed clean is dipped for a trial, and the liquid is heated up until fair confidence is achieved. A ruddy colour is inferior to a blackish one. The fleece is allowed to soak for five hours and after it has

[a] § 126.

carminata, donec omnem ebibat saniem. bucinum
per se damnatur, quoniam fucum remittit: pelagio
ad modum alligatur, nimiaeque eius nigritiae dat
austeritatem illam nitoremque qui quaeritur cocci;
ita permixtis viribus alterum altero[1] excitatur aut
135 astringitur. summa medicaminum in M[2] libras
vellerum bucini ducenae et e pelagio CXI; ita fit
amethysti colos eximius ille. at Tyrius pelagio
primum satiatur inmatura viridique cortina, mox
permutatur in bucino. laus ei summa in colore[3]
sanguinis concreti, nigricans aspectu idemque
suspectu refulgens; unde et Homero purpureus
dicitur sanguis.

136   LXIII. Purpurae usum Romae semper fuisse video,
sed Romulo in trabea: nam toga praetexta et latiore
clavo Tullum Hostilium e regibus primum usum
137 Etruscis devictis satis constat.   Nepos Cornelius, qui
divi Augusti principatu obiit: ' Me,' inquit, ' iuvene
violacea purpura vigebat, cuius libra denariis centum
venibat, nec multo post rubra Tarentina. huic
successit dibapha Tyria, quae in libras denariis
mille non poterat emi. hac P. Lentulus Spinther
aedilis curulis primus in praetexta usus improbabatur,
qua purpura quis non iam,' inquit, ' tricliniaria
facit?'   Spinther aedilis fuit urbis conditae anno

---

[1] ⟨ab⟩ altero? *Rackham.*   [2] M *add. Mayhoff.*
[3] color est *vel* ut sit colore? *Mayhoff.*

been carded is dipped again, until it soaks up all the juice. The whelk by itself is not approved of, as it does not make a fast dye; it is blended in a moderate degree with sea-purple and it gives to its excessively dark hue that hard and brilliant scarlet which is in demand; when their forces are thus mingled, the one is enlivened, or deadened as the case may be, by the other. The total amount of dye-stuffs required for 1,000 lbs. of fleece is 200 lbs. of whelk and 111 lbs. of sea-purple; so is produced that remarkable amethyst colour. For Tyrian purple the wool is first soaked with sea-purple for a preliminary pale dressing, and then completely transformed with whelk dye. Its highest glory consists in the colour of congealed blood, blackish at first glance but gleaming when held up to the light; this is the origin of Homer's phrase, ' blood of purple hue.'

LXIII. I notice that the use of purple at Rome dates from the earliest times, but that Romulus used it only for a cloak; as it is fairly certain that the first of the kings to use the bordered robe and broader purple stripe was Tullus Hostilius, after the conquest of the Etruscans. Cornelius Nepos, who died in the principate of the late lamented Augustus, says: ' In my young days the violet purple dye was the vogue, a pound of which sold at 100 denarii; and not much later the red purple of Taranto. This was followed by the double-dyed Tyrian purple, which it was impossible to buy for 1000 denarii per pound. This was first used in a bordered robe by Publius Lentulus Spinther, curule aedile, but met with disapproval, though who does not use this purple for covering dining-couches now-a-days?' Spinther was

History of use of purple at Rome.

DCXCI Cicerone cos. dibapha tunc dicebatur quae
bis tincta esset, veluti magnifico impendio, qualiter
nunc omnes paene commodiores purpurae tinguuntur.
138 LXIV. In conchyliata veste cetera eadem sine
bucino, praeterque ius temperatur aqua et pro
indiviso humani potus excremento; dimidia et
medicamina adduntur. sic gignitur laudatus ille
pallor saturitate fraudata tantoque dilutior[1] quanto
magis vellera esuriunt.

Pretia medicamento sunt quidem pro fertilitate
litorum viliora, non tamen usquam pelagii centenas
libras quinquagenos nummos excedere et bucini
139 centenos sciant qui ista mercantur inmenso. LXV.
set alia e fine initia, iuvatque ludere impendio et
lusus geminare miscendo iterumque et ipsa adult-
erare adulteria naturae, sicut testudines tinguere,
argentum auro confundere ut electra fiant, addere
his aera ut Corinthia. non est satis abstulisse gem-
mae nomen amethystum; rursum absolutus[2] ine-
briatur Tyrio, ut sit ex utroque nomen improbum
simulque luxuria duplex; et cum confecere con-
140 chylia, transire melius in Tyrium putant. paenitentia hoc primum debet invenisse artifice mutante quod
damnabat; inde ratio nata, votumque[3] factum e
vitio portentosis ingeniis et gemina demonstrata via

[1] dilucidior? *edd.*
[2] *Edd.*: absolutum (ablutus? *Rackham*).
[3] -que? *Mayhoff*: quisque.

---

[a] The Greek name *amethystos* was also used of a herb supposed to ward off intoxication.
[b] Tyriamethystus.

aedile in the consulship of Cicero, 63 B.C. Stuff dipped twice over used at that time to be termed 'double-dyed,' and was regarded as a lavish extravagance, but now almost all the more agreeable purple stuffs are dyed in this way.

LXIV. In a purple-dyed dress the rest of the process is the same except that trumpet-shell dye is not used, and in addition the juice is diluted with water and with human urine in equal quantities; and only half the amount of dye is used. This produces that much admired paleness, avoiding deep colouration, and the more diluted the more the fleeces are stinted. *The other variety of purple.*

The prices for dyestuff vary in cheapness with the productivity of the coasts, but those who buy them at an enormous price should know that deep-sea purple nowhere exceeds 50 sesterces and trumpet-shell 100 sesterces per 100 lbs. LXV. But every end leads to fresh starts, and men make a sport of spending, and like doubling their sports by combining them and re-adulterating nature's adulterations, for instance staining tortoiseshells, alloying gold with silver to produce amber-metal ware, and adding copper to these to make Corinthian ware. It is not enough to have stolen for a dye the name of a gem, 'sober-stone,'[a] but when finished it is made drunk again with Tyrian dye, so as to produce from the combination an outlandish name[b] and a twofold luxury at one time; and when they have made shell-dye, they think it an improvement for it to pass into Tyrian. Repentance must have discovered this first, the artificer altering a product that he disapproved of; but reason sprang up next, and a defect was turned into a success by marvellous inventions, and a double *Elaborate varieties of dyes.*

luxuriae, ut color alius operiretur alio, suavior ita
fieri leniorque dictus; quin et terrena miscere cocco-
que tinctum Tyrio tinguere ut fieret hysginum.
141 coccum Galatiae rubens granum, ut dicemus in terrestribus aut circa Emeritam Lusitaniae in maxima
laude est. verum, ut simul peragantur nobilia
pigmenta, anniculo grano languidus sucus, idem
a quadrimo evanidus: ita nec recenti vires neque
senescenti.

Abunde tractata est ratio qua se virorum iuxta
feminarumque forma credit amplissimam fieri.

142 LXVI. Concharum generis et pina est. nascitur
in limosis, subrecta semper nec umquam sine comite
quem pinoteren vocant, alii pinophylacem; id est
squilla parva, aliubi cancer, dapis adsectator. pandit
se pina luminibus orbum corpus intus minutis piscibus
praebens; adsultant illi protinus et, ubi licentia
audacia crevit, implent eam. hoc tempus speculatus
index morsu levi significat. illa conpressu [1] quicquid
inclusit exanimat partemque socio tribuit.

143 LXVII. Quo magis miror quodam existimasse
aquatilibus nullum inesse sensum. novit torpedo
vim suam ipsa non torpens, mersaque in limo se

---

[1] *Chiffl.* : compresso.

---

[a] The *coccus* is really a scale-insect which lives on the oak; it
resembles a scale pressed against the stem. Pliny and most of
the ancients confused it with seed.

path pointed out for luxury, so that one colour might be concealed by another, being pronounced to be made sweeter and softer by this process; and also a method to blend minerals, and dye with Tyrian a fabric already dyed with scarlet, to produce *hysgine* colour. The kermes,[a] a red kernel of Galatia, as we shall say when dealing with the products of the earth, or else in the neighbourhood of Merida in Lusitania, is most approved. But, to finish off these famous dyes at once, the kernel when a year old has a viscous juice, and also after it is four years old the juice tends to disappear, so that it lacks strength both when fresh and when getting old.

We have amply dealt with the method whereby the beauty of men and women alike believes that it is rendered most abundant.

LXVI. The genus shell-fish also includes the fan- *The pina* mussel. It occurs in marshy places, always in an *and its* upright position, and never without a companion *attendant the* which is called the pea-crab, or by others the sea- *squill.* pen-protector: this is a small shrimp, elsewhere called a crab, its attendant at the feast. The sea-pen opens, presenting the dark inside of its body to the tiny fishes; these at once dart forward, and when their courage has grown by license, they fill up the sea-pen. Her marker having watched for this moment gives her a signal with a gentle nip. She by shutting up kills whatever she has enclosed, and bestows a share on her partner.

LXVII. This makes me all the more surprised that *The torpeda,* some people have held the view that aquatic animals *sea-frog,* possess no senses. The torpedo knows her power, *ray—their* and does not herself possess the torpor she inflicts; *cunning.* she hides by plunging into the mud, and snaps up

occultat piscium qui securi supernatantes obtorpuere corripiens. huius iecori teneritas nulla praefertur. nec minor sollertia ranae quae in mari piscatrix vocatur: eminentia sub oculis cornicula turbato limo exerit, adsultantibus pisciculis retrahens,[1]

144 donec tam prope accedant ut adsiliat. simili modo squatina et rhombus abditi pinnas exertas movent specie vermiculorum, item quae vocantur raiae. nam pastinaca latrocinatur ex occulto transeuntes radio. quod telum est ei, figens; argumenta sollertiae huius, quod tardissimi piscium hi mugilem velocissimum habentes in ventre reperiuntur.

145 Scolopendrae terrestribus similes quas centipedes vocant hamo devorato omnia interanea evomunt donec hamum egerant, deinde resorbent. at vulpes marinae simili in periculo gluttiunt amplius usque ad infirma lineae qua facile praerodant. cautius qui glanis vocatur aversos mordet hamos nec devorat sed esca spoliat.

Grassatur aries ut latro, et nunc grandiorum navium in salo stantium occultatus umbra si quem nandi voluptas invitet expectat, nunc elato extra aquam capite piscantium cumbas speculatur occultusque adnatans mergit.

146 LXVIII. Equidem et iis inesse sensum arbitror quae neque animalium neque fruticum sed tertiam

---

[1] retrahens *aut* praetrahens *edd.* : pertrahens.

a Obviously a worm, such as Eunice or Nereis.
b The fox-shark, *Alopecias vulpes*.
c Probably a dolphin.

any fish that have received a shock while swimming carelessly above her. No tender morsel is preferred to the liver of this fish. The sea-frog called the angler-fish is equally cunning: it stirs up the mud and puts out the little horns that project under its eyes, drawing them back when little fishes frisk towards them till they come near enough for it to spring upon them. In like manner the angel-shark and the turbot while in hiding put out their fins and wave them about to look like worms, and so also do the fish called skate. For the prickly ray acts as a freebooter, from its hiding place transfixing fish passing by with its sting, which is its weapon; there are proofs of this cunning, because these fish, though the slowest there are, are found with mullet, the swiftest of all fish, in their belly.

The *scolopendra*,[a] which resembles the land animal *Other curious species.* called the centipede, when it has swallowed a hook vomits up the whole of its inwards until it succeeds in disgorging it, and then sucks them back again. Sea-foxes[b] on the other hand in a similar emergency gulp down more of the line till they reach its weak part where they may easily gnaw it off. The fish called the catfish more cautiously nibbles at hooks from behind and strips them of the bait without swallowing them.

The sea-ram[c] goes around like a brigand, and now hides in the shadow of the larger vessels riding at anchor and waits in case somebody may be tempted by the pleasure of a swim, now raises its head out of the water and watches for fishermen's boats, and secretly swimming up to them sinks them.

LXVIII. For my own part I hold the view that *The sea-nettle.* even those creatures which have not got the nature of either animals or plants, but some third nature

quandam ex utroque naturam habent, urticis dico et spongeis.

Urticae noctu vagantur locumque [1] mutant. carnosae frondis his natura, et carne vescuntur. vis pruritu mordax est eademque quae terrestris urticae. contrahit ergo se quam maxime rigens ac praenatante pisciculo frondem suam spargit complectensque devorat. alias marcenti similis et iactari se passa fluctu algae vice, contactos piscium attrituque petrae scalpentes pruritum invadit. eadem noctu pectines et echinos perquirit.[2] cum admoveri sibi manum sentit, colorem mutat et contrahitur. tacta uredinem emittit,[3] paulumque si fuit intervalli, absconditur. ora ei in radice esse traduntur, excrementa per summa tenui fistula reddi.

148 LXIX. Spongearum tria genera accepimus: spissum ac praedurum et asperum tragos[4] vocatur, minus[5] spissum et molius manos, tenue densumque, ex quo penicilli, Achillium. nascuntur omnes in petris, aluntur conchis, pisce, limo. intellectum inesse his apparet, quia, ubi avulsorem[6] sensere, contractae multo difficilius abstrahuntur. hoc idem fluctu pulsante faciunt. vivere esca manifesto conchae minutae in his repertae ostendunt. circa Toronem vesci illis avulsas etiam aiunt et ex relictis

---

[1] *Mayhoff ex Aristotele* : noctuque.
[2] *Lacunam* per . . . quaerit *Mayhoff*.
[3] *Mayhoff ?* : mittit.
[4] *Mayhoff* : tragos id.
[5] minus *add. Hermolaus*.
[6] avolsurum ? *Mayhoff*.

147

derived from both, possess sense-perception—I mean jelly-fish and sponges.

Jelly-fish roam about and change their place by night. These have the nature of a fleshy leaf, and they feed on flesh. The itch they cause has a biting power, just like that of the land nettle. Consequently this creature draws itself in as stiffly as possible and when a little fish swims in front of it spreads out its leaf and enfolding it devours it. In other cases it looks as if it were withering up, and allows itself to be tossed about by the waves like seaweed, and attacks any fish that touch it as they try to scrape away the itch by rubbing against a rock. The same creature by night hunts for scallops and sea-urchins. When it feels a hand approach it, it changes colour and draws itself together. When touched it sends out a burning sting, and if there is a moment's interval hides. It is reported to have mouths in its root and to evacuate its excretions by a narrow tube through its topmost parts.

LXIX. We are informed that there are three kinds of sponge: a thick and very hard and rough one is called goat-thorn sponge, a less thick and softer one loose-sponge, and a thin one of close texture, used for making paint-brushes, Achilles sponge. They all grow on rocks, and feed on shells, fish and mud. These creatures manifestly possess intelligence, because when they are aware of a sponge-gatherer they contract and make it much more difficult to detach them. They do the same when much beaten by the waves. The tiny shells found inside them clearly show that they live by eating food. It is said that in the neighbourhood of Torone they can be fed on these shell-fish even after they

The sponge —its three varieties: their habitat:

263

radicibus recrescere in petris; cruoris quoque in-
haeret colos, Africis praecipue quae generantur in
Syrtibus. maximae fiunt manoe sed mollissimae
circa Lyciam, in profundo autem nec ventoso mol-
liores; in Hellesponto asperae, et densae circa
Maleam. putrescunt in apricis locis, ideo optimae in
gurgitibus. viventibus idem qui madentibus nigri-
150 cans colos. adhaerent nec parte nec totae; in-
tersunt enim fistulae quaedam inanes quaternae fere
aut quinae, per quas pasci existimantur. sunt et
aliae, sed superne concretae; et subesse membrana
quaedam radicibus earum intellegitur. vivere
constat longo tempore. pessimum omnium genus
est earum quae aplysiae vocantur, quia elui non
possunt, in quibus magnae sunt fistulae et reliqua
densitas spissa.

151 LXX. Canicularum maxime multitudo circa eas
urinantes gravi periculo infestat. ipsi ferunt et
nubem quandam crassescere super capita (animal
id[1] planorum piscium simile[2]) prementem eos
arcentemque a reciprocando, et ob id stilos praea-
cutos lineis adnexos habere sese, quia nisi perfossae
ita non recedant—caliginis et pavoris, ut arbitror,
opere: nubem enim et nebulam, cuius nomine id

---

¹ *Detlefsen*: animali.   ² *Rackham*: similem.

ᵃ In the Gulf of Sidra and the Gulf of Cabes.
ᵇ Literally ' unwashable.'
ᶜ Probably the large ray.

have been pulled off the rocks, and that fresh sponges grow again on the rocks from the roots left there; also the colour of blood remains on them, especially on the African ones that grow on the Sandbanks.[a] Very large but very soft thin sponges grow round Lycia, though those in deep and calm water are softer; the rough kind grows in the Dardanelles, and the close-textured round Cape Malea. Sponges decay in sunny places, and consequently the best are found in deep pools. Live sponges have the same blackish colour as sponges in use have when wet. They do not cling to the rock with a particular part nor with their entire surface, for they have certain empty tubes, about four or five in number, running through them, through which it is believed that they take their food. They also have other tubes, but these are closed at the upper end; and it is understood that there is a sort of thin skin on the under side of their roots. It is established that they live a long time. The worst of all the species of sponge is one called in Greek the dirty[b] sponge, because it cannot be cleaned; it contains large tubes, and the rest of it is of a very close texture

LXX. The number of dog-fish specially swarming round sponges beset the men that dive for them with grave danger. These persons also report that a sort of ' cloud '[c] thickens above their heads—this a live creature resembling flat-fish—pressing them down and preventing them from getting back, and that because of this they have very sharp spikes attached to cords, because the ' clouds ' will not withdraw unless stabbed through in this way—this story being the result, as I believe, of darkness and fear; for nobody has ever heard of any such creature in the

Diving for sponges: the danger of dog-fish.

malum appellant, inter animalia haut ullam comperit
152 quisquam. cum caniculis atrox dimicatio; inguina
et calces omnemque candorem corporum appetunt.
salus una in adversas eundi ultroque terrendi; pavet
enim hominem aeque ac terret, et ita sors [1] aequa
in gurgite. ut ad summa aquae ventum est, ibi peri-
culum anceps, adempta ratione contra eundi dum
conetur emergere; et salus omnis in sociis. funem
illi religatum ab umeris eius trahunt; hunc
dimicans, ut sit periculi signum, laeva quatit, dextera
153 adprehenso stilo in pugna est. modicus alias trac-
tatus: ut prope carinam ventum est, nisi praeceleri
vi repente eripiunt,[2] absumi spectant. ac saepe iam
subducti e manibus auferuntur, si non trahentium
opem conglobato corpore in pilae modum ipsi
adiuvere. protendunt quidem tridentis alii; sed
monstro sollertia est navigium subeundi atque ita e
tuto proeliandi. omnis ergo cura ad speculandum
hoc malum insumitur; certissima est securitas vidisse
planos pisces, quia numquam sunt ubi maleficae
bestiae, qua de causa urinantes sacros appellant eos.
154   LXXI. Silicea testa inclusis fatendum est nullum
esse sensum, ut ostreis. multis eadem natura quae

---

[1] *Mayhoff*: et in frons.   [2] *Rackham*: rapuit.

list of animals as the ' cloud ' or ' fog,' which is the
name the divers give to this plague. Divers have
fierce fights with the dog-fish; these attack their loins
and heels and all the white parts of the body. The
one safety lies in going for them and frightening
them by taking the offensive; for a dog-fish is as
much afraid of a man as a man is of it, and so they
are on equal terms in deep water. When they come
to the surface, then the man is in critical danger, as
the policy of taking the offensive is not available
while he is trying to get out of the water, and his
only safety is in his comrades. These haul on the
rope tied to his shoulders; this, as he carries on the
duel, he shakes with his left hand to give a signal
of danger, while his right hand grasps his dagger
and is occupied in fighting. Most of the time they
haul gently, but when he gets near the boat, unless
with a quick heave they suddenly snatch him out
of the water, they have to look on while he is made
away with. And often when divers have already
begun to be hauled up they are snatched out of
their comrades' hands, unless they have themselves
supplemented the aid of those hauling by curling up
into a ball. Others of the crew of course thrust
out harpoons, but the vast beast is crafty enough to
go under the vessel and so carry on the battle in
safety. Consequently divers devote their whole attention to keeping a watch against this disaster; the most
reliable token of safety is to have seen some flat-fish,
which are never found where these noxious creatures
are—on account of which divers call them the holy fish.

LXXI. It must be agreed that creatures enclosed *Senses of marine species.*
in a flinty shell, such as oysters, have no senses.
Many have the same nature as a bush, for instance

frutici, ut holothuriis, pulmonibus, stellis. adeoque nihil non gignitur in mari ut cauponarum etiam aestiva animalia, pernici molesta saltu aut quae capillus maxime celat, exsistant ibi [1] et circumglobata escae saepe extrahantur; quae causa somnum piscium in mari noctibus infestare existimatur. quibusdam vero ipsis innascuntur, quo in numero chalcis accipitur.

155 LXXII. Nec venena cessant dira, ut in lepore qui in Indico mari etiam tactu pestilens vomitum dissolutionemque stomachi protinus creat, in nostro offa informis colore tantum lepori similis, in Indis et magnitudine et pilo, duriore tantum; nec vivus ibi capitur. aeque pestiferum animal araneus spinae in dorso aculeo noxius. sed nullum usquam execrabilius quam radius super caudam eminens trygonis quam nostri pastinacam appellant, quincunciali magnitudine; arbores infixus radici necat, arma ut telum perforat vi ferri et veneni malo.

156 LXXIII. Morbos universa genera piscium, ut cetera animalia etiam fera, non accipimus sentire; verum aegrotare singulos manifestum facit aliquorum macies cum in eodem genere praepingues alii capiantur.

157 LXXIV. Quonam modo generent, desiderium et

[1] ibi *add. Rackham.*

a This chapter contains a remarkable mixture of truth and falsehood.

the sea-cucumber, the sea-lung, the starfish. And to *The sea-flea.* such an extent is it the case that everything grows in the sea, that even the creatures found in inns in summer-time,—those that plague us with a quick jump or those that hide chiefly in the hair,—occur there, and are often drawn out of the water clustering round the bait; and their irritation is thought to disturb the sleep of fish in the sea at night. Indeed on some kinds of fish these vermin actually breed as parasites; the herring is believed to be one of these.

LXXII. Nor are there wanting dire poisons, as in *Poisonous* the sea-hare which in the Indian Ocean infects even *fishes.* by its touch, immediately causing vomiting and laxity of the stomach, and in our own seas the shapeless lump resembling a hare in colour only, whereas the Indian variety is also like a hare in size and in fur, only its fur is harder; and there it is never taken alive. An equally pestiferous creature is the weever, which wounds with the sharp point of its dorsal fin. But there is nothing in the world more execrable than the sting projecting above the tail of the prickly ray which our people call the *pastinaca*; it is five inches long, and kills trees when driven into the root, and penetrates armour like a missile, with the force of steel and with deadly poison.

LXXIII. We are not told that the various kinds of *Diseases of* fish suffer from endemic diseases, as do all other even *fish.* wild animals; but that individuals among them are liable to illness is proved by the emaciated condition of some fish contrasted with the extreme fatness of others of the same kind when caught.

LXXIV.[a] The curiosity and wonder of mankind does *Fishes, sexual reproduction.*

admiratio hominum differri non patitur. pisces
attritu ventrium coeunt tanta celeritate ut visum
fallant, delphini et reliqua cete simili modo et paulo
diutius. femina piscis coitus tempore marem sequitur ventrem eius rostro pulsans, sub partum [1] mares
feminas similiter ova vescentes earum. nec satis est
generationi per se coitus, nisi editis ovis interversando
mares vitale adsperserint virus. non omnibus id
contingit ovis in tanta multitudine; alioqui repleren-
tur maria et stagna, cum singuli uteri innumerabilia
concipiant.

158 Piscium ova in mari crescunt, quaedam summa celeritate, ut murenarum, quaedam paulo tardius.
plani piscium quibus cauda non est [2] aculeatique et
testudines in coitu superveniunt, polypi crine uno
feminae naribus adnexo, saepiae et lolligines linguis,
componentes inter se bracchia et in contrarium
nantes; ore et pariunt. sed polypi in terram verso
capite coeunt, reliqua mollium tergis ut canes, item
159 locustae et squillae, cancri ore. ranae superveniunt,
prioribus pedibus alas feminae mare adprehendente,
posterioribus clunes. pariunt minimas carnes nigras,
quas gyrinos vocant, oculis tantum et cauda insignes;
mox pedes figurantur cauda findente se in posteriores.

---

[1] *Gelen* : partu.
[2] *Lacunam hic Mayhoff.*

not allow us to postpone the consideration of these animals' method of reproduction. Fish couple by rubbing their bellies together so quickly as to escape the sight; dolphins and the rest of the large marine species couple in a similar manner, but with rather longer contact. At the coupling season the female fish pursues the male, nudging his belly with her nose, but directly after the eggs are born the males similarly pursue the females and eat their eggs. Copulation is not enough in itself to cause the birth of offspring, unless when the eggs are laid the males swim to and fro sprinkling them with life-giving milt. This is not achieved with all the eggs in so great a multitude —otherwise the seas and marshes would be completely filled, since the uterus of a single fish holds a countless number of eggs.

Fishes' eggs in the sea grow in size, some with extreme rapidity, for instance those of the murena, some a little more slowly. Flat fish not possessing a tail, and sting-ray and tortoises, cover the female in mating, polyps couple by attaching a single feeler to the female's nostrils, the two varieties of cuttle-fish with their tongues, linking their arms together and swimming in opposite directions; they also spawn through the mouth. But polyps couple with their head turned towards the ground, all the other soft fishes with their backs—for instance seadogs, and also langoustes and prawns; crabs with their mouth. Frogs cover the female, the male grasping her shoulder-blades with his fore-feet and her buttocks with his hind feet. They spawn very small lumps of dark flesh that are called tadpoles, possessing only eyes and a tail; but soon feet are formed by the tail dividing into two hind legs. And strange

mirumque, semestri vita resolvuntur in limum nullo
cernente, et rursus vernis aquis renascuntur quae
fuere, naturae perinde occulta ratione, cum omnibus
160 annis id eveniat. et mituli et pectines sponte
naturae in harenosis proveniunt; quae durioris testae
sunt, ut murices, purpurae, salivario lentore, sicut
acescente umore culices; apua spuma maris incales-
cente cum admissus est imber; quae vero siliceo
tegmine operiuntur, ut ostrea, putrescente limo aut
spuma circa navigia diutius stantia defixosque palos
et lignum maxime. nuper compertum in ostreariis
umorem his fetificum lactis modo effluere. anguillae
atterunt se scopulis, ea strigmenta vivescunt, nec alia
161 est earum procreatio. piscium diversa genera
non coeunt praeter squatinam et raiam, ex quibus
nascitur priore parte raiae similis, et nomen ex utroque compositum apud Graecos trahit.

162   Quaedam tempore anni gignuntur et in umore ut
in terra: vere pectines, limaces, hirudines; eadem
tempore evanescunt. piscium lupus et trichias bis
anno parit, et saxatiles omnes; nonnulli[1] ter, ut[2]
chalcis, cyprini sexiens, scorpaenae bis ac sargi, vere
et autumno, ex planis squatina bis sola, autumno,
occasu vergiliarum; plurimi piscium tribus mensibus
Aprili, Maio, Iunio; salpae autumno; sargi, torpedo,

[1] *Detlefsen*: non mulli *aut* mulli.
[2] ut *Mayhoff*: et.

---

[a] *Rhinobatos*, from ῥίνη and βάτος.

to say, after six months of life they melt invisibly
back into mud, and again in the waters of spring-
time are reborn what they were before, equally
owing to some hidden principle of nature, as it occurs
every year. Also mussels and scallops are produced *Non-sexual*
by spontaneous generation in sandy waters; fish with *reproduction.*
harder shells, like the two varieties of purple-fish,
are generated by a sticky juice like saliva, as gnats
are by moisture turning sour; the anchovy by sea-
foam growing warm when rain gets into it; but fish
protected by a flinty covering, like oysters, are
generated by rotting mud, or by the foam round
ships that stay moored for some time, and especially
round stakes fixed in the ground, and timber. It
has recently been discovered in oyster-beds that a
fertilizing moisture flows out of these fish like milk.
Eels rub against rocks and the scrapings come to life;
this is their only way of breeding. Different kinds
of fish do not mate together, except the angel-shark
and the ray, the cross between which is like a ray in
front, and bears in Greece a name [a] derived from the
names of both parents.

Some creatures are born at a fixed season of the *Breeding-*
year, water species as well as those on land: scallops *season of*
and slugs and leeches in the spring; these also pass *various*
away at a fixed season. Among fish the bass and the *species.*
shad breed twice a year, and so do all the rock-fish;
some breed three times, for instance the pilchard;
carp six times; sea-scorpions and sargue twice, in
spring and autumn: of the flat fish only the angel-
shark twice, in the autumn and at the setting of the
Pleiads; most fish in the three months of April,
May and June; the saupe in the autumn, the
sargue, the torpedo and the *squalus* at the season

squali circa aequinoctium, molles vere, saepia omnibus mensibus: ova eius glutino atramenti ad speciem
uvae cohaerentia masculus prosequitur adflatu, alias
163 sterilescunt. polypi hieme coeunt, pariunt vere ova
tortili vibrata pampino, tanta fecunditate ut multitudinem ovorum occisi non recipiant cavo capitis quo
praegnantes tulere.   ea excludunt L die, e quibus
164 multa propter numerum intercidunt. locustae et
reliqua tenuioris crustae ponunt ova subter ipsa[1]
atque ita incubant: polypus femina modo in ovis
sedet, modo cavernam cancellato bracchiorum
inplexu claudit. saepia in terreno parit inter
harundines aut sicubi enata alga, excludit quinto
decimo die. lolligines in alto conserta ova edunt ut
saepiae. purpurae, murices eiusdemque generis
vere pariunt. echini ova pleniluniis habent hieme,
et cocleae hiberno tempore nascuntur.

165   LXXV. Torpedo octogenos fetus habens invenitur,
eaque intra se parit ova praemollia, in alium locum
uteri transferens atque ibi excludens; simili modo
omnia quae cartilaginea appellavimus: ita fit ut sola
piscium et animal pariant et ova concipiant. silurus
mas solus omnium edita custodit ova, saepe et
quinquagenis diebus, ne absumantur ab aliis.
ceterae feminae in triduo excludunt si mas attigit.

_____

[1] *Mayhoff ex Aristotele*: super ova.

_____

ª See § 78.

of the equinox; soft fish in the spring; the cuttle-fish in all the months—its eggs stick together with an inky gum like a bunch of grapes, and the male directs his breath upon them, otherwise they are barren. Polyps mate in winter and lay eggs in spring that cluster in a twisting coil; and they are so prolific that when they are killed the cavity of their head will not hold the multitude of eggs that they carried in it when pregnant. They lay them after seven weeks, many of them perishing because of their number. Langoustes and the rest of the species with rather thin shells deposit their eggs underneath them and so hatch them; the female polyp now sits on the eggs and now forms a closed cavern with her tentacles intertwined in a lattice. The sepia lays on land among reeds or wherever there is seaweed growing, and hatches after a fort-night. The cuttle-fish produces its eggs in deep water clustered together like those of the sepia. The purple-fish, the murex and their kind spawn in spring. Sea-urchins have eggs at the full moons in winter, and snails are born in the winter time.

LXXV. The electric ray is found having broods numbering eighty; also it produces exceedingly small eggs inside it, shifting them to another part of the womb and emitting them there; and similarly all the species that we have designated[a] cartilaginous: thus it comes about that these are the only fish kinds that are both viviparous and oviparous. With the catfish alone of all species the male guards the eggs, often for as long as 50 days at a time, to prevent their being eaten by other fish. The females of all the other species spawn in three days if a male has touched them. *Reproduction of other species of fish.*

275

166   LXXVI. Acus sive belone unus piscium dehiscente
propter multitudinem utero parit; a partu coalescit
vulnus, quod et in caecis serpentibus tradunt.   mus
marinus in terra scrobe effosso parit ova et rursus
obruit terra, tricesimo die refossa aperit fetumque in
aquam ducit.

LXXVII. Erythini et channae volvas habere
traduntur, qui trochos appellatur a Graecis ipse se
inire. fetus omnium aquatilium inter initia visu
carent.

167   LXXVIII. Aevi piscium memorandum nuper
exemplum accepimus. Pausilypum villa est Campaniae haut procul Neapoli; in ea in Caesaris piscinis
a Policne Vedio coniectum piscem sexagensimum
post annum expirasse scribit Annaeus Seneca, duobus aliis aequalibus eius ex eodem genere etiam tunc
viventibus. quae mentio piscinarum admonet ut
paulo plura dicamus hac de re priusquam digrediamur
ab aquatilibus.

168   LXXIX. Ostrearum vivaria primus omnium
Sergius Orata invenit in Baiano aetate L. Crassi
oratoris, ante Marsicum bellum, nec gulae causa sed
avaritiae, magna vectigalia tali ex ingenio suo perci-
piens, ut qui primus pensiles invenerit balineas, ita
mangonicatas villas subinde vendendo. is primus
optimum   saporem   ostreis   Lucrinis   adiudicavit,
quando eadem aquatilium genera aliubi atque aliubi
169 meliora, sicut lupi pisces in Tiberi amne inter duos
pontes, rhombus Ravennae, murena in Sicilia, elops

---

a See § 56.
b Perhaps *Orthagoriscus mola*.
c *I.e.* Sans Souci.
d 91–88 B.C.
e Perhaps the Sublician and the Palatine.

LXXVI. The pipefish or garfish is the only fish so prolific that its matrix is ruptured when it spawns; after spawning the wound grows together, which is said to happen in the case of blindworms also. The filefish digs a trench in the ground to lay its eggs in and covers it again with earth, and a month later digs the earth up again and opens the trench and leads its brood into the water.

LXXVII. The red perch and the sea-perch *a* are said to have wombs. The species called by the Greeks hoop-fish *b* is said to practise self-impregnation. The offspring of all aquatic animals are blind at birth.

LXXVIII. There has recently been sent to us a remarkable case of longevity in fishes. In Campania not far from Naples, there is a country house named Posilipo *c*; Annaeus Seneca writes that in Caesar's fishponds on this property a fish thrown in by Polio Vedius had died after reaching the age of 60, while two others of the same breed that were of the same age were even then living. The mention of fishponds reminds me to say a little more on this topic before leaving the subject of aquatic animals. *Longevity in fish.*

LXXIX. Oyster ponds were first invented by Sergius Orata on the Gulf of Baiae, in the time of the orator Lucius Crassus, before the Marsian war *d*; his motive was not greed but avarice, and he made a great profit out of his practical ingenuity, as he was the first inventor of showerbaths—he used to fit out country houses in this way and then sell them. He was the first to adjudge the best flavour to Lucrine oysters—because the same kinds of fish are of better quality in different places, for example sea-bass in the Tiber between the two bridges *e*, turbot at Ravenna, moray in Sicily, sturgeon at Rhodes, and other kinds *Oyster culture.*

277

Rhodi, et alia genera similiter, ne culinarum censura peragatur. nondum Britannica serviebant litora cum Orata Lucrina nobilitabat; postea visum tanti in extremam Italiam petere Brundisium ostreas, ac ne lis esset inter duos sapores, nuper excogitatum famem longae advectionis a Brundisio conpascere in Lucrino.

170 LXXX. Eadem aetate prior Licinius Murena reliquorum piscium vivaria invenit, cuius deinde exemplum nobilitas secuta est Philippi, Hortensi. Lucullus exciso etiam monte iuxta Neapolim maiore impendio quam villam exaedificaverat euripum et maria admisit, qua de causa Magnus Pompeius Xerxen togatum eum appellabat. |XL| HS e piscina ea[1] defuncto illo veniere pisces.

171 LXXXI. Murenarum vivarium privatim excogitavit ante alios C. Hirrius, qui cenis triumphalibus Caesaris dictatoris sex milia numero murenarum mutua appendit; nam permutare quidem pretio noluit aliave merce. huius villam infra[2] quam

172 modicam |XL| piscinae vendiderunt. invasit dein singulorum piscium amor. apud Baulos in parte Baiana piscinam habuit Hortensius orator in qua murenam adeo dilexit ut exanimatam flesse credatur. in eadem villa Antonia Drusi murenae quam diligebat inaures addidit, cuius propter famam nonnulli Baulos videre concupiverunt.

---

[1] *Mayhoff*: XL hii se pisimae a *aut alia*.
[2] *Mayhoff*: intra.

---

[a] Xerxes made a channel for his fleet through Mount Athos.
[b] 46 and 45 B.C.
[c] The colloquial use of *video*, 'go to see,' survives in Italian, *e.g.* 'Vede Napoli e poi mori.'

likewise—not to carry out this census of the larder to its conclusion. The coasts of Britain were not yet in service when Orata used to advertise the fame of the products of the Lago Lucrino; but subsequently it was deemed worth while to send to the end of Italy, to Brindisi, for oysters, and to prevent a quarrel between the two delicacies the plan has lately been devised of feeding away in the Lago Lucrino the hunger caused by the long porterage from Brindisi.

LXXX. In the same period the elder Licinius *Fishponds.* Murena invented fishponds for all the other sorts of fish, and his example was subsequently followed by the celebrated record of Philip and Hortensius. Lucullus had built a channel that cost more than a country house, by actually cutting through a mountain near Naples and letting in the sea; this was why Pompey the Great used to call him ' Xerxes [a] in Roman dress.' After his decease the fish from this pond sold for 4,000,000 sesterces.

LXXXI. The first person to devise a separate *Moray-ponds.* pond for morays was Gaius Hirrius, who added to the triumphal banquets [b] of Caesar morays to the number of 6000—as a loan, because he would not exchange them for money or for any other commodity. His less than moderate country estate was sold by its fishponds for 4,000,000 sesterces. Subsequently affection for individual fishes came into fashion. At Baculo in the Baiae district the pleader Hortensius had a fishpond containing a moray which he fell so deeply in love with that he is believed to have wept when it expired. At the same country house Drusus's wife Antonia adorned his favourite moray with earrings, and its reputation made some people extremely eager to visit Baculo.[c]

173   LXXXII. Coclearum vivaria instituit **Fulvius
Lippinus** in Tarquiniensi paulo ante civile bellum
quod cum Pompeio Magno gestum est, distinctis
quidem generibus earum, separatim ut essent albae
quae in Reatino agro nascuntur, separatim Illyricae
quibus magnitudo praecipua, Africanae quibus
174 fecunditas, Solitanae quibus nobilitas. quin et
saginam earum commentus est sapa et farre aliisque
generibus, ut cocleae quoque altiles ganeam im-
plerent: cuius artis gloriam in eam magnitudinem
perductam esse ut[1] LXXX quadrantes caperent
singularum calyces auctor est M. Varro.

175   LXXXIII. Piscium genera etiamnum a Theophrasto mira produntur, circa Babylonis rigua dece-
dentibus fluviis in cavernis aquas habentibus
remanere quosdam, inde exire ad pabula pinnulis
gradientes crebro caudae motu, contraque venantes
refugere in suas cavernas et in his obversos stare,
capita eorum esse ranae marinae similia, reliquas
partes gobionum, branchias ut ceteris piscibus.
176 circa Heracleam et Cromnam et multifariam in Ponto
unum genus esse quod extremas fluminum aquas
sectetur cavernasque sibi faciat in terra atque in his
vivat, etiam reciprocis amnibus siccato litore, effodi
ergo motu demum corporum vivere eos adprobante.
177 circa eandem Heracleam [eodemque][2] **Lyco** amne

---

[1] *Rackham* : perducta sit.   [2] *seclusit Mayhoff.*

---

[a] Begun in 49 B.C.   [b] A type of burrowing goby.

LXXXII. Ponds for keeping snails were first made *Snail-* by Fulvius Lippinus in the Trachina district a little *breeding.* before the civil war *a* fought with Pompey the Great; indeed he kept the different kinds of snails separate, with different compartments for the white snails that grow in the Rieti territory and for the Illyrian variety distinguished for size, the African for fecundity and the Solitane for breed. Moreover he devised a method of fattening them with new wine boiled down and spelt and other kinds of fodder, so that gastronomy was enriched even by fattened oysters; and according to Marcus Varro this ostentatious science was carried to such lengths that a single snail-shell was large enough to hold 80 quarts.

LXXXIII. Moreover some wonderful kinds of fish *Remarkable* are reported by Theophrastus. He says that (1) *foreign fish.* where the rivers debouch around the water-meadows of Babylon a certain fish *b* stays in caverns that contain springs and goes out from them to feed, walking with its fins by means of a repeated movement of the tail, and guards against being caught by taking refuge in its caves and remaining in them facing towards the opening, and that these fishes' heads resemble a sea-frog's and the rest of its parts a goby's, though the gills are the same as in other fish. (2) In the neighbourhood of Heraclea and Cromna and in many parts of the Black Sea there is one kind that frequents the water at the edge of rivers and makes itself caverns in the ground and lives in these, and also in the shore of tidal rivers when left dry by the tide; and consequently they are only dug up when the movement of their bodies shows that they are alive. (3) In the same neighbourhood of Heraclea

decedente ovis relictis in limo generari pisces qui ad
pabula petenda palpitent exiguis branchiis, quo fieri
non indigos umoris, propter quod et anguillas diutius
vivere exemptas aquis, ova autem in sicco maturari
ut testudinum. eadem in Ponti regione adprehendi
glacie piscium maxime gobiones non nisi patinarum
178 calore vitalem motum fatentis. est in his quidem,
tametsi mirabilibus,[1] tamen aliqua ratio. idem
tradit in Paphlagonia effodi pisces gratissimos cibis
terrenos altis scrobibus in iis locis in quibus nullae
restagnent aquae; miratusque[2] ipse gigni sine
coitu umoris quidem vim aliquam inesse quam puteis
arbitratur—ceu vero in ullis[3] reperiantur pisces!
quicquid est hoc, certe minus admirabilem talparum
facit vitam, subterranei animalis, nisi forte vermium
terrenorum et his piscibus natura inest.

179   LXXXIV. Verum omnibus his fidem Nili inundatio
adfert omnia excedente miraculo: quippe detegente
eo musculi reperiuntur inchoato opere genitalis aquae
terraeque, iam parte corporis viventes novissima
effigie etiamnum terrena.

180   LXXXV. Nec de anthia pisce silere convenit ea
quae plerosque adverto credidisse. Chelidonias

---

[1] *Rackham*: mirabilis.   [2] *v.l.* miraturque.
[3] *Jan*: vero nullis.

at the outflow of the river Lycus fishes are born from eggs left in the mud that seek their fodder by flapping with their little gills, and this makes them not need moisture, which is the reason why eels also live comparatively long when taken out of the water, while eggs mature in a dry place, for instance tortoise's eggs. (4) In the same region of the Black Sea the fish most frequently caught in the ice is the goby, which is only made to reveal the movement of life by the heat of the saucepan. These accounts indeed, however marvellous, do nevertheless embody a certain principle. The same authority reports that in Paphlagonia earth-fish extremely acceptable for food are dug out of deep trenches in places where there is no overflow from streams; and after himself expressing surprise at their being propagated without coupling, he gives the view that at all events they have a supply of moisture in them similar to that in wells—but as if fish were found in any wells! Whatever the fact is as to this, it certainly makes the life of moles, an underground animal, less remarkable, unless perhaps these fishes also possess the nature of earth-worms.

LXXXIV. But credibility is given to all these statements by the flooding of the Nile, with a marvel that surpasses them all: this is that, when the river withdraws its covering, water-mice are found with the work of generative water and earth uncompleted— they are already alive in a part of their body, but the most recently formed part of their structure is still of earth. *Nile water-mice.*

LXXXV. Nor is it proper to omit the stories about the *anthias* fish that I notice to have won general acceptance. We have mentioned the Swallow *The anthias*

insulas diximus Asiae scopulosi maris ante promunturium Tauri[1] sitas; ibi frequens hic piscis et
celeriter capitur uno genere. parvo navigio et concolori veste eademque hora per aliquot dies con-
tinuos piscator enavigat certo spatio escamque
proicit; quicquid vero[2] mutetur suspecta fraus
praedae est, cavetque quod timuit. cum id saepe
factum est, unus aliquando consuetudine invitatus
181 anthias escam appetit. notatur hic intentione
diligenti ut auctor spei conciliatorque capturae;
neque est difficile, cum per aliquot dies solus accedere
audeat. tandem et alios[3] invenit, paulatimque
comitatior postremo greges adducit innumeros, iam
vetustissimis quibusque adsuetis piscatorem agnos-
cere et e manu cibum rapere. tum ille paulum
ultra digitos in esca iaculatus hamum singulos
involat verius quam capit, ab umbra navis brevi
conatu rapiens[4] ita ne ceteri sentiant, alio intus
excipiente centonibus raptum ne palpitatio ulla aut
182 sonus ceteros abigat. conciliatorem nosse ad hoc
prodest, ne capiatur, fugituro in reliquum grege.
ferunt discordem socium duci insidiatum pulchre noto
cepisse malefica voluntate; agnitum in macello a socio
cuius injuria erat et damni formulam editam con-

---

[1] Tauri *add. post* ante *Hermolaus, hic Mayhoff.*
[2] *Mayhoff*: quicquid ex eo.
[3] alios? *Mayhoff*: aliquos.
[4] *Gelen*: conatur absens.

---

[a] Now Allah Dagh, in south-east Asia Minor.

Islands, situated off a promontory of Mt. Taurus[a] in the rocky sea of Asia; this fish is frequent there, and is quickly caught, in one variety. A fisherman sails out a certain distance in a small boat, wearing clothes that match the boat in colour, and at the same time for several days running, and throws out bait; but if any alteration whatever be made, the prey suspects a trick and avoids the thing that has frightened it. When this has been done a number of times, at last one *anthias* is tempted by familiarity to try to get the bait. This one is marked down with careful attention as a foundation for hope and as a decoy for a catch; and it is not difficult to mark it, as for several days only this one ventures to come close. At last it finds others as well, and gradually enlarging its company finally brings shoals too big to count, as by this time all the oldest fish have got used to recognizing the fisherman and snatching the bait out of his hand. Then he throws a hook fixed in the bait a little beyond his fingers, and catches or rather rushes them one by one, snatching them with a short jerk away from the shadow of the boat so that the others may not notice it, while another man in the boat receives the catch in some rags so that no flapping or noise may drive away the others. It pays to know the decoy fish for this purpose, so that he may not be caught, as thenceforward the shoal will swim away. There is a story that a disaffected partner in a fishery lay in wait for the leader fish, which was very well known, and caught it, with malicious intent; Mucianus adds that it was recognized in the market by the partner who was being victimized, and that proceedings for damage were instituted and

demnatumque addit Mucianus aestimata lite. idem
anthiae, cum unum hamo teneri viderint, spinis quas
in dorso serratas habent lineam secare traduntur eo
qui teneatur extendente ut praecidi possit. at inter
sargos ipse qui tenetur ad scopulos lineam terit.

183 LXXXVI. Praeter haec claros sapientia auctores
video mirari stellam in mari: ea figura est, parva
admodum caro intus, extra duriore callo. huic tam
igneum fervorem esse tradunt ut omnia in mari
contacta adurat, omnem cibum statim peragat.
quibus sit hoc cognitum experimentis haud facile
dixerim, multoque memorabilius duxerim [1] id cuius
experiendi cotidie occasio est.

184 LXXXVII. Concharum e genere sunt dactyli, ab
humanorum unguium similitudine appellati. his
natura in tenebris remoto lumine alio fulgere claro,[2]
et quanto magis umorem habeant lucere in ore
mandentium, lucere in manibus atque etiam in solo
ac veste decidentibus guttis, ut procul dubio pateat
suci illam naturam esse quam miraremur etiam in
corpore.

185 LXXXVIII. Sunt et inimicitiarum atque
concordiae miracula. mugil et lupus mutuo odio
flagrant, conger et murena, caudam inter se praero-

---

[1] *Gelen*: dicerim.   [2] *v.l.* clare.

a I.e. the star-fish.

a verdict given for the prosecution with damages as assessed. Moreover it is said that when these fishes see one of their number hooked they cut the line with the saw-like prickles that they have on their back, while the one held by the line draws it taut so as to enable it to be severed. With the sargue kind however the captive itself rubs the line against the rocks.

LXXXVI. Besides these cases I observe that *The starfish.* authors renowned for their wisdom express surprise at there being a star in the sea: that is the shape of the fish,^a which has rather little flesh inside it but a rather hard rind outside. They say that this fish contains such fiery heat that it scorches all the things it touches in the sea, and digests all food immediately. I cannot readily say by what experiments this has been ascertained, and I should consider a fact that there is daily opportunity of experiencing to be much more worth recording.

LXXXVII. The class shellfish includes the piddock, *The piddock.* named finger-mussel from its resemblance to a human finger-nail. It is the nature of these fish to shine in darkness with a bright light when other light is removed, and in proportion to their amount of moisture to glitter both in the mouth of persons masticating them and in their hands, and even on the floor and on their clothes when drops fall from them, making it clear beyond all doubt that their juice possesses a property that we should marvel at even in a solid object.

LXXXVIII. There are also remarkable facts as to *Hostility and friendship between different species of fish.* their quarrels and their friendship. Violent animosity rages between the mullet and the sea-bass, and between the conger and the moray, which

dentes. polypum in tantum locusta pavet ut si iuxta viderit omnino moriatur, locustam conger; rursus polypum congri lacerant. Nigidius auctor est praerodere caudam mugili lupum. eosdemque statis[1] mensibus concordes esse, omnes autem 186 vivere quibus caudae sic amputentur. at e contrario amicitiae exempla sunt, praeter illa quorum diximus societatem, ballaena et musculus, quando praegravi superciliorum pondere obrutis eius oculis infestantia magnitudinem vada praenatans demonstrat oculorumque vice fungitur.

Hinc volucrum naturae dicentur.

[1] *v.l.* aestatis.

gnaw each other's tails. The langouste is so terrified of the polyp that it dies if it merely sees one near to it, and so does the conger if it sees a langouste; while on the other hand congers tear a polyp to pieces. Nigidius states that the sea-bass gnaws at the tail of the mullet, although they are friendly together in certain months, but that all the mullets with their tails amputated in this way continue to live. But on the other hand instances of friendship, in addition to the creatures whose alliance we have mentioned,[a] are the whale and the file-fish: because the whale's eyes are over-burdened with the excessively heavy weight of its brows the file-fish swims in front of it and points out the shallows dangerous to its bulky size, so acting as a substitute for eyes.

There will follow an account of the natures of birds.

[a] See § 142.

BOOK X

LIBER X

I. Sequitur natura avium, quarum grandissimi et paene bestiarum generis struthocameli Africi vel Aethiopici altitudinem equitis insidentis equo excedunt, celeritatem vincunt, ad hoc demum datis pinnis ut currentem adiuvent: cetero non sunt volucres nec a terra attolluntur.[1] ungulae iis cervinis similes quibus dimicant, bisulcae et conprehendendis lapidibus utiles quos in fuga contra 2 sequentes ingerunt pedibus. concoquendi sine dilectu devorata mira natura, sed non minus stoliditas in tanta reliqui corporis altitudine cum colla frutice occultaverint latere sese existimantium. praemira[2] ex iis ova propter amplitudinem quibusdam habita pro vasis, conosque bellicos et galeas adornantes pinnae.

3   II. Aethiopiae atque Indis discolores maxime et inenarrabiles esse[3] ferunt aves et ante omnes nobilem Arabiae phoenicem, haut scio an fabulose, unum in toto orbe nec visum magno opere. aquilae narratur magnitudine, auri fulgore circa colla, cetero purpureus, caeruleam roseis caudam pinnis distingu-

---

[1] *Mayhoff*: tolluntur.
[2] *Detlefsen*: praemia.
[3] *sic? Mayhoff*: Aethiopes atque Indi . . . inenarrabiles.

---

[a] This description tallies fairly closely with the golden pheasant of the Far East.

BOOK X

I. The next subject is the Nature of Birds. Of
these the largest species, which almost belongs to the
class of animals, the ostrich of Africa or Ethiopia,
exceeds the height and surpasses the speed of a
mounted horseman, its wings being bestowed upon
it merely as an assistance in running, but otherwise
it is not a flying creature and does not rise from
the earth.   It has talons resembling a stag's hooves,
which it uses as weapons; they are cloven in two,
and are useful for grasping stones which when in
flight it flings with its feet against its pursuers.   Its
capacity for digesting the objects that it swallows
down indiscriminately is remarkable, but not less so
is its stupidity in thinking that it is concealed when
it has hidden its neck among bushes, in spite of the
great height of the rest of its body.   The eggs of the
ostrich are extremely remarkable for their size;
some people use them as vessels, and the feathers for
adorning the crests and helmets of warriors.

II. They say that Ethiopia and the Indies possess
birds extremely variegated in colour and indescribable, and that Arabia has one that is famous before
all others (though perhaps it is fabulous), the phoenix,
the only one in the whole world and hardly ever
seen.   The story is *a* that it is as large as an eagle, and
has a gleam of gold round its neck and all the rest of
it is purple, but the tail blue picked out with rose-

entibus, cristis fauces, caputque plumeo apice
4 honestante. primus atque diligentissime togatorum
de eo prodidit Manilius senator ille maximis nobilis
doctrinis doctore nullo: neminem exstitisse qui
viderit vescentem, sacrum in Arabia Soli esse,
vivere annis DXL, senescentem cassiae turisque
surculis construere nidum, replere odoribus et
superemori; ex ossibus deinde et medullis eius nasci
primo ceu vermiculum, inde fieri pullum, principioque
iusta funera priori reddere et totum deferre nidum
prope Panchaiam in Solis urbem et in ara ibi deponere.
5 cum huius alitis vita magni conversionem anni fieri
prodit idem Manilius, iterumque significationes
tempestatum et siderum easdem reverti, hoc autem
circa meridiem incipere quo die signum arietis
sol intraverit, et fuisse eius conversionis annum
prodente se P. Licinio Cn. Cornelio coss. CCXV.
Cornelius Valerianus phoenicem devolavisse in
Aegyptum tradit Q. Plautio Sexto Papinio coss.;
allatus est et in urbem Claudii principis censura
anno urbis DCCC et in comitio propositus, quod
actis testatum est, sed quem falsum esse nemo
dubitaret.
6 III. Ex his quas novimus aquilae maximus honos,
maxima et vis. sex earum genera, melanaetos a

ᵃ 97 B.C.   ᵇ A.D. 36.   ᶜ A.D. 47.

ᵈ Of these *melanaetos* is either the Golden or the Imperial
Eagle, *pygargus* is the White-tailed Sea-Eagle or erne,
haliaetos the Osprey, *morphnos* or *percnos* the Bald Buzzard;
but *percnopterus* and *gnesius* are unidentifiable as species
separate from the others.

coloured feathers and the throat picked out with tufts, and a feathered crest adorning its head. The first and the most detailed Roman account of it was given by Manilius, the eminent senator famed for his extreme and varied learning acquired without a teacher: he stated that nobody has ever existed that has seen one feeding, that in Arabia it is sacred to the Sun-god, that it lives 540 years, that when it is growing old it constructs a nest with sprigs of wild cinnamon and frankincense, fills it with scents and lies on it till it dies; that subsequently from its bones and marrow is born first a sort of maggot, and this grows into a chicken, and that this begins by paying due funeral rites to the former bird and carrying the whole nest down to the City of the Sun near Panchaia and depositing it upon an altar there. Manilius also states that the period of the Great Year coincides with the life of this bird, and that the same indications of the seasons and stars return again, and that this begins about noon on the day on which the sun enters the sign of the Ram, and that the year of this period had been 215, as reported by him, in the consulship [a] of Publius Licinius and Gnaeus Cornelius. Cornelius Valerianus reports that a phoenix flew down into Egypt in the consulship [b] of Quintus Plautius and Sextus Papinius; it was even brought to Rome in the Censorship of the Emperor Claudius, A.U.C. 800 [c] and displayed in the Comitium, a fact attested by the Records, although nobody would doubt that this phoenix was a fabrication.

III. Of the birds known to us the eagle is the most honourable and also the strongest. Of eagles there are six kinds. [d] The one called by the Greeks the black

Varieties of eagle.

295

Graecis dicta, eadem leporaria,[1] minima magnitudine, viribus praecipua, colore nigricans. sola aquilarum fetus suos alit, ceterae, ut dicemus, fugant; sola sine clangore, sine murmuratione. conversatur autem in 7 montibus. secundi generis pygargus in oppidis et in campis, albicante cauda. tertii morphnos, quam Homerus et percnum vocat, aliqui et plangum et anatariam, secunda magnitudine et vi; huic vita circa lacus. Phemonoe Apollinis dicta filia dentes esse ei prodidit mutae alias carentique lingua, eandem aquilarum nigerrimam, prominentiore cauda. consentit et Boethus.[2] ingenium est ei[3] testudines raptas frangere e sublimi iaciendo, quae fors interemit poetam Aeschylum praedictam fatis, ut ferunt, eius- 8 modi[4] ruinam secura caeli fide caventem. item quarti generis est percnopterus, eadem oripelargus, vul- turina specie alis minimis, reliqua magnitudine antecellens, sed inbellis et degener, ut quam verberet corvus. eadem ieiunae semper aviditatis et querulae murmurationis. sola aquilarum exanimata[5] aufert[6] corpora, ceterae cum occidere considunt. haec facit ut quintum genus γνήσιον vocetur velut verum solumque incorruptae originis, media magnitudine, colore subrutilo, rarum conspectu. superest

---

[1] *Mueller* (cf. λαγωφόνος *Ar.*): in Valeria.
[2] *Edd.* (Boeus. huius *Detlefsen*): Boethuius.
[3] *v.l.* et.
[4] *Rackham* (eius diei *edd.*); eidei *aut* diei.
[5] *Dalecamp*: exanima.
[6] *Rackham*: fert.

---

[a] Aristotle calls it the hare-killing eagle.
[b] Probably the marsh-harrier.
[c] Priestess at Delphi.
[d] *I.e.* by keeping in the open and avoiding trees and buildings from which objects might fall on him.

eagle, and also the hare-eagle,[a] is smallest in size and of outstanding strength; it is of a blackish colour. It is the only eagle that rears its own young, whereas all the others, as we shall describe, drive them away; and it is the only one that has no scream or cry. Its haunt is in the mountains. To the second kind belongs the white-rump eagle found in towns and in level country; it has a whitish tail. To the third the *morphnos*,[b] which Homer also calls the dusky eagle, and some the *plangos* and also the duck-eagle; it is second in size and strength, and it lives in the neighbourhood of lakes. Phemonoe,[c] who was styled Daughter of Apollo, has stated that it possesses teeth, but that it is mute and voiceless; also that it is the darkest of the eagles in colour, and has an exceptionally prominent tail. Boethus also agrees. It has a clever device for breaking tortoise-shells that it has carried off, by dropping them from a height; this accident caused the death of the poet Aeschylus, who was trying to avoid a disaster of this nature that had been foretold by the fates, as the story goes, by trustfully relying on the open sky.[d] Next, the fourth class comprises the hawk-eagle, also called the mountain stork, which resembles a vulture in having very small wings but exceeds it in the size of its other parts, and yet is unwarlike and degenerate, as it allows a crow to flog it. It is always ravenously greedy, and keeps up a plaintive screaming. It is the only eagle that carries away the dead bodies of its prey; all the others after killing alight on the spot. This species causes the fifth kind to be called the ' true eagle,' as being the genuine kind and the only pure-bred one; it is of medium size and dull reddish colour, and it is rarely seen. There remains

haliaëtus, clarissima oculorum acie, librans ex alto
sese visoque in mari pisce praeceps in eum ruens et
9 discussis pectore aquis rapiens. illa quam tertiam
fecimus aquaticas aves circa stagna adpetit mergentes
se subinde, donec sopitas lassatasque rapiat. spectanda dimicatio, ave ad perfugia litorum tendente,
maxime si condensa harundo sit, aquila inde ictu
abigente alae et, cum adpetat in lacu, scandente [1]
umbramque suam nanti sub aqua a litore ostendente,
rursus ave in diversa [2] et ubi minime se credat expec-
tari emergente. haec causa gregatim avibus natandi,
quia plures simul non infestantur respersu pinnarum hostem occaecantes. saepe et aquilae ipsae non
tolerantes pondus adprehensum una merguntur.
10 haliaëtus tantum inplumes etiamnum pullos suos
percutiens subinde cogit adversos intueri solis radios
et, si coniventem humectantemque animadvertit,
praecipitat e nido velut adulterinum atque degene-
rem; illum cuius acies firma contra stetit educat.
11 haliaëti suum genus non habent, sed ex diverso
aquilarum coitu nascuntur; id quidem quod ex his
natum est in ossifragis genus habet e quibus vultures
minores progenerantur, et ex his magni qui omnino
non generant. quidam adiciunt genus aquilae
quam barbatam vocant, Tusci vero ossifragam.
12   IV. Tribus primis et quinto aquilarum generi

---

[1] *Mayhoff*: cadente.   [2] *v.l.* diverso.

[a] Perhaps the lämmergeier, *gypaetus barbatus.*

the osprey, which has very keen eye-sight, and which hovers at a great height and when it sees a fish in the sea drops on it with a swoop and cleaving the water with its breast catches it. The species that we made the third hunts round marshes for water-birds, which at once dive, till they become drowsy and exhausted, when it catches them. The duel is worth watching, the bird making for refuge on the shore, especially if there is a dense reed-bed, and the eagle driving it away from the shore with a blow of its wing; and when it is hunting its quarry in a lake, soaring and showing its shadow to the bird swimming under water away from the shore, so that the bird turns back again and comes to the surface at a place where it thinks it is least expected. This is the reason why birds swim in flocks, because several are not attacked at the same time, since they blind the enemy by splashing him with their wings. Often even the eagles themselves cannot carry the weight of their catch and are drowned with it. The sea-eagle only compels its still unfledged chicks by beating them to gaze full at the rays of the sun, and if it notices one blinking and with its eyes watering flings it out of the nest as a bastard and not true to stock, whereas one whose gaze stands firm against the light it rears. Sea-eagles have no breed of their own but are born from cross-breeding with other eagles; but the offspring of a pair of sea-eagles belongs to the osprey genus, from which spring the smaller vultures, and from these the great vultures which do not breed at all. Some people add a species of eagle which they call the bearded eagle,[a] but which the Tuscans call an ossifrage.

IV. The three first and the fifth kinds of eagle have *Eagles' nests.*

inaedificatur nido lapis aëtites (quem aliqui dixere gagiten[1]) ad multa remedia utilis, nihil igne deperdens. est autem lapis iste praegnans intus alio, cum quatias velut in urceo[2] sonante. sed vis illa
13 medica non nisi nido dereptis. nidificant in petris et arboribus, pariunt et ova terna, excludunt pullos binos, visi sunt et tres aliquando. alterum expellunt taedio nutriendi: quippe eo tempore ipsis cibum negavit natura prospiciens ne omnium ferarum fetus raperentur; ungues quoque earum invertuntur diebus iis, albescunt inedia pinnae, ut merito partus suos oderint. sed eiectos ab his cognatum genus
14 ossifragi excipiunt et educant cum suis. verum adultos quoque persequitur parens et longe fugat, aemulos scilicet rapinae. et alioquin unum par aquilarum magno ad populandum tractu, ut satietur, indiget; determinant ergo spatia, nec in proximo praedantur. rapta non protinus ferunt, sed primo deponunt, expertaeque pondus tunc demum avehunt.[3]
15 oppetunt non senio nec aegritudine sed fame, in tantum superiore adcrescente rostro ut aduncitas aperiri non queat. a meridiano autem tempore operantur et volant, prioribus horis diei, donec

---

[1] *V.ll.* gagyten, gagaten.   [2] *Mueller*: utero.
[3] *Pintianus*: abeunt.

---

[a] See § 11 *n.*

the stone called eagle-stone (named by some *gagites*)
built into their nests, which is useful for many cures,
and loses none of its virtue by fire. The stone in
question is big with another inside it, which rattles
as if in a jar when you shake it. But only those
taken from a nest possess the medicinal power
referred to. They build their nests in rocks and
trees, and lay as many as three eggs at a time, but
they shut out two chicks of the brood, and have been
seen on occasion to eject even three. They drive
out the other chick when they are tired of feeding it :
indeed at this period nature has denied food to the
parent birds themselves as a precaution, so that the
young of all the wild animals should not be plundered ;
also during those days the birds' talons turn inward,
and their feathers grow white from want of food, so
that with good reason they hate their own offspring.
But the chicks thrown out by these birds are received
by the kindred breed, the bearded eagles,[a] who
rear them with their own. However the parent bird
pursues them even when grown up, and drives them
far away, doubtless because they are competitors in
the chase. And apart from this a single pair of eagles
in order to get enough food requires a large tract of
country to hunt over ; consequently they mark out
districts, and do not poach on their neighbours' preserves. When they have made a catch they do not
carry it off at once, but first lay it on the ground, and
only fly away with it after first testing its weight.
They meet their end not from old age nor sickness but
from hunger, as their upper mandible grows to such a
size that it is too hooked for them to be able to open it.
They get busy and fly in the afternoon, but in the
earlier hours of the day they perch quite idle till the

impleantur hominum conventu fora, ignavae sedent.
aquilarum pinnae mixtas reliquarum alitum pinnas
devorant. negant umquam solam hanc alitem
fulmine exanimatam; ideo armigeram Iovis consuetudo iudicavit.

16 V. Romanis eam legionibus Gaius Marius in
secundo consulatu suo proprie dicavit. erat et antea
prima cum quattuor aliis: lupi, minotauri, equi
aprique singulos ordines anteibant; paucis ante annis
sola in aciem portari coepta erat, reliqua in castris
relinquebantur; Marius in totum ea abdicavit. ex
eo notatum non fere legionis umquam hiberna esse
castra ubi aquilarum non sit iugum.

17 Primo et secundo generi non minorum tantum
quadripedum rapina sed etiam cum cervis proelia.
multum pulverem volutatu collectum insidens cornibus excutit in oculos, pinnis ora verberans, donec
praecipitet in rupes. nec unus hostis illi satis: est
acrior[1] cum dracone pugna multoque magis anceps,
etiamsi in aere. ova hic consectatur aquilae aviditate
malefica; aquila[2] hoc rapit ubicumque visum. ille
multiplici nexu alas ligat ita se inplicans ut simul
decidat ipse.[3]

18 VI. Celebris apud Seston urbem aquilae gloria
est: educatam a virgine retulisse gratiam aves primo,

---

[1] v.l. satis est; acrior est.
[2] Mayhoff: ab illa aut at illa.
[3] ipse Mayhoff: saepe (aut est percelebris).

---

[a] Pliny is translating περὶ ἀγορὰν πλήθουσαν.
[b] 104 B.C.

market-places fill with a gathering of people.ᵃ If eagles' feathers have the feathers of any other birds mixed with them, they swallow them up. It is stated that this is the only bird that is never killed by a thunderbolt; this is why custom has deemed the eagle to be Jupiter's armour-bearer.

V. The eagle was assigned to the Roman legions as their special badge by Gaius Marius in his second consulship.ᵇ Even previously it had been their first badge, with four others, wolves, minotaurs, horses and boars going in front of the respective ranks; but a few years before the custom had come in of carrying the eagles alone into action, the rest being left behind in camp. Marius discarded them altogether. Thenceforward it was noticed that there was scarcely ever a legion's winter camp without a pair of eagles being in the neighbourhood. *The eagle as a military badge.*

The first and second kinds not only carry off the smaller four-footed animals but actually do battle with stags. The eagle collects a quantity of dust by rolling in it, and perching on the stag's horns shakes it off into its eyes, striking its head with its wings, until it brings it down on to the rocks. Nor is it content with one foe: it has a fiercer battle with a great serpent, and one that is of much more doubtful issue, even though it is in the air. The serpent with mischievous greed tries to get the eagle's eggs; consequently the eagle carries it off wherever seen. The serpent fetters its wings by twining itself round them in manifold coils so closely that it falls to the ground itself with the snake. *Eagles v. stags and snakes.*

VI. At the city of Sestos the fame of an eagle is celebrated, the story being that it was reared by a maiden and that it repaid its gratitude by bringing *The eagle of Sestos.*

mox deinde venatus adgerentem, defuncta postremo
in rogum accensum eius iniecisse sese et simul
conflagrasse. quam ob causam incolae quod vocant
heroum in eo loco fecere appellatum Iovis et virginis,
quoniam illi deo ales adscribitur.

19   VII. Vulturum praevalent nigri. nidos nemo
attigit; ideo et fuere qui putarent illos ex adverso
orbe advolare, falso: nidificant in excelsissimis
rupibus. fetus quidem saepe cernuntur, fere bini.
Umbricius haruspicum in nostro aevo peritissimus
parere tradit ova tredecim, uno ex his reliqua ova
nidumque lustrare, mox abicere; triduo autem ante
advolare eos ubi cadavera futura sunt.

20   VIII. Sanqualem avem atque inmusulum augures
Romani magna in quaestione habent. inmusulum
aliqui vulturis pullum arbitrantur esse et sanqualem
ossifragae. Masurius sanqualem ossifragam esse
dicit, inmusulum autem pullum aquilae priusquam
albicet cauda. quidam post Mucium augurem visos
non esse Romae confirmavere, ego, quod veri similius,
in desidia rerum omnium arbitror non agnitos.

21   IX. Accipitrum genera sedecim invenimus: ex his
aegithum claudum altero pede prosperrimi augurii
nuptialibus negotiis et pecuariae rei: triorchem a
numero testium, cui principatum in auguriis Phemo-

---

to her first birds and soon afterwards big game, and when finally she died it threw itself upon her lighted pyre and was burnt with her. On account of this the inhabitants made what is called a *heroon* in that place, which is named the Shrine of Jupiter and the Maiden, because the bird is assigned to that deity.

VII. Of vultures the black are the strongest. No one has ever reached their nests, and consequently there have actually been persons who have thought that they fly here from the opposite side of the globe. This is a mistake: they make their nests on extremely lofty crags. Their chicks indeed are often seen, usually in pairs. The most learned augur of our age, Umbricius, states that they lay thirteen eggs, but use one of them for cleaning the remaining eggs and the nest and then throw it away; but that three days before they lay the eggs they fly to some place where there will be dead bodies. *The vulture*

VIII. There is great question among the Roman augurs about the sanqualis and the immusulus. Some think that the immusulus is the chick of the vulture and the sanqualis of the bearded vulture. Masurius says that the sanqualis is a bearded vulture and the immusulus an eagle's chick before its tail turns white. Some persons have asserted that they have not been seen at Rome since the time of the augur Mucius,[a] but for my own part I think it more probable that in the general slackness that prevails they have not been recognized. *The sanqualis and the immusulus.*

IX. Of hawks we find sixteen kinds, and among these the aegithus, which when lame in one foot is of very fortunate omen for marriage contracts and for property in cattle, and the triorchis, named from the number of its testicles, the bird to which Phemonoe *Varieties of hawk: the aegithus;*

305

noe dedit. buteonem hunc appellant Romani,
familia etiam ex eo cognominata, cum prospero
auspicio in ducis navi sedisset. epileum Graeci
vocant qui solus omni tempore apparet, ceteri hieme
22 abeunt. distinctio generum ex aviditate: alii non
nisi e terra rapiunt avem, alii non nisi circa arbores
volitantem, alii sedentem in sublimi, aliqui volantem
in aperto. itaque et columbae novere ex his pericula,
visoque considunt, vel subvolant, contra naturam eius
auxiliantes sibi. in insula Africae Cerne in oceano
accipitres totius Massaesyliae humi fetificant, nec
alibi nascuntur, illis adsueti gentibus.
23   X. In Thraciae parte super Amphipolim homines
et accipitres societate quadam aucupantur: hi ex
silvis et harundinetis excitant aves, illi supervolantes
deprimunt rursus; captas aucupes dividunt cum his.
traditum est missas in sublime ibi[1] excipere eos, et
cum sit tempus capturae, clangore ac volatus genere
invitare ad occasionem. simile quiddam lupi ad
Maeotim paludem faciunt; nam nisi partem a
piscantibus suam accepere, expansa eorum retia
lacerant.
24   Accipitres avium non edunt corda. nocturnus
accipiter cybindis vocatur, rarus etiam in silvis, interdiu minus cernens. bellum internecivum gerit cum
aquila, cohaerentesque saepe prenduntur.

---

[1] *v.l.* sibi.

---

[a] *I.e.* buzzard.
[b] Some way down the N.W. African coast outside the Straits
of Gibraltar.

gave primacy among auguries. The Roman name for it is *buteo,*[a] which is also the surname of a family, assumed because one perched on an admiral's ship with good omen. The Greeks give the name of merlin to the only species that appears at every *the merlin.* season, whereas all the others go away in winter. The varieties of hawks are distinguished by their appetite for food: some only snatch a bird off the ground, others only one fluttering round a tree, others one that perches high in the branches, others one flying in the open. Consequently even the doves know the risks that they run from hawks, and when they see one they alight, or else fly upward, safeguarding themselves by going counter to the hawk's nature. The hawks of the whole of Massaesylia lay their eggs on the ground in Cerne,[b] an island of Africa in the Ocean, and they do not breed elsewhere, as they are accustomed to the natives of that island.

X. In the district of Thrace inland from Amphipolis *Hawking.* men and hawks have a sort of partnership for fowling: the men put up the birds from woods and reed-beds and the hawks flying overhead drive them down again; the fowlers share the bag with the hawks. It is reported that when the birds have been put up the hawks intercept them in the air, and when it is time for a catch invite the sportsmen to take the opportunity by their screaming and their way of flying. Wolf-fish at the Maeotic Marsh act somewhat in the same way, for unless they get their share from fishermen they tear their nets when spread.

Hawks do not eat the hearts of birds. The night-hawk is called *cybindis*; it is rare even in forests, and cannot see very well in the daytime. It wages war to the death with the eagle, and they are often taken clinging together in each other's clutches. *The night-hawk.*

25 XI. Coccyx videtur ex accipitre fieri tempore anni
figuram mutans, quoniam tunc non apparent reliqui
nisi perquam paucis diebus, ipse quoque modico
tempore aestatis visus non cernitur postea. est
autem neque aduncis unguibus, solus accipitrum,
nec capite similis illis neque alio quam colore, habitu [1]
columbi potius. quin et absumitur ab accipitre, si
quando una apparuere, sola omnium avis a suo genere
26 interempta. mutat autem et vocem. procedit vere,
occultatur caniculae ortu, inter quae [2] parit in alienis
nidis, maxime palumbium, maiore ex parte singula
ova, quod nulla alia avis, raro bina. causa pullos
subiciendi putatur quod sciat se invisam cunctis
avibus, nam minutae quoque infestant; ita non fore
tutam generi suo stirpem opinatur ni fefellerit, quare
nullum facit nidum, alioqui [3] trepidum animal.
27 educat ergo subditum adulterato feta nido. ille
avidus ex natura praeripit cibos reliquis pullis, itaque
et nitidus in se nutricem convertit. illa gaudet eius
specie miraturque sese ipsam quod talem pepererit;
suos comparatione eius damnat ut alienos. absu-
mique etiam se inspectante patitur, donec corripiat

[1] *Dellefsen*: ac visu *aut* ac victu.
[2] *Mayhoff*: interque (semperque *edd.*).
[3] ⟨et⟩ alioqui? *Mayhoff.*

---

a This belief is held at the present time in some parts of
Britain. Of course the cuckoo is not of the hawk species.
b It is really a migrant.
c As a matter of fact this is never the case.
d All of what follows is untrue.

XI. The cuckoo seems to be made by changing its shape out of a hawk *a* at a certain season of the year, as the rest of the hawks do not appear then, except on a very few days, and the cuckoo itself also after being seen for a moderate period of the summer is not observed afterwards. But the cuckoo is alone among the hawks in not having crooked talons, and also it is not like the other hawks in the head or in anything else but colour: it rather has the general appearance of the pigeon. Moreover a hawk will eat a cuckoo, if ever both have appeared at the same time: the cuckoo is the only one of all the birds that is killed by its own kind. And it also changes its voice. It comes out in the spring and goes into hiding *b* at the rising of the dog-star, between which dates it lays its eggs in the nests of other birds, usually *c* wood-pigeons, for the most part one egg at a time, as does no other bird; it seldom lays two. Its reason for foisting its chicks on other birds is supposed to be that it knows itself to be hated by the whole of the birds, for even the very small birds attack it; consequently it thinks that a progeny will not be secured for its race unless it has escaped notice, for which reason it makes no nest; it is a timid creature in general. Therefore the brooding hen in the nest thus cuckolded rears the changeling. The young cuckoo *d* being by nature greedy snatches the bits of food away from the rest of the chicks, and so gets fat and attracts the mother bird to itself by its sleek appearance. She delights in its beauty and admires herself for having borne such a child, while in comparison with it she convicts her own chicks of not belonging to her, and lets them be eaten up even under her own eyes, until finally the cuckoo,

PLINY: NATURAL HISTORY

ipsam quoque iam volandi potens.   nulla tunc avium
suavitate carnis comparatur illi.

28   XII. Milvi ex eodem accipitrum genere magnitudine differunt. notatum in his rapacissimam et
famelicam semper alitem nihil esculenti rapere
umquam ex funerum ferculis nec Olympiae ex ara,
ac ne ferentium quidem manibus nisi lugubri manci-
piorum [1] immolantium ostento.   idem videntur artem
gubernandi docuisse caudae flexibus, in caelo
monstrante natura quod opus esset in profundo.
milvi et ipsi hibernis mensibus latent, non tamen ante
hirundinem abeuntes; traduntur autem et a solstitiis
adfici podagra.

29   XIII. Volucrum prima distinctio pedibus maxime
constat; aut enim aduncos ungues habent aut digitos,
aut palmipedum in genere sunt ut anseres et aquaticae fere aves. aduncos ungues habentia carne
30 tantum vescuntur ex parte magna; (XIV) cornices et
alio pabulo, ut quae duritiam nucis rostro repugnan-
tem volantes in altum in saxa tegulasve iaciant
iterum ac saepius, donec quassatam perfringere
queant. ipsa ales est inauspicatae garrulitatis, a
quibusdam tamen laudata. ab arcturi sidere ad
hirundinum adventum notatur eam in Minervae lucis
templisque raro, alicubi omnino non aspici, sicut
Athenis: inauspicatissima fetus tempore, hoc est
post solstitium.[2] praeterea sola haec etiam volantes

----
[1] *Detlefsen*: municipiorum.
[2] inauspicatissima . . . solstitium *hic Mueller*: *post* pascit *codd.*

----
[a] Crows as a matter of fact have no talons.

310

now able to fly, seizes the mother bird herself as well. At this stage no sort of bird will compare with a young cuckoo for savoury flavour.

XII. Kites belong to the same genus as hawks *The kite.* but differ in size. It has been noticed in regard to this species that though a most rapacious bird and always hungry it never steals any edible from the oblations at funerals nor from the altar at Olympia and not even out of the hands of the people bringing the offsprings except with a gloomy portent for the slaves performing the sacrifice. Also it seems that this bird by its manipulation of its tail taught the art of steersmanship, nature demonstrating in the sky what was required in the deep. Kites themselves also are not seen in the winter months, though not departing before the swallow; it is reported however that they suffer from gout even from midsummer onward.

XIII. The primary distinction between birds is *Taloned* established especially by the feet; for either they *birds : the* have hooked talons or claws or they are in the web- *crow ;* footed class like geese and water-fowl generally. If they have hooked talons they live for the most part only on flesh; (XIV) though crows *a* eat other food as well, as if a nut is so hard that it resists their beak they fly up aloft and drop it two or more times on to rocks or roof-tiles, till it is cracked and they can break it open. The bird itself has a persistent croak that is unlucky, although some people speak well of it. It is noticed that from the rising of Arcturus to the arrival of the swallows it is rarely seen in groves and temples of Minerva and never at all elsewhere, as is the case at Athens; it is most unlucky at its breeding season, that is, after midsummer. Moreover this bird alone

31 pullos aliquamdiu pascit; (XV) ceterae omnes ex
eodem genere pellunt nidis pullos ac volare cogunt,
sicut et corvi; qui et ipsi non carne tantum aluntur
sed robustos quoque fetus suos fugant longius.
itaque parvis in vicis non plus bina coniugia sunt,
circa Crannonem quidem Thes- saliae singula
perpetuo; genitores suboli loco cedunt.

32   Diversa in hac et supradicta alite quaedam.
corvi ante solstitium generant, idem aegrescunt
sexagenis diebus, siti maxime, antequam fici co-
quantur autumno; cornix ab eo tempore corripitur
morbo.

Corvi pariunt cum plurimum quinos. ore eos
parere aut coire vulgus arbitratur (ideoque gravidas,
si ederint corvinum ovum, per os partum reddere,
atque in totum difficulter parere si tecto inferantur);
Aristoteles negat, non Hercule magis quam in
Aegypto ibim, sed illam exosculationem (quae saepe

33 cernitur) qualem in columbis esse. corvi in auspiciis
soli videntur intellectum habere significationum
suarum; nam cum [1] Medi hospites occisi sunt,
omnes e Peloponneso et Attica regione volaverunt.
pessima eorum significatio cum gluttiunt vocem velut
strangulati.

[1] cum ⟨ad Pharsalam⟩? *Mayhoff ex Ar. Post. An.* IX
619b 14.

---

[a] This is from Aristotle *Hist. An.* IX 618b 14. Medus or
Medeios, son of Medea, was supposed to have given the
Medes their name.

continues feeding its chicks for some time even when they can fly; (XV) whereas all the other birds of the same class drive their chicks out of the nests and compel them to fly, as also do ravens. These not only feed on flesh themselves too, but also drive away their chicks when strong to a considerable distance. Consequently in small villages there are not more than two pairs of ravens, and in fact in the neighbourhood of Crannon in Thessaly there is one pair permanently in each place; the parents retire to make room for their offspring.

There are certain points of difference between this *the raven;* bird and the one mentioned above. Ravens breed before midsummer, also they have 60 days of illhealth, principally owing to thirst, before the figs ripen in the autumn; whereas the crow is seized with sickness from that day onward.

Ravens produce broods of five at most. There is a popular belief that they lay eggs, or else mate, with the beak (and that consequently if women with child eat a raven's egg they bear the infant through the mouth, and that altogether they have a difficult delivery if raven's eggs are brought into the house); but Aristotle says that this is not true of the raven, any more indeed than it is of the ibis in Egypt, but that the billing in question (which is often noticed) is a form of kissing, like that which takes place between pigeons. Ravens seem to be the only birds that have an understanding of the meanings that they convey in auspices; for when the guests of Medus were murdered, all the ravens in the Peloponnese and Attica flew away.[a] It is a specially bad omen when they gulp down their croak as if they were choking.

34　XVI. Uncos ungues et nocturnae aves habent, ut noctuae, bubo, ululae. omnium horum hebetes interdiu oculi. bubo funebris et maxime abominatus publicis praecipue auspiciis deserta incolit nec tantum desolata sed dira etiam et inaccessa, noctis monstrum, nec cantu aliquo vocalis sed gemitu.

35 itaque in urbibus aut omnino in luce visus dirum ostentum est; privatorum domibus insidentem plurium scio non fuisse feralem. volat numquam quo libuit, sed traversus aufertur. Capitolii cellam ipsam intravit Sexto Palpellio Histro L. Pedanio coss., propter quod nonis Martiis urbs lustrata est eo anno.

36　XVII. Inauspicata est et incendiaria avis, quam propter saepenumero lustratam urbem in annalibus invenimus, sicut L. Cassio C. Mario coss., quo anno et bubone viso lustratam esse. quae sit avis ea non reperitur nec traditur. quidam ita interpretantur, incendiariam esse quaecumque apparuerit carbonem ferens ex aris vel altaribus: alii spinturnicem eam vocant, sed haec ipsa quae esset inter aves

37 qui se scire diceret non inveni. cliviam quoque avem ab antiquis nominatam animadverto ignorari—quidam clamatoriam dicunt, Labeo prohibitoriam; et apud

---

a A.D. 43.　　　　*b* 107 B.C.
c Σπινθαρίς.

XVI. Night birds also have hooked talons, for *owls.* instance the little owl, the eagle-owl and the screech-owl. All of these are dim-sighted in the daytime. The eagle-owl is a funereal bird, and is regarded as an extremely bad omen, especially at public auspices; it inhabits deserts and places that are not merely unfrequented but terrifying and inaccessible; a wierd creature of the night, its cry is not a musical note but a scream. Consequenlty when seen in cities or by daylight in any circumstances it is a direful portent; but I know several cases of its having perched on the houses of private persons without fatal consequences. It never flies in the direction where it wants to go, but travels slantwise out of its course. In the consulship *a* of Sextus Palpellius Hister and Lucius Pedanius an eagle-owl entered the very shrine of the Capitol, on account of which a purification of the city was held on March 7th in that year.

XVII. There is also a bird of ill-omen called the *Unknown* fire-bird, on account of which we find in the annals *birds of ill-omen.* that the city has often had a ritual purification, for instance in the consulship *b* of Lucius Cassius and Gaius Marius, in which year the appearance of an eagle-owl also occasioned a purification. What this bird was I cannot discover, and it is not recorded. Some persons give this interpretation, that the fire-bird was any bird that was seen carrying a coal from an altar or altar-table; others call it a 'spinturnix,' *c* but I have not found anybody who professes to know what particular species of bird that is. I also notice that the bird named by the ancients 'clivia' is unidentified—some call it 'screech-owl,' Labeo 'warning owl'; and moreover

315

Nigidium insuper [1] appellatur avis quae aquilarum
ova frangat. sunt praeterea conplura genera depicta
in Etrusca disciplina saeculis non visa, quae nunc
defecisse mirum est cum abundent etiam quae gula
humana populatur.

38   XVIII. Externorum de auguriis peritissime scrip-
sisse Hylas nomine putatur. is tradit noctuam,
bubonem, picum arbores cavantem, trygonam,
cornicem a cauda ovo [2] exire, quoniam pondere
capitum perversa ova posteriorem partem corporum
fovendam matri adplicent.

39   XIX. Noctuarum contra aves sollers dimicatio.
maiore circumdatae multitudine resupinae pedibus
repugnant collectaeque in artum rostro et unguibus
totae teguntur. auxiliatur accipiter collegio quodam naturae bellumque partitur. noctuas sexagenis
diebus hiemis cubare et novem voces habere tradit
Nigidius.

40   XX. Sunt et parvae aves uncorum unguium, ut
pici Martio cognomine insignes et in auspicatu [3]
magni. quo in genere arborum cavatores scandentes
in subrectum felium modo, illi vero et supini, percussi
corticis sono pabulum subesse intellegunt. pullos in
cavis educant avium soli. adactos cavernis eorum
a pastore cuneos admota quadam ab iis herba elabi

---

[1] insuper? *Mayhoff*: super.
[2] ovo? *Mayhoff*: de ovo.
[3] *Hardouin*: auspicatis *aut* auspiciis.

---

[a] An unknown bird.
[b] The red-headed Black Woodpecker.
[c] Repeated XXV 14 and there rejected.

a bird is cited in Nigidius that breaks eagles' eggs. There are besides a number of kinds described in Tuscan lore that have not been seen for generations, though it is surprising that they should have now become extinct when even kinds that are ravaged by man's greed continue plentiful.

XVIII. On the subject of the auguries of foreign races the writings of an author named Hylas are deemed to be the most learned. He states that the night-owl, eagle-owl, woodpecker, trygona[a] and raven come out of the egg tail first, because the eggs are turned the wrong way up by the weight of the heads and present the hinder part of the chicks' bodies to the mother to cherish. *Foreign birds of omen.*

XIX. Night-owls wage a crafty battle against other birds. When surrounded by a crowd that outnumbers them they lie on their backs and defend themselves with their feet, and bunching themselves up close are entirely protected by their beak and claws. Through a kind of natural alliance the hawk comes to their aid and takes part in the war. Nigidius relates that night-owls hibernate for 60 days every winter, and that they have nine cries. *The night-owl.*

XX. There are also small birds with hooked claws, for instance the variety of woodpeckers called Birds of Mars[b] that are important in taking auguries. In this class are the tree-hollowing woodpeckers that climb nearly straight upright in the manner of cats, but also the others that cling upside down, which know by the sound of the bark when they strike it that there is fodder underneath it. They are the only birds that rear their chicks in holes. There is a common belief[c] that when wedges are driven into their holes by a shepherd the birds by applying a *The woodpecker.*

PLINY: NATURAL HISTORY

creditur vulgo. Trebius auctor est clavum cuneumve
adactum quanta libeat vi arbori in qua nidum
habeat statim exilire cum crepitu arboris cum
41 insederit.[1] ipsi principales Latio sunt in auguriis a rege qui nomen huic avi dedit. unum
eorum praescitum transire non queo. in capite
praetoris urbani Aelii Tuberonis in foro iura pro
tribunali reddentis sedit ita placide ut manu pre-
henderetur. respondere vates exitium imperio por-
tendi si dimitteretur, at si exanimaretur praetori.
ille autem [2] protinus concerpsit, nec multo post implevit prodigium.
42   XXI. Vescuntur et glande in hoc genere pomisque
multae, sed quae carne tantum, non bibunt,[3] excepto
milvo, quod ipsum in auguriis dirum est. uncos
ungues habentes omnino non congregantur, et sibi
quaeque praedantur. sunt autem omnes fere altivolae praeter nocturnas, et magis maiores. omnibus
alae grandes, corpus exiguum. ambulant difficulter.
in petris raro consistunt curvatura unguium pro-
hibente.
43   XXII. Nunc de secundo genere dicamus, quod in
duas dividitur species, oscines et alites. illarum
generi cantus oris, his magnitudo differentiam dedit ;
itaque praecedent et ordine, omnesque reliquas in iis

---

[1] *Pintianus* : insederit clavo aut cuneo.
[2] *v.l.* et ille avem.   [3] *Mayhoff* : vivunt.

---

[a] Picus, father of Latinus, was changed into a woodpecker
by Circe, whose love he had slighted.
[b] Viz. *digitatae,* § 29.
[c] Cicero *N.D.* II 160, *Div.* I 120 gives the same classification.
The inclusion of the peacock in the latter class shows that the
term *ales* refers rather to display of the wings than to actual
flight ; and the inclusion of the cock is justified by pointing
318

kind of grass make them slip out again. Trebius
states that if you drive a nail or wedge with as much
force as you like into a tree in which a woodpecker
has a nest, when the bird perches on it it at once
springs out again with a creak of the tree. Woodpeckers themselves have been of the first importance
among auguries in Latium from the time of the king [a]
who gave his name to this bird. One presage of
theirs I cannot pass over. When Aelius Tubero,
City Praetor, was giving judgements from the bench
in the forum, a woodpecker perched on his head so
fearlessly that he was able to catch it in his hand.
In reply to enquiry the seers declared that disaster
was portended to the empire if the bird were released,
but to the praetor if it were killed. Tubero however
at once tore the bird in pieces; and not long afterwards he fulfilled the portent.

XXI. Many birds in this class feed also on acorns *Habits of*
and fruit, but those that eat only flesh do not drink, *taloned*
excepting the kite, and for a kite to drink counts in *species.*
itself as a direful augury. The birds having talons
never live in flocks, and each hunts for itself. But
they almost all except the night-birds among them
fly high, and the bigger ones higher. All have large
wings and a small body. They walk with difficulty.
They rarely perch on rocks, as the curve of their
talons prohibits this.

XXII. Now let us speak about the second class [b], *Clawed birds*
which is divided into two kinds, song-birds and *notable for*
plumage-birds.[c] The former kind are distinguished *their*
by their song and the latter by their size; so the *plumage.*
latter shall come first in order also, and among them

out that its *cantus* is preceeded by *plausus laterum,* and by
reference to its *tripudia,* §§ 46, 49.

319

pavonum genus cum forma tum intellectu eius et
gloria. gemmantes laudatus expandit colores adverso maxime sole, quia sic fulgentius radiant;
simul umbrae quosdam repercussus ceteris, qui et
in opaco clarius micant, conchata quaerit cauda,
omnesque in acervum contrahit pinnarum quos
44 spectari gaudet oculos. idem cauda annuis vicibus
amissa cum foliis arborum, donec renascatur alia cum
flore, pudibundus ac maerens quaerit latebram.
vivit annis xxv, colores fundere incipit in trimatu.
ab auctoribus non gloriosum tantum animal hoc
traditur, sed et malivolum, sicut anserem verecun-
dum—quoniam has quoque quidam addiderunt notas
in iis, haud probatas mihi.

45   XXIII. Pavonem cibi gratia Romae primus occidit
orator Hortensius aditiali cena sacerdotii. saginare
primus instituit circa novissimum piraticum bellum
M. Aufidius Lurco, eoque ex quaestu reditus HS.
sexagena milia habuit.

46   XXIV. Proxime gloriam sentiunt et hi nostri vigiles
nocturni quos excitandis in opera mortalibus rum-
pendoque somno natura genuit. norunt sidera et
ternas distinguunt horas interdiu cantu, cum sole eunt
cubitum, quartaque castrensi vigilia ad curas labor-
emque revocant nec solis ortum incautis patiuntur

ᵃ Piracy was put down by Pompey in 67 B.C.
ᵇ *I.e.* the fourth quarter of the night.

before all the rest will come the peacock class, both
because of its beauty and because of its consciousness
of and pride in it. When praised it spreads out its
jewelled colours directly facing the sun, because in
that way they gleam more brilliantly; and at the
same time by curving its tail like a shell it contrives
as it were reflexions of shadow for the rest of its
colours, which actually shine more brightly in the
dark, and it draws together into a cluster all the eyes
of its feathers, as it delights in having them looked at.
Moreover when it moults its tail feathers every year
with the fall of the leaves, it seeks in shame and
sorrow for a place of concealment until others are
born again with the spring flowers. It lives for 25
years, but it begins to shed its colours at the age of
three. The authorities relate that this creature is
not only ostentatious but also spiteful, just as the
goose is said to be modest—since some writers have
added these characteristics also in that species,
though I do not accept them.

XXIII. The first person at Rome to kill a peacock *The peacock for the table.*
for the table was the orator Hortensius, at the
inaugural banquet of his priesthood. Fattening
peacocks was first instituted about the time of the
last pirate war [a] by Marcus Aufidius Lurco, and he
made 60,000 sesterces profit from this trade.

XXIV. Nearly equally proud and self-conscious are *The farm-yard cock.*
also our Roman night-watchmen, a breed designed
by nature for the purpose of awakening mortals
for their labours and interrupting sleep. They are
skilled astronomers, and they mark every three-
hour period in the daytime with song, go to bed with
the sun, and at the fourth camp-watch [b] recall us
to our business and our labour and do not allow

obrepere, diemque venientem nuntiant cantu, ipsum
47 vero cantum plausu laterum. imperitant suo generi,
et regnum in quacumque sunt domo exercent. dimicatione paritur hoc inter ipsos, velut ideo tela agnata
cruribus suis intellegentium, nec finis saepe nisi [1]
commorientibus. quod si palma contigit,[2] statim in
victoria canunt seque ipsi principes testantur;
victus occultatur silens aegreque servitium patitur.
et plebs tamen aeque superba graditur ardua cervice,
cristis celsa, caelumque sola volucrum aspicit crebra,
in sublime caudam quoque falcatam erigens. itaque terrori sunt etiam leonibus ferarum generosissi-
48 mis. iam ex his quidam ad bella tantum et proelia
adsidua nascuntur—quibus etiam patrias nobilitarunt,
Rhodum aut Tanagram; secundus est honos habitus
Melicis et Chalcidicis,—ut plane dignae aliti tantum
49 honoris perhibeat Romana purpura. horum sunt
tripudia sollistima, hi magistratus nostros cotidie
regunt domusque ipsis suas claudunt aut reserant,
hi fasces Romanos inpellunt aut retinent, iubent acies
aut prohibent, victoriarum omnium toto orbe
partarum auspices; hi maxime terrarum imperio im-
perant, extis etiam fibrisque haut aliter quam opimae
victimae diis gratae. habent ostenta et [3] praeposteri
eorum vespertinique cantus: namque totis noctibus

---

[1] nisi *add. edd.*
[2] *Mayhoff* : contingit.
[3] *v.l.* ex se et (ex re cognita ? *Mayhoff*).

---

[a] Omens were taken from the way in which chickens kept
for the purpose ate grain given to them; it was a good sign
if they ate greedily, letting grain drop on the ground in a
'perfectly regular three-step,' *tripudium sollistimum*, like the
triple beat of the foot in a ritual dance.

the sunrise to creep upon us unawares, but herald the coming day with song, while they herald that song itself with a flapping of their wings against their sides. They lord it over their own race, and exercise royal sway in whatever household they live. This sovereignty they win by duelling with one another, seeming to understand that weapons grow upon their legs for this purpose, and often the fight only ends when they die together. If they win the palm, they at once sing a song of victory and proclaim themselves the champions, while the one defeated hides in silence and with difficulty endures servitude. Yet even the common herd struts no less proudly, with uplifted neck and combs held high, and alone of birds casts frequent glances at the sky, also rearing its curved tail aloft. Consequently even the lion, the noblest of wild animals, is afraid of the cock. Moreover some cocks are born solely for constant wars and battles—by which they have even conferred fame on their native places, Rhodes or Tanagra; the fighting cocks of Melos and Chalcidice have been awarded second honours—so that the Roman purple confers its high honour on a bird full worthy of it. These are the birds that give the Most-Favourable Omens [a]; these birds daily control our officers of state, and shut or open to them their own homes; these send forward or hold back the Roman rods of office, and order or forbid battle formation, being the auspices of all our victories won all over the world; these hold supreme empire over the empire of the world, being as acceptable to the gods with even their inward parts and vitals as are the costliest victims. Even their later and their evening songs contain portents; for by

323

canendo Boeotiis nobilem illam adversus Lacedaemonios praesagivere victoriam, ita coniecta inter-
pretatione quoniam victa ales illa non caneret.

50   XXV. Desinunt canere castrati, quod duobus fit
modis, lumbis adustis candente ferro aut imis
cruribus, mox ulcere oblito figlina creta.   facilius ita
pinguescunt.   Pergami omnibus annis spectaculum
gallorum   publice   editur   ceu   gladiatorum.   invenitur in annalibus in agro Ariminensi M. Lepido Q.
Catulo coss.   in villa Galerii locutum gallinaceum,
semel, quod equidem sciam.

51   XXVI. Est et anseri vigil cura Capitolio testata
defenso, per id tempus canum silentio proditis
rebus, quam ob causam cibaria anserum censores in
primis locant.   quin et fama amoris Aegii dilecta
forma pueri nomine Olenii Amphilochi,[1] et Glauces
Ptolomaeo regi cithara canentis quam eodem tempore et aries amasse proditur.   potest et sapientiae
videri intellectus his esse : ita comes perpetuo adhaesisse Lacydi philosopho dicitur, nusquam ab eo,
non in publico non in balineis, non noctu non interdiu digressus.

52   XXVII. Nostri sapientiores qui eos iecoris bonitate
novere.   fartilibus in magnam amplitudinem crescit,

---

[1] Amphilochi *add.* (*ex Ael. Hist. An.* V 29) *Hardouin.*

---

[a] Leuctra, 371 B.C.: Cicero *Div.* I 74, II 56 (from Callis-
thenes).

[b] 78 B.C.

[c] In 390 B.C., when Rome had been taken by the Gauls,
Manlius the ex-consul was awakened by the cackling of the
geese in the temple of Juno just in time to save the Capitol
from the enemy who were storming it.

crowing all the nights long they presaged to the Boeotians that famous victory *a* against the Spartans, conjecture thus interpreting the sign because this bird when conquered does not crow.

XXV. Cocks when gelt stop crowing; the opera- *Cock-*
tion is performed in two ways—by searing with a *fattening.*
glowing iron either the loins or the bottom parts of the legs, and then smearing the wound with potter's clay. This operation makes them easier to fatten. At Pergamum every year a public show is given of cocks fighting like gladiators. It is found in the Annals that in the consulship *b* of Marcus Lepidus and Quintus Catulus, at the country house of Galerius in the Rimini district, a farmyard cock spoke—the only occasion, so far as I know, on which this has occurred.

XXVI. The goose also keeps a careful watch, as is *The goose.*
evidenced by its defence of the Capitol *c* during the time when our fortunes were being betrayed by the silence of the dogs; for which reason food for the geese is one of the first contracts arranged by the censors. Moreover there is the story of the goose at Aegium that fell in love with the supremely beautiful boy Amphilochus of Olenus, and also the goose that loved Glauce, the girl that played the harp for King Ptolemy, whom at the same time also a ram is said to have fallen in love with. These birds may possibly be thought also to possess the power of understanding wisdom: thus there is a story that a goose attached itself continually as a companion to the philosopher Lacydes, never leaving his side by night or day, either in public or at the baths.

XXVII. Our countrymen are wiser, who know the *Foie gras.*
goose by the excellence of its liver. Stuffing the

exemptum quoque lacte mulso augetur. nec sine causa in quaestione est quis tantum bonum invenerit, Scipione[1] Metellus vir consularis an Marcus Seius eadem aetate eques Romanus, sed, quod constat, Messalinus Cotta, Messalae oratoris filius, palmas pedum ex iis torrere atque patinis cum gallinaceorum cristis condire reperit; tribuetur enim a me culinis
53 cuiusque palma cum fide. mirum in hac alite a Morinis usque Romam pedibus venire: fessi proferuntur ad primos, ita ceteri stipatione naturali propellunt eos.

Candidorum alterum vectigal in pluma. velluntur quibusdam locis bis anno, rursus plumigeri vestiuntur. mollior quae corpori proxima, et e Germania laudatissima. candidi ibi, verum minores; gantae
54 vocantur; pretium plumae eorum in libras denarii quini. et inde crimina plerumque auxiliorum praefectis a vigili statione ad haec aucupia dimissis cohortibus totis; eoque deliciae processere ut sine hoc stramento[2] durare iam ne virorum quidem cervices possint.

55 XXVIII. Aliud repperit Syriae pars quae Commagene vocatur, adipem eorum in vase aereo cum

---

[1] *v.l.* Scipio. [2] *Dalec.* : instrumento.

bird with food makes the liver grow to a great size, and also when it has been removed it is made larger by being soaked in milk sweetened with honey. Not without reason is it a matter of enquiry who was the discoverer of so great a boon—was it Scipio Metellus the consular, or his contemporary Marcus Seius, Knight of Rome? But it is an accepted fact that Messalinus Cotta, son of the orator Messala, invented the recipe for taking from geese the soles of the feet and grilling them and pickling them in dishes with the combs of domestic cocks; for I will award the palm scrupulously to each man's culinary achievement. A remarkable feat in the case of this bird is its coming on foot all the way to Rome from the Morini in Gaul: the geese that get tired are advanced to the front rank, and so all the rest drive them on by instinctively pressing forward in their rear.

White geese yield a second profit in their feathers. *Goose feathers.* In some places they are plucked twice a year, and clothe themselves again with a feather coat. The plumage closest to the body is softer, and that from Germany is most esteemed. The geese there are a bright white, but smaller; the German word for this bird is *Gans*; the price of their feathers is five-pence per pound. And owing to this officers in command of auxiliary troops frequently get into trouble for having sent whole cohorts away from outpost sentry duty to capture these fowls; and luxury has advanced to such a pitch that now not even the male neck can endure to be without goose-feather bedding.

XXVIII. The part of Syria called Commagene *Goose-fat for medicine.* has made another discovery, goose-fat mixed with

327

cinnamo nive multa obrutum ac rigore gelido macera-
tum ad usum praeclari medicaminis quod ab gente
dicitur Commagenum.

56   XXIX. Anserini[1] generis sunt chenalopeces et,
quibus lautiores epulas non novit Britannia, chene-
rotes, fere ansere minores. decet et tetraonas suus
nitor absolutaque nigritia, in superciliis cocci rubor.
alterum eorum genus vulturum magnitudinem
excedit quorum et colorem reddit, nec ulla ales
excepto struthocamelo maius corpore implens pondus,
in tantum aucta ut in terra quoque immobilis pre-
hendatur. gignunt eos Alpes et septentrionalis
regio. in vivariis saporem perdunt, moriuntur
57 contumacia spiritu revocato. proximae iis sunt
quas Hispania aves tardas appellat, Graecia ὠτίδας,
damnatas in cibis; emissa enim ossibus medulla
odoris taedium extemplo sequitur.

58   XXX. Indutias habet gens Pygmaea abscessu
gruum, ut diximus, cum iis dimicantium. inmensus
est tractus quo veniunt, si quis reputet, a mari Eoo.
quando proficiscantur consentiunt, volant ad pro-
spiciendum alte, ducem quem sequantur eligunt, in
extremo agmine per vices qui adclament dispositos
59 habent et qui gregem voce contineant. excubias
habent nocturnis temporibus lapillum pede sustin-
entes, qui laxatus somno et decidens indiligentiam

---

[1] *Gelen* : anseris.

---

[a] ' Birds with ears,' the bustard.
[b] VI 70, VII 26 ff.

cinnamon in a bronze bowl, covered with a quantity of snow and steeped in the icy mixture, to supply the famous medicine that is called after the tribe Commagenum.

XXIX. To the goose kind belong the sheldrake and the barnacle-goose, the latter the most sumptuous feast that Britain knows, both rather smaller than the domestic goose. The black grouse also makes a fine show with its gloss and its absolute blackness, with a touch of bright scarlet above the eyes. Another variety of these exceeds the size of vultures and also reproduces their colour, nor is there any bird except the ostrich that attains a greater weight of body, growing to such a size that it is actually caught motionless on the ground. They are a product of the Alps and the northern region. When kept in fishponds they lose their flavour, and obstinately hold their breath till they die. Next to these are the birds that Spain calls *tardae* and Greece *otides,*[a] which are condemned as an article of diet, because when the marrow is drained out of their bones a disgusting smell at once follows.

Varieties of the goose kind.

XXX. The race of Pygmies have a cessation of hostilities on the departure of the cranes that, as we have said,[b] carry on war with them. It is a vast distance, if one calculates it, over which they come from the eastern sea. They agree together when to start, and they fly high so as to see their route in front of them; they choose a leader to follow, and have some of their number stationed in turns at the end of the line to shout orders and keep the flock together with their cries. At night time they have sentries who hold a stone in their claws, which if drowsiness makes them drop it falls and convicts

The crane— a migrant.

coarguat: ceterae dormiunt capite subter alam
condito alternis pedibus insistentes; dux erecto
60 providet collo ac praedicit. (eaedem mansuefactae
lasciviunt, gyrosque quosdam in decoro[1] cursu
vel singulae peragunt.[2]) certum est Pontum trans-
volaturas primum omnium angustias petere inter
duo promunturia Criumetopon et Carambim, mox
saburra stabiliri; cum medium transierint, abici
lapillos e pedibus, cum attigerint continentem, et c
gutture harenam. Cornelius Nepos, qui divi Augusti principatu obiit, cum scriberet turdos paulo
ante coeptos saginari, addidit ciconias magis placere
quam grues, cum haec nunc ales inter primas expeta-
tur, illam nemo velit attigisse.
61   XXXI. Ciconiae quonam e loco veniant aut quo
se referant incompertum adhuc est. e longinquo
venire non dubium eodem quo grues modo, illas
hiemis, has aestatis advenas. abiturae congregantur
in loca certa, comitataeque sic ut nulla generis sui
relinquatur (nisi captiva et serva) ceu lege praedicta
die recedunt. nemo vidit agmen discedentium,
cum discessurum appareat, nec venire sed venisse
cernimus; utrumque nocturnis fit temporibus, et

---

[1] indecoro *edd.*, ⟨haud⟩ indecoro ? Mayhoff.
[2] eaedem . . . peragunt *infra post* attigisse *tr. Urlichs.*

---

[a] This sentence seems to belong to the end of § 60.
[b] At the end of the Tauric Chersonese.

them of slackness, while the rest sleep with their
head tucked under their wing, standing on either
foot by turns; but the leader keeps a lookout with
neck erect and gives warning. (The same birds
when tamed are fond of play, and execute certain
circles in a graceful swoop, even one bird at a
time [a]). It is certain that when they are going to
fly across the Black Sea they first of all make for the
straits between the two promontories of Ramsbrow [b]
and Carambis, and proceed to ballast themselves
with sand; and that when they have crossed the
middle of the sea they throw away the pebbles out
of their claws and, when they have reached the
mainland, the sand out of their throats as well.
Cornelius Nepos, who died in the principate of the *The crane*
late lamented Augustus, when he wrote that the *for the table.*
practice of fattening thrushes was introduced a little
before his time, added that storks were more in
favour than cranes, although the latter bird is now
one of those most in request, whereas nobody will
touch the former.

XXXI. Where exactly storks come from or where *The stork—*
they go to has not hitherto been ascertained. There *its migra-*
is no doubt that they come from a distance, in the *tion.*
same manner as do cranes, the former being winter
visitors and the latter arriving in summer. When
about to depart they assemble at fixed places, and
forming a company, so as to prevent any of their
class being left behind (unless one captured and in
slavery), they withdraw as if at a date fixed in advance
by law. No one has seen a band of storks departing,
although it is quite clear that they are going to depart,
nor do we see them arrive, but only see that they have
arrived; both arrival and departure take place in

quamvis ultra citrave pervolent, numquam tamen
62 advenisse usquam nisi noctu existimantur. Pytho-
nos Comen vocant in Asia patentibus campis ubi
congregatae inter se conmurmurant, eamque quae
novissima advenit lacerant, atque ita abeunt;
notatum post idus Augustas non temere visas ibi.
sunt qui ciconiis non inesse linguam confirment.
honos iis serpentium exitio tantus ut in Thessalia
capital fuerit occidisse eademque legibus poena
quae in homicidam.
63   XXXII. Simili anseres quoque et olores ratione
commeant, sed horum volatus cernitur. Liburnicarum more rostrato impetu feruntur, facilius ita
findentes aera quam si recta fronte inpellerent;
a tergo sensim dilatante se cuneo porrigitur agmen
largeque inpellenti praebetur aurae. colla inponunt
praecedentibus, fessos duces ad terga recipiunt.
(ciconiae nidos eosdem repetunt. genetricum
senectam invicem educant.)[1] olorum morte narratur
flebilis cantus, falso, ut arbitror aliquot experimentis.
idem mutua carne vescuntur inter se.
64   XXXIII. Verum haec commeantium per maria
terrasque peregrinatio non patitur differri minores
quoque quibus est natura similis. utcumque enim
supra dictas magnitudo et vires corporum invitare
65 videri possint, coturnices ante etiam semper adveniunt

----

[1] ciconiae . . . educant *supra post* visas ibi §62 *tr.?*
Mayhoff.

----

[a] This passage seems to belong to § 62 mid.
[b] The story is true of the Whooper Swan but not of the
ordinary Mute Swan.

the night-time, and although they fly to and fro across the country, it is thought that they have never arrived anywhere except by night. There is a place in Asia called Snakesdorp with a wide expanse of plains where cranes meet in assembly to hold a palaver, and the one that arrives last they set upon with their claws, and so they depart; it has been noticed that they have not frequently been seen there after the first fortnight of August. Some persons declare that storks have no tongue. They are held in such high esteem for destroying snakes that in Thessaly to kill them was a capital crime, for which the legal penalty was the same as for homicide.

XXXII. Geese and swans also migrate on a similar principle, but the flight of these is seen. They travel *Other migrants of this class.* in a pointed formation like fast galleys, so cleaving the air more easily than if they drove at it with a straight front; while in the rear the flight stretches out in a gradually widening wedge, and presents a broad surface to the drive of a following breeze. They place their necks on the birds in front of them, and when the leaders are tired they receive them to the rear. (Storks return to the same nest. They nourish their parents' old age in their turn.) [a] A story is told about the mournful song of swans at their death—a false story as I judge on the strength of a certain number of experiences.[b] Swans are cannibals, and eat one another's flesh.

XXXIII. But this migration of birds of passage over seas and lands does not allow us to postpone *Smaller migrants: the quail, the ortolan.* the smaller breeds as well that have a similar nature. For however much the size and strength of body of the kinds above mentioned may appear to invite them to travel, the quails always actually arrive

quam grues, parva avis et cum ad nos venit terrestris
potius quam sublimis; advolant et hae simili modo,
non sine periculo navigantium cum adpropinquavere
terris: quippe velis saepe insidunt,[1] et hoc semper
66 noctu, merguntque navigia. iter est iis per hospitia
certa. austro non volant, umido scilicet et graviore
vento; aura tamen vehi volunt propter pondus
corporum viresque parvas (hinc volantium illa con-
questio labore expressa); aquilone ergo maxime
volant ortygometra duce. primam earum terrae
adpropinquantem accipiter rapit; semper hinc remeantes comitatum sollicitant, abeuntque una
67 persuasae glottis et otus et cychramus. glottis
praelongam exerit linguam, unde ei nomen. hanc
initio blandita peregrinatione avide provectam
paenitentia in volatu cum labore scilicet subit:
reverti incomitatam piget, et sequi, nec umquam
plus uno die, pergit—in proximo hospitio deserit.
verum invenitur alia, antecedente anno relicta
66 simili modo, in singulos dies. cychramus persever-
antior festinat etiam pervenire ad expetitas sibi
terras; itaque noctu[2] eas excitat admonetque
itineris. otus bubone minor est, noctuis maior,

[1] *Caesarius*: incidunt *Mayhoff*.
[2] *Mayhoff*: noctuis.

---

[a] Unknown.
[b] This identification is uncertain.

before the cranes, though the quail is a small bird and when it has come to us remains on the ground more than it soars aloft; but they too get here by flying in the same way as the cranes, not without danger to seafarers when they have come near to land: for they often perch on the sails, and they always do this at night, and sink the vessels. Their route follows definite resting places. They do not fly in a south wind, doubtless because it is damp and rather heavy, yet they desire to be carried by the breeze, because of the weight of their bodies and their small strength (this is the reason for that mournful cry they give while flying, which is wrung from them by fatigue); consequently they fly mostly in a north wind, a landrail leading the way. The first quail approaching land is seized by a hawk; from the place where this happens they always return and try to get an escort, and the tongue-bird,[a] eared owl and ortolan[b] are persuaded to make the journey with them. The tongue-bird takes its name from the very long tongue that it puts out of its beak. At the start the charm of travelling lures this bird to sail on eagerly, but in the course of the flight repentance comes to it, no doubt with the fatigue; but it does not like to return unaccompanied, and it goes on following, though never for more than one day—at the next resting place it deserts. But day after day the company find another one, left behind in a similar manner the year before. The ortolan is more persevering, and hurries on actually to complete the journey to the lands which they are seeking; consequently it rouses up the birds in the night and reminds them of their journey. The eared owl is smaller than the eagle-owl and

auribus plumeis eminentibus, unde et nomen illi—
quidam Latine axionem vocant; imitatrix alias
avis ac parasita et quodam genere saltatrix. capitur
haut difficulter ut noctuae, intentam in aliquem
69 circumeunte alio. quod si ventus agmen adverso
flatu coepit inhibere, pondusculis lapidum adprehensis aut gutture harena repleto stabilitae volant.
coturnicibus veneni semen gratissimus cibus, quam
ob causam eas damnavere mensae; simulque
comitialem propter morbum despui suetum, quem
solae animalium sentiunt praeter hominem.

70 XXXIV. Abeunt et hirundines hibernis mensibus,
sola carne vescens avis ex iis quae aduncos ungues
non habent; sed in vicina abeunt apricos secutae
montium recessus, inventaeque iam sunt ibi nudae
atque deplumes. Thebarum tecta subire negantur,
quoniam urbs illa saepius capta sit, nec Bizyes in
71 Threcia propter scelera Terei. Caecina Volaterranus
equestris ordinis quadrigarum dominus conprehensas
in urbem secum auferens victoriae nuntias amicis
mittebat in eundem nidum remeantes inlito victoriae
colore. tradit et Fabius Pictor in annalibus suis,
cum obsideretur praesidium Romanum a Ligustinis
hirundinem a pullis ad se adlatam, ut lino ad pedem

---

^a Swallows eat insects.

larger than night-owls; it has projecting feathery
ears, whence its name—some give it the Latin name
'axio'; moreover it is a bird that copies other
kinds and is a hanger-on, and it performs a kind of
dance. Like the night-owl it is caught without
difficulty if one goes round it while its attention is
fixed on somebody else. If a wind blowing against
them begins to hold up a flight of these birds, they
pick up little stones as ballast or fill their throat with
sand to steady their flight. Quails are very fond of
eating poison seed, on account of which our tables
have condemned them; and moreover it is customary
to spit at the sight of them as a charm against
epilepsy, to which they are the only living creatures
that are liable besides man.

XXXIV. Swallows, the only flesh-eating *a* bird *The swallow; its use for messages.*
among those that have not hooked talons, also
migrate in the winter months; but they only retire
to places near at hand, making for the sunny gulleys
in the mountains, and they have before now been
found there moulted and bare of feathers. It is
said that they do not enter under the roofs of Thebes,
because that city has been so often captured, nor at
Bizye in Thrace on account of the crimes of Tereus.
A man of knightly rank at Volterra, Caecina, who
owned a racing four-in-hand, used to catch swallows
and take them with him to Rome and despatch
them to take the news of a win to his friends, as they
returned to the same nest; they had the winning
colour painted on them. Also Fabius Pictor
records in his Annals that when a Roman garrison
was besieged by the Ligurians a swallow taken from
her nestlings was brought to him for him to indicate
by knots made in a thread tied to its foot how

cius adligato nodis significaret quoto die adveniente auxilio eruptio fieri deberet.

72 XXXV. Abeunt et merulae turdique et sturni simili modo in vicina; sed hi plumam non amittunt, nec occultantur, visi saepe ibi quo hibernum pabulum petunt. itaque in Germania hieme maxime turdi cernuntur. verius turtur occultatur, pinnasque amittit. abeunt et palumbes; quonam et in his

73 incertum. sturnorum generi proprium catervatim volare et quodam pilae orbe circumagi omnibus in medium agmen tendentibus. volucrum soli hirundini flexuosi volatus velox celeritas, quibus ex causis neque rapinae ceterarum alitum obnoxia est. eadem[1] sola avium nonnisi in volatu pascitur.

XXXVI. Temporum magna differentia avibus: perennes, ut columbae, semestres, ut hirundines, trimenstres, ut turdi, turtures et quae cum fetum eduxere abeunt, ut galguli, upupae.

74 XXXVII. Auctores sunt omnibus annis advolare Ilium ex Aethiopia aves et confligere ad Memnonis tumulum, quas ob id Memnonidas vocant. hoc idem quinto quoque anno facere eas in Aethiopia circa regiam Memnonis exploratum sibi Cremutius tradit.

XXXVIII. Simili modo pugnant meleagrides in Boeotia; Africae hoc est gallinarum genus gibberum,

[1] *Mayhoff*: ea demum.

---

a Guinea-hens.

many days later help would arrive and a sortie must be made.

XXXV. Blackbirds, thrushes and starlings also *Other migrants.* migrate in a similar way to neighbouring districts; but these do not moult their plumage, and do not go into hiding, being often seen in the places where they forage for winter food. Consequently in Germany thrushes are most often seen in winter. The turtle-dove goes into hiding in a truer sense, and moults its feathers. Wood-pigeons also go into retreat, though in their case also it is not certain exactly where. It is a peculiarity of the starling kind that they fly in flocks and wheel round in a sort of circular ball, all making towards the centre of the flock. The swallow is the only bird that has an extremely swift and swerving flight, owing to which it is also not liable to capture by the other kinds of birds. Also the swallow is the only bird that only feeds when on the wing.

XXXVI. There is a great difference in the seasons *Their periods.* of birds; some stay all the year round, *e.g.* pigeons, some for six months, *e.g.* swallows, some for three months, *e.g.* thrushes and turtle-doves and those that migrate when they have reared their brood, such as woodpeckers and hoopoes.

XXXVII. Some authorities state that every year *An African migrant.* birds fly from Ethiopia to Troy and have a fight at Memnon's tomb, and consequently they call them ' Memnon's daughters.' Cremutius records having discovered that every four years they do the same things in Ethiopia round the royal palace of Memnon.

XXXVIII. The meleagrides[a] in Boeotia fight in a *Another.* similar manner; this is a kind of hen belonging to Africa, hump-backed and with speckled plumage.

339

variis sparsum plumis. quae novissimae sunt pere-
grinarum avium in mensas receptae propter ingratum
virus; verum Meleagri tumulus nobiles eas fecit.

75   XXXIX. Seleucides aves vocantur quarum adventum ab Iove precibus inpetrant Cadmi montis incolae
fruges eorum locustis vastantibus; nec unde veniant
quove abeant compertum, numquam conspectis nisi
cum praesidio earum indigetur. XL. invocant et
Aegyptii ibis suas contra serpentium adventum, et
Elei Myiacoren deum muscarum multitudine pesti-
lentiam adferente, quae protinus intereunt quam
litatum est ei deo.

76   XLI. Sed in secessu avium et noctuae paucis
diebus latere traduntur; quarum genus in Creta
insula non esse,[1] etiam, si qua invecta sit, emori.
nam haec quoque mira naturae differentia: alia aliis
locis negat, tamquam genera frugum fruticumve
sic et animalium. non nasci tralaticium, invecta
emori mirum. quod[2] illud est unius generis saluti
adversum, quaeve ista naturae invidia? aut qui terra-
77 rum dicti avibus termini? Rhodos aquilam non
habet; Transpadana Italia iuxta Alpes Larium
lacum appellat amoenum arbusto agro ad quem
ciconiae non permeant, sicuti nec octavum citra
lapidem ab eo inmensa alioqui finitimo Insubrum

---

[1] *Mayhoff*: est.   [2] *v.l.* quid.

This is the latest of the migratory birds admitted to the menu, because of its unpleasant pungent flavour; but the Tomb of Meleager has made it famous.

XXXIX. There is a species called birds of Seleucis *Other migrants.* for whose arrival prayers are offered to Jupiter by the inhabitants of Mount Cadmus when locusts destroy their crops; it is not known where they come from, nor where they go to when they depart, and they are never seen except when their protection is needed. XL. Also the people of Egypt invoke their ibis to guard against the arrival of snakes, and those of Elis invoke the god Myiacores when a swarm of flies brings plague, the flies dying as soon as a sacrifice to this god has been performed.

XLI. But in the matter of the withdrawal of birds, *The night-owl. Local distribution of species.* it is stated that even night-owls go into retreat for a few days. It is said that this kind does not exist in the island of Crete and even that if one is imported there it dies off. For this also is a remarkable point of variety established by nature: to various places she denies various species of animals as well as of crops and shrubs. For those animals not to be born there is in the ordinary course of things, but their dying off when imported there is remarkable. What is the factor adverse to the health of a single genus that is involved, or what is the jealousy of nature that is indicated? Or what frontiers are prescribed for birds? Rhodes does not possess the eagle; Italy north of the Po gives the name of Como to a lake near the Alps graced with a wooded tract to which storks do not come; and similarly jays and jackdaws—a bird whose unique fondness for stealing especially silver and gold is remarkable—though swarming in enormous numbers

tractu examina graculorum monedularumque (cui soli
avi furacitas argenti aurique praecipue mira est).
picus Martius in Tarentino agro negatur esse.
78 nuper et adhuc tamen rara ab Appennino ad urbem
versus cerni coepere picarum genera quae longa
insignes cauda variae appellantur; proprium his
calvescere omnibus annis cum seritur rapa. perdices
non transvolant Boeotiae fines in Atticam,[1] nec ulla
avis in Ponti insula qua sepultus est Achilles sacratam
ei aedem. in Fidenate agro iuxta urbem ciconiae nec
pullos nec nidum faciunt. at in agrum Volaterranum
79 palumbium vis e mari quotannis advolat. Romae in
aedem Herculis in foro Boario nec muscae nec canes
intrant. multa praeterea similia, quae prudens subinde
omitto in singulis generibus, fastidio parcens, quippe
cum Theophrastus tradat invecticias esse in Asia etiam
columbas et pavones et corvos[2] et in Cyrenaica
vocales ranas.
80   XLII. Alia admiratio circa oscines: fere mutant
colorem vocemque tempore anni, ac repente fiunt
aliae, quod in grandiore alitum genere grues tantum:
hae enim senectute nigrescunt. merula ex nigra
rufescit; canit aestate, hieme balbutit, circa solstitium muta; rostrum quoque anniculis in ebur trans-
figuratur, dumtaxat maribus. turdis colos aestate
circa cervicem varius, hieme concoloribus.[3]

---

[1] *Gesner*: Attica.   [2] *v.l.* cervos.
[3] *Mayhoff*: concolor.

---

* Leuce.

in the adjacent region of the Insubrians, do not come within eight miles of Lake Como. It is said that Mars's woodpecker is not found in the district of Taranto. The kinds of pie called chequered pies and distinguished for their long tail, though hitherto rare, have lately begun to be seen between the Apennines and Rome; this bird has the peculiarity of moulting its feathers yearly at the time when the turnip is sown. Partridges do not fly across the frontier of Boeotia into Attica; nor does any bird fly across the temple dedicated to Achilles on the island ^a of the Black Sea where he is buried. In the district of Fidenae near Rome storks do not hatch chicks or make nests. But a quantity of pigeons every year fly from the sea to the district of Volterra. Neither flies nor dogs enter the temple of Hercules in the Cattle-market at Rome. There are many similar facts besides, which I am continually careful to omit in my account of the several kinds, to avoid being wearisome—for example Theophrastus states that even pigeons and peacocks and ravens are not indigenous in Asia, nor croaking frogs in Cyrenaica.

XLII. There is another remarkable fact about song-birds; they usually change their colour and note with the season, and suddenly become different—which among the larger class of birds only cranes do, for these grow black in old age. The blackbird changes from black to red; and it sings in the summer, and chirps in winter, but at midsummer is silent; also the beak of yearling blackbirds, at all events the cocks, is turned to ivory colour. Thrushes are of a speckled colour round the neck in summer but self-coloured in winter. *Song-birds: seasonal change of plumage.*

81   XLIII. Luscinis diebus ac noctibus continuis xv
garrulus sine intermissu cantus densante se frondium
germine, non in novissimis [1] digna miratu ave.
primum tanta vox tam parvo in corpusculo, tam
pertinax spiritus; deinde in una perfecta musicae [2]
scientia: modulatus editur sonus, et nunc continuo
spiritu trahitur in longum, nunc variatur inflexo,
nunc distinguitur conciso, copulatur intorto, pro-
82   mittitur revocato; infuscatur ex inopinato, interdum
et secum ipse murmurat, plenus,[3] gravis, acutus,
creber, extentus, ubi visum est vibrans—summus,
medius, imus; breviterque omnia tam parvulis in
faucibus quae tot exquisitis tibiarum tormentis ars
hominum excogitavit, ut non [4] sit dubium hanc
suavitatem praemonstratam efficaci auspicio cum in
ore Stesichori cecinit infantis. ac ne quis dubitet
artis esse, plures singulis sunt cantus, nec iidem
83   omnibus, sed sui cuique. certant inter se, palamque
animosa contentio est; victa morte finit saepe
vitam, spiritu prius deficiente quam cantu. medi-
tantur aliae iuveniores versusque quos imitentur
accipiunt; audit discipula intentione magna et
reddit, vicibusque reticent; intellegitur emendatae
correctio [5] et in docente quaedam reprehensio.
84   ergo servorum illis pretia sunt, et quidem ampliora

---

[1] *edd.*: novissimum.   [2] *v.l.* musica.
[3] plenus ⟨inanis⟩? *Rackham.*   [4] non ut *Mayhoff.*
[5] *edd.*: correptio.

---

a Some antithesis to *plenus* seems to have been lost in the
Latin text.
b Famous Sicilian Greek poet, 632–552 B.C., on whose lips
in infancy a nightingale perched and sang.

XLIII. Nightingales pour out a ceaseless gush of song for fifteen days and nights on end when the buds of the leaves are swelling—a bird not in the lowest rank remarkable. In the first place there is so loud a voice and so persistent a supply of breath in such a tiny little body; then there is the consummate knowledge of music in a single bird: the sound is given out with modulations, and now is drawn out into a long note with one continuous breath, now varied by managing the breath, now made staccato by checking it, or linked together by prolonging it, or carried on by holding it back; or it is suddenly lowered, and at times sinks into a mere murmur, loud, low,[a] bass, treble, with trills, with long notes, modulated when this seems good—soprano, mezzo, baritone; and briefly all the devices in that tiny throat which human science has devised with all the elaborate mechanism of the flute, so that there can be no doubt that this sweetness was foretold by a convincing omen when it made music on the lips of the infant Stesichorus.[b] And that no one may doubt its being a matter of science, the birds have several songs each, and not all the same but every bird songs of its own. They compete with one another, and there is clearly an animated rivalry between them; the loser often ends her life by dying, her breath giving out before her song. Other younger birds practise their music, and are given verses to imitate; the pupil listens with close attention and repeats the phrase, and the two keep silence by turns: we notice improvement in the one under instruction and a sort of criticism on the part of the instructress. Consequently they fetch the prices that are given for slaves, and indeed larger prices than were paid

The nightingale: range and variety of its song.

Trade in trained nightingales

quam quibus olim armigeri parabantur. scio HS.
vi candidam alioquin, quod est prope invisitatum,[1]
venisse quae Agrippinae Claudii principis coniugi
dono daretur. visum iam saepe iussas canere
coepisse et cum symphonia alternasse, sicut homines
repertos qui sonum earum addita in transversas
harundines aqua foramina [2] inspirantes linguave [3]
parva aliqua opposita mora indiscreta redderent
85 similitudine. sed hae tantae tamque artifices
argutiae a xv diebus paulatim desinunt—nec ut
fatigatas possis dicere aut satiatas; mox aestu aucto
in totum alia vox fit, nec modulata aut varia. mutatur et color, postremo hieme ipsa non cernitur.
linguis earum tenuitas illa prima non est quae
ceteris avibus. pariunt vere primo cum plurimum
sena ova.

86   XLIV. Alia ratio ficedulis, nam formam simul
coloremque mutant; hoc nomen autumno habent,
postea melancoryphi vocantur. sic et erithacus
hieme, idem phoenicurus aestate. mutat et upupa,
ut tradit Aeschylus poeta, obscena alias pastu avis,
crista visenda plicatili contrahens eam subrigensque
per longitudinem capitis.

87   XLV. Oenanthe quidem etiam statos latebrae dies
habet: exoriente sirio occultata ab occasu eiusdem

---

[1] v.l. inusitatam (cf. § 132).   [2] Rackham : foramen.
[3] v.l. linguaeve.

---

[a] Fr. quoted Ar. Hist. An. 633a 19.

for armour-bearers in old days. I know of one bird, a white one it is true, which is nearly unprecedented, that was sold for 600,000 sesterces to be given as a present to the emperor Claudius's consort Agrippina. Frequent cases have been seen before now of nightingales that have begun to sing when ordered, and have sung in answer to an organ, as there have been found persons who could reproduce the birds' song with an indistinguishable resemblance by putting water into slanting reeds and breathing into the holes or by applying some slight check with the tongue. But these exceptional and artistic trills after a fortnight gradually cease, though not in such a way that the birds could be said to be tired out or to have had enough of singing; and later on when the heat has increased their note becomes entirely different, with no modulations or variations. Their colour also changes, and finally in winter the bird itself is not seen. Their tongues do not end in a point like those of all other birds. They lay in early spring, six eggs at most.

XLIV. It is otherwise with the fig-pecker, as it changes its shape and colour at the same time; it has this name in the autumn, but afterwards is called the blackcap. Similarly also the bird known as the robin in winter is called redstart in summer. The hoopoe also changes its appearance, as the poet Aeschylus[a] records; it is moreover a foul-feeding bird, noticeable for its flexible crest, which it draws together and raises up along the whole length of its head.

The beca-fico and other species that change their plumage, or go into retreat.

XLV. The wheatear indeed actually has fixed days of retirement: it goes into hiding at the rising of the dogstar and comes out after its setting, doing both

prodit, quod miremur, ipsis diebus utrumque.
chlorion quoque, qui totus est luteus, hieme non
visus, circa solstitia procedit. merulae circa Cylle-
nen Arcadiae nec usquam aliubi candidae nascuntur.
ibis circa Pelusium tantum nigra est, ceteris omnibus
locis candida.

88 XLVI. Oscines praeter exceptas non temere fetus
faciunt ante aequinoctium vernum aut post autumn-
ale, ante solstitium autem dubios, post solstitium
vitales.

89 XLVII. Eo maxime sunt insignes halcyones:
dies earum partus maria quique [1] navigant novere.
ipsa avis paulo amplior passere, colore cyanea et
parte inferiore [2] tantum purpurea, candidis admixta
pinnis collo, gracili ac procero rostro.[3] alterum
genus earum magnitudine distinguitur et cantu;

90 minores in harundinetis canunt. halcyonem videre
rarissimum est, nec nisi vergiliarum occasu et circa
solstitia brumamve, nave aliquando circumvolata
statim in latebras abeuntem. fetificant bruma,
qui dies halcyonides vocantur, placido mari per eos et
navigabili, Siculo maxime. faciunt autem septem
ante brumam diebus nidos, et totidem sequentibus

91 pariunt. nidi earum admirationem habent pilae
figura paulum eminenti ore perquam angusto,
grandium spongearum similitudine; ferro intercidi
non queunt, franguntur ictu valido, ut spuma arida

---

[1] quiqui *anon.*
[2] *Mayhoff*: cyanea ex parte maiore *aut alia.*
[3] rostro *add. ex Aristotele Mayhoff.*

---

[a] This larger variety is the Pied Kingfisher.
[b] About the beginning of November.

on the actual days, which is surprising. Also the golden oriole, which is yellow all over, is not seen in winter but comes out about midsummer. Blackbirds are born white at Cyllene in Arcadia, but nowhere else. The ibis is black only in the neighbourhood of Pelusium, being white in all other places.

XLVI. Songbirds apart from some exceptions do not ordinarily breed before the spring equinox or after the autumn one; and their eggs laid before midsummer are doubtful, but those after midsummer are fertile. *Breeding of song-birds*

XLVII. Kingfishers are especially remarkable for this: the seas and those who sail them know the days when they breed. The bird itself is a little larger than a sparrow, sea-blue in colour and reddish only on the underside, blended with white feathers in the neck, with a long slender beak.[a] There is another kind of kingfisher different in size and note; this smaller kind sings in beds of rushes. A kingfisher is very rarely seen, and only at the setting [b] of the Pleiads and about midsummer and midwinter, when it occasionally flies round a ship and at once goes away to its retreat. They breed at midwinter, on what are called 'the kingfisher days,' during which the sea is calm and navigable, especially in the neighbourhood of Sicily. They make their nests a week before the shortest day, and lay a week after it. Their nests are admired for their shape, that of a ball slightly projecting with a very narrow mouth, resembling very large sponges;[c] they cannot be cut with a knife, but break at a strong blow, like *The kingfisher; its seasons and habits.*

[c] The so-called nests on which this story is based are clearly a kind of sponge.

maris; nec unde confingantur invenitur: putant ex
spinis aculeatis,[1] piscibus enim vivunt. subeunt et
in amnes. pariunt ova quina.

XLVIII. Gaviae in petris nidificant, mergi et in
arboribus. pariunt cum [2] plurimum terna, sed gaviae
aestate, mergi incipiente vere.

92 XLIX. Halcyonum nidi figura reliquarum quoque
sollertiae admonet; neque alia parte ingenia avium
magis admiranda sunt. hirundines luto construunt,
stramento roborant; si quando inopia est luti,
madefactis multa aqua pinnis pulverem spargunt.
ipsum vero nidum mollibus plumis floccisque con-
sternunt tepefaciendis ovis, simul ne durus sit
infantibus pullis. in fetum [3] summa aequitate
alternant cibum. notabili munditia egerunt excrementa pullorum, adultioresque circumagi docent
93 et foris saturitatem emittere. alterum est hirundinum genus rusticarum et agrestium quae raro in
domibus diversos figura sed eadem materia confingunt
nidos, totos supinos, faucibus porrectis in angustum,
utero capaci, mirum qua peritia et occultandis
94 habiles pullis et substernendis molles. in Aegypti
Heracleotico ostio molem continuatione nidorum
evaganti Nilo inexpugnabilem opponunt stadii fere
unius spatio, quod humano opere perfici non posset.

[1] acularum (cf.XXXII 11 belonae, quos aculas vocamus
Gronovius.
[2] cum add. ? Mayhoff.
[3] Rackham coll. Tac. Ann. II. 67 : fetu.

[a] I.e. the βελόνη, Ar. Hist. An. 616a32, garfish.
[b] I.e. cormorants.
[c] Our house-martin.

dry sea-foam; and it cannot be discovered of what they are constructed: people think they are made out of the spines of fishes' *a* prickles, for the birds live on fish. They also go up rivers. They lay five eggs at a time.

XLVIII. Gulls nest on rocks, divers *b* also in trees. They lay at most three eggs at a time, seamews laying in summer and divers at the beginning of spring.

The gull.

XLIX. The conformation of the kingfisher's nest reminds one of the skill of all the other birds as well; and the ingenuity of birds is in no other department more remarkable. Swallows build with clay and strengthen the nest with straw; if ever there is a lack of clay, they wet their wings with a quantity of water and sprinkle it on the dust. The nest itself, however, they carpet with soft feathers and tufts of wool, to warm the eggs and also to prevent it from being hard for the infant chicks. They dole out food in turns among their offspring with extreme fairness. They remove the chicks' droppings with remarkable cleanliness, and teach the older ones to turn round and relieve themselves outside of the nest. There is another kind of swallow *c* that frequents the country and the fields, which seldom nests on houses, and which makes its nest of a different shape though of the same material—entirely turned upward, with orifices projecting to a narrow opening and a capacious interior, and adapted with remarkable skill both to conceal the chicks and to give them a soft bed to lie on. In Egypt, at the Heracleotic Mouth of the Nile, they block the outflow of the river with an irremovable mole of contiguous nests almost two hundred yards long, a thing that could not be achieved

The swallow, its varieties and methods of nesting.

in eadem Aegypto iuxta oppidum Copton insula est
sacra Isidi quam ne laceret amnis idem muniunt
opere, incipientibus vernis diebus palea et stramento
rostrum eius firmantes, continuatis per triduum
noctibus tanto labore ut multas in opere et [1] mori
constet; eaque militia illis cum anno redit semper.
95 tertium est earum genus quae ripas excavant atque
ita in terra nidificant.[2] (harum pulli ad cinerem
ambusti mortifero faucium malo multisque aliis
morbis humani corporis medentur.) non faciunt hae
nidos, migrantque multis diebus ante si futurum est
ut auctus amnis attingat.
96 L. In genere vitiparrarum est cui nidus ex musco
arido ita absoluta perficitur pila ut inveniri non
possit aditus. acanthyllis appellatur eadem figura
ex lino intexens. picorum aliquis suspenditur
surculo primis in ramis cyathi modo, ut nulla quadripes
possit accedere. galgulos quidem ipsos dependentes
pedibus somnum capere confirmant quia tutiores ita
97 se sperent. iam publicum quidem omnium est
tabulata ramorum sustinendo nido provide eligere,
camarare ab imbri aut fronde protegere densa. in
Arabia cinnamolgus avis appellatur, cinnami surculis
nidificans.[3] plumbatis eos sagittis decutiunt indigenae
mercis gratia. in Scythis avis magnitudine otidis

---

[1] *v.l.* opere emori.   [2] *v.l.* ita internidificant.
        [3] *Mayhoff*: nidificant *aut* -at.

---

[a] Our sand-martin.   [b] Our long-tailed tit.
[c] Our goldfinch.   [d] This is an unfounded story.

by human labour. Also in Egypt near the town of
Coptos there is an island sacred to Isis which they
fortify with a structure to prevent its being destroyed
by the same river, strengthening its point with chaff
and straw when the spring days begin, going on for
three days all through the nights with such industry
that it is agreed that many birds actually die at the
work; and this spell of duty always comes round again
for them with the returning year. There is a third
kind of swallows *a* that make holes in banks and so
construct their nests in the ground. (Their chicks
when burnt to ashes are a medicine for a deadly
throat malady and many other diseases of the human
body.) These birds do not build proper nests, and
if a rise of the river threatens to reach their holes,
they migrate many days in advance.

L. There is a species of titmouse *b* that makes
its nest of dry moss finished off in such a perfect
ball that its entrance cannot be found. The bird
called the thistle-finch *c* weaves its nest out of flax
in the same shape. One of the woodpeckers hangs
by a twig at the very end of the boughs, like a ladle
on a peg, so that no four-footed animal can get to it.
It is indeed asserted that the witwall purposely
takes its sleep while hanging suspended by the feet,
because it hopes thus to be safer. Again, it is a
common practice of them all carefully to choose a
flooring of branches to support their nest, and
to vault it over against the rain or roof it with a
penthouse of thick foliage. In Arabia *d* a bird called
cinnamolgus makes a nest of cinnamon twigs;
the natives bring these birds down with arrows
weighted with lead, to use them for trade. In
Scythia a bird of the size of a bustard lays two eggs

Other species remarkable for their nests.

bina[1] parit in leporina pelle semper in cacuminibus
98 ramorum suspensa. picae cum diligentius visum ab
homine nidum sensere, ova transgerunt alio. hoc
in his avibus quarum digiti non sint accommodati
complectendis transferendisque ovis miro traditur
modo: namque surculo super bina ova inposito ac
ferruminato alvi glutino subdita cervice medio
aequa utrimque libra deportant alio.

99   LI. Nec vero iis minor sollertia quae cunabula in
terra faciunt corporis gravitate prohibitae sublime
petere. merops vocatur genitores suos reconditos
pascens, pallido intus colore pennarum, superne
cyaneo, priore parte[2] subrutilo. nidificat in specu
sex pedum defossa altitudine.

100   Perdices spina et frutice sic muniunt receptaculum
ut contra feras abunde vallentur; ovis stragulum
molle pulvere contumulant, nec in quo loco peperere
incubant; ne cui frequentior conversatio suspecta
sit, transferunt alio. illae quidem et maritos suos
fallunt, quoniam intemperantia libidinis frangunt
earum ova ne incubando detineantur, tunc inter se
dimicant mares desiderio feminarum; victum aiunt
101 venerem pati. id quidem et coturnices Trogus et
gallinaceos aliquando, perdices vero a domitis feros

---

[1] *Dalecamp*: binos.
[2] *Mayhoff ex Aristotele*: priori.

at a time in a hare-skin, which is always hung on the top boughs of trees. When magpies notice a person observing their nest with special attention, they transfer the eggs somewhere else. It is reported that in the case of these birds, as their claws are not adapted for grasping and carrying the eggs, this is effected in a remarkable manner: they place a sprig on the top of two eggs at a time, and solder it with glue from their belly, and placing their neck under the middle of it so as to make it balance equally on both sides, carry it off somewhere else.

LI. Nor yet are those species less cunning which, because the weight of their body forbids their soaring aloft, make their nests on the ground. The name of bee-eater is given to a bird that feeds its parents in their lair; its wings are a pale colour inside and dark-blue above, reddish at the tip. It makes its nest in a hole dug in the ground to a depth of ten feet. *Nests on the ground.*

Partridges fortify their retreat with thorn and bush in such a way as to be completely entrenched against wild animals; they heap a soft covering of dust on their eggs. and they do not sit on them at the place where they laid them but remove them somewhere else, lest their frequently resorting there should cause somebody to suspect it. Hen partridges in fact deceive even their own mates, because these in the intemperance of their lust break the hens' eggs so that they may not be kept away by sitting on them; and then the cocks owing to their desire for the hens fight duels with each other; it is said that the one who loses has to accept the advances of the victor. Trogus indeed says this also occurs occasionally with quails and farmyard cocks, but *Habits of the partridge in mating and hatching.*

et novos aut victos iniri promiscue. capiuntur quoque pugnacitate eiusdem libidinis, contra aucupis inlicem exeunte in proelium duce totius gregis, capto eo procedit alter ac subinde singuli. rursus circa conceptum feminae capiuntur contra aucupum 102 feminam exeuntes ut rixando abigant eam. nec in alio animali par opus libidinis. si contra mares steterint feminae, aura ab his flante praegnantes fiunt, hiantes autem exerta lingua per id tempus aestuant. concipiunt et supervolantium adflatu, saepe voce tantum audita masculi. adeoque vincit libido etiam fetus caritatem, ut illa furtim et in occulto incubans, cum sensit feminam aucupis accedentem ad marem, recanat revocetque et ultro praebeat se libidini. rabie quidem tanta feruntur ut in capite aucupantium 103 saepe caecae impetu[1] sedeant. si ad nidum is coepit accedere, procurrit ad pedes eius feta, praegravem aut delumbem sese simulans, subitoque in procursu aut brevi aliquo volatu cadit fracta ut ala aut pedibus, procurrit iterum iam iam prensurum effugiens spemque frustrans, donec in diversum abducat a nidis. eadem in pavore libera ac materna

---

[1] *Jan* (motu, initu *alii*; *an* caeco impetu ?) : metu.

that wild partridges are promiscuously covered by
tame ones, and also new-comers or cocks that have
been beaten in a fight. They are also captured
owing to the fighting instinct caused by the same
lust, as the leader of the whole flock sallies out to
battle against the fowler's decoy, and when he has
been caught number two advances, and so on one
after another in succession. Again about breeding
time the hens are caught when they sally out against
the fowlers' hen to hustle and drive her away.
And in no other creature is concupiscence so active.
If the hens stand facing the cocks they become
pregnant by the afflatus that passes out from them,
while if they open their beaks and put out their tongue
at that time they are sexually excited. Even the
draught of air from cocks flying over them, and
often merely the sound of a cock crowing, makes them
conceive. And even their affection for their brood
is so conquered by desire that when a hen is quietly
sitting on her eggs in hiding, if she becomes aware
of a fowler's decoy hen approaching her cock she
chirps him back to her and recalls him and voluntarily
offers herself to his desire. Indeed they are subject
to such madness that often with a blind swoop they
perch on the fowler's head. If he starts to go towards
a nest, the mother bird runs forward to his feet,
pretending to be tired or lame, and in the middle
of a run or a short flight suddenly falls as if with a
broken wing or damaged feet, and then runs forward
again, continually escaping him just as he is going to
catch her and cheating his hope, until she leads him
away in a different direction from the nests. On
the other hand if the hen thus scared is free and
not possessed with motherly anxiety she lies on her

vacans cura in sulco resupina glaeba se terrae pedibus
adprehensa operit.

Perdicum vita et ad sedecim annos durare existimatur.

104   LII. Ab iis columbarum maxime spectantur
simili ratione mores. inest [1] pudicitia illis plurima,[2]
et neutri nota adulteria: coniugii fidem non violant,
communemque servant domum: nisi caelebs aut
vidua nidum non relinquit. et imperiosos mares,
subinde etiam iniquos ferunt, quippe suspicio est
adulterii, quamvis natura non sit; tunc plenum
querelae [3] guttur saevique rostro ictus, mox in
satisfactione exosculatio et circa veneris preces

105 crebris pedum orbibus adulatio. amor utrique subolis aequalis; saepe et ex hac causa castigatio
pigrius intrante femina ad pullos. parturienti
solatia et ministeria ex mare. pullis primo salsiorem
terram collectam gutture in ora inspuunt praepa-
rantes tempestivitatem cibo. proprium generis eius
et turturum cum bibant colla non resupinare, largeque
bibere iumentorum modo.

106   Vivere palumbes ad tricensimum annum, aliquas
et ad quadragensimum, habemus auctores, uno
tantum incommodo unguium—eodem et argumento
senectae—qui citra perniciem reciduntur. cantus
omnibus similis atque idem trino conficitur versu,

---

[1] *Mayhoff*: inde sed.   [2] *Mayhoff*: prima.
[3] *Mayhoff* (?): querela.

back in a furrow and catches hold of a clod of earth with her claws and covers herself with it.

The life of partridges is believed to extend to as much as sixteen years.

LII. Next to partridges the habits of pigeons *Mating of pigeons.* are most noticeable for a similar reason. These possess the greatest modesty, and adultery is unknown to either sex; they do not violate the faith of wedlock, and they keep house in company—unless unmated or widowed a pigeon does not leave its nest. Also they say that the cock pigeon is domineering, and occasionally even unkind, as he is suspicious of adultery although not himself prone to it; in this state his throat is full of complaining and his beak deals savage pecks, and upon his satisfaction there follows billing and fawning with repeated twirlings of his feet during his entreaties for indulgence. Both partners have equal affection for their offspring; this also often gives occasion for chastisement, when the hen is too slack in coming home to the chicks. When she is producing a brood she receives comfort and attendance from the cock. For the chicks at first they collect saltish earth in their throat and disgorge it into their beaks, to get them into proper condition for food. It is a peculiarity of this species and of the turtle-dove not to raise the neck backward when drinking, and to take copious draughts like cattle.

We have authorities for saying that wood-pigeons *The wood-pigeon.* live to be thirty and in some cases forty years old, only with the single inconvenience of their claws—this also a sign of old age—which have to be cut to prevent damage. The cooing of all is alike and the same, composed of a phrase repeated three times and

praeterque in clausula gemitu, hieme mutis, a vere vocalibus. Nigidius putat, cum ova incubet sub tecto, nominatam palumbem relinquere nidos. 107 pariunt autem post solstitium. columbae et turtures octonis annis vivunt. contra passeri minimum vitae, cui salacitas par: mares negantur anno diutius durare, argumento quia nulla veris initio appareat nigritudo in rostro, quae ab aestate incipit; feminis 108 longiusculum spatium. verum columbis inest quidam et gloriae intellectus: nosse credas suos colores varietatemque dispositam; quin etiam ex volatu quaeritur: plaudere in caelo varieque sulcare. qua in ostentatione ut vinctae praebentur accipitri, inplicatis strepitu pennis qui non nisi ipsis alarum umeris eliditur, alioquin soluto volatu multum velociores. speculatur occultus fronde latro et 109 gaudentem in ipsa gloria rapit. ob id cum his habenda est avis quae tinnungulus vocatur; defendit enim illas terretque accipitres naturali potentia in tantum ut visum vocemque eius fugiant. hac de causa praecipuus columbis amor eorum, feruntque, si in quattuor angulis defodiantur in ollis novis oblitis, non mutare sedem columbas (quod et auro insectis alarum articulis quaesivere aliqui, non aliter

then a sigh at the close; in winter they are silent, but begin singing in spring. Nigidius thinks that a wood-pigeon when sitting on her eggs under a roof will leave her nest in answer to her name. They lay after midsummer. Pigeons and turtle-doves live eight years. On the other hand the sparrow, their equal in salaciousness, has a very small span of life: the cocks are said not to last longer than a year, the proof being that at the beginning of spring no black colouring is seen on their beak, which begins with summer; but the hens have a rather longer span of life. However pigeons actually possess a certain sense of vanity—you would fancy them to be conscious of their own colours and the pattern of their marking; indeed this can be inferred from their flight—it is observed that they flap their wings in the sky and trace a variety of lines. During this *Pigeons and* display they expose themselves to the hawk as if *hawks.* fettered, folding their wings with a flapping noise that is only produced from the actual wing joints, though otherwise when flying freely they are much swifter. The highwayman hawk watches concealed in foliage, and seizes the exultant pigeon in the very act of showing off. For that reason the bird *Pigeons and* called kestrel must be classed with these; for it *kestrels.* defends the pigeons, and scares the hawks by its natural powerfulness so much that they fly from sight and sound of it. For this reason wood-pigeons have a special love for kestrels, and they say that if kestrels put in new jars with their mouths sealed up are hidden in the four corners of the dovecot the pigeons do not change their abode (a result that some people have also sought to obtain by cutting the joints of their wings with gold, the only way of making a

innoxiis vulneribus) multivagam alioquin avem.[1] est
enim ars illis inter se blandiri et corrumpere alias
110 furtoque comitatiores reverti. LIII. quin et inter-
nuntiae in magnis rebus fuere, epistulas adnexas
earum pedibus obsidione Mutinensi in castra con-
sulum Decumo Bruto mittente; quid vallum et
vigil obsidio atque etiam retia in amne praetenta
profuere Antonio per caelum eunte nuntio? et
harum amore insaniunt multi; super tecta exaedificant turres his, nobilitatemque singularum et
origines narrant, vetere iam exemplo: L. Axius
eques Romanus ante bellum civile Pompeianum
denariis cccc singula paria venditavit, ut M.
Varro tradit. quin et patriam nobilitavere in Campania grandissimae provenire existimatae.

111 LIV. Harum volatus in reputationem ceterarum
quoque volucrum inpellit. omnibus animalibus
reliquis certus et unius modi et in suo cuique genere
incessus est: aves solae vario meatu feruntur et in
terra et in aere. ambulant aliquae, ut cornices;
saliunt aliae, ut passeres, merulae; currunt, ut
perdices, rusticulae; ante se pedes iaciunt, ut
ciconiae, grues. expandunt aliae [2] alas pendentesque
raro intervallo quatiunt, aliae crebrius sed et primas
dumtaxat pennas, aliae tota latera plaudunt;

---

[1] *Rackham* : multivaga . . . ave.
[2] aliae *add. Rackham.*

---

[a] By Mark Antony 44–43 B.C.
[b] Begun in 49 B.C.

wound that does no harm), although otherwise the pigeon is a bird much given to straying. For they have a trick of exchanging blandishments and enticing other pigeons and coming back with a larger company won by intrigue. LIII. Moreover *Carrier-* also they have acted as go-betweens in important *pigeons.* affairs, when at the siege *a* of Modena Decimus *fanciers.* Brutus sent to the consuls' camp despatches tied to their feet; what use to Antony were his rampart and watchful besieging force, and even the barriers of nets that he stretched in the river, when the message went by air? Also pigeon-fancying is carried to insane lengths by some people: they build towers on their roofs for these birds, and tell stories of the high breeding and pedigrees of particular birds, for which there is now an old precedent: before Pompey's civil war *b* Lucius Axius, Knight of Rome, advertised pigeons for sale at 400 denarii per brace—so Marcus Varro relates. Moreover the largest birds, which are believed to be produced in Campania, have conferred fame on their native place.

LIV. The flight of these birds prompts one to turn *Flight and* to the consideration of the other birds as well. All *gait of* the rest of the animals have one definite and uniform *various* mode of progression peculiar to their particular kind, *species of* but birds alone travel in a variety of ways both on *birds.* land and in the air. Some walk, as crows; others hop, as sparrows and blackbirds; run, as partridges and black grouse; throw out their feet in front of them, as storks and cranes. Some spread their wings and at rare intervals let them droop and shake them; others do so more frequently, but also only the tips of the wings; others flap the whole of their

112 quaedam vero maiore ex parte compressis volant percussoque semel, aliquae et gemino ictu, aere feruntur; velut inclusum eum prementes eiaculantur sese in sublime, in rectum, in pronum. impingi putes aliquas aut rursus ab alto cadere has, illas salire. anates solae quaeque sunt eiusdem generis in sublime protinus sese tollunt atque e vestigio caelum petunt, et hoc etiam ex aqua; itaque in foveas quibus

113 feras venamur delapsae solae evadunt. vultur et fere graviores nisi ex procursu aut altiore cumulo inmissae non evolant; cauda reguntur. aliae circumspectant, aliae flectunt colla; nec nullae[1] vescuntur ea quae rapuere pedibus. sine voce non volant multae, aliae e[2] contrario semper in volatu silent. subrectae, pronae, obliquae, in latera, in ora, quaedam et resupinae feruntur, ut, si pariter cernantur genera plura, non in eadem natura meare videantur.

114 LV. Plurimum volant quae apodes (quia careant usu pedum), ab aliis cypseli appellantur hirundinum specie. nidificant in scopulis. hae sunt quae toto mari cernuntur, nec umquam tam longo naves tamque continuo cursu recedunt a terra ut non circumvolitent eas apodes. cetera genera residunt et insistunt, his quies nisi in nido nulla: aut pendent aut iacent.

---

[1] *v.ll.* nec ullae, nonnullae.
[2] *Mueller*: aut e.

---

[a] Swifts.

sides; but there are some that fly with their wings
for the greater part folded, and after giving one
stroke, or others also a repeated stroke, are borne by
the air: by as it were squeezing it tight between
their wings, they shoot upward or horizontally or
downward. Some you would think to be flung forward, or again in some cases to fall from a height and
in other cases to leap upward. Only ducks and birds
of the same kind soar up straight away, and move
skyward from the start, and this even from water;
and consequently they alone when they have fallen
into the pits that we use for trapping wild animals
get out again. Vultures and the heavier birds in
general cannot fly upward except after a run forward
or when launching from a higher eminence; they
steer with their tail. Some birds turn their gaze
round, others bend their necks; and some eat things
they have snatched with their feet. Many do not
fly without a cry, others on the contrary are always
silent when in flight. They move upward, downward,
slanting, sideways, straight forward, and some even
with the head bent backward; consequently if
several kinds are seen at the same time, they might
be thought not to be travelling in the same
element.

LV. The greatest flyers are the species resembling *Flight of*
swallows called *apodes*[a] (because they lack the use of *swifts.*
feet) and by others 'cypseli.' They build their
nests on crags. These are the birds seen all over
the sea, and ships never go away from land on so
long or so unbroken a course that they do not have
apodes flying round them. All the other kinds alight
and perch, but these never rest except on the nest:
they either hover or lie on a surface.

115 LVI. Et ingenia aeque varia, ad pastum maxime. caprimulgi appellantur, grandioris merulae aspectu, fures nocturni—interdiu enim visu carent. intrant pastorum stabula caprarumque uberibus advolant suctum propter lactis, qua iniuria uber emoritur caprisque caecitas quas ita mulsere oboritur. platea nominatur advolans ad eas quae se in mari mergunt et capita illarum morsu corripiens, donec capturam extorqueat. eadem cum devoratis se implevit conchis, calore ventris coctas evomit, atque ita ex iis esculenta eligit testas excernens.

116 LVII. Villaribus gallinis et religio inest: inhorrescunt edito ovo excutiuntque sese et circumactae purificant ac[1] festuca aliqua sese et ova lustrant. minimae avium cardueles imperata faciunt, nec voce tantum sed pedibus et ore pro manibus. est quae boum mugitus imitetur, in Arelatensi agro taurus appellata, alioquin parva est. equorum quoque hinnitus anthus nomine herbae pabulo adventu eorum pulsa imitatur ad hunc modum se ulciscens.

117 LVIII. Super omnia humanas voces reddunt, psittaci quidem etiam sermocinantes. India hanc avem mittit, siptacen vocat, viridem toto corpore, torque tantum miniato in cervice distinctam. imperatores[2] salutat et quae accipit verba pronuntiat, in vino praecipue lasciva. capiti eius duritia eadem

---

[1] *Gelen*: aut.   [2] imperatorem? *Rackham.*

---

[a] There is no foundation for this story.
[b] This is a mistake.   [c] Our bittern.
[d] Probably the yellow wagtail.
[e] The ring-necked parrakeet is meant.
[f] A mistake for *psittacus*, parrot.
[g] Or possibly, emending the text ' gives the salute to the emperor ', says ' Ave, Caesar ! '

LVI. Birds' dispositions also are equally varied, *The goat-sucker and especially in respect of food. Those called goat- *the shoveller-suckers, which resemble a rather large blackbird, *duck—modes are night thieves—for they cannot see in the daytime. They enter the shepherds' stalls and fly to the goats' udders in order to suck their milk, which injures the udder and makes it perish, and the goats they have milked in this way gradually go blind.[a] There is a bird called the shoveller-duck which flies up to the sea-divers and seizes their heads in its bill till it wrings their catch from them. The same bird after filling itself by swallowing shells brings them up again when digested by the warmth of the belly and so picked out from them the edible parts, discarding the shells.

LVII. Farmyard hens actually have a religious *Curious ritual: after laying an egg they begin to shiver and *other birds. shake, and purify themselves by circling round, and make use of a straw as a ceremonial rod to cleanse themselves and the eggs. The smallest[b] of birds, the goldfinches, perform their leader's orders, not only with their song but by using their feet and beak instead of hands. One bird in the Arles district, called the bull-bird[c] although really it is small in size, imitates the bellowing of oxen. Also the bird[d] whose Greek name is ' flower,' when driven away from feeding on grass by the arrival of horses, imitates their neighing, in this way taking its revenge.

LVIII. Above all, birds imitate the human voice, *Talking parrots indeed actually talking. India sends us this *parrots. bird[e]; its name in the vernacular is *siptaces*[f]; its whole body is green, only varied by a red circlet at the neck. It greets its masters,[g] and repeats words given to it, being particularly sportive over the wine. Its head

quae rostro; hoc, cum loqui discit, ferreo verberatur
radio: non sentit aliter ictus. cum devolat, rostro
se excipit, illi innititur levioremque ita se pedum
infirmitati facit.

118   LIX. Minor nobilitas, quia non ex longinquo
venit, sed expressior loquacitas certo generi picarum
est. adamant verba quae loquantur nec discunt
tantum [1] sed diligunt, meditantesque intra semet
cura atque cogitatione [2] intentionem non occultant.
constat emori victas difficultate verbi ac, nisi subinde
eadem audiant, memoria falli, quaerentesque mirum
in modum hilarari si interim audierint id verbum.
nec vulgaris [3] forma, quamvis non spectanda: satis
119 illis decoris in specie [4] sermonis humani est. verum
addiscere alias negant posse quam ex genere earum
quae glande vescantur, et inter eas facilius quibus
quini sint digiti in pedibus, ac ne eas quidem ipsas
nisi primis duobus vitae annis. latiores linguae
omnibus in suo cuique genere quae sermonem
imitantur humanum, quamquam id paene in omnibus
120 contingit: Agrippina Claudii Caesaris turdum
habuit, quod numquam ante, imitantem sermones
hominum. cum haec proderem, habebant et Caesares
iuvenes sturnum, item luscinias, Graeco ac Latino
sermone dociles, praeterea meditantes assidue et
in diem [5] nova loquentes, loquentes, longiore etiam
contextu. docentur secreto et ubi nulla alia vox

---

[1] tantum *om. plurimi.*
[2] *v.l.* curam atque cogitationem.
[3] *Mayhoff* (?): vulgaris his.
[4] *Mayhoff*: spe.
[5] *Mayhoff*: in diem et assidue.

---

[a] Britannicus, Claudius's son, and Nero, his stepson.

is as hard as its beak; and when it is being taught to speak it is beaten on the head with an iron rod—otherwise it does not feel blows. When it alights from flight it lands on its beak, and it leans on this and so reduces its weight for the weakness of its feet.

LIX. A certain kind of magpie is less celebrated, *Talking magpies and other birds.* because it does not come from a distance, but it talks more articulately. These birds get fond of uttering particular words, and not only learn them but love them, and secretly ponder them with careful reflexion, not concealing their engrossment. It is an established fact that if the difficulty of a word beats them this causes their death, and that their memory fails them unless they hear the same word repeatedly, and when they are at a loss for a word they cheer up wonderfully if in the meantime they hear it spoken. Their shape is unusual, though not beautiful: this bird has enough distinction in its power of imitating the human voice. But they say that none of them can go on learning except ones of the species that feeds on acorns, and among these those with five claws on the feet learn more easily, and not even they themselves except in the two first years of their life. All the birds in each kind that imitate human speech have exceptionally broad tongues, although this occurs in almost all species; Claudius Caesar's consort Agrippina had a thrush that mimicked what people said, which was unprecedented. At the time when I was recording these cases, the young princes[a] had a starling and also nightingales that were actually trained to talk Greek and Latin, and moreover practised diligently and spoke new phrases every day, in still longer sentences. Birds are taught to talk in private and where no other utterance can

misceatur, adsidente qui crebro dicat ea quae condita velit ac cibis blandiente.

121 LX. Reddatur et corvis sua gratia, indignatione quoque populi Romani testata, non solum conscientia. Tiberio principe ex fetu supra Castorum aedem genito pullus in adpositam sutrinam devolavit, etiam religione commendatus officinae domino. is mature sermoni adsuefactus, omnibus matutinis evolans in rostra in forum versus Tiberium, dein Germanicum et Drusum Caesares nominatim, mox transeuntem populum Romanum salutabat, postea ad tabernam remeans, plurium annorum adsiduo 122 officio mirus. hunc sive aemulatione vicinitatis manceps proximae sutrinae sive iracundia subita, ut voluit videri, excrementis aspersa¹ calceis macula, exanimavit tanta plebei consternatione ut primo pulsus ex ea regione, mox et interemptus sit, funusque aliti innumeris celebratum exequiis, constratum lectum super Aethiopum duorum umeros praecedente tibicine et coronis omnium generum ad rogum usque qui constructus dextra viae Appiae ad secundum lapi- 123 dem in campo Rediculi appellato fuit. adeo satis iusta causa populo Romano visa est exequiarum ingenium avis ac² supplicii de cive Romano in ea urbe in qua

---

¹ *Mayhoff (?)* : eius posita.
² ac ? *Mayhoff* : aut.

---

a Here Hannibal turned back (*rediit*) from marching on Rome, and there was a chapel to Rediculus, a deity whose name commemorated the event.

interrupt, with the trainer sitting by them to keep on repeating the words he wants retained, and coaxing them with morsels of food.

LX. Let us also repay due gratitude to the ravens the gratitude that is their due, evidenced also by the indignation and not only by the knowledge of the Roman nation. When Tiberius was emperor, a young raven from a brood hatched on the top of the Temple of Castor and Pollux flew down to a cobbler's shop in the vicinity, being also commended to the master of the establishment by religion. It soon picked up the habit of talking, and every morning used to fly off to the Platform that faces the forum and salute Tiberius and then Germanicus and Drusus Caesar by name, and next the Roman public passing by, afterwards returning to the shop; and it became remarkable by several years' constant performance of this function. This bird the tenant of the next cobbler's shop killed, whether because of his neighbour's competition or in a sudden outburst of anger, as he tried to make out, because some dirt had fallen on his stock of shoes from its droppings; this caused such a disturbance among the public that the man was first driven out of the district and later actually made away with, and the bird's funeral was celebrated with a vast crowd of followers, the draped bier being carried on the shoulders of two Ethiopians and in front of it going in procession a flute-player and all kinds of wreaths right to the pyre, which had been erected on the right hand side of the Appian Road at the second milestone *a* on the ground called Rediculus's Plain. So adequate a justification did the Roman nation consider a bird's cleverness to be for a funeral procession and for the punishment of a Roman

A talking raven.

371

multorum principum nemo deduxerat funus, Scipionis vero Aemiliani post Carthaginem Numantiamque deletas ab eo nemo vindicaverat mortem. hoc gestum M. Servilio C. Cestio coss. a. d. v kal.

124 Aprilis. nunc quoque erat in urbe Roma haec prodente me equitis Romani cornix e Baetica primum colore mira admodum nigro, dein plura contexta verba exprimens et alia atque alia crebro addiscens. nec non et recens fama Crateri Monocerotis cognomine in Erizena regione Asiae corvorum opera venantis eo quod devehebat in silvas eos insidentes corniculo umerisque; illi vestigabant agebantque, eo perducta consuetudine ut exeuntem sic comitarentur

125 et feri. tradendum putavere memoriae quidam visum per sitim lapides congerentem in situlam monimenti in qua pluvia aqua duraret[1] sed quae attingi non posset; ita descendere paventem expressisse tali congerie quantum poturo sufficeret.

126 LXI. Nec Diomedias praeteribo aves. Iuba cataractas vocat, et eis esse dentes oculosque igneo colore, cetero candidis, tradens. duos semper his duces, alterum ducere agmen, alterum cogere;

---

[1] *Rackham* : durabat *aut mutila*.

[a] 129 B.C.   [b] 146 B.C.   [c] 133 B.C.
[d] A horn-shaped ornament, the reward of bravery.
[e] Perhaps the gannet.

372

citizen, in the city in which many leading men had
had no obsequies at all, while the death [a] of Scipio
Aemilianus after he had destroyed Carthage [b] and
Numantia [c] had not been avenged by a single person.
The date of this was 28 March, A.D. 36, in the consulship of Marcus Servilius and Gaius Cestius.   At the
present day also there was in the city of Rome at the *A talking*
time when I was publishing this book a crow belong- *crow.*
ing to a Knight of Rome, that came from Southern
Spain, and was remarkable in the first place for
its very black colour and then for uttering sentences
of several words and frequently learning still more
words in addition.   Also there was recently a report *Ravens*
of one Crates surnamed Monoceros in the district of *trained for*
Eriza in Asia hunting with the aid of ravens, to such *hawking.*
an extent that he used to carry them down into the
forests perched on the crest [d] of his helmet and on his
shoulders; the birds used to track out and drive the
game, the practice being carried to such a point
that even wild ravens followed him in this way when
he left the forest.   Certain persons have thought it
worth recording that a raven was seen during a
drought dropping stones into a monumental urn in
which some rain water still remained but so that the
bird was unable to reach it; in this way as it was
afraid to go down into the urn, the bird by piling up
stones in the manner described raised the water high
enough to supply itself with a drink.

LXI. Nor will I pass by the birds [e] of Diomede. *The*
Juba calls them Plungers-birds, also reporting that *plunger.*
they have teeth, and that their eyes are of a fiery red
colour but the rest of them bright white.   He states
that they always have two leaders, one of whom leads
the column and the other brings up the rear;. that

scrobes excavare rostro, inde crate consternere et operire terra quae ante fuerit egesta; in his fetificare; fores binas omnium scrobibus: orientem spectare quibus exeant in pascua, occasum quibus redeant; alvum exoneraturas subvolare semper et contrario
127 flatu. uno hae in loco totius orbis visuntur, in insula quam diximus nobilem Diomedis tumulo atque delubro, contra Apuliae oram, fulicarum similes. advenas barbaros clangore infestant, Graecis tantum adulantur miro discrimine, velut generi Diomedis hoc tribuentes, aedemque eam cotidie pleno gutture madentibus pennis perluunt atque purificant, unde origo fabulae Diomedis socios in earum effigies mutatos.

128   LXII. Non omittendum est, cum de ingeniis disserimus, e volucribus hirundines indociles esse, e terrestribus mures, cum elephanti iussa faciant, leones iugum subeant, in mari vituli totque piscium genera mitescant.

129   LXIII. Bibunt aves suctu ex iis quibus longa colla intermittentes et capite resupinato velut infundentes sibi. porphyrio solus morsu bibit. idem est proprio genere, omnem cibum aqua subinde tinguens, deinde pede ad rostrum veluti manu adferens. laudatissimi in Commagene; rostra his et praelonga crura rubent.

---

* III 151.

they hollow out trenches with their beaks and then roof them over with lattice and cover this with the earth that they have previously dug from the trenches, and in these they hatch their eggs; that the trenches of all of them have two doors, that by which they go out to forage facing east and that by which they return west; and that when about to relieve themselves they always fly upwards and against the wind. These birds are commonly seen in only one place in the whole world, in the island which we spoke of [a] as famous for the tomb and shrine of Diomede, off the coast of Apulia, and they resemble coots. Barbarian visitors they beset with loud screaming, and they pay deference only to Greeks, a remarkable distinction, as if paying this tribute to the race of Diomede; and every day they wash and purify the temple mentioned by filling their throats with water and wetting their wings, which is the source of the legend that the comrades of Diomede were transformed into the likeness of these birds.

LXII. In a discussion of mental faculties it must not be omitted that among birds swallows and among land animals mice are unteachable, whereas elephants execute orders and lions are yoked to chariots, and in the sea seals and ever so many kinds of fish can be tamed. *Docile and indocile species.*

LXIII. Birds of the kinds that have long necks drink by suction, stopping now and then and so to speak pouring the water into themselves by bending their head back. Only the porphyrio drinks by beakfuls; it also eats in a peculiar way of its own, continually dipping all its food in water and then using its foot as a hand with which to bring it to its beak. The most admired variety of sultana-hen is in Commagene; this has a red beak and very long red legs. *Birds' modes of drinking.*

130   LXIV. Haec quidem et himantopodi multo minori, quamquam eadem crurum altitudine. nascitur in Aegypto. insistit ternis digitis. praecipue ei pabulum muscae. vita in Italia paucis diebus.

LXV. Graviores omnes et[1] fruge vescuntur, altivolae carne tantum, inter aquaticas mergi, soliti avide vorare[2] quae ceterae reddunt.

131   LXVI. Olorum similitudinem onocrotali habent, nec distare existimarentur omnino, nisi faucibus ipsis inesset alterius uteri genus. huc omnia inexplebile animal congerit, mira ut sit capacitas. mox perfecta rapina sensim inde in os reddita in veram alvum ruminantis modo refert. Gallia hos septentrionali proxima oceano mittit.

132   LXVII. In Hercynio Germaniae saltu inusitata[3] genera alitum accepimus quarum plumae ignium modo conluceant noctibus; in ceteris nihil praeter nobilitatem longinquitate factam memorandum occurrit. phalerides in Seleucia Parthorum et in Asia aquaticarum laudatissimae, rursus phasianae in Colchis—geminas ex pluma aures submittunt subriguntque—, Numidicae in parte Africae Numidia, omnes quae[4] iam in Italia.

133   LXVIII. Phoenicopteri linguam praecipui saporis esse Apicius docuit nepotum omnium altissimus gurges. attagen maxime Ionius celeber et vocalis

1 et add. ? Mayhoff.
2 Mayhoff : solida ut devorare.
3 v.l. invisitata (cf. § 84).
4 Mayhoff (vel omnes) : omnesque.

---

a The Black Forest and the Hartz.
b The guinea-fowl, above called meleagrides. .

LXIV. The long-legged plover has the same, *The himantopus.* much smaller bird although with equally long legs. It is born in Egypt. It stands on three toes of each foot. Its food consists chiefly of flies. When brought to Italy it lives only for a few days.

LXV. All the heavier birds feed also on grain, but *Flesh-diet of birds.* the scaring species on flesh only, and so among aquatic birds the cormorants, who regularly devour what the rest disgorge.

LXVI. Pelicans have a resemblance to swans, and *The pelican.* would be thought not to differ from them at all were it not that they have a kind of second stomach in their actual throats. Into this the insatiable creature stows everything, so that its capacity is marvellous. Afterwards when it has done plundering it gradually returns the things from this pouch into its mouth and passes them into the true stomach like a ruminant animal. These birds come to us from the extreme north of Gaul.

LXVII. We have been told of strange kinds of *Other remarkable birds.* birds in the Hercynian Forest *a* of Germany whose feathers shine like fires at night-time; but in the other forests nothing noteworthy occurs beyond the notoriety caused by remoteness. The most celebrated water-bird in Parthian Seleucia and in Asia is the phalaris-duck, the most celebrated bird in Colchis the pheasant—it droops and raises its two feathered ears—and in the Numidian part of Africa the Numidic fowl*b*; all of these are now found in Italy.

LXVIII. Apicius, the most gluttonous gorger of *Rare birds for the table.* all spendthrifts, established the view that the flamingo's tongue has a specially fine flavour. The francolin of Ionia is extremely famous. Normally it is

alias, captus vero obmutescens, quondam existimatus inter raras aves, iam et in Gallia Hispaniaque. capitur circa [1] Alpes etiam, ubi et phalacrocoraces, avis Baliarium insularum peculiaris, sicut Alpium pyrrhocorax luteo rostro niger et praecipua sapore lagopus. pedes leporino villo nomen hoc dedere

134 cetero candidae, columbarum magnitudine. non extra terram eam vesci facile, quando nec vita mansuescit et corpus ocissime marcescit. est et alia nomine eodem a coturnicibus magnitudine tantum differens, croceo tinctu, cibis gratissima. visam in Alpibus ab se peculiarem Aegypti et ibim Egnatius Calvinus praefectus earum prodidit.

135 LXIX. Venerunt in Italiam Bedriacensibus bellis civilibus trans Padum et novae aves—ita enim adhuc vocantur—turdorum specie, paulum infra columbas magnitudine, sapore gratae. Baliares insulae nobiliorem etiam supra dicto porphyrionem mittunt. ibi et buteo accipitrum generis in honore mensarum est, item vipiones [2]—sic enim vocant minorem gruem.

136 LXX. Pegasos equino capite volucres et gryphas [3] auritos ac dira [4] aduncitate rostri fabulosos reor, illos in Scythia, hos in Aethiopia; equidem et tragopana de qua plures adfirmant, maiorem

----

[1] circa *Mayhoff*: et.
[2] *v.ll.* viviones, vibiones.
[3] *v.l.* grypas.
[4] auritos ac dira ? *Mayhoff*: auritos *aut* aurita.

----

[a] Cevedale between Cremona and Verona, where in A.D. 69 Otho was defeated by the troops of Vitellius, and a few months later these in turn by those of Vespasian.

[b] Probably the sand-grouse.

[c] Perhaps Pliny has got them the wrong way round—at all events the griffin was usually placed in Scythia. But in point of fact the reference of the pronouns is not quite certain.

vocal, though when caught it keeps silent. It was once considered one of the rare birds, but now it also occurs in Gaul and Spain. It is even caught in the neighbourhood of the Alps, where also cormorants occur, a bird specially belonging to the Balearic Islands, as the chough, black with a yellow beak, and the particularly tasty willow-grouse belong to the Alps. The latter gets its name of 'hare-foot' from its feet which are tufted like a hare's, though the rest of it is bright white; it is the size of a pigeon. Outside that region it is not easy to keep it, as it does not grow tame in its habits and very quickly loses flesh. There is also another bird with the same name that only differs from quails in size, yellow-coloured, very acceptable for the table. Egnatius Calvinus, Governor of the Alps, has stated that also the ibis, which properly belongs to Egypt, has been seen by him in that region.

LXIX. There also came into Italy during the battles of the civil war round Bedriacum *a* north of the Po the 'new birds'*b*—for so they are still called—which are like thrushes in appearance and a little smaller than pigeons in size, and which have an agreeable flavour. The Balearic Islands send the porphyrio, an even more splendid bird than the one mentioned above. In those islands the buzzard of the hawk family is also in repute for the table, and the *vipio* as well— that is their name for the smaller crane. *Birds imported for the table.*

LXX. The pegasus bird with a horse's head and the griffin with ears and a terrible hooked beak—the former said to be found in Scythia and the latter in Ethiopia*c*—I judge to be fabulous; and for my own part I think the same about the bearded eagle*d* *Fabulous birds.*

d Cf. § 11 n., § 13.

aquila, cornua in temporibus curvata habentem, ferruginei coloris, tantum capite phoeniceo. nec sirenes impetraverint fidem, adfirmet licet Dinon Clitarchi celebrati auctoris pater in India esse mulcerique earum cantu quos gravatos somno lacerent.

137 qui credat ista, et Melampodi profecto auguri aures[1] lambendo dedisse intellectum avium sermonis dracones non abnuat, vel quae Democritus tradit nominando aves quarum confuso sanguine serpens gignatur, quem quisquis ederit intellecturus sit alitum colloquia, quaeque de una ave galerita privatim commemorat, etiam sine his inmensa vitae

138 ambage circa auguria. nominantur ab Homero scopes, avium genus: neque harum satyricos motus, cum insidientur, plerisque memoratos facile conceperim mente, neque ipsae iam aves noscuntur. quamobrem de confessis disseruisse praestiterit.

139 LXXI. Gallinas saginare Deliaci coepere, unde pestis exorta opimas aves et suopte corpore unctas devorandi. hoc primum antiquis cenarum interdictis exceptum invenio iam lege Gai Fanni consulis undecim annis ante tertium Punicum bellum, ne quid volucrum poneretur praeter unam gallinam quae non esset altilis, quod deinde caput translatum per

140 omnes leges ambulavit. inventumque deverticulum

---

[1] auguri aures *Detlefsen* : aures *aut* augures.

---

[a] *Odyssey* V 66.   [b] A genus of owl.
[c] B.C. 161.

attested by a number of people, a bird larger than an eagle, having curved horns on the temples, in colour a rusty red, except that its head is purple-red. Nor should the sirens obtain credit, although Dinon the father of the celebrated authority Clitarchus declares that they exist in India and that they charm people with their song and then when they are sunk in a heavy sleep tear them in pieces. Anybody who would believe that sort of thing would also assuredly not deny that snakes by licking the ears of the augur Melampus gave him the power to understand the language of birds, or the story handed down by Democritus, who mentions birds from a mixture of whose blood a snake is born, whoever eats which will understand the conversations of birds, and the things that he records about one crested lark in particular, as even without these stories life is involved in enormous uncertainty with respect to auguries. Homer [a] mentions a kind of bird called the scops [b]; many people *The dancing* speak of its comic dancing movements when it is *scops.* watching for its prey, but I cannot easily grasp these in my mind, nor are the birds themselves now known. Consequently a discussion of admitted facts will be more profitable.

LXXI. The people of Delos began the practice of *Fattening* fattening hens, which has given rise to the pestilential *and dressing* fashion of gorging fat poultry basted with its own *poultry for* gravy. I find this first singled out in the old inter- *the table.* dicts dealing with feasts as early as the law of the consul Gaius Fannius eleven years [c] before the Third Punic War, prohibiting the serving of any bird course beside a single hen that had not been fattened—a provision that was subsequently renewed and went on through all our sumptuary legislation. And a

est in fraudem earum gallinaceos quoque pascendi
lacte madidis cibis : multo ita gratiores adprobantur.
feminae quidem ad saginam non omnes eliguntur,
nec nisi in cervice pingui cute. postea culinarum
artes, ut clunes spectentur, ut dividantur in tergora,
ut a pede uno dilatatae repositoria occupent. dedere
et Parthi cocis suos mores. nec tamen in hoc
mangonio quicquam totum placet, clune, alibi
pectore tantum laudatis.

141 LXXII. Aviaria primus instituit inclusis omnium
generum avibus M. Laenius Strabo Brundisi equestris
ordinis. ex eo coepimus carcere animalia coercere
quibus rerum natura caelum adsignaverat. maxime
tamen insignis est in hac memoria Clodii Aesopi,
tragici histrionis, patina HS c taxata, in qua posuit
aves cantu aliquo aut humano sermone vocales, HS
142 vī singulas coemptas, nulla alia inductus suavitate
nisi ut in iis imitationem hominis manderet, ne
quaestus quidem suos reveritus illos opimos et voce
meritos, dignus prorsus filio a quo devoratas diximus
margaritas, non sic tamen ut verum facere velim [1]
inter duos iudicium turpitudinis, nisi [2] quod minus
est summas rerum naturae opes quam hominum
linguas cenasse.

---

[1] velim *Mueller* : vi.   [2] *edd.* : si.

[a] IX 122.

way round so as to evade them was discovered, that
of feeding male chickens also with foodstuffs soaked
in milk, a method that makes them esteemed as
much more acceptable. As for hens, they are not
all chosen for fattening, and not unless they have
fat skin on the neck. Subsequently came elaborate
methods of dressing fowls, so as to display the
haunches, so as to split them along the back, so as
to make them fill the dishes by spreading them out
from one foot. Even the Parthians bestowed their
fashions on our cooks. And nevertheless with all
this showing off, no entire dish finds favour, only the
haunch or in other cases the breast being esteemed.

LXXII. Aviaries with cages containing all kinds *Cage-birds*
of birds were first set up by Marcus Laenius Strabo *and
aviaries.*
of the Order of Knighthood at Brindisi. From him
began our practice of imprisoning within bars living
creatures to which Nature had assigned the open sky.
Nevertheless the most remarkable instance in this
record is the dish belonging to the tragic actor
Clodius Aesop, rated at the value of 100,000 sesterces,
in which he served birds that sang some particular
song or talked with human speech, which he acquired
at the price of 6000 sesterces apiece, led by no
other attraction except the desire to indulge in a
sort of cannibalism in eating these birds, and not even
showing any respect for that lavish fortune of his,
even though won by his voice—in fact a worthy father
of a son whom we have spoken of [a] as swallowing
pearls, though not so much so as to make me wish to
give a true decision in the competition in baseness
between the two, unless in so far as it is a smaller
thing to have dined on the most bounteous resources
of Nature than on the tongues of men.

143 LXXIII. Generatio avium simplex videtur esse, cum et ipsa habeat sua miracula, quoniam et quadripedes ova gignunt, chamaeleontes, lacertae et quae diximus in aquatilibus,[1] item serpentes. pennatorum autem infecunda sunt quae aduncos habent ungues. cenchris sola ex his supra quaterna edit ova. tribuit hoc avium generi natura ut fecundiores essent fugaces earum quam fortes; plurima pariunt struthocameli, gallinae, perdices soli. coitus avibus duobus modis, femina considente humi ut in gallinis aut stante ut in gruibus.

144 LXXIV. Ovorum alia sunt candida, ut columbis, perdicibus, alia pallida, ut aquaticis, alia punctis distincta, ut meleagridum, alia rubri coloris, ut phasianis, cenchridi. intus autem omne ovum volucrum bicolor, aquaticis lutei plus quam albi, idque ipsum magis luridum quam ceteris; piscium
145 unus color, in quo nihil candidi. avium ova ex calore fragilia, serpentium ex frigore lenta, piscium ex liquore mollia. aquatilium rotunda, reliqua fere fastigio cacuminata. exeunt a rotundissima sui parte, dum pariuntur, molli putamine sed protinus durescente quibuscumque emergunt portionibus. quae oblonga sint ova gratioris saporis putat Horatius Flaccus. feminam edunt quae rotundiora gignun-

---

[1] in aquatilibus *add. Mueller.*

---

a IX 37, 78.   *b* Sat. II. 4. 12.

LXXIII. The reproductive system of birds appears *Mating of birds.* to be simple, although even this possesses marvels of its own, since even four-footed creatures produce eggs—chamaeleons and lizards and those we have specified[a] among aquatic species, and also snakes. But among feathered creatures those that have hooked talons are unfertile. Of these only the lesser kestrel produces more than four eggs at a time. Nature has bestowed on the bird kind the attribute that the species among them that are shy are more prolific than the brave ones; only ostriches, hens and partridges bear very numerous broods. Birds have two methods of coupling, the hen sitting on the ground as in the case of the domestic fowl or standing up as in the case of the crane.

LXXIV. The eggs are in some cases white, as *Colours and* with the dove and partridge, in others pale-coloured, *shapes of eggs.* as with waterfowl, in others spotted, as those of the guinea-hen, in others of a red colour, as in the case of the pheasant and the lesser kestrel. The inside of every bird's egg is of two colours; in that of the aquatic birds there is more yellow than white, and that yellow is brighter than with the other species. Fishes' eggs are of one colour, which contains no bright white. Birds' eggs are made easily breakable by heat, snakes' eggs are made flexible by cold, and fishes' eggs are softened by liquid. Aquatic species have round eggs, but almost all others oval-shaped ones. They are laid with their roundest part in front, the shell of whatever portions they emerge with being soft but becoming hard immediately after the process. Long-shaped eggs are thought by Horace[b] to have a more agreeable flavour. Eggs of a rounder formation produce a hen chicken and

tur, reliqua marem. umbilicus ovis a cacumine inest,
ceu gutta eminens in putamine.

146 Quaedam omni tempore coeunt, ut gallinae, et
pariunt praeterquam duobus mensibus hiemis bruma-
libus. ex his iuvencae plura quam veteres sed
minora, et[1] in eodem fetu prima ac novissima. est
autem tanta fecunditas ut aliquae et sexagena
parient, aliquae cotidie, aliquae bis die, aliquae in
147 tantum ut effetae moriantur. Hadrianis laus maxima. columbae deciens anno pariunt, quaedam et
undeciens, in Aegypto vero etiam brumali mense.
hirundines et merulae et palumbi et turtures bis anno
pariunt, ceterae aves fere semel. turdi in cacuminibus arborum luto nidificantes paene contextim,
in secessu generant. a coitu decem diebus ova
maturescunt in utero, vexatis autem gallinae et
columbae pinna evulsa aliave simili iniuria diutius.
148 omnibus ovis medio vitelli parva inest velut san-
guinea gutta, quod esse cor avium existimant,
primum in omni corpore id gigni opinantes: in ovo
certe gutta ea salit palpitatque. ipsum animal ex
albo liquore ovi corporatur; cibus eius in luteo est.
omnibus initio[2] caput maius toto corpore, oculi
compressi capite maiores. increscente pullo candor
149 in medium vertitur, luteum circumfunditur. vicensimo die si moveatur ovum, iam viventis intra puta-

____
[1] et ⟨minima⟩ in ? *Rackham.*
[2] initio ? *ex Aristotele Mayhoff* : intus.

____
[a] Near Venice, on the coast of the sea named after it. We
learn elsewhere that the birds were bantams.

386

the rest a cock. The navel in eggs is at the top end, projecting like a speck in the shell.

Some birds mate in any season, for instance the domestic fowl, and lay, except in the two midwinter months. Of these kinds the young hens lay more eggs than the old, but smaller ones, and in the same brood those laid first and last are the smallest. But they are so fertile that some even lay eggs sixty times, some lay daily, some twice daily, some so much that they die of exhaustion. Adria [a] birds are most highly spoken of. Pigeons lay ten times a year, some even eleven times, while in Egypt they even lay in a midwinter month. Swallows and blackbirds and woodpigeons and turtle-doves lay twice a year, all other birds as a rule only once. Thrushes build their nests of mud in an almost continuous mass on the tops of trees, and breed in retirement. The eggs grow to full size in the uterus in ten days from pairing, but in the case of the domestic fowl and the pigeon, if the hen is disturbed by having a feather torn out or by some similar damage, it takes longer. In all eggs the middle of the yolk contains a small drop of a sort of blood, which people think is the heart of birds, supposing that the heart is the first part that is produced in every body: in an egg undoubtedly this drop beats and throbs. The animal itself is formed out of the white of the egg, but its food is in the yolk.[b] In all cases at the beginning the head is larger than the whole body, and the eyes, which are pressed together, are larger than the head. As the chick grows in size the white turns to the middle and the yolk spreads round it. If on the twentieth day the egg be moved, the voice of the

Fertility of bird species. Modes of laying and hatching. Physiology of the egg.

[b] Actually it is both the yolk and the white.

men vox auditur. ab eodem tempore plumescit, ita positus ut caput supra dextrum pedem habeat, dextram vero alam supra caput. vitellus paulatim deficit. aves omnes in pedes nascuntur, contra
150 quam reliqua animalia. quaedam gallinae omnia gemina ova pariunt et geminos interdum excludunt, ut Cornelius Celsus auctor est, alterum maiorem; aliqui negant omnino geminos excludi. plus vicena quina incubanda subici vetant. parere a bruma incipiunt; optima fetura ante vernum aequinoctium: post solstitium nata non implent magnitudinem iustam, tantoque minus quanto serius provenere.

151 LXXV. Ova incubari intra decem dies edita utilissimum; vetera aut recentiora infecunda. subici impari numero debent. quarto die postquam coepere incubari, si contra lumen cacumine ovorum adprehenso ima [1] manu purus et uniusmodi perluceat color, sterilia existimantur esse proque eis alia substituenda. et in aqua est experimentum: inane fluitat, itaque sidentia, hoc est plena, subici volunt. concuti vero experimento vetant, quoniam non gignant confusis
152 vitalibus venis. incubationi datur initium decima demum [2] post novam lunam, quia prius inchoata non proveniant. celerius excluduntur calidis diebus; ideo aestate undevicensimo educent fetum, hieme xxv. si incubitu tonuit, ova pereunt, et accipitris

---

[1] v.l. una.   [2] decima demum add. e Columella Mayhoff.

[a] Romans called the day after an event *secunda dies* and the day after that *tertia*.

chick already alive is heard inside the shell. At the same time it begins to grow feathers, its posture being such that it has its head above its right foot but its right wing above its head. The yolk gradually disappears. All birds are born feet first, the opposite way to the remaining animals. Some domestic hens lay all their eggs in pairs, and according to Cornelius Celsus occasionally hatch twin chicks, one larger than the other; though some assert that twin chicks are never hatched out. They lay down a rule that the hen should not be required to sit on more than 25 eggs at a time. Hens begin to lay at midwinter, and breed best before the spring equinox: chickens born after midsummer do not attain the proper size, and the later they are hatched the more they fall short of it.

LXXV. It pays best for eggs to be sat on within ten days of laying; older or fresher ones are infertile. An odd number should be put under the hen. If three days after they began to be sat on the top of the eggs held in the tips of the fingers against the light shows a transparent colour of a single hue, the eggs are judged to be barren, and others should be substituted for them. They may also be tested in water: an empty egg floats, and consequently people prefer eggs that sink, that is, are full, to put under the hens. But they warn against their being tested by shaking, on the ground that if the vital veins are displaced the eggs are sterile. The ninth[a] day after a new moon is assigned for starting a hen's sitting, as eggs begun earlier do not hatch out. The chicks are hatched more quickly when the days are warm, and consequently eggs will hatch out in 18 days in summer but 24 in winter. If it thunders while the

Rules for managing sitting hens.

389

cudita voce vitiantur; remedium contra tonitrus
clavus ferreus sub stramine ovorum positus aut terra
153 ex aratro. quaedam autem et citra incubitum
sponte natura[1] gignit,[2] ut in Aegypti fimetis.
scitum de quodam potore reperitur Syracusis tamdiu
potare solitum donec cooperta terra fetum ederent
ova.

154   LXXVI. Quin et ab homine perficiuntur. Iulia
Augusta prima sua iuventa Ti. Caesare ex Nerone
gravida, cum parere virilem sexum admodum cuperet,
hoc usa est puellari augurio, ovum in sinu fovendo
atque, cum deponendum haberet, nutrici per sinum
tradendo ne intermitteretur tepor; nec falso augu-
rata proditur. nuper inde fortassis inventum ut ova
calido in loco imposita paleis igne modico foverentur
homine versante, pariterque et stato die vivus[3]
155 erumperet fetus. traditur quaedam ars gallinarii
cuiusdam dicentis quod ex quaque esset. narrantur
et mortua gallina mariti earum visi succendentes in
vicem et reliqua fetae more facientes abstinentesque
se cantu. super omnia est anatum ovis subditis
atque exclusis admiratio prima non plane agnoscentis

---

[1] naturae *Gelen.*   [2] *v.l.* gignunt.
[3] vivus? *Mayhoff*: milium *aut* illi-nc.

ᵃ Livia Drusilla was thus styled after her marriage with
Augustus. Her first husband, Tiberius Claudius Nero, was
the father of the Emperor Tiberius.

hen is sitting the eggs die, and if she hears the cry
of a hawk they go bad. A remedy against thunder
is an iron nail placed under the straw in which the
eggs lie, or some earth from the plough. In some
cases Nature hatches of her own accord even without
the hen sitting, as on the dunghills of Egypt. We
find a clever story about a certain toper at Syracuse,
that he used to go on drinking for as long a time as it
would take for eggs covered with earth to produce a
hatch.

LXXVI. Moreover eggs can be hatched even by *Birth-control*
a human being. Julia Augusta [a] in her early woman- *for women*
hood was with child with Tiberius Caesar by Nero, *and for*
and being specially eager to a bear a baby of the *poultry.*
male sex she employed the following method of
prognostication used by girls—she cherished an egg
in her bosom and when she had to lay it aside passed
it to a nurse under the folds of their dresses, so that
the warmth might not be interrupted; and it is said
that her prognostication came true. It was perhaps
from this that the method was lately invented of
placing eggs in chaff in a warm place and cherishing
them with a moderate fire, with somebody to keep
turning them over, with the result that all the live
brood breaks the shell at once on a fixed day. It is
recorded that a certain poultry-keeper had a
scientific method of telling which egg was from which
hen. It is related also that when a hen has died the
cocks of the farmyard have been seen taking on her
duties in turn and generally behaving in the manner
of a broody hen, and abstaining from crowing.
Above all things is the behaviour of a hen when ducks'
eggs have been put under her and have hatched out
—first her surprise when she does not quite recognize

fetum, mox incerti singultus sollicite convocantis, postremo lamenta circa piscinae stagna mergentibus se pullis natura duce.

156   LXXVII. Gallinarum generositas spectatur crista recta, interim et gemina, pennis nigris, ore rubicundo, digitis inparibus, aliquando et super quattuor digitos traverso uno. ad rem divinam luteo rostro pedibusque purae non videntur, ad opertanea sacra[a] nigrae. est et pumilionum genus non sterile in his, quod non in alio genere alitum, sed quibus certa[1] fecunditas rara et incubatio ovis noxia.

LXXVIII. Inimicissima autem omni[2] generi pituita, maximeque inter messis ac vindemiae tempus.
157 medicina in fame et cubitus in fumo, utique si e lauru aut herba sabina fiat, penna per traversas inserta nares et per omnes dies mota, cibus alium cum farre, aut aqua perfusus in qua maduerit noctua aut cum semine vitis albae coctus, ac quaedam alia.

158   LXXIX. Columbae proprio ritu osculantur ante coitum. pariunt fere bina ova, ita natura moderante ut aliis crebrior sit fetus, aliis numerosior. palumbus et turtur plurimum terna nec plus quam bis vere pariunt, atque ita ut,[3] si prior fetus corruptus est, et quamvis tria pepererint, numquam plus duobus educant; tertium quod inritum est urinum vocant.

---

  ¹ v.ll. contra, centra.   ² Mayhoff: omnium.
                ³ ut add. Detlefsen.

  ᵃ Sacrifices to the Bona Dea.

her brood, then her puzzled sobs as she anxiously calls them to her, and finally her lamentations round the margin of the pond when the chicks under the guidance of instinct take to the water.

LXXVII. Marks of good breeding in hens are an upstanding comb, which is occasionally double, black feathers, red beak, and uneven claws, sometimes one lying actually across the four others. Fowls with yellow beak and feet seem not to be unblemished for purposes of religion, and black ones for the mystery rites.[a] Even the dwarf variety is not sterile in the case of the domestic fowl, which is not the case in any other breeds of birds, though with the dwarf fowl reliability in laying is unusual, and sitting on the eggs is harmful to the hen. *Signs of breed in fowls.*

LXXVIII. But the worst enemy of every kind is the pip, and especially between the time of harvest and vintage. The cure is in hunger, and they must lie in smoke, at all events if it be produced from bay-leaves or savin, a feather being inserted right through the nostrils and shifted daily; diet garlic mixed with spelt, either steeped in water in which an owl has been dipped or else boiled with white vine seed, and certain other substances. *Poultry disease.*

LXXIX. Pigeons go through a special ceremony of kissing before mating. They usually lay two eggs at a time, nature so regulating as to make some produce larger chicks and others more numerous. The woodpigeon and the turtle-dove lay at most three eggs at a time, and never more than twice in a spring, and keeping a rule that, if the former lay goes bad, even although they lay three eggs they never rear more than two chicks; the third egg, which is unfertile, they call a wind-egg. The hen wood- *Mating of pigeons.*

palumbis incubat femina post meridianam[1] in
159 matutinum, cetero mas. columbae marem semper
et feminam pariunt, priorem marem, postridie
feminam. incubant in eo genere ambo, interdiu mas,
noctu femina. excludunt xx die, pariunt a coitu V.
aestate quidem interdum binis mensibus terna
educunt paria, namque xviii die excludunt statimque concipiunt; quare inter pullos saepe ova inveniuntur et alii provolant, alii erumpunt. ipsi
160 deinde pulli quinquemenstres fetificant. et ipsae
autem inter se, si mas non sit, feminae aeque saliunt,
pariuntque ova inrita ex quibus nihil gignitur, quae
hypenemia Graeci vocant.

161   Pavo a trimatu parit. primo anno unum aut
alterum ovum, sequenti quaterna quinave, ceteris
duodena, non amplius, intermittens binos dies
ternosve parit, et ter anno, si gallinis subiciantur
incubanda. mares ea frangunt desiderio incuban-
tium; quapropter noctu et in latebris pariunt aut in
excelso cubantes, et nisi molli strato excepta franguntur. mares singuli quinis sufficiunt coniugibus;
cum singulae aut binae fuere, corrumpitur salacitate
fecunditas. partus excluditur diebus ter novenis,
aut tardius tricensimo.

              [1] *Mayhoff ?* : meridiana.

pigeon sits from noon till the next morning and the cock the rest of the time. Pigeons always lay a male and a female egg, the male first and the female a day later. In this species both birds sit, the cock in the daytime and the hen at night. They hatch in about three weeks, and they lay four days after mating. In summer indeed they sometimes produce three pairs of chickens every two months, for they hatch on the 17th[a] day and breed immediately; consequently eggs are often found among the chickens, and some are beginning to fly just when others are breaking the egg. Then the chicks themselves begin laying when five months old. However in the absence of a cock hen birds actually mate with one another indifferently, and produce unfertile eggs from which nothing is produced, which the Greeks call wind-eggs.

The peahen begins to lay when three months old. In the first year it lays one egg or a second one, but in the following year four or five at a time, and in the remaining years twelve at a time, but not more, with intervals of two or three days between the eggs, and three times in the year, provided that the eggs are put under farmyard hens to sit on. The male peacock breaks the eggs, out of desire for the female sitting on them; consequently the hen bird lays at night, and in hiding or when perching on a high place—and unless the eggs are caught on a bed of straw they are broken. One cock can serve five hens, and when there have been only one or two hens for each cock their fertility is spoiled by its salaciousness. The chickens are hatched in 27 days or at latest on the 29th.

Mating of peacocks.

<hr />

[a] See note [a] on c. LXXV.

162 Anseres in aqua coeunt, pariunt vere aut, si bruma coiere, post solstitium, xl prope, bis anno si priorem fetum gallinae excludant, alio plurima ova sedecim, paucissima septem. si quis subripiat, pariunt donec

163 rumpantur. aliena non excludunt. incubanda subici utilissimum novem aut undecim. incubant feminae tantum tricenis diebus, si vero tepidiores sint, xxv. pullis eorum urtica contactu mortifera, nec minus aviditas, nunc satietate nimia, nunc suamet vi, quando adprehensa radice morsu saepe conantes avellere ante colla sua abrumpunt. contra urticam remedium est stramento ab incubitu subdita radix earum.

164 Ardeolarum tria genera: leucon, asterias, pellos. hi in coitu anguntur: mares quidem cum vociferatu sanguinem etiam. ex oculis profundunt; nec minus

165 aegre pariunt gravidae. aquila tricenis diebus incubat, et fere maiores alites, minores vicenis, ut milvus et accipiter. milvus binos [1] fere parit, numquam plus ternos, is qui aegolios vocatur et quaternos, corvus aliquando et quinos; incubant totidem diebus. cornicem incubantem mas pascit. pica novenos, melancoryphus supra xx parit, semper numero inpari, nec alia plures: tanto fecunditas maior parvis.

---

[1] *Gesner*: accipiter. singulos.

Geese mate in the water; they lay in spring, or *Mating of geese.* if they mated in midwinter, after midsummer; they lay nearly 40 eggs, twice in a year if the hens turn the first brood out of the nest, otherwise sixteen eggs at the most and seven at the fewest. If somebody removes the eggs, they go on laying till they burst. They do not turn strange eggs out of the nest. It pays best to put nine or eleven eggs for them to sit on. The hens sit only 30 days at a time, or if the days are rather warm, 25. The touch of a nettle is fatal to goslings, and not less so is their greediness, sometimes owing to their excessive gorging and sometimes owing to their own violence, when they have caught hold of a root in their beak and in their repeated attempts to tear it off break their own necks before they succeed. A nettle-root put under their straw after they have lain in it is a cure for nettle-sting.

There are three kinds of heron, the white, the *Mating of herons, eagles, kites, crows, magpies and swallows.* speckled and the dark.[a] These birds suffer pain in mating, indeed the cocks give loud screams and even shed blood from their eyes; and the broody hens lay their eggs with equal difficulty. The eagle sits on her eggs for thirty days at a time, and so do the larger birds for the most part, but the smaller ones, for instance the kite and hawk, sit for twenty days. A kite's brood usually numbers two chicks, never more than three, that of the bird called the merlin as many as four, and the raven's occasionally even five; they sit for the same number of days. The hen crow is fed by the cock while sitting. The magpie's brood numbers nine, the blackcap's[b] over twenty and always an odd number, and no other bird has a larger brood: so much more prolific are

397

hirundini caeci primo pulli sunt et fere omnibus quibus numerosior fetus.

166 LXXX. Inrita ova, quae hypenemia diximus, aut mutua feminae inter se libidinis imaginatione concipiunt aut pulvere, nec columbae tantum, sed et gallinae, perdices, pavones, anseres, chenalopeces. sunt autem sterilia, et minora ac minus iucundi saporis et magis umida. quidam et vento putant ea generari, qua de causa etiam zephyria appellantur; urina autem vere tantum fiunt incubatione derelicta,

167 quae alii cynosura dixere. ova aceto macerata in tantum emolliuntur ut per anulos transeant. servari ea in lomento aut hieme in paleis, aestate furfuribus utilissimum; sale exinaniri creduntur.

168 LXXXI. Volucrum animal parit vespertilio tantum, cui et membranae ceu pennae; eadem sola volucrum lacte nutrit ubera admovens. parit[1] geminos; volitat amplexa infantes secumque portat. eidem coxendix una traditur esse.[2] in cibatu culices gratissimi.

169 LXXXII. Rursus in terrestribus ova pariunt serpentes, de quibus nondum dictum est. coeunt complexu, adeo circumvolutae sibi ipsae ut una

---

[1] *Mueller*: parens.   [2] *Mayhoff*: traditur et.

ª See § 160.

the small species. A swallow's first chicks are blind, as are those of almost all species that have a comparatively large brood.

LXXX. Unfertile eggs, which we have designated *a* *Wind-eggs.* wind-eggs, are conceived by the hen birds mating together in a pretence of sexual intercourse, or else from dust, and not only by hen pigeons but also by farmyard hens, partridges, peahens, geese and ducks. But these eggs are sterile, and of smaller size and less agreeable flavour, and more watery. Some people think they are actually generated by the wind, for which reason they are also called Zephyr's eggs; but wind-eggs are only produced in spring, when the hens have left off sitting: another name for them is addle-eggs. When steeped in vinegar eggs become so much softer that they can be passed through rings. It pays best to keep them in bean meal, or else chaff in winter and bran in summer; it is believed that keeping them in salt drains them quite empty.

LXXXI. The only viviparous creature that flies *The bat.* is the bat, which actually has membranes like wings; it is also the only flyer that nourishes its young with milk, bringing them to its teats. It bears twins, and flits about with its children in its arms, carrying them with it. The bat is said to have a single hip-bone. Gnats are its favourite fodder.

LXXXII. On the other hand among land animals, *Mating of* the snake is oviparous; we have not yet described *snakes and* *of crocodiles.* this species. Snakes mate by embracing, intertwining so closely that they could be taken to be a single animal with two heads. The male viper inserts its head into the female viper's mouth, and the female is so enraptured with pleasure that she

existimari biceps possit. viperae mas caput inserit
170 in os, quod illa abrodit voluptatis dulcedine. terrestrium eadem sola intra se parit ova unius coloris
et mollia ut pisces. tertio die intra uterum catulos
excludit, dein singulis diebus singulos parit, xx fere
numero; itaque ceteri tarditatis inpatientes perrum-
punt latera occisa parente. ceterae serpentes
contexta ova in terra incubant, et fetum sequenti
excludunt anno. crocodili vicibus incubant, mas et
femina.

Sed reliquorum quoque terrestrium reddatur
generatio.

171 LXXXIII. Bipedum solus homo animal gignit.
homini tantum primi coitus paenitentia, augurium
scilicet vitae a paenitenda origine. ceteris animalibus stati per tempora anni concubitus, homini, ut
dictum est, omnibus horis dierum noctiumque.
172 ceteris satias in coitu, homini prope nulla; Messalina
Claudii Caesaris coniunx regalem hanc existimans
palmam elegit in id certamen nobilissimam e prosti-
tutis ancillam mercenariae stipis, eamque nocte ac
die superavit quinto atque vicensimo concubitu.
in hominum genere maribus deverticula veneris
excogitata omnia, scelera [1] naturae, feminis vero
abortus. quantum in hac parte multo nocentiores
quam ferae sumus! viros avidiores veneris hieme,
feminas aestate Hesiodus prodidit.

[1] v.l. scelere.

---

[a] Ar. Probl. IV, 8779, Διὰ τί οἱ νέοι ὅταν πρῶτον ἀφροδισιάζειν
ἄρχωνται, οἷς ἂν ὁμιλήσωσι, μετὰ τὴν πρᾶξιν μισοῦσιν.
[b] VII 38.
[c] Works and Days 586.

gnaws it off. The viper is the only land animal that bears eggs inside it; they are of one colour and soft like fishes' roe. After two days she hatches the young inside her uterus, and then bears them at the rate of one a day, to the number of about twenty; the consequence is that the remaining ones get so tired of the delay that they burst open their mother's sides, so committing matricide. All the other kinds of snakes incubate their eggs in a clutch on the ground, and hatch out the young in the following year. Crocodiles take turns to incubate, male and female.

But let us give an account of the mode of reproduction of the remaining land animals as well.

LXXXIII. Man is the only viviparous biped. *Mating periods of animals.* Man is the only animal with which mating for the first time is followed by repugnance,[a] which is doubtless an augury of life as sprung from regrettable source. All the other animals have fixed seasons of the year for mating, but man, as has been said,[b] mates at every hour of the day and night. All the others experience satiety in coupling, but with man this is almost entirely absent. Claudius Caesar's consort Messalina, thinking that this would be a truly regal triumph, selected for a competition in it a certain maid who was the most notorious of the professional prostitutes, and beat her in a twenty-four hours' match, with a score of twenty-five. In the human race the males have devised every out-of-the-way form of sexual indulgence, crimes against nature, but the females have invented abortion. How much more guilty are we in this department than the wild animals! Hesiod[c] has stated that men have stronger sexual appetites in winter and women in summer.

173 Coitus aversis elephantis, camelis, tigribus, lyncibus,
rhinoceroti, leoni, dasypodi, cuniculis, quibus aversa
genitalia. cameli etiam solitudines aut secreta certe
petunt, neque intervenire datur sine pernicie; coitus
toto die, et his tantum ex omnibus. quibus solida
ungula in quadrupedum genere, mares olfactus
accendit, avertuntur et canes, phocae, lupi in medio [1]
174 coitu invitique [2] etiam cohaerent. supra dictorum
dasypodum [3] plerumque feminae priores superveniunt, in reliquis mares; ursi autem, ut dictum
est, humanitus [4] strati, irenacei stantes ambo inter
se complexi, feles mare stante, femina subiacente,
vulpes in latera proiectae maremque femina amplexa.
taurorum cervorumque feminae vim non tolerant;
ea de causa ingrediuntur in coitu.[5] cervi vicissim ad
alias transeunt et ad priores redeunt. lacertae ut
ea quae sine pedibus sunt circumflexu venerem
novere.

175 Omnia animalia quo maiora corpore hoc minus
fecunda. singulos gignunt elephanti, cameli, equi;
acanthis duodenos, avis minima. ocissime pariunt
quae plurumos gignunt; quo maius est animal, tanto
diutius formatur in utero; diutius gestantur quibus
longiora sunt vitae spatia. neque crescentium tem-
176 pestiva ad generandum aetas. quae solidas habent

---

[1] *Rackham*: medioque.
[2] inviti *Urlichs.*
[3] dasypodum *add. ex Ar. Mueller.*
[4] humi *secundum Ar. Pintianus.*
[5] *Gelen*: conceptu.

Species with the genital organs behind them, *Quadrupeds*
elephants, camels, tigers, lynxes, the rhinoceros, the *various*
lion, the hairy-footed and the common rabbit *coupling.*
couple back to back. Camels even make for
deserts or else places certain to be secret, and
one is not allowed to interrupt them without disaster; the coupling lasts a whole day, and this is the
case with these alone of all animals. With the
solid-hooved species in the quadruped class the
males are excited by scenting the female. Also
dogs, seals and wolves turn away in the middle of
coupling and still remain coupled against their will.
Among the above-mentioned^a species, of hares the
females usually cover first, but with all the others the
males; but bears, as was said, couple, like human
beings, lying down, hedgehogs both standing up and
embracing each other, cats with the male standing
and the female lying beneath it, foxes lying down on
their sides and the female embracing the male.
Cows and does resent the violence of the bulls and
stags, and consequently walk forward in pairing.
Stags pass across to other hinds and return to the
former ones alternately. Lizards like the creatures
without feet practise intercourse by intertwining.

All animals are less fertile the larger they are in *Fertility*
bulk. Elephants, camels and horses produce off- *varies*
spring one at a time, but the thistle-finch, the smallest *with size*
of birds, twelve at a time. Those that produce most *of species.*
young bear them most quickly; the larger the animal,
the longer it takes to be shaped in the womb; the
more long-lived ones are carried longer by the
mother. Also animals are not of an age suitable for
procreation while they are still growing. Solid-

<hr>

^a VIII 126.

ungulas singulos, quae bisulcas et geminos pariunt;
quorum in digitos pedum fissura divisa est, et[1]
numerosiora in fetu. sed superiora omnia perfectos
edunt partus, haec inchoatos, in quo sunt genere
leaenae, ursae; et vulpes informe etiam magis quam
supradicta parit, rarumque est videre parientem.
postea lambendo calefaciunt fetus omnia ea et
177 figurant. pariunt plurimum quaternos. caecos
autem gignunt canes, lupi, pantherae, thoes.

Canum plura genera. Laconicae octavo mense
utrumque generant; ferunt sexaginta diebus et
plurimum tribus. ceterae canes et semenstres
coitum patiuntur. inplentur omnes uno coitu.
quae ante iustum tempus concepere diutius caecos
habent catulos, et omnes totidem diebus. existimantur in urina attollere crus fere semenstres; id est
signum consummati virium roboris. feminae hoc
178 idem sidentes. partus duodeni quibus numerosis-
simi, cetero quini, seni, aliquando singuli, quod pro-
digiosum putant, sicut omnes mares aut omnes
feminas gigni. primos quosque mares pariunt, in
ceteris alternant. ineuntur a partu sexto mense.
octonos Laconicae pariunt. propria in eo genere
maribus laboris alacritas.[2] vivunt Laconici anni
denis, feminae duodenis, cetera genera xv aliquando

---

[1] *Mayhoff*: e.   [2] *edd.* : labore salacitas.

hoofed animals bear one child at a time, those with cloven hooves also bear two, but those whose feet are divided into separate toes also produce a larger number. But whereas all those above bear their offspring fully formed, these produce them un-finished—in this class being lionesses and bears; and a fox bears its young in an even more unfinished state than the species above-mentioned, and it is rare to see one in the act of giving birth. After-wards all these species warm their offspring and shape them by licking them. Their litters number four at the most. Dogs, wolves, panthers and jackals bear their young blind. *Species born immature.*

There are several kinds of dogs. The Spartan hounds breed when both sexes are seven months old; the bitches carry for 60 days, and 63 at most. The bitches of the other breeds are willing to couple, even when six months old. They all conceive from a single coupling. Those that are bred from before the proper time have puppies that stay blind longer, and all of them for the same number of days. They are believed to raise the leg in making water when about six months old; this is a sign of fully matured strength. Bitches relieve themselves sitting. The most prolific have litters of twelve, but usually they have five or six, and sometimes only one: this is considered portentous, as are litters that are all males or all females. Male puppies are born first in each litter, whereas in all other animals the sexes come in turns. Bitches couple five months after their last litter. The Spartan hounds have litters of eight. The males of that breed are marked by keenness for work. Spartan dog hounds live ten years, bitches twelve; all the other breeds live fifteen years, some- *Breeding of dogs.*

et xx, nec tota sua aetate generant, fere a duodecimo desinentes.

179 Felium et ichneumonum reliqua ut canum; vivunt annis denis.[1] dasypodes omni mense pariunt, et superfetant, sicut lepores; a partu statim implentur. concipiunt quamvis ubera siccante fetu; pariunt vero[2] caecos. elephanti, ut diximus, pariunt singulos magnitudine vituli trimenstris. cameli duodecim mensibus ferunt, a trimatu pariunt vere

180 iterumque post annum implentur a partu. equas autem post tertium demum aut post unum ab enixu utiliter admitti putant; coguntque invitas. asinas[3] et septimo[4] die concipere facillime creditur. equarum iubas tondere praecipiunt ut asinorum coitum patiantur humilitate, comantes enim gloria superbire. a coitu solae animalium currunt exadversus aquilonem austrumve prout marem aut feminam concepere. colorem ilico mutant rubriore pilo vel quicumque sit pleniore: hoc argumento desinunt admittere, etiam volentes.[5] nec impedit partus quasdam ab opere, falluntque gravidae. vicisse Olympia praegnantem

181 Echecratidis Thessali invenimus. equos et canes et sues initum matutinum adpetere, feminas autem post meridiem blandiri diligentiores tradunt; equas

---

[1] *Brotier*: senis.   [2] *Hardouin*: non.
[3] asinas *add. Pintianus.*
[4] *Mueller*: et mulier septimo.
[5] *v.l.* nolentes.

---

[a] The MSS. give ' six.'   [b] VIII 28.

times even twenty. But they do not breed all their lives, ceasing usually at the age of twelve.

The cat and the mongoose resemble dogs in other respects, but their length of life is ten [a] years. Rabbits breed in every month of the year, and superfetate, as do hares; after giving birth they pair again at once. They conceive although still suckling their previous litter, but the young are blind. Elephants, as we have said,[b] bear one young one at a time, of the size of a three months old calf. Camels carry their young twelve months; they begin breeding at the age of three, in the spring, and mate again a year after giving birth. Mares on the other hand are believed not to be profitably sired till three years old, and not before a year after their last foaling; when they are unwilling, compulsion is used. It is believed that she-asses conceive quite easily even a week after delivery. It is said that mares' manes ought to be clipped to make them submit to allow coupling with asses, as having long manes makes them proud and high-spirited. Mares are the only animals that after coupling run in a northerly or southerly direction according as they have conceived a male or a female foal. Immediately afterwards they change the colour of their coat for a deeper red or a darker hue of whatever their colour is: this marks their ceasing to be able to couple, even if willing to do so. Some are not hindered from work by foaling, and are in foal without its being known. We find it on record that a mare in foal belonging to a Thessalian named Echecratides won a race at Olympia. It is stated by exceptionally careful authorities that horses, dogs and swine like mating in the morning, but that the females make approaches in the afternoon; that

Breeding of various other species.

Horse-breeding.

407

domitas sexaginta diebus equire ante quam gregales ;
sues tantum in [1] coitu spumam ore fundere ; verrem
subantis audita voce, ni admittatur, cibum non capere
usque in maciem, feminas autem in tantum efferari
ut hominem lancinent, candida maxime veste
indutum. rabies ea aceto mitigatur naturae asperso.

182 aviditas coitus putatur et cibis fieri, sicut viro eruca,
pecori caepa. quae ex feris mitigentur non concipere, ut anseres, apros vero tarde et cervos nec nisi
ab infantia educatos mirum est. quadripedum
praegnantes venerem arcent praeter equam et suem ;
sed superfetant dasypus et lepus tantum.

183 LXXXIV. Quaecumque animal pariunt in capita
gignunt circumacto fetu sub enixum alias in utero
porrecto. quadripedes gestantur extensis ad longitudinem cruribus et ad alvum suam applicatis, homo
in semet conglobatus inter duo genua naribus sitis.

184 molas, de quibus ante diximus, gigni putant ubi
mulier non ex mare verum ex semetipsa tantum
conceperit ; ideo nec animari quia non sit ex duobus,
altricemque habere per se vitam illam quae satis
arboribusque contingat. ex omnibus quae perfectos fetus sues tantum et numerosos edunt,

---

[1] in *add. ? Mayhoff.*

---

[a] The eye-cavities in the human face were supposed to be
created by the pressure of the knees in the womb.
[b] VII 63.

mares that have been broken are in heat 60 days sooner than those running with the herd; that swine only foam at the mouth when mating; that when a boar-pig has heard a sow in heat grunting it refuses food to the point of losing flesh entirely unless it is admitted to her, while sows get so fierce that they will gore a human being, especially one wearing white clothes. This madness can be reduced by sprinkling the organs with vinegar. It is believed that desire for mating is also stimulated by articles of diet, for instance rocket in the case of a man and onions in the case of cattle. It is a remarkable fact that wild species when domesticated refuse to breed, for instance wild geese, and wild boars and stags do so reluctantly and only if they have been reared from infancy. Female animals refuse intercourse when pregnant, except the mare and the sow; but only the common rabbit and the hairy-footed rabbit allow superfetation.

LXXXIV. All viviparous species produce their young head foremost, the embryo turning round shortly before delivery, but otherwise lying stretched at length in the womb. Four-footed species are carried with the legs stretched out to full length and folded against their own belly, but the human embryo curled up in a ball, with the nostrils placed between the two knees.[a] It is thought that moon calves, about which we have spoken before,[b] are produced when a woman has conceived not from a male but from herself alone, and that they do not come alive because they are not produced from two parents, and they possess the self-nourishing vitality that belongs to plants and trees. Of all the species bearing fully developed offspring pigs alone have litters that are numerous as well as developed, for it

Posture of the embryo at birth.

409

nam[1] plures[2] contra naturam solidipedum aut
bisulcorum.

185 LXXXV. Super cuncta est murium fetus, haut sine
cunctatione dicendus, quamquam sub auctore Aristotele et Alexandri Magni militibus. generatio eorum
lambendo constare, non coitu, dicitur. ex una
genitos cxx tradiderunt, apud Persas vero praegnantes in ventre parentis[3] repertas; et salis gustatu
186 fieri praegnantes opinantur. itaque desinit mirum
esse unde vis tanta messes populetur murium agrestium; in quibus illud quoque adhuc latet quonam
modo illa multitudo repente occidat: nam nec
exanimes reperiuntur neque extat qui murem hieme
in agro effoderit. plurimi ita ad Troada proveniunt,
et iam inde fugaverunt incolas. proventus eorum
siccitatibus. tradunt etiam obituris vermiculum in
capite gigni. Aegyptiis muribus durus pilus sicut
irenaceis; idem bipedes ambulant ceu Alpini quoque.
187 —Cum diversi generis coiere animalia, ita demum
generant si tempus nascendi par habent.—Quadripedum ova gignentium lacertas ore parere, ut creditur vulgo, Aristoteles negat. neque incubant
eaedem, oblitae quo sint in loco enixae, quoniam
huic animali nulla memoria; itaque per se catuli
erumpunt.

188 LXXXVI. Anguem ex medulla hominis spinae

---

[1] *Mayhoff*: item.   [2] item mures *Detlefsen*.
[3] *Hermolaus Barbarus*: in praegnantis ventre parientis.

---

[a] This sentence appears to be out of place here.

is against the nature of those with solid or cloven hoofs to produce several young.

LXXXV. The most prolific of all animals whatever *Fertility of* is the mouse—one hesitates to state its fertility, even *the mouse.* though on the authority of Aristotle and the troops of Alexander the Great. It is stated that with it impregnation takes place by licking and not by coupling. There is a record of 120 being born from a single mother, and in Persia of mice already pregnant being found in the parent's womb; and it is believed that they are made pregnant by tasting salt. Accordingly it ceases to be surprising how so large an army of field-mice ravages the crops; and in the case of field-mice it is also hitherto unknown exactly how this vast multitude is suddenly destroyed: for they are never found dead, and nobody exists who ever dug up a mouse in a field in winter. Vast numbers thus appear in the Troad, and they have by now banished the inhabitants from that country. They appear during droughts. It is also related that when a mouse is going to die a worm grows in its head. The mice in Egypt have hard hair like hedgehogs, and also they walk on two feet, as also do the Alpine mice.—When animals of a different *Other facts* kind pair, the union is only fertile when the two species *as to breed-* have the same period of gestation.[a]—There is a *ing.* popular belief that of the oviparous quadrupeds the lizard bears through the mouth, but this is denied by Aristotle. Lizards do not hatch their eggs, but forget where they laid them, as this animal has no memory; and consequently the young ones break the shell without assistance.

LXXXVI. We have it from many authorities that *Marvellous* a snake may be born from the spinal marrow of a *births.*

411

gigni accepimus a multis. pleraque enim occulta et caeca origine proveniunt, etiam in quadripedum genere, sicut salamandrae, animal lacertae figura, stellatum, numquam nisi magnis imbribus proveniens et serenitate deficiens.[1] huic tantus rigor ut ignem tactu restinguat non alio modo quam glacies. eiusdem sanie, quae lactea ore vomitur, quacumque parte corporis humani contacta toti defluunt pili, idque quod contactum est colorem in vitiliginem mutat.

189 LXXXVII. Quaedam ergo gignuntur ex non genitis et sine ulla simili origine, ut supra dicta et quaecumque [2] ver statumque tempus anni generat. ex his quaedam nihil gignunt, ut salamandrae, neque est in his masculum femininumve, sicut neque in anguillis omnibusque quae nec animal nec ovum ex sese generant; neutrum est et ostreis genus et

190 ceteris adhaerentibus vado vel saxo. quae autem per se generantur, si in mares et feminas discripta sunt, generant quidem aliquid coitu, sed inperfectum ac dissimile et ex quo nihil amplius gignatur, ut vermiculos muscae. id magis declaravit natura eorum quae insecta dicuntur, arduae explanationis omnia et privatim dicato opere narranda. quapropter ingenium praedictorum et reliqua subtexetur edissertatio.

191 LXXXVIII. Ex sensibus ante cetera homini tactus, dein gustatus; reliquis superatur a multis.

---

[1] v.l. desinens.
[2] v.l. aestas aut ver.

---

[a] Doubtless ' molluscs ', i.e. any shell-fish, are meant.

human being. For a number of animals spring from some hidden and secret source, even in the quadruped class, for instance salamanders, a creature shaped like a lizard, covered with spots, never appearing except in great rains and disappearing in fine weather. It is so chilly that it puts out fire by its contact, in the same way as ice does. It vomits from its mouth a milky slaver, one touch of which on any part of the human body causes all the hair to drop off, and the portion touched changes its colour and breaks out in a tetter.

LXXXVII. Consequently some creatures are born *Other* from parents that themselves were not born and *curiosities* were without any similar origin, like the ones men- *duction.* tioned above and all those that are produced by the spring and a fixed season of the year. Some of these are infertile, for instance the salamander, and in these there is no male or female, as also there is no sex in eels and all the species that are neither vivi-parous nor oviparous; also oysters *a* and the other creatures clinging to the bottom of shallow water or to rocks are neuters. But self-generated creatures if divided into males and females do produce an off-spring by coupling, but it is imperfect and unlike the parent and not productive in its turn: for instance flies produce maggots. This is shown more clearly by the nature of the creatures called insects, all of which are difficult to describe and must be discussed in a work devoted specially to them. Consequently the psychology of the beforesaid creatures, and the remainder of the discussion, must be appended.

LXXXVIII. Among the senses, that of touch in *Keenness of* man ranks before all the other species, and taste *the senses* next; but in the remaining senses he is surpassed *species.*

413

aquilae clarius cernunt, vultures sagacius odorantur, liquidius audiunt talpae—obrutae terra, tam denso atque surdo naturae elemento, praeterea voce omni in sublime tendente, sermonem exaudiunt et, si de iis loquare, intellegere etiam dicuntur et profugere.

192 auditus cui hominum primo negatus est, huic et sermonis usus ablatus, nec sunt naturaliter surdi ut non idem sint et muti. in marinis ostreis auditum esse non est verisimile; sed ad sonum mergere se dicuntur solenes; ideo et silentium in more [1]

193 piscantibus. LXXXIX. pisces quidem auditus nec membra habent nec foramina, audire tamen eos palam est, utpote cum plausu congregari feros ad cibum adsuetudine in quibusdam vivariis spectetur, et in piscinis Caesaris genera piscium ad nomen venire, quosdamve [2] singulos. itaque produntur etiam clarissime audire mugil, lupus, salpa, chromis, et ideo in vado vivere.

194 XC. Olfactum iis esse manifeste patet, quippe non omnes eadem esca capiuntur et prius quam adpetant odorantur. quosdam et speluncis latentes salsamento inlitis faucibus scopuli piscator expellit velut sui cadaveris agnitionem fugientes; conveniunt-que ex alto etiam ad quosdam odores, ut sepiam ustam et polypum, quae ideo coiciuntur in nassas. sentinae quidem navium odorem procul fugiunt,

---

[1] v.l. in mari.
[2] *Mayhoff*: quosdam *aut* quosdamque.

by many other creatures. Eagles have clearer sight, vultures a keener sense of smell, moles acuter hearing—although they are buried in the earth, so dense and deaf an element of nature, and although moreover all sound travels upward, they can overhear people talking, and it is actually said that if you speak about them they understand and run away. Among men, when one is first of all denied hearing he also is robbed of the power of talking, and there are no persons deaf from birth who are not also dumb. The sea-oyster probably has no sense of hearing; but it is said that the razor-shell dives at a sound: consequently people fishing make a practice of silence. LXXXIX. Fish indeed have no auditory *Fishes sensitive is sound.* organs or passages, but nevertheless it is obvious that they hear, inasmuch as it can be observed that in some fishponds wild fish have a habit of flocking together to be fed at the sound of clapping, and in the Emperor's aquarium the various kinds of fish come in answer to their names, or in some cases individual fish. Consequently it is also stated that the mullet, the wolf-fish, the stockfish and the *chromis* hear very clearly, and therefore live in shallow water.

XC. It is clearly obvious that fish possess a sense *Fishes' sense of smell.* of smell, as they are not all attracted by the same food, and they smell a thing before they seize it. Some fish even when hiding in caves are driven out by a fisherman who smears the mouth of the crag with brine used in pickling—they run away as it were from the recognition of their own dead body; and they also flock together from the deep water to certain smells, for instance a burnt cuttle-fish or polyp, which are thrown into wicker creels for this purpose. Indeed the stench of a ship's bilge makes

415

195 maxime tamen piscium sanguinem. non potest ab escis[1] avelli polypus; idem cunila admota ab odore[2] protinus resilit. purpurae quoque faetidis capiuntur. nam de reliquo animalium genere quis dubitet? cornus cervini usti[3] odore serpentes fugantur, sed maxime styracis; origani aut calcis aut sulpuris formicae necantur. culices acida petunt, ad dulcia non advolant.

Tactus sensus omnibus est, etiam quibus nullus alius; nam et ostreis et terrestrium vermibus
196 quoque. XCI. existimaverim omnibus sensum et gustatus esse; cur enim alios alia sapores adpetant? in quo vel praecipua naturae artificia[4]: alia dentibus praedantur, alia unguibus, alia rostri aduncitate carpunt, alia latitudine eruunt, alia acumine excavant; alia sugunt, alia lambunt, sorbent, mandunt, vorant. nec minor varietas in pedum ministerio, ut rapiant, distrahant, teneant, premant, pendeant, tellurem scabere non cessent.

197 XCII. Venenis capreae et coturnices, ut diximus, pinguescunt, placidissima animalia, at serpentes ovis, spectanda quidem draconum arte: aut enim solida hauriunt, si iam fauces capiunt, quae deinde in semet

---

[1] ab escis *Rackham* (escis? *Mayhoff*): petris.
[2] ob odorem? *Mayhoff*.
[3] usti *add. Mayhoff*.
[4] artificia *Detlefsen* (varietas et lusus *Mayhoff*): *fragmenta varia codd.*

---

[a] The MSS. give 'from the rocks,' but *cf.* Ar. *Hist. An.* 534b 27.
[b] § 69.

them flee far away, but most of all the blood of fishes. The polyp cannot be dragged away from the bait [a]; but when a sprig of marjoram is brought near to it, it at once darts away from the scent. *Sense of* Purple-fish also can be caught by means of things *smell in* with a foul smell. As to the rest of the animal class *species.* who could have any doubt? Snakes are driven away by the stench of burnt stag's horn, but especially by that of styrax-tree gum; the scent of marjoram or lime or sulphur kills ants. Gnats seek for sour things and are not attracted by sweet things.

All creatures have the sense of touch, even those *Touch and* that have none of the others; it is possessed even *taste.* by molluscs, and also, among land animals, by worms. XCI. I am inclined to believe that all possess the sense of taste also; for why are different species attracted by different flavours? In the matter of taste nature's handicraft is outstanding: some creatures catch their prey with their teeth, others with their claws, others snatch their food with the curve of the beak, others root it up with the flat of the beak, others dig it out with the point; some suck it in, others lick it, sup it up, chew it, gulp it down. Nor is there less variety in the service rendered by their feet, in snatching, tearing asunder, holding, squeezing, hanging, or incessantly scratching the earth.

XCII. Wild goats and quails, the most peaceful *Varieties of* of creatures, grow fat, as we have said, on poisons,[b] *nutrition.* but snakes batten on eggs, serpents having a remarkably skilful trick—they either gulp the eggs down whole, if their throats have grown large enough to hold them, and then break them inside them by

convoluti frangunt intus atque ita putamina extus-
siunt, aut si tenerior est catulis adhue aetas, orbe
adprehensa spirae ita sensim vehementerque praes-
tringunt ut amputata parte ceu ferro e reliqua quae
amplexu tenetur sorbeant. simili modo avibus
devoratis solidis contentione plumam et ossa revo-
munt.

198 XCIII. Scorpiones terra vivunt. serpentes cum
occasio est vinum praecipue adpetunt, cum alioqui
exiguo indigeant potu; eaedem minimo et paene
nullo cibo cum adservantur inclusae; sicuti aranei
quoque, alioqui suctu viventes. ideo nullum interit
fame aut siti venenatum; nam neque calor iis nec
sanguis, nec sudor, qui[1] aviditatem naturali sale
auget.[2] in quo genere omnia magis exitialia si
199 suum genus edere antequam noceant. condit in
thesauros maxillarum cibum sphingiorum et satyro-
rum genus, mox inde sensim ad mandendum
manibus expromit—et quod formicis in annum,
sollemne est his in dies vel horas. unum animal
digitos habentium herba alitur lepus; ea[3] et fruge
solidipedes, et e bisulcis sues omni cibatu et radicibus.
solidipedum volutatio propria. serratorum dentium
carnivora sunt omnia. ursi et fruge, fronde, vindemia, pomis vivunt et apibus, cancris etiam ac formicis.
200 lupi, ut diximus, et terra in fame. pecus potu

---

[1] *Rackham* : quae.   [2] *Rackham* : augent.
[3] ea *Mayhoff* : sed.

---

[a] VIII 83.

rolling themselves up in a coil, and so cough out the bits of eggshell, or if they are young snakes as yet of too tender an age, they catch hold of the eggs in the ring of their coil and squeeze them so gradually and forcibly that part is cut off as if with a knife from the remainder which is held in their folds and then they suck it in. In a like manner they swallow birds whole and then with a heave bring up again the feathers and the bones.

XCIII. Scorpions live on earth. Snakes are specially fond of wine when they have the chance, though otherwise they need little drink; they also need very little food, and almost none at all when they are kept shut up; just as do spiders also, which otherwise live by suction. Consequently no venomous creature dies of hunger or thirst; for they have neither heat nor blood, nor yet sweat, which increases appetite by its natural salt. All in this class are more deadly if they have eaten their own kind before they attack somebody. The class of dog-headed apes and ourang-outangs stores food in the recesses of the jaw-bones, and then gradually takes it out from there with its hands to chew it—and what with ants is an annual ceremony is for these a daily or hourly practice. The only animal with toes that lives on grass is the hare; solid-hooved animals live on grass and corn, and among animals with cloven feet the pig eats all kinds of fodder and also roots. Rolling on the ground is peculiar to animals with solid hooves. All species with serrated teeth are carnivorous. Bears also eat grain, leaves, grapes and fruits and bees, and even crabs and ants. Wolves, as we have said,[a] when hungry even eat earth. Cattle grow fat with drinking,

Curious facts as to nutrition of different species.

Ruminants.

pinguescit, ideo sal illis aptissimus, item veterina, quamquam et fruge et herba, scilicet[1] ut bibere sic edunt. ruminant praeter iam dicta silvestrium cervi, cum a nobis aluntur; omnia autem iacentia potius quam stantia, et hieme magis quam aestate, septenis fere mensibus. Pontici quoque mures simili modo remandunt.

201 XCIV. In potu autem quibus serrati dentes lambunt, et mures hi vulgares, quamvis ex alio genere sint; quibus continui dentes sorbent, ut equi, boves; neutrum ursi, sed aquam quoque morsu vorant. in Africa maior pars ferarum aestate non bibunt inopia imbrium, quam ob causam capti mures Libyci si bibere moriuntur. orygem perpetuo sitientia Africae generant ex natura loci potu carentem et mirabili modo ad remedia sitientium: namque Gaetuli latrones eo durant auxilio repertis in[2] corpore corum saluberrimi liquoris vesicis.

202 Insidunt in eadem Africa pardi condensas arbores[3] occultatique earum ramis in practereuntia desiliunt, atque e volucrum sede grassantur. feles quidem quo silentio, quam levibus vestigiis obrepunt avibus! quam occulte speculatae in musculos exiliunt! excrementa sua effossa obruunt terra intellegentes 203 odorem illum indicem sui esse. XCV. ergo et alios

---

[1] scilicet *Mayhoff*: sed.
[2] *v.l.* pro: aperto *Mayhoff*.
[3] *Rackham* (-am arborem *Mayhoff*): condensa arbore.

---

[a] Perhaps the ermine is meant.

and consequently salt is specially suitable for them.
So also do beasts of burden, although they also
fatten on corn and grass; in fact they eat in
proportion to what they have drunk. Beside the
ruminants already mentioned, of forest animals stags
ruminate when they are kept by us; but they all
ruminate lying down in preference to standing, and
in winter more than in summer, for a period of about
seven months. The mice of Pontus [a] also remasticate
their food in a similar manner.

XCIV. In drinking, animals with serrated teeth *Modes of*
lap, and so does our common mouse, though it *drinking.*
really belongs to another class; those with teeth
that touch suck, for instance horses and cattle;
bears do neither, but gulp water as well as food in
bites. In Africa the greater part of the wild animals
do not drink at all in summer, owing to lack of
rains for which reason Libyan mice in captivity
die if given drink. The perpetually dry parts of
Africa produce the antelope, which owing to the
nature of the region goes without drink in quite a
remarkable fashion, for the assistance of thirsty
people, as the Gaetulian brigands rely on their
help to keep going, bladders containing extremely
healthy liquid being found in their body.

In Africa also leopards crouch in the thick foliage *Feline*
of the trees and hidden by their boughs leap down *modes of*
on to animals passing by, and stalk their prey from *stalking.*
the perches of birds. Then how silently and with
what a light tread do cats creep up to birds! how
stealthily they watch their chance to leap out on
tiny mice! They scrape up the earth to bury their
droppings, realizing that the smell of these gives
them away. XCV. Consequently it is easily manifest

quosdam sensus esse quam supra dictos haud difficulter apparet.

Sunt enim quaedam iis bella amicitiaeque, unde
et adfectus, praeter illa quae de quibusque eorum
suis diximus locis. dissident olores et aquilae;
corvus et chloreus noctu invicem ova exquirentes;
simili modo corvus et milvus, illo praeripiente huic
cibos; cornices atque noctuae,[1] aquila[2] et trochilus
—si credimus, quoniam rex appellatur avium; noctuae
204 et ceterae minores; aves rursus cum terrestribus[3]—
mustela et cornix, turtur et pyrallis, ichneumones
[vespae][4] et phalangia [aranei][5] aquaticae brenthos et
gavia et harpe et triorchis [accipiter][6]; sorices et
ardiolae invicem fetibus insidiantes, aegithus avis
minima cum asino—spinetis enim se scabendi causa
atterens nidos eius dissipat, quod adeo pavet ut voce
omnino rudentis audita ova eiciat, pulli ipsi metu
cadant; igitur advolans ulcera eius rostro excavat—
205 volpes et milvi, angues et mustelae et sues. aesalon
vocatur parva avis ova corvi frangens, cuius pulli
infestantur a vulpibus; invicem haec catulos volpis[7]
ipsamque vellit; quod ubi viderunt corvi, contra
auxiliantur velut adversus communem hostem. et
acanthis in spinis vivit: idcirco asinos et ipsa odit

---

[1] *Rackham* : noctua.
[2] aquila ? *Mayhoff* : aquilae.
[3] rursus cum trochilo *ex Ar. Mayhoff.*
[4], [5], [6] *secl. Rackham.*
[7] volpis ? *Mayhoff* : eius.

---

[a] χλωρεύς: the hen is bright green.
[b] *I.e.* the long-tailed titmouse, the only one that nests in
bushes.

that there are also certain senses other than those mentioned above.

For animals have certain kinds of warfare and of friendships, and the feelings that result from them, besides the various facts that we have stated about each species in their places. There are quarrels between swans and eagles; between the raven and the golden oriole ^a when searching for one another's eggs by night; similarly between the raven and the kite when the former snatches the latter's food before he can get it; between crows and owls, the eagle and the gold-crest—if we can believe it, as the eagle is called the king of birds; between owls and the other smaller birds; again birds with land animals—the weasel and the crow, the turtle-dove and the *pyrallis*, ichneumon-flies and spiders; the water-birds *brenthos* and gull and goshawk and buzzard; shrewmice and herons lying in wait for each other's young; that very tiny bird the titmouse ^b with the ass, which by rubbing itself against thorns for the sake of scratching dislodges the nests of the titmouse, which is so scared that when it merely hears the sound of an ass braying it throws its eggs out of the nest, and the chicks themselves in fear fall out, and consequently the bird flies at the ass and hollows out its sores with its beak; foxes and kites; snakes and weasels and pigs. There is a small bird called the aesalon that breaks a raven's eggs, whose chicks are preyed upon by foxes, and it retaliates by pecking the fox-cubs and the vixen herself; when the ravens see this they come to their aid against the aesalon as against a common foe. Also the gold-finch lives in thorn-bushes and consequently it also hates asses

Hostility between species.

flores spinae devorantes; aegithum vero anthus [1] in tantum ut sanguinem eorum credant non coire multisque ob id veneficiis infament. dissident thoes

206 et leones. et minima aeque ac maxima. formicosam arborem erucae cavent; librat araneus se filo in caput serpentis porrectae sub umbra arboris suae tantaque vi morsu cerebrum adprehendit ut stridens subinde et vertigine rotata ne filum quidem pendentis rumpere, adeo non fugere queat, nec finis ante mortem est.

207 XCVI. Rursus amici pavones et columbae, turtures et psittaci, merulae et turtures, cornix et ardiola [2] contra vulpium genus communibus inimicitiis, harpe et milvus contra triorchin. quid, non et affectus indicia sunt etiam in serpentibus, inmitissimo animalium genere? dicta sunt quae Arcadia narrat de domino a dracone servato et agnito voce

208 [draconis].[3] de aspide miraculum Phylarcho reddatur: is enim auctor est, cum ad mensam cuiusdam veniens in Aegypto aleretur adsidue, enixam [4] catulos, quorum ab uno filium hospitis interemptum; illam reversam ad consuetudinem cibi intellexisse culpam et necem intulisse catulo, nec postea in tectum id reversam.

209 XCVII. Somni quaestio non obscuram coniectationem habet. in terrestribus omnia quae coniveant

---

[1] anthus *add. ex Ar. Hermolaus.*
[2] *Rackham :* ardiolae.
[3] *secl. Mayhoff.*
[4] *v.l.* enixa.

---

that devour the flowers of the thorn; but the yellow wagtail hates the titmouse so bitterly that people believe that their blood will not mix, and consequently they give it a bad name as used for many poisons. The thos and the lion quarrel. Also the smallest animals quarrel as much as the largest: a tree infested with ants is hollowed out by caterpillars; a spider swings by a thread on to the head of a snake stretched out beneath the shade of its tree, and nips its brain with its jaws so violently that it at once gives a hiss and whirls giddily round, but cannot even break the thread by which the spider hangs, much less get away, and there is no end to it before its death.

XCVI. On the other hand friendships occur *Friendships between species;* between peacocks and pigeons, turtle-doves and parrots, blackbirds and turtle-doves, the crow and *between snakes and man.* the little heron in a joint enmity against the fox kind and the goshawk and kite against the buzzard. Why, are there not signs of affection even in snakes, the most hostile kind of animals? we have mentioned [a] the story that Arcady tells about the snake that saved his master's life and recognized him by his voice. Let us place to the credit of Phylarchus a marvellous tale about an asp: he relates that in Egypt, when it used to come regularly to be fed at someone's table, it was delivered of young ones, and that its hosts's son was killed by one of these; and that when the mother came back for its usual meal it realized the young one's guilt and killed it, and never came back to the house again afterwards.

XCVII. The question of sleep does not involve *Sleep of aquatic species.* any obscure conjecture. It is clear that among land

dormire manifestum est. aquatilia quoque exiguum quidem etiam qui de ceteris dubitant dormire tamen existimant, non oculorum argumento, quia non habent genas, verum ipsa quiete: cernuntur placida ceu soporata, neque aliud quam caudas moventia, et

210 ad tumultum aliquem expavescentia. de thynnis confidentius adfirmatur, iuxta ripas enim aut petras dormiunt; plani autem piscium in vado, ut manu saepe tollantur. nam delphini ballaenaeque stertentes etiam audiuntur. insecta quoque dormire silentio apparet, quae ne luminibus quidem admotis excitentur.

211 XCVIII. Homo genitus premitur somno per aliquot menses, dein longior in dies vigilia. somniat statim infans, nam et pavore expergiscitur et suctum imitatur. quidam vero numquam, quibus mortiferum fuisse signum contra consuetudinem somnium invenimus exempla. magnus hic invitat locus et diversis refertus documentis, utrumne sint aliqua praescita animi quiescentis, quaque[1] fiant ratione, an fortuita res sit ut pleraque. si exemplis agatur, profecto paria fiant. a vino et a cibis proxima, atque in redormitione, vana esse visa prope convenit; est autem somnus nihil aliud quam animi in medium sese

212 recessus. praeter hominem somniare equos, canes,

---

[1] que add. *Sillig.*

animals all those that close the eyes sleep. That also water animals sleep at all events a little is held even by those who doubt about the other kinds; they do not infer this from the eyes, as these creatures have no eyelids, but merely by their quietness : they are seen reposing as if sunk in slumber, and only moving their tails, and waking up in alarm at any disturbance. It is affirmed with more confidence about tunny-fish, because they sleep close to banks or rocks; while flatfish sleep in shallow water, so that they are often taken out by hand. Dolphins and whales, in fact, are heard actually snoring. That insects also sleep is shown by their silence, and by their not even being roused by having lights brought near them.

XCVIII. Man when born is beset by sleep for *Sleep of* some months, and then day by day his waking period *man.* gets longer. An infant begins to dream at once, for *man and of* it wakes up in a fright, and also imitates sucking. *animals.* But some children never dream, and with these we find instances in which their dreaming contrary to their usual habit was a sign of approaching death. Here an important topic invites us and one fully supplied with arguments on both sides—whether there are certain cases of foreknowledge present in the mind during repose, and what causes them, or whether it is a matter of chance like most things. If the question be argued by instances, these would doubtless be found to be equal on both sides. It is practically agreed that dreams occurring directly after drinking wine and eating food, and those that come in dozing off to sleep a second time, are false; but sleep is really nothing but the retirement of the mind into its innermost self. It is manifest that,

427

boves, pecora, capras, palam est; ob hoc creditur et in omnibus quae animal pariant. de his quae ova gignunt incertum est, sed dormire ea certum.

Verum et ad insecta transeamus; haec namque restant, inmensae subtilitatis animalia.[1]

[1] haec—animalia (*cf.* XI 1 *init.*) *om. Caesarius.*

beside human beings, horses, dogs, oxen, sheep and goats dream; it is consequently believed that, dreams also occur in all viviparous species. As to the oviparous creatures it is uncertain. but it is certain that they sleep.

But let us also pass to insects, for these remain. creatures of immeasurably minute structure.

BOOK XI

LIBER XI

I. Restant immensae subtilitatis animalia, quando aliqui ea neque spirare et sanguine etiam carere prodiderunt. multa haec et multigenera terrestrium volucrumque vita, alia. . . .[1] pennata. ut apes, alia utroque modo, ut formicae, aliqua et pennis et pedibus carentia, iure omnia insecta appellata ab incisuris quae nunc cervicium loco, nunc pectorum atque alvi, praecincta separant membra, tenui modo fistula cohaerentia, aliquis vero non tota incisurae[2] ambiente ruga, sed in alvo aut superne tantum, imbricatis flexilibus vertebris, nusquam alibi spectatiore natu-

2 rae rerum artificio : in magnis siquidem corporibus aut certe maioribus facilis officina sequaci materia fuit, in his tam parvis atque tam nullis quae ratio, quanta vis, quam inextricabilis perfectio ! ubi tot sensus collocavit in culice ?—et sunt alia dictu minora,—sed ubi visum in eo praetendit ? ubi

---

[1] *lacunam, fort.* ⟨pinnis carentia, ut iuli, alia⟩ *Mayhoff.*
[2] *Mayhoff* : incisura eam.

---

[a] In respect of insects etc. the ancients, handicapped by not having microscopes, were even more at fault than in other departments.
[b] This clause is a conjectural insertion from Aristotle 523 b 19.

BOOK XI

I. There remain some creatures of immeasurably *Insects :*
minute structure [a]—in fact some authorities have *their habits*
stated that they do not breathe and also that they *and*
are actually devoid of blood. These are of great *structure—*
sense-organs,
number and of many kinds; they have the habits *limbs and*
of land-animals and of flying animals, some lacking *stings.*
wings, for instance centipedes,[b] others winged, for
instance bees, others of both kinds, for instance ants,
some lacking both wings and feet; and all are rightly
termed insects, from the incisions which encircle
them in some cases in the region of their necks and
in others of their chests and stomach and separate
off their limbs, these being only connected by a thin
tube, with some however the crease of the incision
not entirely encircling them, but only at the belly
or higher up, with flexible vertebrae shaped like
gutter-tiles—showing a craftsmanship on the part
of Nature that is more remarkable than in any other
case: inasmuch as in large bodies or at all events
the larger ones the process of manufacture was
facilitated by the yielding nature of the material,
whereas in these minute nothings what method,
what power, what labyrinthine perfection is displayed! Where did Nature find a place in a flea
for all the senses?—and other smaller creatures
can be mentioned,—but at what point in its surface
did she place sight? where did she attach taste?

433

gustatum adplicavit? ubi odoratum inseruit? ubi
vero truculentam illam et portione maximam vocem
3 ingeneravit? qua subtilitate pennas adnexuit, prae-
longavit pedum crura, disposuit ieiunam caveam uti
avidam sanguinis et potissimum humani
sitim [1] accendit! telum vero perfodiendo tergori quo
spiculavit ingenio, atque ut in capaci, cum cerni non
possit exilitas, reciproca generavit arte ut fodiendo
acuminatum pariter sorbendoque fistulosum esset!
quos teredini ad perforanda robora cum [2] sono teste
dentes adfixit potissimumque e ligno cibatum fecit!
4 sed turrigeros elephantorum miramur umeros taurorumque colla et truces in sublime iactus, tigrium
rapinas, leonum iubas, cum rerum natura nusquam
magis quam in minimis tota sit. quapropter quaeso
ne nostra legentes, quoniam ex his spernunt multa,
etiam relata fastidio damnent, cum in contemplatione
naturae nihil possit videri supervacuum.
5 II. Insecta multi negarunt spirare, idque ratione
persuadentes quoniam viscera interiora [3] nexus
spirabilis non inessent,[4] itaque vivere ut fruges
arboresque, sed plurimum interesse spiret aliquid an
vivat; eadem de causa nec sanguinem iis esse, qui sit
nullis carentibus corde atque iecore; sic nec spirare
ea quibus pulmo desit. unde numerosa quaestio-

[1] siti *Detlefsen*.
[2] robora ⟨terebrar⟩um *Mayhoff*
[3] inter et ora *Detlefsen*.
[4] *Mayhoff*: inesset.

---

[a] This may mean the ship-worm, mistaken for an insect, or
the goat-moth caterpillar which bores into living trees.
[b] An emendation of the text gives 'as is evidenced by a
sound as of gimlets.'

where did she insert smell? and where did she implant that truculent and relatively very loud voice? with what subtlety she attached the wings, extended the legs that carry the feet, placed a ravenous hollow to serve as a stomach, kindled a greedy thirst for blood and especially human blood! Then with what genius she provided a sharp weapon for piercing the skin, and as if working on a large object, although really it is invisibly minute, created it with alternating skill so as to be at once pointed for digging and tubed for sucking! What teeth she attached to the wood-borer [a] for boring through timber, with the accompanying sound as evidence,[b] and made its chief nutriment to consist of wood! But we marvel at elephants' shoulders carrying castles, and bulls' necks and the fierce tossings of their heads, at the rapacity of tigers and the manes of lions, whereas really Nature is to be found in her entirety nowhere more than in her smallest creations. I consequently beg my readers not to let their contempt for many of these creatures lead them also to condemn to scorn what I relate about them, since in the contemplation of Nature nothing can possibly be deemed superfluous.

II. Many people have asserted that insects do not breathe, also arguing in support of this from the fact that they do not possess the internal organs of a respiratory system, and saying that consequently they live like plants and trees, whereas there is a very great difference between breathing and living; it is for the same reason, they argue, that they do not contain blood either, as this is found in no species lacking a heart and a liver; similarly, they say, things that have not got lungs do not breathe. This

They have no respiratory organs but presumably they breathe, and though they have no voice, they buzz.

435

6 num series exoritur. iidem enim et vocem esse his
negant in tanto murmure apium, cicadarum sono, et
quae alia suis aestimabuntur locis. nam mihi
contuenti semper suasit rerum natura nihil incredibile existimare de ea; nec video cur magis
possint non trahere animam talia et vivere quam
spirare sine visceribus, quod etiam in marinis docui-
mus quamvis arcente spiritum densitate et altitudine
7 umoris. volare quidem aliqua et animatu carere in
ipso spiritu viventia, habere sensum victus, genera-
tionis, operis, atque etiam de futuro curam, et
quamvis non sint membra quae velut carina ¹ sensus
invehant, esse tamen iis auditum, olfactum, gustatum,
eximia praeterea naturae dona, sollertiam, animum,
8 artem, quis facile crediderit? sanguinem non esse iis
fateor, sicut ne ² terrestribus quidem cunctis inter se
similem; verum ut saepiae in mari sanguinis vicem ³
atramentum optinet, purpurarum generi infector ille
sucus, sic et insectis quisquis est vitalis umor hic erit
sanguis. denique existimatio sua cuique sit, nobis
propositum est naturas rerum manifestas indicare,
non causas indagare dubias.
9   III. Insecta, ut intellegi possit, non videntur
habere nervos nec ossa nec spinas nec cartilaginem

----

¹ canali? *Mayhoff.*
² ne *om. v.l.*
³ vicem *aut* vices *edd. vett.* : vires.

ᵃ Cf. IX 16 ff.
ᵇ A variant gives ' that they have not all got the same kind
of blood, as all land animals have.'

gives rise to a long list of questions. For the same
people actually say that these creatures have not
got a voice, in spite of all the buzzing of bees and
chirping of tree-crickets, and make other statements
the value of which will be judged in their places.
For when I have observed Nature she has always
induced me to deem no statement about her
incredible; nor do I see why such creatures should
be more able to live without breathing than to
breathe without vital organs, which we have proved [a]
to occur even in the case of marine creatures in
spite of the fact that their breath is barred by the
density and depth of the water. At all events that
any creatures fly and yet have no capacity of
breathing in spite of their living in the very breath
of the air, and that they have consciousness of
nutrition, generation and work, and even interest
in the future, and that although they have no organs
to carry the senses as in a vessel, they nevertheless
possess hearing, smell, taste, and those outstanding
gifts of nature, intelligence, brain, science, into
the bargain—who would easily believe this? I
admit that they have not got blood, as even land
animals have not all got blood of the same kind [b];
but just as in the sea the black fluid of the cuttle-
fish takes the place of blood, as also does the famous
juice of the genus purple-fish that supplies a dye,
similarly also whatever is the life-giving fluid
possessed by insects, this will be their blood. Finally
let each man form his own opinion, but our purpose
is to point out the manifest properties of objects,
not to search for doubtful causes.

III. So far as is perceptible, insects do not appear
to possess sinews or bones or spines or cartilage or fat

nec pinguia nec carnes, ne crustam quidem fragilem,
ut quaedam marina, nec quae iure dicatur cutis, sed
mediae cuiusdam inter omnia haec naturae corpus,
arenti simile, in [1] nervo mollius, in reliquis partibus
tutius vere quam durius. et hoc solum iis est, nec
practerea aliud; nihil intus nisi admodum paucis
10 intestinum inplicatum. itaque divolsis praecipua
vivacitas et partium singularum palpitatio, quia
quaecumque est ratio vitalis illa non certis inest
membris sed toto in corpore, minime tamen capite,
solumque non movetur nisi cum pectore avolsum.
in nullo genere plure sunt pedes, et quibus ex his
plurimi, diutius vivunt divulsa, ut in scolopendris
videmus. habent autem oculos praeterque e sensibus tactum atque gustatum, aliqua et odoratum,
pauca et auditum.

11   IV. Sed inter omnia ea principatus apibus et iure
praecipua admiratio, solis ex eo genere hominum
causa genitis. mella contrahunt sucumque dulcissi-
mum atque subtilissimum ac saluberrimum; favos
confingunt et ceras mille ad usus vitae, laborem
tolerant, opera conficiunt, rempublicam habent,
consilia privatim ac duces gregatim, et quod maxime
12 mirum sit, mores habent praeter cetera,[2] cum sint
neque mansueti generis neque feri. tanta est natura

---

[1] in add. *Rackham.*
[2] *Mayhoff*: habent praeterea.

---

^a The bee kept by the Greeks and Romans was Apis
Ligustica, somewhat smaller than our bee.

or flesh, and not even a fragile rind, such as some sea creatures have, nor anything that can properly be termed a skin, but a substance of a nature intermediate between all of these, as it were dried up, softer in the sinew but harder or rather more durable in all the other parts. And this is all that they possess, and nothing else in addition; they have no internal organs except, in the case of quite a few, a twisted intestine. Consequently when torn asunder they display a remarkable tenacity of life, and the separate parts go on throbbing, because whatever their vital principle is it certainly does not reside in particular members but in the body as a whole—least of all in the head, and this alone does not move unless it has been torn off with the breast. No other kind of creature has a greater number of feet, and of this species the ones that have more feet live longer when torn asunder, as we see in the case of the multipede. But they possess eyes, and also of the other senses touch and taste, and some have smell as well, and a few hearing also.

Exceptional physiological structure; sense-organs.

IV. But among all of these species the chief place belongs to the bees,[a] and this rightly is the species chiefly admired, because they alone of this genus have been created for the sake of man. They collect honey, that sweetest and most refined and most health-giving of juices, they model combs and wax that serves a thousand practical purposes, they endure toil, they construct works, they have a government and individual enterprises and collective leaders, and, a thing that must occasion much surprise, they have a system of manners that outstrips that of all the other animals, although they belong neither to the domesticated nor to the wild class. Nature is

The bee the chief insect species. Its industry and its social organization.

rerum ut prope ex umbra minima animalis incomparabile effecerit quiddam. quos efficaciae industriaeque tantae comparemus nervos, quas vires? quos ratione medius fidius iis [1] viros, hoc certe praestantioribus quod [2] nihil novere nisi commune? non sit de anima quaestio: constet et de sanguine; quantulum tamen esse in tantulis potest! aestimemus post ea ingenium.

13   V. Hieme conduntur—unde enim ad pruinas nivesque et aquilonum flatus perferendos [3] vires?— sane et insecta omnia, sed minus diu quae parietibus nostris occultata mature tepefiunt. circa apes aut temporum locorumve ratio mutata est, aut erraverunt priores. conduntur a vergiliarum occasu, et latent ultra exortum—adeo non ad veris initium, ut dixere—nec quisquam in Italia de alvis existimat

14 ante fabas florentes. exeunt ad opera et labores, nullusque, cum per caelum licuit, otio perit dies. primum favos construunt, ceram fingunt, hoc est domos cellasque faciunt, dein subolem, postea mella, ceram ex floribus, melliginem a lacrimis arborum quae glutinum pariunt, salicis, ulmi, harundinis suco,

15 cummi, resina. his primum alvum ipsam intus totam [4] ut quodam tectorio inlinunt, et aliis amariori-

---

[1] iis add. Mayhoff.   [2] Mayhoff: quo.
[3] edd.: perferre.   [4] Sillig: totum (in totum edd.).

---

[a] As a matter of fact nearly all insects die in winter.
[b] About the beginning of November.
[c] About the beginning of May.

so mighty a power that out of what is almost a tiny ghost of an animal she has created something incomparable! What sinews or muscles can we match with such efficacy and industry as that of the bees? What men, I protest, can we rank in rationality with these insects, which unquestionably excel mankind in this, that they recognize only the common interest? Not raising the question of breath, suppose we agree as to their possessing even blood; yet what a tiny quantity can there be in these tiny creatures! After these points let us estimate their intelligence.

V. In winter insects go into retirement [a]—for whence could they obtain strength to endure frost and snow and the blasts of the north wind?—all species alike, no doubt, but not for so long a period the ones that hide in our house-walls and are warmed earlier than others are. In regard to bees, either seasons or else climates have changed, or previous writers have been mistaken. They go into retirement after the setting [b] of the Pleiads and remain in hiding till after their rise [c]—so not till the beginning of spring, as writers have said,—and nobody in Italy thinks about hives before the bean is in flower. They go out to their works and to their labours, and not a single day is lost in idleness when the weather grants permission. First they construct combs and mould wax, that is, construct their homes and cells, then produce offspring, and afterwards honey, wax from flowers, bee-glue from the droppings of the gum-producing trees—the sap, glue and resin of the willow, elm and reed. They first smear the whole interior of the hive itself with these as with a kind of stucco, and then with other bitterer juices

Hibernation of bees.

Construction of the hive.

441

bus sucis contra aliarum bestiolarum aviditates, id
se facturas consciae quod concupisci possit; isdem
fores quoque latiores circumstruunt.

16 VI. Prima fundamenta commosin vocant periti,
secunda pissoceron, tertia propolin, inter coria
cerasque, magni ad medicamina usus. commosis
crusta est prima saporis amari. pissoceros super eam
venit, picantium modo, ceu dilutior cera. e vitium
populorumque mitiore cummi propolis crassioris iam
materiae additis floribus, nondum tamen cera, sed
favorum stabilimentum, qua omnes frigoris aut
iniuriae aditus obstruuntur, odore et ipsa etiamnum [1]
gravi, ut qua plerique pro galbano utantur.

17 VII. Praeter haec convehitur erithace quam
aliqui sandaracam, alii cerinthum vocant: hic erit
apium dum operantur cibus, qui saepe invenitur
in favorum inanitatibus sepositus, et ipse amari
saporis, gignitur autem rore verno et arborum
suco cummium modo. capitur in ficis [2]—austri
flatu nigrior, aquilonibus melior et rubens—
plurimus in Graecis nucibus. Menecrates florem
esse dicit, sed nemo praeter eum.

18 VIII. Ceras ex omnium arborum satorumque
floribus confingunt excepta rumice et echinopode:
herbarum haec genera. falso excipitur et spartum,

[1] *edd.* : etiamnunc.
[2] *Mayhoff* : capitur fici (capitur Africi *Sillig*).

[a] *I.e.* ' gumming,' ' pitch-waxing ' and ' bee-glue.'
[b] Perhaps bugloss.

as a protection against the greed of other small creatures, as they know that they are going to make something that may possibly be coveted; with the same materials they also build wider gateways round the structure.

VI. The first foundations are termed by experts *Three materials.* *commosis*, the second *pissoceros*, the third *propolis*,[a] between the outer cover and the wax, substances of great use for medicaments. Commosis is the first crust, of a bitter flavour. Pissoceros comes above it, as in laying on tar, as being more fluid than wax. Propolis is obtained from the milder gum of vines and poplars, and is made of a denser substance by the addition of flowers, and though not as yet wax it serves to strengthen the combs; with it all approaches of cold or damage are blocked, and besides it has itself a heavy scent, being in fact used by most people as a substitute for galbanum.

VII. Besides these things a collection is made of *Store of food.* *erithace*, which some people call sandarach and others bee-bread; this will serve as food for the bees while they are at work, and it is often found stored up in the hollows of the combs, being itself also of a bitter flavour, but it is produced out of spring dew of trees like the gums. It is obtained in fig trees—blacker in colour when an east wind is blowing and of better quality and a reddish colour when north winds blow—and in the largest quantity in Greek nut-trees. Menecrates says that it is a flower, but he is the only authority that makes that statement.

VIII. They make their wax from the flowers of *Collection of wax.* all trees and plants except the sorrel and the echinopod[b]; these are kinds of herbs. It is a mistake to say that esparto grass is also an exception, because

quippe cum in Hispania multa in spartariis mella
herbam eam sapiant. falso et oleas excipi arbitror,
quippe olivae proventu plurima examina gigni
certum est. fructibus nullis nocetur. mortuis ne
floribus quidem, non modo corporibus, insidunt.
19 operantur intra LX passus et subinde consumptis in
proximo floribus speculatores ad pabula ulteriora
mittunt. noctu deprehensae in expeditione excu-
bant supinae, ut alas a rore protegant.

IX. Ne quis miretur amore earum captos Aristo-
machum Solensem duodesexaginta annis nihil aliud
egisse, Philiscum vero Thasium in desertis apes
colentem Agrium cognominatum, qui ambo scripsere
de iis.

20 X. Ratio operis mire divisi[1]: statio ad portas
more castrorum; quies in matutinum, donec una
excitet gemino aut triplici bombo ut bucino aliquo;
tunc universae provolant, si dies mitis futurus est—
praedivinant enim ventos imbresque, cum[2] se
continent tectis, itaque temperiei[3] caeli otium[4]
hoc inter praescita habent. cum agmen ad opera
processit, aliae flores adgerunt pedibus, aliae aquam
21 ore guttasque lanugine totius corporis. quibus est
earum adulescentia ad opera exeunt et supradicta
convehunt, seniores intus operantur. quae flores
conportant, prioribus pedibus femina onerant prop-

---

[1] *Mayhoff, cf.* §§ 23, 25 : operis interdiu.
[2] *Mayhoff* : ni.
[3] *Rackham* : temperies (temperie *edd.*).
[4] *Mayhoff* : cum *aut* tum.

a great deal of the honey obtained in the broom-thickets in Spain tastes of that plant. I also think that olives are wrongly excepted, as it is certain that the largest number of swarms are produced where olive-trees are growing. No harm is done to any kind of fruit. They do not settle even on dead flowers, let alone dead bodies. They work within a range of sixty paces, and subsequently when the flowers in the vicinity have been used up they send scouts to further pastures. If overtaken by nightfall on an expedition they camp out, reclining on their backs to protect their wings from the dew.

IX. Nobody must be surprised that love for bees inspired Aristomachus of Soli to devote himself to nothing else for 58 years, and Philiscus of Thasos to keep bees in desert places, winning the name of the Wild Man; both of these have written about them.

X. Their work is marvellously mapped out on the following plan: a guard is posted at the gates, after the manner of a camp; they sleep till dawn, until one bee wakes them up with a double or triple buzz as a sort of bugle-call; then they all fly forth in a body, if the day is going to be fine—for they forecast winds and rain, in case of which they keep indoors; and consequently men consider this inaction on the part of the bees as one of the prognostics of the weather. When the band has gone out to its tasks, some bring home flowers in their feet and others water in their mouth and drops clinging to the down all over their body. While the youthful among them go out to their tasks and collect the things mentioned above, the older ones work indoors. Those collecting flowers with their front feet load

Their organization of their work.

445

ter id natura scabra, pedes priores rostro, totaeque
22 onustae remeant sarcina pandatae. excipiunt eas
ternae quaternae quae exonerant: sunt enim intus
quoque officia divisa—aliae struunt, aliae poliunt, aliae
suggerunt, aliae cibum conparant ex eo quod adla-
tum est; neque enim separatim vescuntur, ne
inaequalitas operis et cibi fiat et temporis. struunt
orsae a concamaratione alvi, textumque velut a
summa tela deducunt, limitibus binis circa singulos
23 actus, ut aliis intrent, aliis exeant. favi superiori
parti[1] adfixi et paulum etiam lateribus simul
haerent et pendent, imam[2] alvum non contingunt,
tunc[3] oblongi,[4] tunc rotundi, qualiter poscit alvus,
aliquando et duorum generum, cum duo examina
concordibus populis dissimiles habuere ritus. ruentes
ceras fulciunt, pilarum intergerivis a solo fornicatis
24 ne desit aditus ad sarciendum. primi fere tres
versus inanes struuntur, ne promptum sit quod
invitet furantem, novissimi maxime implentur melle:
ideo aversa alvo favi eximuntur. gerulae secundos
flatus captant. si cooriatur procella, adprehensi
pondusculo lapilli se librant; quidam in umeros eum

---

[1] *Rackham*: superiore parte.   [2] *Detlefsen*: ima.
[3] tunc *Detlefsen*: nunc.

their thighs, which are covered with scales so as to
serve this purpose, and with their beak load their
front feet, and when fully loaded return bulging
with their burden. Each is received by three or
four others who relieve him of his load: for indoors
also the duties are divided—some build, others
polish, others bring up material, others prepare
food from what is brought to them; for they do not
feed separately, so that there shall be no inequality
of work or food or time. In building they begin
with the vaulting of the hive, and they bring down
as it were a web from the top of a loom, with two
balks round each square of work, so that some may
come in and others go out. The combs hang firmly
attached to the upper part and also a little to the
sides at the same time, but they do not reach to the
floor of the hive; sometimes they are oblong and
sometimes round, according as the shape of the
hive requires, and occasionally also of both kinds,
when two swarms whose members are friendly
have different customs. They prop up combs that
are inclined to fall, the party-walls between the
pillars being arched from the ground level so as to
supply access for the purpose of repairing. The
first three rows or so are arranged empty, so that
there may not be any obvious temptation to a thief;
the last ones are filled fullest with honey;
consequently the combs are taken out from the back
of the hive. Carrier bees wait for favourable breezes.
If a storm arises, they steady themselves with the
weight of a little pebble held in their feet; some
authorities say that it is placed on their shoulders.

Pintianus (e Columella): obliqui.

inponi tradunt. iuxta vero terram volant in ad-
25 verso flatu vepribus evitatis. mira observatio operis:
cessantium inertiam notant, castigant, mox et
puniunt morte. mira munditia: amoliuntur omnia e
medio, nullaeque inter opera spurcitiae iacent;
quin et excrementa operantium intus, ne longius
recedant, unum congesta in locum turbidis diebus
26 et operis otio egerunt. cum adversperascit, in alvo
strepunt minus ac minus, donec una circumvolet
·eodem quo excitavit bombo ceu quietem capere
imperitans, et hoc castrorum more; tunc repente
omnes conticescunt.

Domos primum plebei exaedificant, deinde regibus. si speratur largior proventus, adiciuntur
contubernia et fucis; hae cellarum minimae, sed
27 ipsis[1] maiores apibus. XI. sunt autem fuci sine
aculeo, velut inperfectae apes novissimaeque, a
fessis et iam emeritis inchoatae. serotinus fetus
et quasi servitia verarum apium; quamobrem im-
perant is primosque expellunt in opera, tardantis sine
clementia puniunt. neque in opere tantum, sed in
fetu quoque adiuvant eas, multum ad calorem

---

[1] *Rackham*: ipsi.

---

[a] *I.e.* the queen-bees.
[b] *Fucus*, 'pretence,' 'sham bee,' was used as a name for
the drones because of their supposed sterility (*cf.* § 49), although
just below here Pliny seems aware that their presence has
something to do with the size of the population of the hive.
They are in fact the males, who impregnate the queens, and
are then idle consumers until, when the harvest of honey

448

However in a wind against them they fly close to the ground, carefully avoiding the brambles. They keep a wonderful watch on the work in hand; they mark the idleness of any who are slack and chastise them, and later even punish them with death. They are wonderfully clean: they remove everything out of the way and no refuse is left lying among their work; indeed the droppings of those working inside are heaped in one place so that they may not have to retire too far, and they carry them out on stormy days and when work is suspended. When evening approaches, the buzzing inside the hive grows less and less, till one bee flies round as though giving the order to take repose with the same loud buzz with which she woke them, and this in the manner of a military camp; thereupon they all suddenly become quiet.

They build homes for the commonalty first, and for the kings[a] afterwards. If a specially large production of honey is expected, quarters are added for the drones as well; these are the smallest of the cells, but those for the worker-bees themselves are larger. XI. The drones [b] have no stings, being so to say imperfect bees and the newest made, the incomplete product of those that are exhausted and now discharged from service, a late brood, and as it were the servants of the true bees, who consequently order them about, and drive them out first to the works, punishing laggards without mercy. And the drones are of service to the bees not only in work but also when breeding, as their crowd

Construction of hives.

Function of drones.

begins to fail in autumn, they are killed and cast out of the colony by the worker-bees. The workers are females not specialized like the queens for reproduction.

28 conferente turba; certe quo maior eorum fuit multitudo, hoc maior fit et [1] examinum proventus.   cum
mella coeperunt maturescere, abigunt eos, multaeque
singulos adgressae trucidant.   nec id genus nisi vere
conspicitur.   fucus ademptis alis in alvum reiectus
29 ipse ceteris adimit.   XII. regias imperatoribus
futuris in ima parte alvi exstruunt amplas, magnificas,
separatas, tuberculo eminentes; quod si exprimatur,
non gignuntur.[2]   sexangulae omnes cellae a singulorum pedum opere.   nihil horum stato tempore,
sed rapiunt diebus serenis munia.   melle uno alterove
summum die cellas replent.

30   Venit hoc ex aere et maxime siderum exortu,
praecipueque ipso Sirio explendescente fit [3] nec
omnino prius vergiliarum exortu, sublucanis temporibus.   itaque tum prima aurora folia arborum melle
roscida inveniuntur, ac si qui matutino sub divo [4]
fuere, unctas liquore vestis capillumque concretum
sentiunt, sive ille est caeli sudor sive quaedam
siderum saliva sive purgantis se aeris sucus.   utinam-
que esset purus ac liquidus et suae naturae, qualis
31 defluit primo! nunc vero a tanta cadens altitudine
multumque dum venit sordescens et obvio terrae
halitu infectus, praeterea e fronde ac pabulis potus et

---

[1] *Mayhoff*: fiet *aut* fit.   [2] *v.l.* gignuntur suboles.
[3] *edd.*: explendescente *aut* exsplendescit.
[4] *v.l.* sub diu.

contributes much to their warmth: it is certain
that the larger number of drones there has been,
the larger production of swarms also occurs. When
the honey has begun to ripen, the bees drive the
drones away, and falling on them many to one kill
them. Moreover this class of bee is only seen in
spring. If a drone is stripped of its wings and afterwards thrown back into the hive it itself strips
the wings off the others. XII. They build large *King-bees'*
and splendid separate palaces for those who are to be *palaces.*
their rulers, in the bottom of the hive; these project
with a protuberance, and if this be squeezed out,
no offspring is born. All the cells are hexagonal,
each side being made by one of the bee's six feet.
None of these tasks are done at a fixed time, but they
snatch their duties on fine days. They fill their
cells with honey on one or at most two days.

Honey comes out of the air, and is chiefly formed *They collect*
at the rising of the stars, and especially when the *honey-dew*
from foliage
Dogstar itself shines forth, and not at all before the *and carry it*
rising of the Pleiads, in the periods just before *in their*
stomachs.
dawn. Consequently at that season at early dawn
the leaves of trees are found bedewed with honey,
and any persons who have been out under the
morning sky feel their clothes smeared with damp
and their hair stuck together, whether this is the
perspiration of the sky or a sort of saliva of the stars
or the moisture of the air purging itself. And
would it were pure and liquid and homogeneous,
as it was when it first flowed down! But as it is,
falling from so great a height and acquiring a great
deal of dirt as it comes and becoming stained with
vapour of the earth that it encounters, and moreover
having been sipped from foliage and pastures and

in utriculos congestus apium—ore enim eum vomunt, ad hoc suco florum corruptus et alvi vitiis[1] maceratus, totiensque mutatus, magnam tamen caelestis naturae voluptatem adfert.

32   XIII. Ibi optumus semper ubi optimorum doliolis florum conditur. fit[2] Atticae regionis hoc et Siculae Hymetto et Hybla, apricis locis,[3] mox Calydna in[4] insula.   est autem initio mel ut aqua dilutum, et primis diebus fervet ut musta seque purgat, vicensimo die crassescit, mox obducitur tenui membrana quae fervoris ipsius spuma concrescit.   sorbetur optimum et minime fronde infectum e quercus, tiliae, harundinum foliis.

33   XIV. Summa quidem bonitatis ratione[5] constat, ut supra diximus, pluribus modis.   aliubi enim favi cera spectabiles gignuntur, ut in Sicilia, Paelignis, aliubi copia mellis, ut in Creta, Cypro, Africa, aliubi magnitudine, ut in septentrionalibus, viso iam in Germania octo pedum longitudinis favo in

34   cava parte nigro.   in quocumque tamen tractu terna sunt genera mellis.   vernum ex floribus constructo favo, quod ideo vocatur anthinum.   hoc quidam attingi vetant, ut largo alimento valida exeat suboles; alii ex nullo minus apibus relinquunt, quoniam magna sequatur ubertas magnorum siderum

----

[1] *Mayhoff*: alvinis *aut* alveis.   [2] fit *add. Mayhoff.*
[3] *Mayhoff ?*: ab locis *aut* locis.   [4] in *add. ? Mayhoff.*
                [5] *v.l.* natione.

ᵃ At § 33.

having been collected into the stomachs of bees—
for they throw it up out of their mouths, and in
addition being tainted by the juice of flowers, and
soaked in the curruptions of the belly, and so often
transformed, nevertheless it brings with it the great
pleasure of its heavenly nature.

XIII. It is always of the best quality where it is *Varieties of*
stored in the calyces of the best flowers. This takes *honey.*
place at Hymettus and Hybla in the region of
Attica and of Sicily, which are sunny localities
and also on the island of Calydna. But at the
start it is honey diluted as it were with water, and
in the first days it ferments like must and purifies
itself, while on the twentieth day it thickens and
then is covered with a thin skin which forms from
the foam of the actual boiling. The best kind and
that least stained with the foliage is sucked from the
leaves of the oak and lime and of reeds.

XIV. Indeed it is constituted on a supreme *Local*
principle of excellence, as we have said,[a] in a variety *varieties.*
of ways. In some places honeycombs distinguished
for their wax are formed, as in Sicily and the Abruzzi,
in other places for quantity of honey, as in Crete,
Cyprus, Africa, in others for size, as in the northern
countries, a comb having before now been seen in
Germany that was 8 ft. long, and black in its hollow
part. Yet in any region there are three kinds of *Seasonal*
honey. There is spring honey with the comb made *varieties.*
from flowers, which is consequently called flower-
honey. Some people say this ought not to be
touched, so that a progeny made strong by plentiful
nourishment may be produced; but others leave
less of this honey than of any other kind for the bees,
on the ground that a great profusion follows at the

exortu, praeterea solstitio, cum thymum et uva
35 florere incipiunt, praecipua cellarum materia. est
autem in eximendis favis necessaria dispensatio,
quoniam inopia cibi desperant moriunturque aut
diffugiunt, contra copia ignaviam adfert, ac iam melle,
non erithace, pascuntur; ergo diligentiores ex hac
vindemia xv partem apibus relinquont. dies status
inchoandae ut quadam lege naturae, si scire aut
observare homines vellent, tricensimus ab educto
examine; fereque Maio mense includitur haec
vindemia.

36 Alterum genus est mellis aestivi, quod ideo vocatur
horaeon a tempestivitate praecipua, ipso sirio ex-
splendescente, post solstitium diebus xxx fere. inmensa circa hoc subtilitas naturae mortalibus pate-
facta est, nisi fraus hominum cuncta pernicie corrum-
37 peret. namque ab exortu sideris cuiuscumque,
sed nobilium maxime, aut caelestis arcus, si non
sequantur imbres sed ros tepescat solis radiis,
medicamenta, non mella, gignuntur, oculis, ulceribus
internisque visceribus dona caelestia. quod si
servetur hoc Sirio exoriente casuque congruat in
eundem diem, ut saepe, Veneris aut Iovis Mer-
curive exortus, non alia suavitas visque mortalium
malis a morte revocandis quam divini nectaris
fiat.

38 XV. Mel plenilunio uberius capitur, sereno die
pinguius. in omni melle quod per se fluxit ut

rising of the great stars, and also at the solstice, when thyme and grape-vines begin to flower, the outstanding material for the cells. It is however necessary to practice economy in taking away the combs, as lack of food causes the bees to despair and die or fly away, and on the other hand a large supply brings sloth, and then the bees feed on the honey and not on bee-bread; consequently the more careful beekeepers leave a fifteenth part of this vintage to the bees. The day fixed for beginning by a sort of law of nature, if only men would know or keep it, is the thirtieth after the leading out of the swarm; and this vintage usually falls within the month of May.

The second kind of honey is summer honey, the Greek name for which consequently is ' ripe honey,' because it is produced in the most favourable season, when the dogstar is shining in its full splendour, about thirty days after midsummer. In respect of this, immense subtlety on the part of nature has been displayed to mortals, did not man's dishonesty spoil everything with its banefulness. For after the rising of each star, but particularly the principal stars, or of a rainbow, if rain does not follow but the dew is warmed by the rays of the sun, not honey but drugs are produced, heavenly gifts for the eyes, for ulcers and for the internal organs. And if this substance is kept when the dogstar is rising, and if, as often happens, the rise of Venus or Jupiter or Mercury falls on the same day, its sweetness and potency for recalling mortals' ills from death is equal to that of the nectar of the gods.

XV. Honey is obtained more copiously at full *Other varieties.* moon, and of thicker substance in fine weather. In all honey the portion that has flowed by itself like

mustum oleumque—appellatur acetum—maxime
laudabile est. aestivum omne rutilum, ut siccioribus
confectum diebus. album mel non fit ubi thymum
est, sed oculis et ulceribus aptissimum existimatur e
thymo, coloris aurei, saporis gratissimi. coit [1] palam
39 e violis [2] pingue, e marino rore spissum, quod concrescit autem minime laudatur. thymosum non
coit et tactu praetenuia fila remittit,[3] quod primum
bonitatis argumentum est; abrumpi statim et
resilire guttas vilitatis indicium habetur. sequens
probatio ut sit odoratum et ex dulci acre, glutinosum,
40 perlucidum. ex [4] aestiva mellatione x partem Cassio
Dionysio apibus relinqui placet, si plenae fuerint
alvi; si minus, pro rata portione aut, si inanes,
omnino non attingi. huic vindemiae Attici signum
dedere initium caprifici, alii diem Volcano sacrum.

41 Tertium genus mellis minime probatum silvestre,
quod ericaeum vocant. convehitur post primos
autumni imbres, cum erice sola floret in silvis, ob id
harenoso simile. gignit id maxume Arcturi exortus
ex a. d. pr. id. Septembris. quidam aestivam mella-
tionem ad Arcturi exortum proferunt, quoniam ad
aequinoctium autumni ab eo supersint dies xiv, et
ab aequinoctio ad Vergiliarum occasum diebus
42 xxxxviii plurima sit erice. Athenienses eam

---

[1] *Detlefsen* : cofit *aut* quo fit.
[2] e violis ? *Mayhoff* : doliolis.
[3] ? *Mayhoff* : mittit.   [4] ex *add. Ian.*

---

[a] About midsummer.   [b] August 23.

must and olive oil—it is called honey-vinegar—is the most commendable. All summer honey is reddish, as it has been made in a comparatively dry period. White honey is not made where there is thyme, but honey made from thyme is thought most suitable for the eyes and for ulcers—it is of a gold colour and has an extremely agreeable taste. The fat honey from violets and the thick kind from rosemary can be seen to condense, but honey that thickens is least praised. Honey from thyme does not condense, and when touched sends out very thin threads, which is the first proof of goodness; it is considered a mark of poor quality for the drops to break off at once and fall back. The next test is for it to have a fragrant scent and a sweet taste leaving a tang, and to be sticky and transparent. Cassius Dionysius holds that a tenth part of the summer honey-crop should be left to the bees, if the hives were full, and that if they were not, a proportionate amount should be left, or if they were empty, they should not be touched at all. The population of Attica have given the first ripening of the wild fig [a] as the signal for this vintage, but others say Vulcan's holy day.[b]

A third, very little valued, kind of honey is wild honey, called heath-honey. It is collected after the first autumn rains, when only the heath is in flower in the woods, and consequently it resembles sandy honey. It is produced mostly by the rise of Arcturus after September 12. Some people advance the summer honey-making to the rise of Arcturus, since that leaves fourteen days to the autumnal equinox, and in the forty-eight days from the equinox to the setting of the Pleiads heath is most plentiful. The Athenian name for it is *tetralice*, and

Wild honey of autumn.

tetralicen[1] appellant, Euboea sisyrum, putantque
apibus esse gratissimam, fortassis quia tunc nulla alia
sit copia. haec ergo mellatio fine vindemiae et
Vergiliarum occasu idibus Novembribus fere includitur. relinqui ex ea duas partes apibus ratio persuadet,
et semper eas partes favorum quae habeant erithacen.
43 a bruma ad Arcturi exortum diebus LX somno
aluntur sine ullo cibo; ab Arcturi exortu ad aequinoctium vernum tepidiore tractu iam vigilant, sed
etiamnum alvo se continent servatosque in id tempus
cibos repetunt. in Italia vero hoc idem a Vergi-
44 liarium exortu faciunt; in eum dormiunt. alvos
quidam in eximendo melle expendunt, ita diribentes
quantum relinquant. aequitas quidem etiam in iis
obstringitur, feruntque societate fraudata alvos
mori. in primis ergo praecipitur ut lauti purique
eximant mella; et furfurem[2] mulierumque menses
45 odere. cum eximantur mella, apes abigi fumo
utilissimum, ne irascantur aut ipsae avide vorent.
fumo crebriore et ignavia earum excitatur ad opera,
nam nisi incubavere, favos lividos faciunt. rursus
fumo nimio inficiuntur, quando iniuriam celerrime
sentiunt mella vel minimo contactu roris acescentia;
et ob id inter genera servatur quod acapnum vocant.

---

[1] edd. ex Theophrasto: tetradicen.
[2] Mueller: furem (faetorem Mayhoff).

the Euboean *sisyrus*, and they believe it to be very acceptable to bees, perhaps because at that season there is no other supply for them. Consequently this honey-gathering is roughly in the period between the end of vintage and the setting of the Pleiads on November 13. Reason advises leaving two-thirds of the honey then procured for the bees, and always the parts of the combs that contain bee-bread. In the sixty days from midwinter to the rising of Arcturus they live on sleep, without any food; in the warmer period from the rising of Arcturus to the spring equinox they now keep awake, but still keep inside the hive and have recourse to the food kept for this time. But in Italy they do the same after the rising of the Pleiads, sleeping till then. Some people in taking out the honey weigh the hives, so separating the amount to be left behind. There is indeed a bond of equity even in the case of bees, and it is said that if the partnership is defrauded the hives perish. Consequently it is one of the first rules that people must wash themselves clean before they take the honey; also bees hate scurf, and women's menstruation. When honey is being removed it is very useful for the bees to be driven away by smoke, so that they may not get angry or greedily devour it themselves. Also denser smoke is employed to arouse their sloth to their tasks, for if they have not gone on incubating, the combs they make are discoloured. On the other hand excessive smoke kills them, as honey very quickly undergoes deterioration if turned sour by the least touch of moisture; and for this reason among the kinds of honey there is a special sort called by the Greek word meaning ' smokeless.'

Hibernation of bees.

Methods of taking honey.

459

46 XVI. Fetus quonam modo progenerarent magna inter eruditos et subtilis fuit quaestio; apium enim coitus visus est numquam. plures existimavere ore confingi floribus compositis [1] calami [2] atque olivae [3]; aliqui coitu unius, qui rex in quoque appelletur examine; hunc esse solum marem, praecipua magnitudine, ne fatiscat: ideo fetum sine eo non edi, apesque reliquas tamquam marem feminas comitari, non tamquam ducem. quam probabilem alias sententiam fucorum proventus coarguit; quae enim ratio ut idem coitus alios perfectos,[4] inperfectos

47 generet alios? propior vero prior existimatio fieret, ni rursus alia difficultas ocurreret: quippe nascuntur aliquando in extremis favis apes grandiores quae ceteras fugant. oestrus vocatur hoc malum—

48 quonam modo nascens si ipsae fingunt? quod certum est, gallinarum modo incubant. id quod exclusum est primo vermiculus videtur candidus, iacens transversus adhaerensque ita ut pars cerae videatur. rex statim mellei coloris, ut electo flore ex omni copia factus, neque vermiculus sed statim pinniger. cetera turba cum formam capere coepit,

49 nymphae vocantur, ut fuci sirenes aut cephenes. si

---

[1] *v.l.* compositas.
[2] calami *add. Detlefsen.*
[3] olivae *ex Aristotele Detlefsen*: utiliter.
[4] *v.l. om.* alios perfectos.

---

[a] *Cf.* § 27 *n.*

XVI. There has been a great deal of minute *Reproduction* enquiry among the learned as to the manner in *of bees—* which bees reproduce their species; for sexual *various views* intercourse among them has never been observed. *as to.* A majority of authorities have held the view that the offspring are formed in the mouth, by blending together blossoms of the reed and the olive; some think it is by copulation with a single male which in each swarm is called the king; and that this is the only male, and is of exceptional size, so as not to grow weary; and that consequently offspring is not produced without him, and the rest of the bees accompany him as women accompany a husband, not as their leader. This view, though probable *Selection of* on other grounds, is refuted by the production of *future king.* drones; for what reason can there be why the same act of union should engender some perfect offspring and others imperfect? The former opinion would be nearer to the truth, were it not that again another difficulty meets us: it is a fact that sometimes larger bees are born in the extremities of the combs which drive away all the rest. This mischievous creature is *Varieties of* called a gadfly—being born in what possible manner if *offspring.* the female bees themselves shape it? One certain fact is that they sit on their eggs in the way that hens do. The offspring hatched at first looks like a white maggot, lying crosswise and sticking so closely to the wax that it seems to be part of it. The king is from the start of the colour of honey, as if made from a special blossom chosen out of the whole supply, and is not a maggot but has wings from the start. The remaining throng when they begin to take shape are called pupae, while the sham ones *a* are called sirens or drones. If anybody takes the heads

461

quis alterutris capita demat priusquam pennas habeant, pro gratissimo sunt pabulo matribus. tempore procedente instillant cibos atque incubant, tum maxime murmurantes, caloris, ut putant, faciendi gratia necessarii excludendis pullis, donec ruptis membranis quae singulos cingunt ovorum modo universum agmen emergat. spectatum hoc Romae consularis cuiusdam suburbano alvis cornu lanternae
50 tralucido factis. fetus intra xLV diem peragitur. fit in favis quibusdam qui vocatur clavus, amarae duritia cerae, cum fetum inde non eduxere, morbo aut ignavia aut infecunditate naturali; hic est abortus apium. protinus autem educti operantur quadam disciplina cum matribus, regemque iuvenem
51 aequalis turba comitatur. reges plures inchoantur, ne desint[1]; postea ex his suboles cum adulta esse coepit, concorde suffragio deterrimos necant, ne distrahant agmina. duo autem genera eorum, melior rufus, deterior[2] niger variusque. omnibus forma semper egregia et duplo quam ceteris maior, pennae breviores, crura recta, ingressus celsior, in fronte macula quodam diademate candicans; multum etiam nitore a volgo differunt.
52   XVII. Quaerat nunc aliquis, unusne Hercules fuerit et quot Liberi patres et reliqua vetustatis situ

---

[1] *Hermolaus*: nec desunt.
[2] rufus deterior *add. Jan* (rufus quam *Hermolaus*).

off specimens of either kind before they have wings, they serve as very acceptable food for their mothers. As time goes on they give them drops of food and sit on them, buzzing more than at any other time, with the object, it is thought, of producing the warmth needed for hatching out the grubs, until they break the membranes that enclose each of them like eggshells and the whole band emerges. This was observed at Rome on the suburban estate of a certain ex-consul, who had hives made of the transparent horn of a lantern. The brood grows up in about six weeks. In some hives what is called a wart is formed, a hard lump of bitter wax, when the bees have not produced offspring out of the comb, owing to disease or sloth or natural infertility; this is the bees' form of abortion. But as soon as they are hatched out they get to work with their mothers under some sort of tuition, and the youthful king is escorted by a retinue of his peers. Several kings are begun to be produced, so that there may not be a lack of them; but afterwards, when the offspring sprung from these has begun to be grown up, by a unanimous vote they kill the worst of them so that they may not divide up the forces. They are of two kinds, the better sort red and the inferior kind black or speckled. All of them are always exceptionally well-formed and twice as large as the others; their wings are shorter, their legs straight, their bearing more lofty, and they have a spot on their brow that shines white in a kind of fillet; they also differ from the common herd a great deal by their brilliant colour.

XVII. Now let somebody raise the questions whether Hercules was one person and how many Father Libers there were, and all the other puzzles

Hatching of grubs.

Selection of future king.

'as a king-bee a sting? His office and privileges.

obruta! ecce in re parva villisque nostris adnexa,
cuius adsidue copia est, non constat inter auctores,
rex nullumne solus habeat aculeum maiestate
tantum armatus, an dederit quidem eum natura, sed
usum eius illi tantum negaverit. illud constat,
53 imperatorem aculeo non uti. mira plebei circa eum
obedientia. cum procedit, una est totum examen
circaque eum globatur, cingit, protegit, cerni non
patitur. reliquo tempore, cum populus in labore est,
ipse opera intus circumit, similis exhortanti, solus
immunis. circa eum satellites quidam lictoresque
54 adsidui custodes auctoritatis. procedit foras non
nisi migraturo examine; id multo intellegitur ante,
aliquot diebus murmure intus strepente, apparatus
indice diem tempestivum eligentium. si quis alam
ei detruncet, non fugiat examen. cum processere,
se quaeque proximam illi cupit esse et in officio
conspici gaudet; fessum umeris sublevant, validius
fatigatum ex toto portant. si qua lassata defecit aut
forte aberravit, odore persequitur. ubicumque ille
consedit, ibi cunctarum castra sunt.

55　　XVIII. Tunc ostenta faciunt privata ac publica

buried beneath the litter of antiquity! Here on a
trifling matter connected with our own country-
houses, a thing constantly in evidence, there is no
agreement among the authorities—the question
whether the king bee alone has no sting and is
armed only with the grandeur of his office, or whether
nature has indeed bestowed one upon him but has
merely denied him the use of it. It is a well
established fact that the ruler does not use a sting.
The commons surround him with a marvellous
obedience. When he goes in procession, the whole
swarm accompanies him and is massed around him
to encircle and protect him, not allowing him to be
seen. During the rest of the time, while the people
are engaged in labour, he himself goes the circuit
of the works inside, with the appearance of
urging them on, while he alone is free from duty.
He is surrounded by certain retainers and lictors as
the constant guardians of his authority. He only
issues abroad when the swarm is about to migrate;
intelligence of this is given long before, as a buzzing
noise has been going on for some days in the hive, a
sign of their preparation while they are selecting a
suitable day. If anybody should cut off one of his
wings, the swarm would not run away. When they
have started, each one wants to be next him and
delights to be seen on duty; when he is tired they
support him with their shoulders, and carry him
entirely if he is more completely exhausted. Any
bee that falls out from weariness or happens to stray
from the main body, follows on by scent. Wherever
the king alights is the camping place of the whole
body.

XVIII. Moreover they supply private and public

465

uva dependente in domibus templisque, saepe ex-
piata magnis eventibus. sedere in ore infantis tum
etiam Ptatonis, suavitatem illam praedulcis eloquii
portendentes; sedere in castris Drusi imperatoris
cum prosperrime pugnatum apud Arbalonem est,
haut quaquam perpetua haruspicum coniectura, qui
56 dirum id ostentum existimant semper. duce prenso
totum tenetur agmen, amisso dilabitur migratque
ad alios; esse utique sine rege non possunt. invitae
autem interemunt eos cum plures fuere, potiusque
nascentium domos diruunt. si proventus desperatur,
57 tunc et fucos abigunt. quamquam et de his video
dubitari propriumque iis genus esse aliquos existimare, sicut furibus, grandissimis inter illos sed nigris
lataque alvo, ita appellatis quia furtim devorent
mella. certum est ab apibus fucos interfici; utique
regem non habent aequo modo [1]; si [2] sine aculeo
nascantur in quaestione est.
58   Umido vere melior fetus, sicco mel copiosius.
quod si defecit aliquas alvos cibus, impetum in proxi-
mas faciunt rapinae proposito; at illae contra
dirigunt aciem, et si custos adsit, alterutra pars quae
sibi favere sensit non adpetit eum. ex aliis quoque

[1] aequo modo *cum praec. edd.* : et quo modo.
[2] si *add. Jan.*

portents when a cluster of them hangs suspended in *Portents given by bees.* houses and temples, portents that have often been expiated by great events. They alighted on the mouth of Plato even when he was still an infant, portending the charm of that matchless eloquence; and they alighted in the camp of General Drusus on the occasion of the very successful battle of Arbalo—as there are certainly exceptions to the interpretation of the augurs, who invariably think this a direful portent. The capture of the leader *A king indispensable.* holds up the whole body, and when they have lost him they separate and migrate to other lords; in any case they are unable to be without a king. But when the kings have become too numerous they reluctantly destroy them, and by preference they destroy their homes while they are being born. If a supply of honey is despaired of, then they even drive away the drones. Nevertheless I see that *Function of drones.* there is a doubt about these also, and that some persons think them to form a breed of their own, like the robber-bees, the largest in size among the drones but black and with a broad belly, which have this designation because they steal and devour the honey. It is certain that the drones are killed by the bees; at all events they do not have a king in the same way as the other bees do; but whether they are born without a sting is a doubtful point.

Bees breed better in a damp spring, but produce *How affected by weather.* more honey in a dry one. If there is a dearth of food for some hives, they make a raid on their *Battles of bees.* neighbours for the purpose of plunder; but the bees attacked form in line of battle to resist, and if the bee-keeper is present whichever side thinks that he favours it does not attack him. They also often

467

saepe dimicant causis, duasque acies contrarias duo imperatores instruunt, maxime rixa in convehendis floribus exorta et suos quibusque evocantibus; quae dimicatio iniectu pulveris aut fumo tota discutitur, reconciliatur vero lacte vel aqua mulsa.

59 XIX. Apes sunt et rusticae silvestresque. horridae aspectu, multo iracundiores, sed opere ac labore praestantes. urbanarum duo genera: optimae breves variaeque et in rotunditatem conpactiles, deteriores longae et quibus similitudo vesparum, etiamnum deterrimae ex iis pilosae. in Ponto sunt quaedam albae quae bis in mense mella faciunt; circa Thermodontem autem fluvium duo genera, aliarum quae in arboribus mellificant, aliarum quae sub terra triplici cerarum ordine, uberrimi proventus.

60 Aculeum apibus dedit natura ventri consertum ad unum ictum; hoc infixo quidam eas statim emori putant, aliqui non nisi in tantum adacto ut intestini quippiam sequatur, sed fucos postea esse nec mella facere velut castratis viribus pariterque et nocere et prodesse desinere. est in exemplis

61 equus [1] ab iis occisus.[2] odere foedos odores proculque fugiunt, sed et fictos; itaque unguenta redolentes infestant. ipsae plurimorum animalium iniuriis ob-

---

[1] *Mayhoff* : equos.
[2] *v.l.* occisos.

fight battles for other reasons, and form in two opposing lines under two commanders, the chief source of quarrel arising while they are collecting flowers, and each party calling out their friends; but the combat can be entirely scattered by some dust being thrown on it or by smoke, while a reconciliation can be effected by some milk or water sweetened with honey.

XIX. There are also wild and forest bees, which *Wild bees and domesticated bees.* are of a bristly appearance, and are much more irascible but of superior industry and diligence. Domesticated bees are of two kinds; the best are short and speckled and of a compact round shape, and the inferior ones are long and have a resemblance to wasps, and also the worst among them are hairy. In Pontus there is a white kind that makes honey twice in a month; and in the neighbourhood of the river Thermodon there are two kinds, one that makes honey in trees and the other that makes it underground in a threefold arrangement of combs, and is most lavishly productive.

Nature has given bees a sting attached to the *Bees' use of sting.* stomach, designed for a single blow; certain persons think that when they have planted their sting they at once die, while some hold that this only occurs if it is driven in so far that some of the gut follows it, but that afterwards the bees are drones and do not make honey, as though their strength had been castrated, and they cease at the same time both to hurt and to benefit. There is a case of a horse being killed by bees. Bees hate foul smells and flee far away from them, even those not due to natural causes; consequently they attack people scented *Dangers of bees.* with perfumes. They themselves are liable to

noxiae. inpugnant eas naturae eiusdem degeneres
vespae atque crabrones, etiam e culicum genere qui
vocantur muliones, populantur hirundines et quaedam
aliae aves; insidiantur aquantibus ranae, quae
maxima earum est operatio tum cum subolem
62 faciunt. nec eae tantum quae stagna rivosque
obsident, verum et rubetae veniunt ultro adrepentes-
que foribus per eas sufflant; ad hoc statio provolat
confestimque abripitur; nec sentire ictus apium
ranae traduntur. inimicae et oves difficile se e lanis
earum explicantibus. cancrorum etiam odore, si
quis iuxta coquat, exanimantur.

63 XX. Quin et morbos suapte natura sentiunt.
index eorum tristitia torpens, et cum ante fores in
teporem solis promotis aliae cibos ministrant et [1] cum
defunctas progerunt funerantiumque more comitantur exequias. rege ea peste consumpto maeret
plebes ignavo dolore, non cibos convehens, non
procedens; tristi tantum murmure glomeratur circa
corpus eius. subtrahitur itaque diductae multitu-
dini; alias spectantes exanimem luctum non minuunt.
tunc quoque, ni subveniatur, fame moriuntur.
hilaritate igitur et nitore sanitas aestimatur.

64 Sunt et operis morbi: cum favos non explent,

---

[1] et add. Rackham.

injuries from very many creatures. Wasps and hornets which are degenerate species of the same nature attack them, as also do the species of gnat called mule-flies. Swallows and some other birds ravage them. Frogs lie in wait for them when they are getting water, which is their most important task at the period when they are producing offspring. And not only the frogs that beset ponds and rivers but also toads come of their own accord and crawling up to the doorways blow through them; thereupon the guard flies out and is immediately snapped up; and it is said that frogs do not feel a bee's sting. Sheep too are the enemies of bees, which with difficulty disentangle themselves from their wool. Also the smell of crabs being boiled near them is fatal to them.

XX. Moreover bees suffer diseases due to their own *Diseases of bees.* nature. A symptom of these is a gloomy torpidity, both when they are brought out before the doorway into the warmth of the sun and food is served to them by others and when they die and the others carry them out and escort their obsequies in the manner of persons conducting a funeral. When this pestilence carries off the king the commons mourn with abject grief, not collecting food and not going out of the hive; they only mass themselves round his body with a sorrowful buzzing. Consequently the throng is separated and he is taken away from it; otherwise they keep gazing at his lifeless body and never stop mourning. Then also, unless help is brought to them, they die of hunger. Consequently their health is judged by their gaiety and brightness.

There are also diseases that affect their work:

claron vocant, item blapsigonian si fetum non
peragant.

65   XXI. Inimica et echo est resultanti sono qui
pavidas alterno pulset ictu; inimica et nebula.
aranei quoque vel maxime hostiles: cum praevaluere
ut intexant, enecant alvos. papilio etiam, hic[1]
ignavus et inhonoratus luminibus accensis advolitans,
pestifer, nec uno modo, nam et ipse ceras depascitur
et relinquit excrementa e quibus teredines gignuntur; fila etiam araneosa, quacumque incessit,
66 alarum maxime lanugine obtexit. nascuntur et in
ipso ligno teredines quae ceras praecipue adpetunt.
infestat et aviditas pastus, nimia florum satietate
verno maxume tempore alvo cita. oleo quidem non
apes tantum sed omnia insecta exanimantur, praeci-
67 pue si capite uncto in sole ponantur. aliquando et
ipsae contrahunt mortis sibi causas, cum sensere
eximi mella, avide vorantes, cetero praeparcae et
quae alioqui prodigas atque edaces non secus ac
pigras et ignavas proturbent. nocent et sua mella
ipsis, inlitaeque ab aversa parte moriuntur. tot
hostibus, tot casibus—et quotam portionem eorum
commemoro?—tam munificum animal expositum est.
remedia dicemus suis locis; nunc enim sermo de
natura est.

---

[1] hic *om. v.l.*

---

[a] The disease now called ' foul brood.'
[b] *Papilio* includes moths; here it means the pipe-moth,
which breeds in bee-hives.

when they do not fill the combs full, it is called *claron*, and *blapsigonia* [a] if they do not bring their offspring to maturity.

XXI. Also an echo is detrimental to bees with its repercussion that alarms them by striking them with an alternating blow; fog too is detrimental. Also spiders are in the highest degree hostile; when they have succeeded in weaving a web over the combs they kill the grubs. Even the moth,[b] that cowardly and ignoble creature that flutters up to lamps when they are lit, brings disaster, and not in one way only, for it both devours the combs itself and leaves excrement from which grubs are produced; also wherever it walks it weaves a covering of cobwebs chiefly made from the down on its wings. Moreover moths are born in the wood itself that specially attack the combs. And another bane is their greed for food, as their belly is moved, specially in the spring time, by their devouring a surfeit of flowers. Olive oil indeed kills not only bees but all insects, especially if they are placed in the sun after their head has been anointed. Sometimes also they themselves cause their own death, by greedily devouring honey when they perceive that it is being taken away, whereas normally they are extremely thrifty and make a practice of driving away wasteful and greedy bees just the same as lazy and slothful ones. Also their own honey is noxious to them, and if it is smeared on their backs they die. To so many foes and so many disasters—and how small a fraction of them I am recounting!—is this beneficent creature exposed. The remedies we will speak of in their proper places; for at present we are discussing their nature.

Enemies of bees; other dangers.

68 XXII. Gaudent plausu atque tinnitu aeris, eoque convocantur; quo manifestum est auditus quoque inesse sensum. effecto opere, educto fetu, functae munere omni exercitationem tamen sollemnem habent, spatiataeque in aperto et in altum elatae, gyris volatu editis, tum demum ad cibum redeunt.
69 vita iis longissima, ut prospere inimica ac fortuita cedant, septenis annis. universas[1] alvos numquam ultra decem annos durasse proditur. sunt qui mortuas, si intra tectum hieme serventur, dein sole verno torreantur ac ficulneo cinere tepido foveantur,
70 putent revivescere; XXIII. in totum vero amissas reparari ventribus bubulis recentibus cum fimo obrutas,[2] Vergilius iuvencorum corpore exanimato, sicut equorum vespas atque crabrones, sicut asinorum scarabaeos, mutante natura ex aliis quaedam in alia. sed horum omnium coitus cernuntur, et tamen in fetu eadem prope natura quae apibus.
71 XXIV. Vespae in sublimi e luto nidos faciunt, in his ceras; crabrones cavernis aut sub terra; et horum omnium sexangulae cellae, cerae autem e cortice, araneosae. fetus ipse inaequalis et[3] varius,[4] alius evolat, alius in nympha est, alius in vermiculo; et autumno, non vere, omnia ea. plenilunio maxime
72 crescunt. vespae quae ichneumones vocantur—

[1] *Madvig*: universa.   [2] *Mayhoff?*: obrutis.
[3] *v.l.* ut.
[4] *Detlefsen*: barbarus *aut* barbaris.

_____

ᶜ *Georgics* IV 284 ff.

XXII. They delight in the clash and clang of bronze, and collect together at its summons; which shows that they also possess the sense of hearing. When their work is done and their brood reared, though they have accomplished all their duty they nevertheless have a ritual exercise to perform, and they range abroad in the open and soar on high, tracing circles in flight, and only when this is finished do they return to take food. Their life at longest, granted that hostile attacks and accidents are encountered successfully, lasts seven years. It is stated that the hives have never lasted in their entirety beyond ten years. Some people think that dead bees come to life again if they are kept indoors in winter and then exposed to the heat of the sun in spring and kept warm with hot fig-wood ashes; XXIII. but that when entirely lost they can be restored by being covered with fresh ox-paunches together with mud, or according to Virgil *c* with the dead body of bullocks, just as wasps and hornets are brought to life from horses' bodies and beetles from those of asses, since nature can change some things from one kind into another. But all these creatures are seen to pair, and nevertheless their offspring possess almost the same nature as that of bees.

XXIV. Wasps make their nests high up, of mud, and in them make cells of wax; hornets make them in caverns or underground; all of these have hexagonal cells, and make their combs of bark, like spiders' webs. The actual offspring are not uniform but vary—one flies out while another is in the pupa and another in the grub; and all of these stages are in the autumn, not the spring. They grow chiefly at full moon. The wasps called ichneumon-flies—they

Noises to summon bees.

Life period of bees.

Restoration of dead bees.

Wasps.

475

sunt autem minores quam aliae—unum genus ex araneis peremunt phalangium appellatum et in nidos suos ferunt, deinde inlinunt et ex his incubando suum genus procreant. praeterea omnes carne vescuntur contra quam apes quae nullum corpus attingunt. sed vespae muscas grandiores venantur amputatoque iis capite reliquom corpus auferunt.

73 Crabronum silvestres in arborum cavernis degunt, hieme ut cetera insecta conduntur, vita bimatum non transit. ictus eorum haud temere sine febri est. auctores sunt ter novenis punctis interfici hominem. aliorum qui mitiores videntur duo genera: opifices, minores corpore, qui moriuntur hieme, matres 74 quae biennio durant; hi et clementes. nidos vere faciunt fere quadrifores, in quibus opifices generentur. his eductis alios deinde maiores nidos fingunt, in quibus matres futuras iam producant. tum [1] opifices funguntur munere et pascunt eas. latior matrum species, dubiumque an habeant aculeos, quia non egrediuntur. et his sui fuci. quidam opinantur omnibus his ad hiemem decidere aculeos. nec crabronum autem nec vesparum generi reges aut examina, sed subinde renovatur multitudo subole.

75 XXV. Quartum inter haec genus est bombycum, in Assyria proveniens, maius quam supra dicta. nidos luto fingunt salis specie, adplicatos lapidi, tanta duritia ut spiculis perforari vix possint. in his

---

[1] *Mayhoff* (?): producant. iam tum.

---

[a] Three times three times three is of course a magic number.

are smaller than the others—kill one kind of spider called *phalangium* and carry them to their nests and then smear them over, and from these by incubating produce their own species. Moreover they all feed on flesh, contrary to bees which never touch a body. But wasps hunt larger flies and after cutting off their heads carry away the rest of the body.

The forest variety of hornets live in hollow trees, *Hornets.* hibernating in winter like the rest of insects; they do not live beyond the age of two. Their sting is rarely not followed by fever. Some authorities state that twenty-seven [a] hornet-stings will kill a human being. Another kind that seems less fierce has two classes—workers, smaller in size, which die in winter, and mothers, which last two years: these are not fierce at all. They make nests in spring, usually with four entrances, in which to breed the workers. When these have been reared, they then make other larger nests, in which they may now produce those who are to be mothers. Then the workers begin to function, and feed the mothers. The mothers are of a wider shape, and it is doubtful whether they possess stings, because they do not come out. These also have their drones. Some people hold the view that all these insects lose their stings towards winter. Neither the hornet nor the wasp kind have kings, nor do they swarm, but their numbers are continually renewed by offspring.

XXV. Among these is a fourth genus, the silk- *The silk-* moth, which occurs in Assyria; it is larger than the *moth: its* kinds mentioned above. Silk-moths make their nests *two modes of* *reproduction.* of mud like a sort of salt; they are attached to a stone, and are so hard that they can scarcely be pierced with javelins. In these nests they make

ceras largius quam apes faciunt, dein maiorem
vermiculum.

76   XXVI. Et alia horum origo. ex grandiore vermiculo gemina protendens sui generis cornua primum [1]
urica fit, dein quod vocatur bombylis, ex ea necy-
dallus, ex hoc in sex mensibus bombyx. telas
araneorum modo texunt ad vestem luxumque
feminarum, quae bombycina appellatur. prima eas
redordiri rursusque texere invenit in Coo mulier
Pamphile, Plateae filia, non fraudanda gloria excogitatae rationis ut denudet feminas vestis.

77   XXVII. Bombycas et in Coo insula nasci tradunt,
cupressi, terebinthi, fraxini, quercus florem imbribus
decussum terrae halitu animante. fieri autem
primo papiliones parvos nudosque, mox frigorum
inpatientia villis inhorrescere et adversus hiemem
tunicas sibi instaurare densas, pedum asperitate
radentes foliorum lanuginem, in vellera hanc ab iis
cogi subigique unguium carminatione, mox trahi
in tramas,[2] tenuari ceu pectine, postea adprehensam
78   corpori involvi nido volubili. tum ab homine tolli
fictilibusque in [3] vasis tepore et furfurum esca nutriri,
atque ita subnasci sui generis plumas, quibus vestitos
ad alia pensa dimitti. quae vero carpta [4] sint lanicia [5]
umore lentescere, mox in fila tenuari iunceo fuso.

[1] *Hardouin*: cornuum.
[2] *Jan*: inter ramos.
[3] in *add. ? Mayhoff.*
[4] *Detlefsen*: capta.
[5] *Jan*: lanifica *aut* lanificia.

combs on a larger scale than bees do, and then produce a bigger grub.

XXVI. These creatures are also produced in another way. A specially large grub changes into a caterpillar with two projecting horns of a peculiar kind, and then into what is called a cocoon, and this turns into a chrysalis and this in six months into a silk-moth. They weave webs like spiders, producing a luxurious material for women's dresses, called silk. The process of unravelling these and weaving the thread again was first invented in Cos by a woman named Pamphile, daughter of Plateas, who has the undeniable distinction of having devised a plan to reduce women's clothing to nakedness. *Invention of silk.*

XXVII. Silk-moths are also reported to be born in the island of Cos, where vapour out of the ground creates life in the blossom of the cypress, terebinth, ash and oak that has been stripped off by rain. First however, it is said, small butterflies are produced that are bare of down, and then as they cannot endure the cold they grow shaggy tufts of hair and equip themselves with thick jackets against winter, scraping together the down of leaves with the roughness of their feet; this is compressed by them into fleeces and worked over by carding with their claws, and then drawn out into woof-threads, and thinned out as if with a comb, and afterwards taken hold of and wrapped round their body in a coiled nest. Then (they say) they are taken away by a man, put in earthenware vessels and reared with warmth and a diet of bran, and so a peculiar kind of feathers sprout out, clad with which they are sent out to other tasks; but tufts of wool plucked off are softened with moisture and then thinned out into threads with *The Coan silk industry.*

nec puduit has vestes usurpare etiam viros levitatem propter aestivam: in tantum a lorica gerenda discessere mores ut oneri sit etiam vestis. Assyria tamen bombyce adhuc feminis cedimus.

79   XXVIII. Araneorum his non absurde iungatur natura digna vel praecipua admiratione. plura autem sunt genera nec dictu necessaria in tanta notitia. phalangia ex iis appellantur quorum noxii morsus, corpus exiguum, varium, acuminatum, adsultim ingredientium. altera eorum species nigri prioribus cruribus longissimis. omnibus internodia

80 terna in cruribus. luporum minimi non texunt; maiores in terra, et cavernis exigua vestibula praepandunt. tertium eorundem genus erudita operatione conspicuum; orditur telas tantique operis materiae uterus ipsius sufficit, sive ita corrupta alvi natura stato tempore, ut Democrito placet, sive est quaedam intus lanigera fertilitas: tam moderato ungue, tam tereti filo et tam aequali deducit stamina,

81 ipso se pondere usus. texere a medio incipit circinato orbe subtemina adnectens, maculasque paribus semper intervallis sed subinde crescentibus ex angusto dilatans indissolubili nodo inplicat. quanta arte celat pedicas scutulato[1] rete grassantes!

----

[1] *v.l.* a scutulato.

----

[a] The legs have three pieces, *internodia*.
[b] Aristotle *Hist. An.* ix 39, 623a 30; Aristotle adopts the alternative view here given.

a rush spindle. Nor have even men been ashamed to make use of these dresses, because of their lightness in summer: so far have our habits departed from wearing a leather cuirass that even a robe is considered a burden! All the same we so far leave the Assyrian silk-moth to women.

XXVIII. To these may be not ineptly joined the nature of spiders, which deserves even exceptional admiration. There are several kinds of spiders, but they need not be described, as they are so well known. The name of *phalangium* is given to a kind of spider that has a harmful bite and a small body of variegated colour and pointed shape, and advances by leaps and bounds. A second species of spider is black, with very long fore legs. All spiders have legs with two joints.[a] Of the wolf-spiders the smallest do not weave a web, but the larger ones live in the ground and spin tiny ante-rooms in front of their holes. A third kind of the same species is remarkable for its scientific method of construction; it sets up its warp-threads, and its own womb suffices to supply the material needed for this considerable work, whether because the substance of its intestines is thus resolved at a fixed time, as Democritus holds,[b] or because it has inside it some power of producing wool: with such careful use of its claw and such a smooth and even thread it spins the warp, employing itself as a weight. It starts weaving at the centre, twining in the woof in a circular round, and entwists the meshes in an unloosable knot, spreading them out at intervals that are always regular but continually grow less narrow. How skilfully it conceals the snares that lurk in its checkered net! How unintentional

The spider— its varieties, and mode of weaving its web, and dealing with a catch.

quam non ad hoc videtur pertinere crebratae pexitas
telae et quadam politurae arte ipsa per se tenax
ratio tramae! quam laxus ad flatus ad[1] non res-
82 puenda quae veniant sinus! derelicta a[2] lasso
praetendi summa parte arbitrere licia: at illa
difficile cernuntur atque ut in plagis lineae offensae
praecipitant in sinum. specus ipse qua concamaratur
architectura! et contra frigora quanto[3] villosior!
quam remotus a medio aliudque agentis similis,
inclusus vero sic ut sit necne intus aliquis cerni non
83 possit! age firmitas, quando rumpentibus ventis,
qua pulverum mole degravante? latitudo telae saepe
inter duas arbores, cum exercet artem et discit
texere, longitudo fili a cacumine,[4] ac rursus a terra
per illud ipsum velox reciprocatio, subitque pariter ac
fila deducit. cum vero captura incidit, quam vigilans
et paratus accursus! licet extrema haereat plaga,
semper in medium currit, quia sic maxime totum
84 concutiendo implicat. scissa protinus reficit ad
polituram sarciens. ranarumque[5] et lacertarum
catulos venantur os primum tela involventes et tunc
demum labra utraque morsu adprehendentes, amphi-
theatrali spectaculo cum contigit. sunt ex eo et
auguria: quippe incremento amnium futuro telas

---

[1] ad *edd. vet*: ac.
[2] a *add. Rackham.*
[3] *edd.*: quando.
[4] *Detlefsen*: acumine (a culmine *edd.*).
[5] *Mayhoff? cf. Ar.*: namque.

appears to be the density of the close warp and the plan of the woof, rendered by a sort of scientific smoothing automatically tenacious! How its bosom bellies to the breezes so as not to reject things that come to it! You might think the threads had been left by a weary weaver stretching in front at the top; but they are difficult to see, and, like the cords in hunting-nets, when the quarry comes against them throw it into the bosom of the net. With what architectural skill is the vaulting of the actual cave designed! and how much more hairy it is made, to give protection against cold! How distant it is from the centre, and how its intention is concealed, although it is really so roofed in that it is impossible to see whether somebody is inside or not! Then its strength—when is it broken by the winds? what quantity of dust weighs it down? When the spider is practising its art and learning to weave, the breadth of the web often reaches between two trees and the length of the thread stretches down from the top of the tree and there is a quick return right up the thread from the ground, and the spider goes up and brings down the threads simultaneously. But when a catch falls into the web, how watchfully and alertly it runs to it! although it may be clinging to the edge of the net, it always runs to the middle, because in that way it entangles the prey by shaking the whole. When the web is torn it at once restores it to a finished condition by patching it. And spiders actually hunt young frogs and lizards, first wrapping up their mouth with web and then finally gripping both lips with their jaws, giving a show worthy of the amphitheatre when it comes off. Also auguries are *Augury by* obtained from the spider: for instance, when the *spiders.*

suas altius tollunt; idem sereno texunt,[1] nubilo
retexunt,[2] ideoque multa aranea imbrium signa sunt
feminam putant esse quae texat, marem qui venetur;
ita paria fieri merita coniugio.

85   XXIX. Aranei conveniunt clunibus, pariunt vermiculos ovis similes—nam nec horum, differri potest
genitura, quoniam insectorum vix ulla alia ratio[3]
est; pariunt autem omnia in tela, set sparsa, quia
saliunt atque ita emittunt. phalangia tantum in
ipso specu incubant magnum numerum qui. ut
emersit, matrem consumit, saepe et patrem, adiuvat
enim incubare. pariunt autem et tricenos, ceterae
pauciores; et incubant triduo. consummantur
aranei quater septenis diebus.

86   XXX. Similiter his et scorpiones terrestres vermiculos ovorum specie pariunt similiterque pereunt,
pestis inportuna, veneni serpentium nisi quod
graviore supplicio lenta per triduum morte conficiunt,
virginibus letali semper ictu et feminis fere in totum,
viris autem matutino, exeuntes cavernis, priusquam aliquo fortuito ictu ieiunum egerant venenum.

87   semper cauda in ictu est nulloque momento meditari
cessat, ne quando desit occasioni; ferit et obliquo
ictu et inflexo. venenum ab his candidum fundi

----

[1] *v.l.* retexunt.   [2] *Mayhoff*: texunt.
[3] *Mayhoff*: narratio.

rivers are going to rise they raise their webs higher;
also they weave their web in fine weather and reweave
it in cloudy weather, and consequently a number of
spiders' webs is a sign of rain. People think that it
is the female that weaves and the male that hunts,
and that thus the married pair do equal shares of
service.

XXIX. Spiders couple with the haunches, and *Reproduction*
produce grubs resembling eggs—for their mode of *of spiders.*
reproduction also must not be deferred, as insects
have scarcely any other method; and they lay them
all into their webs, but scattered, because they jump
about and lay them in the process. The *phalangium*
spiders only incubate in the actual cave a large
number of grubs which when hatched out devour the
mother, and often the father too, for he helps to
incubate. They produce broods of as many as three
hundred, whereas all the other kinds produce fewer;
and they sit on the eggs three days. They take
four weeks to become full-grown spiders.

XXX. Land scorpions also like spiders produce *Land*
grubs resembling eggs and die in the same way as *scorpions.*
spiders; they are a horrible plague, poisonous like
snakes, except that they inflict a worse torture by
despatching the victim with a lingering death lasting
three days, their wound being always fatal to girls
and almost absolutely so to women, but to men only
in the morning, when they are coming out of their
holes, before they emit their yet unsated poison by
some accidental stroke. Their tail is always engaged in striking and does not stop practising at
any moment, lest it should ever miss an opportunity;
it strikes both a sideway stroke and one with the
tail bent up. Apollodorus states that these insects

Apollodorus auctor est in novem genera discriptis per colores maxime, opere supervacuo,[1] quoniam non est scire quos minime exitiales praedixerit; geminos quibusdam aculeos esse, maresque saevissimos— nam coitum iis tribuit—intellegi autem gracilitate

88 et longitudine; venenum omnibus medio die cum incanduere solis ardoribus, itemque cum sitiunt inexplebile potus. constat et septena caudae internodia saeviorum[2] esse; pluribus enim sena sunt. hoc malum Africae volucre etiam austri faciunt pandentibus bracchia ut remigia sublevantes; Apollodorus idem plane quibusdam inesse pinnas tradit.

89 saepe Psylli, qui reliquarum venena terrarum invehentes quasi quaestus sui causa peregrinis malis implevere Italiam, hos quoque importare conati sunt, sed vivere intra Siculi caeli regionem non potuere. visuntur tamen aliquando in Italia, sed innocui, multisque aliis in locis ut circa Pharum in

90 Aegypto. in Scythia interemunt etiam sues alioquin vivaciores contra venena talia, nigras quidem celerius, si in aquam se inmerserint. homini icto putatur esse remedio ipsorum cinis potus in vino. magnam adversitatem oleo mersis et stellionibus putant esse, innocuis dumtaxat iis, qui et ipsi carent sanguine, lacertarum figura; aeque[3] scorpiones in

---

[1] *Mayhoff* (?): maxime supervacuos.
[2] *Mayhoff* (?): saeviora.   [3] *Mayhoff*: atque.

---

[a] Lit. 'with seven bones intermediate between joints,' vertebrae.
[b] *I.e.* in a more northerly climate than that of Sicily.

486

emit a white poison, and he divides them into
nine kinds, chiefly by their colours, a superfluous
task, since he does not let us know which he pro-
nounces to be the least deadly. He says that some
have a pair of stings, and that the males are fiercest—
for he attributes coupling to these creatures—but
that they can be recognized by their long slender
shape; and that all are poisonous at midday, when
they have got hot from the warmth of the sun, and
also that when they are thirsty they cannot have their
fill of drinking. It is also agreed that those with six
joints [a] in the tail are more savage—for the majority
have five. This curse of Africa is actually given the *Locality of*
power of flight by a south wind, which supports *scorpions.*
their arms when they spread them out like oars;
Apollodorus before mentioned definitely states that
some possess wings. The Psylli tribe, who by im-
porting the poisons of all the other countries for their
own profit have filled Italy with foreign evils, have
tried to bring these creatures here also, but they
have proved unable to live this side of the climate
of Sicily.[b] Nevertheless they are sometimes seen
in Italy, though these are harmless, and in many
other places, for instance in the neighbourhood of
Pharos in Egypt. In Scythia they kill even pigs,
which normally are exceptionally immune to such
poisons, black pigs indeed more quickly, if they
plunge into water. For a human victim the ashes
of the creatures themselves drunk in wine are thought
to be a cure. It is thought that to be dipped in oil
is a great disaster to geckoes as well as scorpions;
but geckoes at least are harmless; these too are
bloodless, and are shaped like a lizard; equally
scorpions are believed to do no harm whatever to

91 totum nullis [1] nocere quibus non sit sanguis. quidam
et ab ipsis fetum devorari arbitrantur; unum modo
relinqui sollertissimum et qui se ipsius matris clunibus
inponendo tutus et a cauda et a morsu loco fiat: hunc
esse reliquorum ultorem, qui postremo genitorem [2]
superne conficiat. pariuntur autem undeni.

XXXI. Chamaeleonum stelliones hi quodammodo
naturam habent, rore tantum viventes praeterque
araneis.

92 XXXII. Similis cicadis vita, quarum duo genera:
minores quae primae proveniunt et novissimae
pereunt—sunt autem mutae; sequens est volatura
earum [3] quae canunt: vocantur achetae et, quae
minores ex his sunt, tettigonia, sed illae magis
canorae. mares canunt in utroque genere, feminae
silent. gentes vescuntur his ad orientem, etiam
Parthi opibus abundantibus; ante coitum mares
praeferunt, a coitu feminas, ovis earum corrupti,
93 quae sunt candida. coitus supinis. asperitas praeacuta in dorso, qua excavant feturae locum in terra.
fit primo vermiculus, deinde ex eo quae vocatur tetti-
gometra, cuius cortice rupto circa solstitia evolant,
noctu semper, primo nigrae atque durae. unum
hoc ex iis quae vivunt et sine ore est; pro eo quiddam
aculeatorum linguis simile, et hoc in pectore, quo
rorem lambunt. pectus ipsum fistulosum; hoc

---

[1] *Dalec.*: nulli.   [2] *Rackham*: genitores.
[3] earum *add. Mayhoff.*

---

[a] *Cicada* here stands for the grass-hopper tribe in general.

any bloodless creatures. Some think that they also devour their own offspring, and that only one is left, a specially clever one that by perching on his mother's haunches secures himself by this position against both her tail and her bite; and that this one is the avenger of the rest, as he finally kills their parent with a blow from above. They are produced in broods of eleven.

XXXI. These geckoes in a certain manner have the nature of chamaeleons, living only on dew and on spiders as well.

XXXII. The life-history of the cicada *a* is similar. Of this there are two kinds: the smaller ones that come out first and perish latest—these however are mute; subsequent is the flight of those that sing: they are called Singers, and the smaller ones among them grass-hoppers, but the former are more vocal. The males in either class sing, but the females are silent. These creatures are used as food by the Eastward races, even the Parthians with their abundant resources; they prefer the males before mating and the females afterwards, being seduced by their eggs, which are white. They couple lying on their backs. They have a very sharp prickliness on the back, with which they hollow a place in the ground for their offspring. This is produced first as a grub, and then from this comes what is called the larva; at the period of the solstices they break the shell of this and fly out, always at night; at first they are black and hard. This is the only living creature actually without a mouth; they have instead a sort of row of prickles resembling tongues, this also being on the breast, with which they lick the dew. The breast itself forms a pipe; the singers use

Geckoes.

The cicada.

94 canunt achetae, ut dicemus. de cetero in ventre nihil est. excitatae cum subvolant, umorem reddunt, quod solum argumentum est rore eas ali; isdem solis nullum ad excrementa corporis foramen. oculis tam hebetes ut, si quis digitum contrahens ac remittens adpropinquet iis, transeant velut folio [1] ludente.[2] quidam duo alia genera faciunt earum, surculariam quae sit grandior, frumentariam quam alii avenariam vocant: apparet enim simul cum
95 frumentis arescentibus. cicadae non nascuntur in raritate arborum—idcirco non sunt Cyrenis nisi [3] circa oppidum—nec in campis nec in frigidis aut umbrosis nemoribus. est quaedam et his locorum differentia: in Milesia regione paucis sunt locis, sed in Cephallania amnis quidam paenuriam earum et copiam dirimit; at in Regino agro silent omnes, ultra flumen in Locrensi canunt. pinnarum illis natura quae apibus, sed pro corpore amplior.

96   XXXIII. Insectorum autem quaedam binas gerunt pinnas, ut muscae, quaedam quaternas, ut apes. membranis et cicadae volant. quaternas habent quae aculeis in alvo armantur, nullum cui telum in ore pluribus quam binis advolat pinnis: illis enim ultionis causa datum est, his aviditatis. nullis eorum pinnae revivescunt avulsae. nullum cui aculeus in alvo bipinne est.

---

[1] *v.l.* folia (in folia *Hermolaus*).
[2] ludente *add. ex Ar. Mayhoff.*   [3] nisi *add. Schlenger.*

---

[a] § 266.

this to sing with, as we shall say.[a] For the rest, there
is nothing on the belly. When they are disturbed
and fly away, they give out moisture, which is the
only proof that they live on dew; moreover they are
the only creatures that have no aperture for the
bodily excreta. Their eyes are so dim that if anybody comes near to them contracting and straightening out a finger, they pass by as if it were a leaf
flickering. Some people make two other classes of
tree-crickets, the twig-cricket which is the larger,
and the corn-cricket, which others call the oat-cricket,
because it appears at the same time as the crops
begin to dry. Tree-crickets do not occur where trees
are scarce—consequently they are not found at
Cyrenae except in the neighbourhood of the town—
nor in plains or in chilly or shady woods. These
creatures also make some difference between localities; in the district of Miletus they occur in few
places, but there is a river in Cephallania which makes
a boundary with a few of them on one side and many
on the other; again in the Reggio territory they are
all silent but beyond the river in the region of Locri
they sing. They have the same wing-structure as
bees, but larger in proportion to the body.

XXXIII. Of insects some have two wings, for *Structure of*
instance, flies, and some four, for instance bees. *various insects.*
The tree-cricket also flies with its membranes.
Those armed with a sting in the belly have four wings,
but none having a weapon in the mouth has more than
two wings to fly with, for the former have this weapon
bestowed on them for the sake of vengeance but the
latter for the purpose of greed. No insects' wings
when torn off grow again. None that has a sting in
the belly is two-winged.

97 XXXIV. Quibusdam pinnarum tutelae crusta
supervenit, ut scarabaeis, quorum tenuior fragilior-
que pinna. his negatus aculeus, sed in quodam genere
eorum grandi cornua praelonga, bisulca dentatis[1]
forficibus in cacumine, cum libuit, ad morsum
coeuntibus, infantium etiam remediis ex cervice
98 suspenduntur; Lucanos vocat hos Nigidius. aliud
rursus eorum genus qui e fimo ingentis pilas aversi
pedibus volutant parvosque in iis contra rigorem
hiemis vermiculos fetus sui nidulantur. volitant alii
magno cum murmure aut mugitu, alii focos et
parietes[2] crebris foraminibus excavant nocturno
stridore vocales. lucent ignium modo noctu laterum
et clunium colore lampyrides, nunc pinnarum hiatu
refulgentes, nunc vero conpressu obumbratae, non
ante matura pabula aut post desecta conspicuae.
99 e contrario tenebrarum alumna blattis vita, lucemque
fugiunt, in balinearum[3] maxime umido vapore
prognatae. fodiunt ex eodem genere rutili atque
praegrandes scarabaei tellurem aridam favosque
parvae et fistulosae modo spongiae medicato melle
fingunt. in Threcia iuxta Olynthum locus est parvus
quo unum hoc anima exanimatur, ob hoc Cantharo-
100 lethrus appellatus. pinnae insectis omnibus sine
scissura. nulli cauda nisi scorpioni. hic eorum
solus et bracchia habet et in cauda spiculum; reli
quorum quibusdam aculeus,[4] ut asilo (sive tabanum
dici placet), item culici et quibusdam muscis, omnibus

---

[1] *Brandis* (cf. IX. 97): bisulcis dentata.
[2] *Detlefsen* (cf. § 13): parata *aut* prata.
[3] *Mayhoff*: balineas *aut* balineis.
[4] *Rackham*: aculeus in ore.

---

[a] The stag-beetle.   [b] The dor-beetle.

XXXIV. In some species the wings are protected *Varieties of* by an outer covering of shell, for instance beetles; *beetle:* in these species the wing is thinner and more fragile. *cockchafers.* They are not provided with a sting, but in one large variety *a* of them there are very long horns, with two prongs and toothed claws at the point which close together at pleasure for a bite; they are actually hung round children's necks as amulets; Nigidius calls these Lucanian oxen.   Another kind of them again is one that rolls up backwards with its feet vast balls of mud and nests its brood of little grubs in these against the rigour of winter.   Others *b* flutter about with a loud murmur or a shrill noise, and others *c* giving out a buzz bore numerous holes in hearths and walls in the night.   Glow worms shine like fires at night time owing to the colour of their sides and loins, now giving a flash of light by opening their wings and now darkened by closing them; they are not much seen before the crops are ripe or after they have been cut.   The cockroaches' life on the contrary is a nurseling of the shadows, and they fly the light, being mostly produced in the damp warmth of bath-houses.   The reddish and very large beetles of the same kind dig dry earth and mould combs that resemble a small porous sponge and contain poisoned honey.   There is a small place near Olynthus in Thrace that is fatal to this animal, and is conse-quently called Beetle-bane.   The wings of all *Varieties of* insects have no cleft.   None has a tail except *insect structure.* the scorpion.   This is the only insect that has arms, and also a spike in the tail; some of the rest have a sting, for instance the gad-fly (or if you like, ' breeze '), and also the gnat and some flies, but with all of these

c The wood-worm and the death-watch beetle.

autem his in ore et pro lingua. sunt hi aculei quibusdam hebetes, neque ad punctum sed ad suctum, ut
muscarum generi, in quo lingua evidens fistula est;
nec sunt talibus dentes. aliis cornicula ante oculos
praetenduntur ignava, ut papilionibus. quaedam
insecta carent pinnis, ut scolopendra.

101 XXXV. Insectorum pedes quibus sunt in obliquum
moventur. quorundam extremi longiores foris curvantur, ut locustis.

Hae pariunt, in terram demisso spinae caule, ova
condensa autumni tempore. ea durant hieme, e
terra subsequenti anno exitu veris emittunt parvas,
nigrantes et sine cruribus, pinnisque reptantes.
itaque vernis [1] aquis intereunt ova, sicco vere maior
102 proventus. alii duplicem earum fetum, geminum [2]
exitium tradunt—vergiliarum exortu parere, deinde
ad canis ortum obire et alias renasci; quidam arcturi
occasu renasci. mori matres cum pepererint certum
est, vermiculo statim circa fauces innascente qui eas
strangulat. eodem tempore mares obeunt. et [3] tam
frivola ratione morientes serpentem cum libuit
necant singulae, faucibus eius adprehensis mordicus.
103 non nascuntur nisi rimosis locis. in India ternum
pedum longitudinis esse traduntur, cruribus et
feminibus serrarum usum praebere cum inaruerint.
est et alius earum obitus: gregatim sublatae vento

---

[1] *An* hibernis? (*Ar.* μετοπωρινῶν) *Mayhoff.*
[2] *Hardouin*: geminumque.
[3] *Mayhoff*: obeunte.

it is in the mouth and serves as a tongue. With some these stings are blunt, and do not serve for pricking but for suction—for instance with a sort of fly, in which the tongue is evidently a tube; and this sort of insect have no teeth. Others, for instance butterflies, have useless little horns projecting in front of their eyes. Some insects, for instance the centipede, have no wings.

XXXV. Insects that have feet can move sideways. *The locust.* Of some, for instance locusts, the hind feet are longer and curve outward.

Locusts in the autumn season give birth to clusters of eggs, by lowering the tube of the prickle to the earth. The eggs last for the winter, but in the ensuing year at the end of spring send out small insects, that are blackish and have no legs, and crawl with their wing-feathers. Consequently spring rains kill the eggs, whereas in a dry spring there are larger broods. Others record that they have two breeding seasons and two seasons when they die off—bearing at the rise of the Pleiads and then dying at the rise of the Dogstar, others being born in their place; some say that this second brood is born at the setting of Arcturus. It is certain that the mothers die when they have given birth to a brood, a maggot immediately forming inside them in the region of the throat that chokes them. The males die at the same time. And although dying for such a trifling reason a single locust when it likes can kill a snake by gripping its throat with its teeth. They are born only in places with chinks in them. There are said to be locusts in India three feet long, with legs and thighs that when they have been dried can be used as saws. They also have another way of dying:

in maria aut stagna decidunt. forte hoc casuque
evenit, non, ut prisci existimavere, madefactis
nocturno umore alis. idem quippe nec volare eas
noctibus propter frigora tradiderunt, ignari etiam
longinqua maria ab iis transiri, continuata plurium
dierum—quod maxime miremur—fame quoque,
104 quam propter externa pabula petere sciunt. deorum
irae pestis ea intellegitur; namque et grandiores
cernuntur et tanto volant pinnarum stridore ut alites
credantur, solemque obumbrant, sollicitis suspectan-
tibus populis ne suas operiant terras. sufficiunt
quippe vires et, tamquam parum sit maria transisse,
inmensos tractus permeant diraque messibus nube
contegunt, multa contactu adurentes, omnia vero
morsu erodentes et fores quoque tectorum.

105   Italiam ex Africa maxime coortae infestant, saepe
populo Romano ad Sibyllina coacto remedia confugere
inopiae metu. in Cyrenaica regione lex etiam est
ter anno debellandi eas, primo ova obterendo, dein
fetum, postremo adultas, desertoris poena in eum
106 qui cessaverit. et in Lemno insula certa mensura
praefinita est quam singuli enecatarum ad magistratus referant. graculos quoque ob id colunt ad-

they are carried away in swarms by the wind and fall into the sea or a marsh. This happens purely by accident and not, as was believed by ancient writers, owing to their wings being drenched by the dampness of night. The same people indeed have also stated that they do not fly by night because of the cold—not being aware that they cross even wide seas, actually, which is most surprising, enduring several days' continuous hunger, to remedy which they know how to seek fodder abroad. This plague is interpreted as a sign of the wrath of the gods; for they are seen of exceptional size, and also they fly with such a noise of wings that they are believed to be birds, and they obscure the sun, making the nations gaze upward in anxiety lest they should settle all over their lands. In fact their strength does not fail, and as though it were not enough to have crossed the seas, they pass over immense tracts of land and cover them with a cloud disastrous for the crops, scorching up many things with their touch and gnawing away everything with their bite, even the doors of the houses as well.

Italy is infested by swarms of them, coming principally from Africa, the Roman nation having often been compelled by fear of dearth to resort to remedies prescribed by the Sibylline Books. In the district of Cyrene there is actually a law to make war upon them three times a year, the first time by crushing the eggs, then the grubs and last the fully grown insects, with the penalty of a deserter for the man who shirks. Also in the Island of Lemnos there is a rule prescribing a definite quantity of locusts killed that each man has to bring in to the magistrates. Also they keep jays for this purpose, *Legislation to keep down locusts.*

verso volatu occurrentes earum exitio. necare et
in Syria militari imperio coguntur. tot orbis partibus
vagatur id malum; Parthis et hae in cibo gratae.

107   Vox earum proficisci ab occipitio videtur; eo loco
in commissura scapularum habere quasi dentes
existimantur eosque inter se terendo stridorem edere,
circa duo maxime aequinoctia, sicut cicadae circa
solstitium. coitus locustarum qui et insectorum
omnium quae coeunt, marem portante femina, in
eum [1] ultumo caudae reflexo tardoque digressu.
minores autem in omni hoc genere feminis mares.

108   XXXVI. Plurima insectorum vermiculum gignunt; nam et formicae similem ovis vere,[2] et hae
communicantes laborem ut apes, sed illae faciunt
cibos, hae condunt. ac si quis conparet onera
corporibus earum, fateatur nullis portione vires esse
maiores. gerunt ea morsu; maiora aversae postremis
pedibus moliuntur umeris obnixae. et his reipub-
109 licae ratio, memoria, cura. semina adrosa condunt ne rursus in frugem exeant e terra, maiora
ad introitum dividunt, madefacta imbre proferunt
atque siccant. operantur et noctu plena luna,

---

[1] *Rackham*: eum feminarum.
[2] *Lacunam fortasse* vere, ⟨mirabiles opere⟩ et *Mayhoff.*

---

[a] A probable suggestion inserts words giving 'These too
are remarkable workers, sharing—.'

which meet them by flying in the opposite direction, to their destruction. In Syria as well people are commandeered by military order to kill them. In so many parts of the world is this plague abroad; but with the Parthians even the locust is an acceptable article of diet.

The locust's voice appears to come from the back *Physiology* of the head: it is believed that in that place at the *of the* *locust.* juncture of the shoulder-blades they have a sort of teeth, and that they produce a grating noise by rubbing them together, chiefly about the two equinoxes, as grasshoppers do about midsummer. Locusts couple in the same manner as all insects that pair, the female carrying the male with the end of her tail bent back to him, and with slow separation. In all this class the males are smaller than the females.

XXXVI. Most of the insects give birth to a *The ant.* maggot; ants for example produce in spring one that resembles an egg, these too sharing *a* their labour as do bees, but bees make the food stuffs, whereas ants collect theirs. And if anybody compared the loads that ants carry with the size of their bodies, he would confess that no creatures have proportionally greater strength; they carry them held in their mouths, but they move larger loads with their hind feet, turning their backs to them and heaving against them with their shoulders. Ants also have a system of government, and possess memory and diligence. They nibble their seeds before they store them away, so that they may not sprout up again out of the earth and germinate; they divide the larger seeds so as to get them in; when they have been wetted by rain they bring them

499

eaedem interlunio cessant. iam in opere qui labor,
quae sedulitas! et quoniam ex diverso convehunt
altera alterius ignarae[1] certi dies[2] ad recognitionem
110 mutuam nundinis dantur. quae tunc earum con-
cursatio, quam diligens cum obviis quaedam con-
locutio atque percontatio! silices itinere earum
adtritos videmus et opere semitam factam, ne quis
dubitet et qualibet in re quid possit quantulacumque
adsiduitas! sepeliunt inter se viventium solae praeter
hominem.—non sunt in Sicilia pinnatae.

111   Indicae formicae cornua Erythris in aede Herculis
fixa miraculo fuere. aurum hae cavernis egerunt
cum[3] terra, in regione septentrionalium Indorum qui
Dardae vocantur. ipsis color felium, magnitudo
Aegypti luporum. erutum hoc ab iis tempore
hiberno Indi furantur aestivo fervore, conditis
propter vaporem in cuniculos formicis, quae tamen
odore sollicitatae provolant crebroque lacerant quamvis praevelocibus camelis fugientes: tanta pernicitas
feritasque est cum amore auri.

112   XXXVII. Multa autem insecta et aliter nascuntur,
atque in primis e rore. insidet hic raphani folio
primo vere et spissatus sole in magnitudinem milii
cogitur. inde porrigitur vermiculus parvus et triduo

---

[1] *v.l.* ignara.   [2] indices *Detlefsen.*
[3] cum *add. ? Mayhoff* (terrae *alii*).

---

[a] It has been suggested that these relics were in reality the
pick-axes of Tibetan gold-miners, and the gold-carrying ants
their dogs.

out and dry them. They even work at night when there is a full moon, although when there is no moon they stop. Again what industry and what diligence is displayed in their work! and since they bring their burdens together from opposite directions, and are unknown to one another, certain days are assigned for market so that they may become acquainted. How they flock together on these occasions! How busily they converse, so to speak, with those they meet and press them with questions! We see rocks worn by their passage and a path made by their labours, so that nobody may doubt how much can be accomplished in any matter by even a trifling amount of assiduity! They are the only living creatures beside man that bury their dead.— Winged ants do not occur in Sicily.

The horns [a] of an Indian ant fixed up in the Temple *The gold-digger ant.* of Hercules were one of the sights of Erythrae. These ants carry gold out of caves in the earth in the region of the Northern Indians called the Dardae. The creatures are of the colour of cats and the size of Egyptian wolves. The gold that they dig up in winter time the Indians steal in the hot weather of summer, when the heat makes the ants hide in burrows; but nevertheless they are attracted by their scent and fly out and sting them repeatedly although retreating on very fast camels: such speed and such ferocity do these creatures combine with their love of gold.

XXXVII. Many insects however are born in *Butterflies produced from dew.* other ways as well, and in the first place from dew. At the beginning of spring this lodges on the leaf of a radish and is condensed by the sun and shrinks to the size of a millet seed. Out of this a small

mox uruca, quae adiectis diebus adcrescit; fit [1] immobilis, duro cortice, ad tactum tantum movetur,
araneo accreta, quam chrysallidem appellant. rupto
deinde eo cortice evolat [2] papilio.

113 XXXVIII. Sic quaedam ex imbre generantur in
terra, quaedam et in ligno. nec enim cossi tantum
in eo, sed etiam tabani ex eo nascuntur et alia [3]
ubicumque umor est nimius, (XXXIX) sicut intra hominem taeniae tricenum pedum, aliquando et plurium,

114 longitudine. iam in carne exanima et viventium
quoque hominum capillo, qua foeditate et Sulla
dictator et Alcman ex clarissimis Graeciae poetis
obiere. hoc quidem et aves infestat, phasianas

115 vero interemit nisi pulverantes sese; pilos habentium
asinum tantum inmunem hoc malo credunt et oves.
gignuntur autem et vestis genere praecipue, lanicio
interemptarum a lupis ovium. aquas quoque quasdam quibus lavemur fertiliores eius generis invenio
apud auctores, quippe cum etiam cerae id gignant
quod animalium minimum existimatur. alia rursus
generantur sordibus a radio solis, posteriorum lascivia
crurum petauristae, alia pulvere umido in cavernis
volucria.

116 XL. Est animal eiusdem temporis infixo semper
sanguini capite vivens atque ita intumescens, unum

---

[1] fit *auctore Warmington add. Rackham.*
[2] *Rackham :* volat.
[3] *v.l.* alibi : alias *edd.*

---

[a] Our cabbage-white   [b] The larvae of flies.
[c] The clothes-moth.   [d] The 'leaper'.

maggot develops, and three days later it becomes
a caterpillar, which as days are added grows larger;
it becomes motionless, with a hard skin, and only moves
when touched, being covered with a cobweb growth—
at this stage it is called a chrysalis. Then it bursts
its covering and flies out as a butterfly.[a]

XXXVIII. In this way some creatures are *Other modes of generation of insects.*
generated from rain in the earth and some even in
wood. For not only is the goatmoth caterpillar born
in wood, but also the horse-fly springs from wood, and
other creatures, wherever there is excessive damp,
(XXXIX) just as tape-worms thirty feet in length,
sometimes even more, grow inside a human being.
Again worms [b] are born in the flesh of dead bodies
and also in the hair of living people, a foul growth that
caused the death of the dictator Sulla and also of one
of the most famous of Greece poets, Alcman. This
indeed also infests birds, and actually kills pheasants
unless they sprinkle themselves with dust; and of
hairy animals it is believed that only the ass and sheep
are immune from this evil. They [c] also breed in one
kind of clothing especially, woollen made from sheep
that have been killed by wolves. Also I find in the
authorities that some springs of water in which
we bathe are specially productive of this kind
of creature; inasmuch as even wax generates
what is believed to be the smallest of animals.
Others[d] again are generated out of dirt by the rays
of the sun, creatures that hop with a frisk of their
hind legs, and others out of damp dust, that fly
about in caves.

XL. There is an animal belonging to the same *Blood-suckers and maggots.*
season that always lives with its head fixed in the *Leeches.*
blood of a host, and consequently goes on swelling,

animalium cui cibi non sit exitus: dehiscit cum nimia satietate, alimento ipso moriens. numquam hoc in iumentis gignitur, in bubus frequens, in canibus aliquando, in quibus omnia, in ovibus et in capris hoc solum. aeque mira sanguinis et hirudinum in palustri aqua sitis; namque et hae toto capite conduntur. est volucre canibus peculiare suum malum, aures maxime lancinans, quae defendi morsu non queunt.

117 XLI. Idem pulvis in lanis et veste tineas creat, praecipue si araneus una includatur; sitiens [1] enim et omnem umorem absorbens ariditatem ampliat. hoc et in chartis noscitur.[2] est earum genus tunicas suas trahentium quo cocleae modo; sed harum pedes cernuntur. spoliatae exspirant; si adcrevere, faciunt 118 chrysallidem. ficarios culices caprificus generat, cantharidas vermiculi ficorum et piri et peuces et cynacanthae et rosae. venenum hoc remedia secum habet: alae medentur, quibus demptis letale est. rursus alia genera culicum acescens natura gignit, quippe cum et in nive candidi inveniantur et vetustiore vermiculi, in media quidem altitudine rutili,[3]—nam et ipsa nix vetustate rufescit,—hirti pilis, grandiores torpentesque.

119 XLII. Gignit aliqua et contrarium naturae elementum. siquidem in Cypri aerariis fornacibus et medio

[1] *Mayhoff*: sititur.

[2] nascitur? *Mayhoff*.

[3] in nive inveniantur vetustiore vermiculi rutili—nam et ipsa nix vetustate rufescit—hirti pilis, in Media quidem candidi *Mayhoff*.

---

[b] The dog-tick.

as it is the only animal that has no vent for its food :
with gorging to excess it bursts, so dying of its very
nutriment. This creature never grows in cart-
horses but occurs frequently in oxen and occasionally
in dogs,[b] in which all creatures breed, whereas this
alone occurs in sheep and goats. Equally remarkable
is the thirst for blood that is even felt by leeches in
marshy water; for they too penetrate with the whole
of their head. Dogs have a special pest of their
own, a maggot that lances particularly their ears,
which they cannot protect by their bite.

XLI. Similarly, dust in woollens and in clothes *Clothes-*
breeds moths, especially if a spider is shut up with *moths, gnats,*
them; for being thirsty and sucking up all the *beetles.*
moisture it increases the dryness. This is also
noticed in papers. There is a kind of moths that
carry their own coats in the same way as snails;
but the moths have visible feet. If stripped of their
coats they die, but if they grow up, they form a
chrysalis. The wild fig-tree breeds fig-gnats;
beetles are produced by the maggots of figs and of
the pear tree, pine, dog-rose and rose. This
poisonous creature brings its remedies with it—
the wings have a healing power; but with these
removed it is deadly. Again, other kinds, namely
gnats, are bred by a substance growing sour, and in
fact white ones are found even in snow, and also in
snow that has been lying for some time maggots,
which in a moderate depth of snow at all events are
ruddy—for even snow itself turns reddish with lapse
of time; these have shaggy hair and are of considerable size, and torpid.

XLII. Some creatures are generated also by *Fire-flies.*
the opposite natural element. Thus in the copper

igni maioris muscae magnitudinis volat pinnatum quadrupes; appellatur pyrallis, a quibusdam pyrotocon.[1] quamdiu est in igne vivit, cum evasit longiore paulo volatu emoritur.

120 XLIII. Hypanis fluvius in Ponto circa solstitium defert acinorum effigie tenues membranas quibus erumpit volucre quadrupes supra dicti modo, nec ultra unum diem vivit, unde hemerobion vocatur. reliquis talium ab initio ad finem septenarii sunt numeri, culici et vermiculis ter septeni, corpus parientibus quater septeni. mutationes et in alias figuras transitus trinis aut quadrinis diebus. cetera ex his pinnata autumno fere moriuntur tabe alarum,[2] tabani quidem etiam caecitate. muscis umore exanimatis, si cinere condantur, redit vita.

121 XLIV. Nunc per singulas corporum partes praeter iam dicta membratim tractetur historia.

Caput habent cuncta quae sanguinem. in capite paucis animalium nec nisi volucribus apices, diversi quidem generis, phoenici plumarum serie e medio eo exeunte alio, pavonibus crinitis arbusculis, stymphalidi cirro, phasianae corniculis, praeterea parvae avi quae, ab illo galerita appellata quondam, postea

---

[1] *Mayhoff*: pyroto (pyrota *Jan*).
[2] tabe alarum *add. ex Aristotele Mayhoff*.

---

[a] A species of May-fly.
[b] 'Of decay of the wings' is added by Mayhoff from Aristotle.
[c] A mythical species.

foundries of Cyprus even in the middle of the fire there flies a creature with wings and four legs, of the size of a rather large fly; it is called the *pyrallis*, or by some the *pyrotocon*. As long as it is in the fire it lives, but when it leaves it on a rather long flight it dies off.

XLIII. The river Bug on the Black Sea at midsummer brings down some thin membranes that look like berries out of which burst a four-legged caterpillar in the manner of the creature mentioned above, but it does not live beyond one day, owing to which it is called the hemerobius.[a] The rest of this sort of creatures have from start to finish seven-day periods, but the gnat and maggots have twenty-one-day, and those whose offspring are fully formed twenty-eight-day periods. Their changes and transformations into other shapes take place every three or every four days. The remaining kinds of this class possessing wings usually die in autumn of decay of the wings,[b] but horse-flies die of blindness also. When flies have been killed by damp they can be resuscitated by being buried in ashes. *Life-periods of various insects.*

XLIV. Now let our investigation treat of the various parts of bodies besides the ones already mentioned, taking limb by limb. *Varieties of structure taking the parts of the body*

All creatures that have blood have a head. On the head a few kinds, and these only birds, have crests, of different sorts it is true—with the phoenix it is a row of feathers spreading out from the middle of the head in a different direction, peacocks have bushy tufts, the bird of Stymphalus[c] a crest, the pheasant little horns, as moreover has the small bird that was formerly named from this peculiarity the crested lark and subsequently was called by the *seriatim: birds' crests.*

507

Gallico vocabulo etiam legioni nomen dederat alaudae.
122 diximus et cui plicatilem cristam dedisset natura.
per medium caput a rostro residentem et fulicarum
generi dedit, cirros pico quoque Martio et grui
Balearicae, sed spectatissimum insigne gallinaceis,
corporeum, serratum; nec carnem id [1] esse nec
cartilaginem nec callum iure dixerimus, verum
peculiare datum: draconum enim cristas qui
viderit non reperitur.

123   XLV. Cornua multis quidem et aquatilium et
marinorum et serpentium variis data sunt modis,
sed quae iure cornua intellegantur quadripedum
tantum generi; Actaeonem enim, et Cipum etiam
in Latia historia, fabulosos reor. nec alibi maior
naturae lascivia; lusit animalium armis: sparsit
haec in ramos, ut cervorum, aliis simplicia tribuit,
ut in eodem genere subulonibus ex argumento
dictis, aliorum fudit in palmas digitosque emisit
124 ex his, unde platycerotas vocant. dedit ramosa
capreis sed parva, nec fecit decidua; convoluta in
anfractum arietum generi, ceu caestus daret;
infesta tauris—in hoc quidem genere et feminis
tribuit, in multis tantum maribus; rupicapris in
dorsum adunca, dammis in adversum; erecta autem

---

[1] *edd.*: ita.

---

[a] Raised by Caesar in Gaul, at his own expense. Presumably a crested lark was the crest on its helmets.
[b] See X. 68.
[c] The black woodpecker.
[d] Actaeon was torn to pieces by his hounds after having seen Diana bathing. Cipus was a fabled Roman praetor who suddenly grew horns: Ovid. *Met.* 15. 565.
[e] Fallow deer.

Gallic word *alauda* and gave that name also to the legion[a] so entitled. We have also said[b] which bird has been endowed by nature with a folding crest. Nature has also bestowed a crest that slopes backwards from the beak down the middle of the neck on the coot species, and also a tufted crest on Mars's woodpecker[c] and on the Balearic crane, but she has given the most distinguished decoration to the poultry-cock—its fleshy, notched comb; and this cannot rightly be described as flesh or gristle or hard skin, but is a gift peculiar to it: for no one can be found who has ever seen serpents' crests.

XLV. Many of the water and marine and snake species are furnished in various ways with horns of a sort, but horns in the proper sense of the term only belong to the genus quadrupeds; for I deem the story of Actaeon,[b d] and also that of Cipus[d] in the history of Latium, to be fabulous. And in no other field does nature allow herself more sport; with the weapons of animals she has made a game—dividing some into branches, for instance, the horns of stags; assigning simple horns to others, for instance, the species in the same genus called from this feature 'flute-stags,'[e] spreading those of others into palms and making fingers shoot out from these, the origin of the designation 'broad-horn.' To goats she has given branching but small horns, and these she has not made to be shed; to the ram class horns twisted into a crooked shape, as if providing them with weighted gauntlets for boxing; to bulls horns for attacking—in this class indeed she has also bestowed horns on the females, although in many she only gives them to the males; to chamois horns curved over the back, to antelopes horns curved the opposite

Horns.

rugarumque ambitu contorta et in leve fastigium
exacuta, ut lyras decerent, strepsiceroti, quem
addacem Africa appellat; mobilia eadem, ut aures,
125 Phrygiae armentis; Trogodytarum in terram derecta,
qua de causa obliqua cervice pascuntur; aliis singula,
et haec medio capite aut naribus, ut diximus; iam
quidem aliis ad incursum robusta, aliis ad ictum,
aliis adunca, aliis redunca, aliis ad iactum pluribus
modis supina, convexa, conversa; omnia in mucro-
nem migrantia; in quodam genere pro manibus ad
scabendum corpus; cocleis ad praetemptandum
iter—corporea haec, sicut cerastis; his [1] aliquando
singula, cocleis semper bina, et ut protendantur ac
resiliant.
126   Urorum cornibus barbari septentrionales potant,
vinisque [2] bina capitis unius cornua inplent; alii
praefixa hastilia cuspidant, apud nos in lamnas
secta tralucent atque etiam lumen inclusum latius
fundunt, multasque alias ad delicias conferuntur,
nunc tincta, nunc sublita, nunc quae cestrota a [3]
127 picturae genere dicuntur. omnibus autem cava et
in mucrone demum concreta sunt, cervis tantum tota
solida et omnibus annis decidua. boum adtritis
ungulis cornua unguendo arvina medentur agricolae,
adeoque sequax natura est ut in ipsis viventium cor-

---

[1] his add. *Mueller.*   [2] *Rackham*: urnisque.
[3] a add. *Hardouin.*

---

[a] This name is still in use.
[b] Herodotus (4. 192) says that the horns of the Libyan
ὄρυξ, a kind of antelope, are used for the πήχεις, horns, or
sides, of a lyre.

way; but to the crook-horn, the African name for which is addax,[a] upright horns twisted with a coil of wrinkles and sharpened at the end into a smooth point, so as to make them suitable for lyres[b]; also horns that are movable, like ears, to the cattle of Phrygia; horns pointing towards the ground to those belonging to the Cave-dwellers, which consequently graze with the neck bent sideways; to other creatures a single horn, and this placed in the middle of the head or between the nostrils, as we have said; moreover some have strong horns for charging, others for striking; some horns curved forward, some backward, some for tossing in various ways—curving backward, curving together, curving outward; all ending in a point; in one kind horns used instead of hands for scratching the body; with snails used for exploring the way in advance—these fleshy, as those of the horned snake; these creatures sometimes have one horn, snails always two, so as both to be stretched forward and to spring back.

The northern barbarians use the horns of the aurochs for drinking, and fill the two horns of a single head with wine; others point their spears with horn tips. With us horn is cut into transparent plates to give a wider diffusion to a light enclosed in it, and it is also applied to many other articles of luxury, sometimes dyed, sometimes painted, sometimes what is called from a certain kind of picture ' engraved.' All animals' horns are hollow and solid solely at the tip, but only stags have horns that are entirely solid and that are shed every year. Farmers heal the hooves of their oxen when worn by greasing the horn of the hoof with fat; and the substance of horn is so ductile that even the horns of living cattle

Uses of horn.

poribus ferventi cera flectantur, atque incisa nascentium in diversas partes torqueantur, ut singulis capitibus quaterna fiant.

128 Tenuiora feminis plerumque sunt, ut in pecore multis, ovium nulla, nec cervorum, nec quibus multifidi pedes, nec solidipedum ulli excepto asino Indico qui uno armatus est cornu. bisulcis bina natura[1] tribuit, at[2] nulli superne primores habenti dentes: qui putant eos in cornua absumi facile coarguuntur cervarum natura, quae nec dentes habent quos[3] neque mares, nec tamen cornua. ceterorum ossibus adhaerent, cervorum tantum cutibus enascuntur.

129 XLVI. Capita piscibus portione corporum maxima, fortassis ut mergantur. ostrearum generi nulla nec spongiis nec aliis fere quibus solus ex sensibus tactus est. quibusdam indiscretum caput, ut cancris.

130 XLVII. In capite animalium cunctorum homini plurimus pilus, iam quidem promiscue maribus ac feminis, apud intonsas utique gentes; atque etiam nomina ex eo Capillatis Alpium incolis, Galliae Comatae, ut tamen sit aliqua in hoc terrarum differentia: quippe Myconii carentes eo gignuntur, sicut in Cauno lienosi (et quaedam animalium naturaliter

---

[1] natura *add. Broterius.*
[2] at *add. ? Mayhoff.*
[3] *Rackham auctore* (?) *Warmington* : habent ut.

can be bent with boiling wax, and they can be slit
at birth and twisted in opposite directions, so as to
produce four horns on one head.

The females usually have thinner horns, as is the *Distribution*
case with many in the cattle class, but the females *structure of*
of sheep and of stags have none, nor have those of the *horns.*
animals with cloven hooves, nor any of those with
solid hooves except the Indian ass that is armed with
a single horn. Nature has bestowed two horns on the
kinds with cloven hooves, but on no kind having
front teeth in the upper jaw: but those who think
that the material to form upper teeth is entirely
used up in horns are easily refuted by the nature of
does, which have no teeth that stags have not also
and nevertheless have no horns. The horns of all
other kinds are attached to the bones, but those of
stags alone grow out of the hide.

XLVI. The heads of fishes are very large in pro- *Heads of*
portion to their bodies, perhaps so as to enable them *fishes.*
to dive. The shell-fish kind have no heads, nor have
sponges nor virtually any of the other creatures
which only possess the sense of touch. Some kinds,
for instance crabs, have the head not separated from
the body.

XLVII. Of all the animals man has most hair *Hair;*
on the head: indeed this is the case indiscriminately *baldness*
with males and females, at all events with the races *in man.*
that do not cut the hair; and the Longhair tribes of
the Alps and Gallia Comata have actually derived
their names from this, though nevertheless there is
in this respect some difference between countries: in
fact the people of Mykoni are born devoid of hair,
like the persons with an affection of the spleen at
Caunus. (Also some kinds of animals are bald by

513

PLINY: NATURAL HISTORY

calvent, sicut struthiocameli et corvi aquatici, quibus
131 apud Graecos nomen inde). defluvium eorum in
muliere rarum, in spadonibus non visum, nec in ullo
ante veneris usum, nec infra cerebrum aut infra
verticem aut circa tempora atque aures. calvitium
uni tantum animalium homini praeterquam innatum;
canities homini tantum et equo, sed homini semper
a priore parte capitis, tum deinde ab aversa.
132   XLVIII. Vertices bini hominum tantum aliquis.
capitis ossa plana, tenuia, sine medullis, serratis
pectinatim structa conpagibus. perfracta non queunt solidari, sed excepta modice non sunt letalia in
vicem eorum succedente corporea cicatrice. infirmis-
sima esse ursis, durissima psittacis, suo diximus loco.
133   XLIX. Cerebrum omnia habent animalia quae
sanguinem, etiam in mari quae mollia appellavimus
quamvis careant sanguine, ut polypus. sed homo
portione maximum et umidissimum omniumque viscerum frigidissimum, duabus supra subterque membranis velatum, quarum alterutram rumpi mortiferum
134 est. cetero viri quam feminae maius. omnibus
hominibus [1] hoc sine sanguine, sine venis, et aliquis [2]
sine pingui. aliud esse quam medullam eruditi

---

[1] *Rackham* : omnibus *aut* hominibus.
[2] *Mueller ?* (*vel ex Aristotele* sebosis) : reliquis.

---

[a] φαλακροκόρακες, c . X. 133.   [b] VIII. 130, X. 117.
      [c] IX. 83.   [d] *I.e.* the octopus.

514

nature, for instance ostriches and cormorants; the Greek name [a] for the latter is derived from this peculiarity.) With these races loss of the hair is rare in the case of a woman and unknown in eunuchs, and never occurs in any case before sexual intercourse has taken place; and they are never bald below the brainpan or the crown of the head, or round the temples and the ears. Man is the only species in which baldness occurs, except in cases of animals born without hair, and only with human beings and horses does the hair turn grey, in the former case always starting at the forehead and only afterwards at the back of the head.

XLVIII. In human beings only a double-crowned *The skull.* skull occurs in some cases. The bones of the human skull are flat and thin and have no marrow; they are constructed with interlockings serrated like the teeth of a comb. When broken they cannot form again, but the removal of a moderate piece is not fatal, as its place is taken by a scar of flesh. The skull of the bear is the weakest and that of the parrot the hardest, as we have stated in the proper place.[b]

XLIX. All blooded animals have a brain, and so *The brain:* also have the sea-creatures that we have designated [c] *its functions.* the soft species, although they are bloodless, for instance the polypus.[d] Man however has the largest brain in proportion to his size and the most moist one, and it is the coldest of all his organs; it is wrapped in two membranes above and below, the fracture of either of which is fatal. For the rest a man's brain is larger than a woman's. With all human beings it has no blood or veins, and in some cases no fat. The learned teach that it is distinct from marrow

docent quoniam coquendo durescat. omnium cerebro
medio insunt ossicula parva. uni homini in infantia
palpitant, nec conroborantur ante primum sermonis
135 exordium. hoc est viscerum excelsissimum custodi-
tumque[1] caelo[2] capitis, sine carne, sine cruore, sine
sordibus. hanc habet sensus arcem, huc venarum
omnis a corde vis tendit, hic desinit, hoc culmen
altissimum, hic mentis est regimen. omnium[3]
autem animalium in priora pronum, quia et sensus
ante nos tendunt. ab eo proficiscitur somnus, hinc
capitis nutatio; quae cerebrum non habent non
dormiunt.

Cervis in capite inesse vermiculi sub linguae
inanitate et circa articulum qua caput iungitur numero
xx produntur.

136 L. Aures homini tantum immobiles (ab his Flac-
corum cognomina). nec in alia parte feminis maius
inpendium margaritis dependentibus; in Oriente
quidem et viris aurum eo loci gestare decus existimatur. animalium aliis maiores aliis minores;
cervis tantum scissae ac velut divisae, sorici pilosae;
sed aliquae omnibus animal dumtaxat generantibus
excepto vitulo marino atque delphino et quae carti-
137 laginea appellavimus et viperis: haec cavernas tantum habent aurium loco praeter cartilaginea et
delphinum, quem tamen audire manifestum est:
nam et cantu mulcentur, et capiuntur attoniti[4] sono.

[1] sic? vel protectumque Mueller (proximumque alii):
excelsissimumque.
[2] an cavo ut IX. 163? Mayhoff.   [3] edd.: omnibus.
[4] attenti? Rackham.

[a] Larvae of the gad-fly.   [b] IX. 78.
[c] Perhaps the text should be altered to give ' while intent
on,' ' absorbed by ': cf. Shakespeare, ' I am never merry when
I hear sweet music.'—' The reason is, your spirits are attentive.'

because boiling makes it hard. In the middle of the brain of all species there are tiny little bones. With man alone the brain throbs in infancy, and does not become firm before the child first begins to talk. The brain is the highest of the organs in position, and it is protected by the vault of the head; it has no flesh or blood or refuse. It is the citadel of sense-perception, and the focus to which all the flow of the veins converges from the heart and at which it stops; it is the crowning pinnacle, the seat of government of the mind. But the brain of all animals slopes forward, because our senses also stretch in front of us. It is the source of sleep and the cause of drowsy nodding; species without a brain do not sleep.

Stags are stated to have maggots [a] to the number of twenty in the head beneath the hollow of the tongue and in the neighbourhood of the juncture of the head with the neck.

L. Only man is unable to move the ears. (The *The ear.* family surname *Flabby* comes from them.) Also women spend more money on their ears, in pearl earrings, than on any other part of their person; in the East indeed it is considered becoming even for men to wear gold in that place. Some animals have larger and others smaller ears; only stags have cleft and as it were divided ears; the shrew-mouse has shaggy ears; but all species, at all events viviparous ones, have some ears, except the seal and dolphin, and those which we have designated [b] cartilaginous, and vipers: these have only holes in place of ears, except the cartilaginous species and the dolphin, although the latter is obviously able to hear; for dolphins are charmed even by music, and are caught while bewildered by [c] the sound. Their precise

quanam audiant mirum. idem nec olfactus vestigia habent, cum olfaciant sagacissime. pinnatorum animalium buboni tantum et oto plumae velut auris, ceteris cavernae ad auditum; simili modo squamigeris atque serpentibus. in equis et omni [1] iumentorum genere indicia animi praeferunt, marcidae fessis, micantes pavidis, subrectae furentibus, resolutae aegris.

138   LI. Facies homini tantum, ceteris os aut rostra. frons et aliis, sed homini tantum tristitiae, hilaritatis, clementiae, severitatis index. in assensu eius supercilia homini et pariter et alterna mobilia, et in his pars animi: his [2] negamus, annuimus, haec maxime indicant fastum; superbia aliubi conceptaculum sed hic sedem habet: in corde nascitur, huc subit, hic pendet—nihil altius simul abruptiusque invenit in corpore ubi solitaria esset.

139   LII. Subiacent oculi, pars corporis pretiosissima et quae lucis usu vitam distinguat a morte. non omnibus animalium hi: ostreis nulli, quibusdam concharum dubii; pectines enim, si quis digitos adversum hiantes eos moveat, contrahuntur ut videntes, et solenes fugiunt admota ferramenta. quadripedum talpis visus non est, oculorum effigies inest, si quis
140 praetentam detrahat membranam. et inter aves

---

[1] *Mayhoff*: omnium.
[2] his *add. Rackham* (iis *Mayhoff*).

---

[a] Or perhaps tracks along which smell passes, ‘smelling-organs.’

method of hearing is a riddle. They also have **no** indications of smell,[a] although they possess a **very** keen scent. Of feathered creatures only the eagle-owl and eared owl have feathers that serve as ears, the rest have apertures for hearing; and similarly with the scaly creatures and with snakes. In horses and every kind of cattle the ears display signs of their feelings, drooping when they are tired, twitching when they are frightened, pricked up when they are angry and relaxed when they are sick.

LI. Only man has a face, all other animals have a *The face and* muzzle or beak. Others also have a brow, but only *features.* with man is it an indication of sorrow and gaiety, mercy and severity. The eyebrows in man can be moved in agreement with it, either both together or alternately, and in them a portion of the mind is situated: with them we indicate assent and dissent, they are our chief means of displaying contempt; pride has its place of generation elsewhere, but here is its abode: it is born in the heart, but it rises to the eyebrows and hangs suspended there—having found no position in the body at once loftier and steeper where it could be sole occupant.

LII. Beneath the brows lie the eyes, the most *The eye.* precious part of the body and the one that distinguishes life from death by the use it makes of daylight. Not all animals have these organs: oysters have no eyes, and some of the shellfish doubtful ones, as scallops, if somebody moves his fingers towards them when they are open, shut up as though seeing them, and razor-shells hurry away from iron hooks brought near them. Of fourfooted creatures moles have no sight, although they possess the semblance of eyes if one draws off the covering membrane. And

519

ardeolarum in[1] genere quos leucos vocant altero oculo
carere tradunt, optimi auguri cum ad austrum volent
septentrionemve; solvi enim pericula et metus
narrant. Nigidius nec locustis, cicadis esse dicit.
cocleis oculorum vicem cornicula bina praetemptatu
implent. nec lumbricis ulli sunt vermiumve generi.

141   LIII. Oculi homini tantum diverso colore, ceteris
in suo cuique genere similes. et equorum quibusdam
glauci; sed in homine numerosissimae varietatis
atque differentiae, grandiores, modici, parvi; pro-
minentes quos hebetiores putant, conditi quos clarissime cernere, sicuti[2] colore caprinos.[a]

142   LIV. Praeterea alii contuentur longinqua, alii nisi
prope admota non cernunt. multorum visus fulgore
solis constat, nubilo die non cernentium nec post
occasus; alii interdiu hebetiores, noctu praeter
ceteros cernunt. de geminis pupillis, aut quibus
noxii visus essent, satis diximus.[3][b] caesi in tenebris

143   clariores. ferunt Ti. Caesari, nec alii genitorum
mortalium, fuisse naturam ut[4] expergefactus noctu
paulisped haut alio modo quam luce clara
contueretur omnia, paulatim tenebris sese obducenti-
bus. divo Augusto equorum modo glauci fuere,
superque hominem albicantis magnitudinis, quam ob

---

[1] in *add. Sillig.*   [2] *Mayhoff*: sicut in.
[3] VII. 16.   [4] ut *add. edd.*

---

[a] *I.e.* egrets.   [b] VII. 16.

among birds the variety of the heron class called in
Greek white herons *a* are said to lack one eye, and
to be a very good omen when they fly North or
South, as they tell that dangers and alarms are being
dissipated. Nigidius says that also locusts and
cicadas have no eyes. For snails their pair of horns
fill the place of eyes by feeling in front of them.
Earth-worms also and worms in general have no
eyes.

LIII. Man alone has eyes of various colours,
whereas with all other creatures the eyes of each
member of a species are alike. Some horses too have
grey eyes; but in man the eyes are of extremely
numerous variety and difference—larger than the
average, medium, small; prominent, which are
thought to be dimmer, or deep-set, which are thought
to see most clearly, as are those with the colour of
goats' eyes.

LIV. Moreover some people have long sight but *Sight.*
others can only see things brought close to them.
The sight of many depends on the brilliance of the
sun, and they cannot see clearly on a cloudy day or
after sunset; others have dimmer sight in the day
time but are exceptionally keen-sighted at night.
We have already said enough *b* about double pupils, *Varieties of*
or persons who have the evil eye. Blue-grey eyes see *eyes.*
more clearly in the dark. It is stated that Tiberius
Caesar alone of all mankind was so constituted that
if he woke up in the night for a short time he could
see everything just as in bright daylight, although
darkness gradually closed over him. The late
lamented Augustus had grey eyes like those of
horses, the whites being larger than usual in a
human being, on account of which he used to be

causam diligentius spectari eos iracunde ferebat;
144 Claudio Caesari ab angulis candore carnoso sanguineis
venis subinde suffusi; Gaio principi rigentes; Neroni,[1]
nisi cum coniveret ad prope admota, hebetes. $\overline{xx}$ [2]
gladiatorum in Gai principis ludo fuere, in his duo
omnino qui contra comminationem aliquam non coni-
verent, et ob id invicti: tantae hoc difficultatis est
homini, plerisque vero naturale ut nictari non cessent,
145 quos pavidiores accepimus. oculus unicolor [3] nulli:
communi [4] candore omnibus medius colos differens.
neque ulla ex parte maiora animi indicia cunctis
animalibus, sed homini maxime, id est moderationis,
clementiae, misericordiae, odii, amoris, tristitiae,
laetitiae. contuitu quoque multiformes, truces, torvi,
flagrantes, graves, transversi, limi, summissi, blandi:
profecto in oculis animus habitat. ardent, inten-
146 duntur, umectant, conivent; hinc illa miseri cordiae
lacrima, hos cum exosculamur animum ipsum videmur
attingere, hinc fletus et rigantis ora rivi. quis ille
est umor in dolore tam fecundus et paratus? aut ubi
reliquo tempore? animo autem videmus, animo
cernimus; oculi ceu vasa quaedam visibilem eius
partem accipiunt atque tramittunt. sic magna

---

[1] *edd.* (Neroni ⟨caesii⟩ at *ex Suetonio Mayhoff*): Neronia.
[2] *Urlichs*: xx.
[3] *v.l.* unicolore (*an* uno colore? *Mayhoff*).
[4] *Mayhoff*: cum.

angry if people watched his eyes too closely; Claudius Caesar's eyes were frequently bloodshot and had a fleshy gleam at the corners; the Emperor Gaius had staring eyes; Nero's eyes were dull of sight except when he screwed them up to look at objects brought close to them. In the training-school of the Emperor Gaius there were 20,000 gladiators, among whom there were only two that did not blink when faced by some threat of danger and were consequently unconquerable: so difficult it is for a human being to stare steadily, whereas for most people it is natural to keep on blinking, and these are traditionally supposed to be more cowardly. Nobody has eyes of only one colour: with everyone the general surface is white but there is a different colour in the middle. No other part of the body *The eye as* supplies greater indications of the mind—this is so *expressing the mind.* with all animals alike, but specially with man— that is, indications of self-restraint, mercy, pity, hatred, love, sorrow, joy. The eyes are also very varied in their look—fierce, stern, sparkling, sedate, leering, askance, downcast, kindly: in fact the eyes are the abode of the mind. They glow, stare, moisten, wink; from them flows the tear of compassion, when we kiss them we seem to reach the mind itself, they are the source of tears and of the stream that bedews the cheek. What is the nature of this moisture that at a moment of sorrow flows so copiously and so promptly? Or where is it in the remaining time? In point of fact it is the mind that is the real instrument of sight and of observation; the eyes act as a sort of vessel receiving and transmitting the visible portion of the consciousness. This explains why deep thought

523

cogitatio obcaecat abducto intus visu, sic in morbo
147 comitiali animo caligante aperti nihil cernunt. quin
et patentibus dormiunt lepores multique hominum,
quos κορυβαντιᾶν Graeci dicunt.

Tenuibus multisque membranis eos natura com-
posuit, callosis contra frigora calorisque in extumo
tunicis, quas subinde purificat lacrimationum salivis,
148 lubricos propterincursantia et mobiles. LV. media
eorum cornua fenestravit pupilla, cuius angustiae
non sinunt vagari incertam aciem ac velut canali
dirigunt, obiterque incidentia facile declinant,
aliis nigri, aliis ravi, aliis glauci coloris orbibus
circumdatis, ut et[1] habili mixtura accipiatur e[2]
circumiecto candore lux et[5] temperato repercussu
non obstrepat; adeoque his absoluta vis speculi ut
tam parva illa pupilla totam imaginem reddat hominis.
ea causa est ut pleraeque alitum e manibus hominum
oculos potissimum appetant, quod effigiem suam in
his cernentes velut ad cognata desideria sua tendunt.
149 veterina tantum quaedam ad incrementa lunae
morbos sentiunt. sed homo solus emisso umore
caecitate liberatur. post vicensimum annum multis
restitutus est visus, quibusdam statim nascentibus
negatus nullo oculorum vitio, multis repente ablatus

---

[1] et *hic Rackham* : *post* mixtura.
[2] e *add. Rackham.*
[5] *v.l.* e.

---

[a] The κορύβαντες were priests of Cybele, who was worshipped in Phrygia with frenzied dancing.

blinds the eyes by withdrawing the vision inward, and why when the mind is clouded during an attack of epilepsy the eyes though open discern nothing. Moreover hares sleep with the eyes wide open, and so do many human beings while in the condition which the Greeks term ' corybantic.'[a]

Nature has constructed them with thin and multiple membranes, and with outside wrappers that are callous against cold and heat, which she repeatedly cleanses with moisture from the tear-glands, and she has made the eyes slippery against objects that encounter them, and mobile. LV. The horny skin in the centre of the eye nature has furnished with the pupil as a window, the narrow opening of which does not allow the gaze to roam uncertain, but so to speak canalizes its direction, and easily averts objects that encounter it on the way; the pupil is surrounded with circles which with some people are coloured black, with others grey and with others blue, so that the light from the surrounding radiance both may be received in a suitable blend and having its reflexion moderated may not be jarring; and the efficacy of the mirror is made so perfect by these means that the small pupil can reflect the entire image of a human being. This is the reason why commonly birds when released from men's hands go first of all for their eyes, because they see their own likeness reflected in them and try to reach as it were a desired object that is akin to themselves. Beasts of burden only experience diseases at certain phases of the moon. Man alone is cured of blindness by the emission of fluid from the eye. Many have had their sight restored after 20 years of blindness; some have been blind at birth owing to no defect in the eyes; similarly, many have

Physiology of the eye.

Cure of blindness.

simili modo nulla praecedente iniuria. venam ab his
pertinere ad cerebrum peritissimi auctores tradunt;
ego et ad stomachum crediderim: certe nulli sine
150 redundatione eius eruitur oculus. morientibus illos
operire rursusque in rogo patefacere Quiritium
magno[1] ritu sacrum est, ita more condito ut neque
ab homine supremum eos spectari fas sit et caelo non
ostendi nefas. uni animalium homini depravantur,
unde cognomina Strabonum et Paetorum. ab iisdem
qui altero lumine orbi nascerentur Coclites voca-
bantur, qui parvis utrisque Ocellae; Luscini iniuriae
151 cognomen habuerunt. nocturnorum animalium
veluti felium in tenebris fulgent radiantque oculi ut
contueri non sit, et capreae[2] lupoque splendent
lucemque iaculantur; vituli marini et hyaenae in
mille colores transeunt subinde; quin et in tenebris
multorum piscium refulgent, aridi sicut robusti
caudices putresque vetustate.[3] non conivere diximus quae non[4] obliquis oculis sed circumacto capite
152 cernerent. chamaeleonis oculos ipsos circumagi
totos tradunt. cancri in oblicum aspiciunt crusta
fragili inclusos gerentes. locustis, squillis magna ex
parte sub eodem munimento praeduri eminent.

---

[1] Magno *v.l. om.*
[2] *Gelen* : caprae.
[3] *Mayhoff* : vetustate putresque.
[4] non *add. ex* VIII. 107 *edd.*

---

[a] *Cocles* and *luscus* both appear to denote a person blind in
one eye.

suddenly lost their sight without any previous injury. The most learned authorities state that the eyes are connected with the brain by a vein; for my own part I am inclined to believe that they are also thus connected with the stomach: it is unquestionable that a man never has an eye knocked out without vomiting. There is a solemn ritual custom among Roman citizens to close the eyes of the dying and to open them again on the funeral pyre, custom having established that it is not right for the eyes to be seen by a human being at the last moment and also wrong for them not to be displayed to the heavens. Man is the only animal whose eyes are liable to distortion, which is the origin of the family names Squint-eye and Blinky. From the eyes also came the name of One-eye that used to be given to persons born blind in one eye, and that of Eyelet given to persons both of whose eyes were small; the One-eye family [a] received the name of an injury done to one of them. The eyes of night-roaming animals like cats shine and flash in the dark so that one cannot look at them, and those of the wild-goat and the wolf gleam and shoot out light; the eyes of the sea-calf and of the hyena change frequently into a thousand colours; moreover those of many fishes shine out even in the dark, like oak-tree stumps when dry and rotten with age. We have stated that creatures that do not direct their gaze by slanting the eyes but by turning the head round do not wink. It is reported that the chamaeleon's eyes turn themselves entirely round. Crabs look sideways, having their eyes enclosed in a fragile shell. Lobsters and shrimps mostly have very hard eyes projecting under a protection of the same kind. Creatures with hard

Sight of various animals.

527

quorum duri sunt minus cernunt quam quorum umidi.
serpentium catulis et hirundinum pullis si quis eruat
153 renasci tradunt. insectorum omnium et testacei
operimenti oculi moventur sicut quadripedum aures.
quibus fragilia operimenta, his oculi duri. omnia
talia et pisces et insecta non habent genas nec
integunt oculos; omnibus membrana vitri modo
tralucida obtenditur.

154   LVI. Palpebrae in genis homini utrimque. mulieri-
bus fuco [1] etiam infectae cotidiano: tanta est
decoris adfectatio ut tinguantur oculi quoque. alia
de causa hoc natura dederat, ceu vallum quoddam
visus et prominens munimentum contra occursantia
animalia aut alia fortuito incidentia. defluere eas
155 haut inmerito venere abundantibus tradunt. ex
ceteris nulli sunt nisi quibus et in reliquo corpore pili,
sed quadripedibus in superiore tantum gena, volucribus in inferiore, et quibus molle tergus, ut serpentibus, et quadripedum quae ova pariunt, ut lacertae.
struthocamelus alitum sola ut homo utrimque
palpebras habet.

156   LVII. Ne genae quidem omnibus, item [2] neque
nictatio nisi [3] his quae animal generant. graviores
alitum inferiore gena conivent, eaedem nictantur ab
angulis membrana obeunte. columbae et similia
utraque conivent. at quadripedes quae ova pariunt,
ut testudines, crocodili, inferiore tantum, sine ulla

_____

[1] *Mayhoff*: vero.   [2] item? *Mayhoff*: ideo.
[3] *Mayhoff ex Aristotele*: nictationis.

eyes have less keen sight than those whose eyes are moist. It is stated that if one removes the eyes of young snakes and swallow chicks, they grow again. The eyes of all insects and of creatures with a covering of shell move like the ears of quadrupeds. Those with fragile coverings have hard eyes. All such creatures, and also fish and insects, have no eyelids and do not close their eyes; withal the eye is covered with a membrane that is transparent like glass.

LVI. Human beings have eyelashes on both eyelids. Women actually have them dyed every day: such is their desire to achieve beauty that they colour even their eyes; but really the lashes were bestowed by nature for another purpose, as a sort of fence to the sight and a barrier projecting against insects meeting the eye, or other things accidentally falling into them. It is said that sexual excess causes them to drop off, not undeservedly. None of the other species have them excepting those with hair on the rest of the body as well, but quadrupeds have them only on the upper lid, birds on the lower, as also do creatures with a soft skin, for instance snakes, and oviparous quadrupeds, for instance lizards. The ostrich is the only bird with lashes on both eyelids like a human being. *The eyelashes.*

LVII. Not all species have eyelids either, and also only viviparous creatures can wink. The heavier birds close the eye with the lower lid, and also wink with a skin that covers the eye from the corner. Pigeons and similar birds close the eyes with both lids. But oviparous quadrupeds, such as tortoises and crocodiles, do so only with the lower lid, without any winking because their eyes are extremely *The eyelids.*

157 nictatione propter praeduros oculos. extremum
ambitum genae superioris antiqui cilium vocavere,
unde et supercilia. hoc vulnere aliquo diductum
non coalescit, ut in paucis humani corporis membris.

LVIII. Infra oculos malae homini tantum (quas
prisci genas vocabant, xii tabularum interdicto radi
a feminis vetantis). pudori shaec sedes : ibi maxume
ostenditur rubor.

158 LIX. Intra eas hilaritatem risumque indicantes
buccae et altior homini tantum, quem novi mores
subdolae inrisioni dicavere, nasus. non alii animalium nares eminent: avibus, serpentibus, piscibus
foramina tantum ad olfactus sine naribus; et hinc
cognomina Simorum, Silonum. septimo mense genitis saepenumero foramina aurium et narium defuere.

159 LX. Labra, a quibus Brocchi, Labeones dicti, et
os probum duriusve animal generantibus. pro his
cornea et acuta volucribus rostra, eadem rapto
viventibus adunca, collecto recta, herbas eruentibus
limumque lata, ut et[1] suum generi. iumentis vice
manus ad colligenda pabula. ora apertiora laniatu
viventibus.

Mentum nulli praeter hominem, ut[2] nec malae.
maxillas crocodilus tantum superiores movet, terrestres quadrupedes eodem quo cetera more praeterque
in oblicum.

---

[1] *Mayhoff*: uti.   [2] ut *add. ? Mayhoff.*

---

[a] When mourning for a death : *Mulieres genas ne radunto,
neve lessum* (wailing) *funeris ergo habento.*

hard. The old name for the edge of the upper eyelid was *cilium*; hence our word for the brows. When the eyelid is cleft by a wound it does not grow together again, as is the case with a few other parts of the human body.

LVIII. Only man has cheeks below the eyes (the *The cheeks* old word for the cheeks was *genae*, used in the Twelve Tables in the prohibition of women's lacerating them).ᵃ The cheeks are the seat of modesty: on them a blush is most visible.

LIX. The face between the cheek-bones displays *The nose.* merriment and laughter, and higher up, but in man only, stands the nose, which modern fashion has made the organ of sly mockery. No other animal has projecting nostrils, birds, snakes and fishes only having apertures for smelling, without nostrils and this is the origin of the surnames Snubby and Pug. Seven-month children have frequently been born lacking the apertures of the ears and nostrils.

LX. The viviparous species have lips—whence the *The mouth.* surnames Lippy and Blubber-lips—and a well-shaped or rather harsh mouth. Instead of lips birds have pointed beaks of horn, which are hooked in birds of prey, straight in those that live by pecking, and broad in those that dig up grass and mud, like the snouts of the swine class. Cattle use their mouths instead of a hand for gathering fodder. Beasts that live by tearing up their prey have mouths that open wider.

No creature but man has a chin, any more than *The jaw.* cheeks. The crocodile moves only the upper jaw; four-footed land animals open the mouth in the same way as all other creatures and in addition move the lower jaw sideways.

160 LXI. Dentium tria genera, serrati aut continui aut exerti serrati: pectinatim coeuntes, ne contrario occursu atterantur, ut serpentibus, piscibus, canibus; continui, ut homini, equo; exerti, ut apro, hippopotamo, elephanto. continuorum qui digerunt cibum lati et acuti, qui conficiunt duplices, qui discriminant

161 eos canini appellantur. hi sunt serratis longissimi. continui aut utraque parte oris sunt, ut equo, aut superiore primores non sunt, ut bubus, ovibus omnibusque quae ruminant. caprae superiores non sunt praeter primores geminos. nulli exerti quibus serrati, raro feminae, et tamen sine usu; itaque cum

162 apri percutiant, feminae sues mordent. nulli cui cornua exerti, sed omnibus concavi; ceteris dentes solidi. piscium omnibus serrati praeter scarum, huic uni aquatilium plani. cetero multis eorum in lingua et toto ore, ut turba vulnerum molliant quae adtritu subigere non queunt. multis et in palato [atque etiam in cauda],[1] praeterea in os vergentes, ne excidant cibi, nullum habentibus retinendi adminiculum.

163 LXII. Similes aspidi et serpentibus, sed duo in supera parte dextra laevaque longissimi, tenui fistula perforati ut scorpionis[2] aculei, venenum

---

[1] secl. coll. Ar. Mayhoff.
[2] Mayhoff (?): scorpioni.

---

[a] This odd addition is lacking in Aristotle.

LXI. There are three kinds of teeth—serrated or *The teeth.* continuous or projecting : serrated teeth closing together like the teeth of a comb, so as not to be worn away by direct collision, as in snakes, fishes and dogs ; continuous, as in man and the horse ; projecting, as in the boar, hippopotamus and elephant. Of continuous teeth those that separate the food (incisors), are called the broad or sharp teeth, those that masticate it double teeth, and those between these dog-teeth. The latter are longest in creatures with serrated teeth. Continuous teeth are either in both jaws, as with the horse, or else there are no front teeth in the upper jaw, as with oxen and sheep and all the ruminants. The goat has no upper teeth except the pair in front. Species having serrated teeth have no projecting teeth, and a female rarely has them, and when she has them does not use them; consequently though boars gore, sows bite. No species with horns has projecting teeth, but all have curved ones; all the other species have solid teeth. All kinds of fish have serrated teeth except the parrot-fish—this is the only aquatic species that has level teeth. Many of them however have teeth on the tongue and all over the mouth, so as to soften by means of a multiplicity of wounds objects that they are unable to reduce by mastication. Many also have teeth on the palate [and also on the tail,][a] and also turned further into the mouth, so as to prevent morsels of food from falling out, as they have no apparatus for retaining it.

LXII. The asp and serpent have similar teeth, *The teeth of poisonous species.* but two extremely long ones on the right and left side of the upper jaw, perforated by a slender tube like the stings of the scorpion, which inject poison.

533

înfundentes. non aliud hoc esse quam fel serpentium, et inde venas sub spina ad os pervenire diligentissimi auctores scribunt; quidam unum esse eum et quia sit aduncus resupinari cum momorderit; aliqui tum decidere eum rursusque recrescere facilem decussu,

164 et sine eo esse quas tractari cernamus; scorpionis caudae inesse eum, ut plerique[1] ternos. viperis dentes gingiva conduntur. haec eodem praegnans veneno inpressum[2] dentium repulsu virus fundit in morsus. volucrum nulli dentes praeter vespertilionem. camelus una ex his quae non sunt cornigera in superiore maxilla primores non habet. cornua habentium nulli serrati. et cocleae dentes habent;

165 indicio est vel[3] a minimis earum derosa vicia. at in marinis crustata et cartilaginea primores habere, item echinis quinos esse unde intellegi potuerit miror. dentium vice aculei sunt[4] insectis. Simiae dentes ut homini. elephanto intus ad mandendum quattuor, praeterque eos qui prominent masculis reflexi, feminis recti atque proni. musculus marinus qui ballaenam antecedit nullos habet, sed pro iis saetis intus os hirtum et linguam etiam ac palatum. terrestrium minutis quadripedibus primores bini utrimque longissimi.

166 LXIII. Ceteris cum ipsis nascuntur, homini

---

[1] *sic ? Mayhoff*: et plerisque.
[2] *Mayhoff*: impresso.
[3] vel *add. ? Mayhoff* (*ipse* et).
[4] *Detlefsen*: aculeis *aut* aculeus.

---

[a] *I.e.* by snake-charmers.
[b] Really this is the case with very few.

The most accurate authorities write that this poison
is nothing else than the serpents' gall, and that veins
pass from the gall-bladder under the spine to the
mouth; certain writers say that it is only one tooth,
and that as it is hooked it is sloped backward when it
has inflicted a bite; some authorities state that it
then falls out and afterwards grows again, as it is
very easy to dislodge, and that the snakes that we
see handled [a] lack this tooth; and that the scorpion
has this tooth in its tail—as according to most
authorities it has three. The vipers' teeth are
concealed in its gum. Their gum is charged with
the same poison, and when squeezed by the pressure
of the teeth pours out its venom into the bites
inflicted. No winged creature except the bat has *The teeth*
teeth. The camel is the only animal without horns *of other*
that has not got front teeth in the upper jaw. No *species.*
horned animal has serrated teeth. Even snails
have teeth; this is proved by the fact that even the
smallest of them gnaw vetches. But I wonder
what possible ground there is for the view that
among marine species shell-fish and cartilaginous
fish have front teeth, and also that sea-urchins have
five. Insects have stings instead of teeth. The
monkey has teeth like those of a human being. The
elephant has four inner teeth for masticating, and
besides these the prominent tusks that are bent
backward in the male and slope straight downward
in the female. The sea-mouse that swims in front
of the whale has no teeth, but instead of them its
mouth inside and also its tongue and palate are set
with bristles. Of land animals very small quadrupeds
have two extremely long front teeth in each jaw.

LXIII. All the other animals are born with teeth,[b]

postquam natus est septimo mense. reliquis perpetui
manent, mutantur homini, leoni, iumento, cani et
ruminantibus, sed leoni et cani non nisi canini
appellati. lupi dexter caninus in magicis [1] habetur
opibus.[2] maxillares, qui sunt a caninis, nullum
animal mutat. homini novissimi qui genuini vocantur, circiter vicensimum annum, gignuntur, multis
et octogensimo, feminis quoque, sed quibus in iuventa
167 non fuere nati. decidere in senecta et mox renasci
certum est. Zoclen Samothracem cui renati essent
post CIV annos Mucianus visum a se prodidit.
cetero maribus plures quam feminis in homine,
pecude, capra, sue. Timarchus Nicoclis filius **Paphi**
duos ordines habuit maxillarium; frater eius non
mutavit primores, ideoque praetrivit. est exemplum
dentis homini et in palato geniti. a caninis [3] amissi
casu aliquo numquam renascuntur. ceteris senecta
rufescunt, equo tantum candidiores fiunt.
168 LXIV. Aetas veterinorum dentibus indicatur.
equo sunt numero XL. amittit tricensimo mense
primores utrimque binos, sequenti anno totidem
proximos, cum subeunt dicti columellares; quinto
anno incipiente amittit binos, qui sexto anno renascuntur; septimo omnes habet et renatos et inmut-
169 abilis. equo castrato prius non decidunt dentes.

---

[1] magicis? *Detlefsen* : magnis.
[2] opibus? *Mayhoff* : operibus.
[3] at canini *vel* a genuinis *edd.*

---

[a] All these statements are erroneous.
[b] *Cf.* XXVIII 257.

but man grows them six months after birth. All the *First and second teeth.* rest keep their teeth permanently, but man, the lion, the beasts of burden, dogs and ruminant animals shed them; with the lion and dog however this only applies to those called dog-teeth.[a] The right dog-tooth of a wolf is held to be valuable as an amulet.[b] No animal sheds its maxillary teeth, the ones next to the dog-teeth. In man those called wisdom-teeth grow latest, at about the age of twenty, and in many cases even at eighty, with females as well, but only in the case of persons who did not grow them in youth. It is certain that in old age they fall out and then grow again. Mucianus has stated that he saw a Samothracian named Zocles who grew a new set of teeth when 140 years old. For the rest, males have more teeth than females in the case of man, ox, goat and pig.[a] Timarchus son of Nicocles at Paphos had two rows of maxillaries; his brother did not shed his front teeth, and consequently wore them down. There is a case of a person even growing a tooth in the palate. Any of the dog teeth lost by some accident never grow again. With all other species the teeth get red in old age, but in the horse alone they become whiter.

LXIV. In beasts of burden the teeth are a sign *Teeth of domestic animals.* of their age. A horse has forty teeth; when two-and-a-half years old it loses two front ones in each jaw, and in the following year the same number of the teeth next these, when they are replaced by those called grinders; at the beginning of its fifth year it looses two teeth, which grow again in its sixth year; in its seventh year it has all of its second teeth and also its permanent ones. A horse previously gelt does not shed its teeth.[a] The ass

537

asinorum genus tricensimo mense similiter amittit, dein senis mensibus; quod si non prius peperere quam decidant postremi, sterilitas certa. boves bimi mutant. subus non decidunt umquam.

Absumpta hac observatione senectus in equis et ceteris veterinis intellegitur dentium brocchitate, superciliorum canitia et circa ea lacunis, cum fere XVI annorum existimantur.

170 Hominum dentibus quoddam inest virus, namque et speculi nitorem ex adverso nudati hebetant et columbarum fetus inplumes necant. reliqua de iis in generatione hominum dicta sunt. erumpentibus morbi corpora infantium afficiunt.¹ [reliqua] ² animalia quae serratos habent saevissime dentiunt ³

171 LXV. Linguae non omnibus eodem modo. tenuissima serpentibus et trisulca, vibrans, atri coloris et, si extrahas, praelonga; lacertis bifida et pilosa, vitulis quoque marinis duplex; sed supra dictis capillamenti tenuitate. ceteris ad circumlambenda ora, piscibus paulo minus quam tota adhaerens,

172 crocodilis tota. sed in gustatu linguae vice carnosum aquatilibus palatum. leonibus, pardis omnibusque generis eius, etiam felibus, imbricatae asperitatis ac limae similis attenuansque lambendo cutem hominis, quae causa etiam mansuefacta, ubi ad vicinum

---

¹ *Detlefsen* : accipiunt.
² *secl. ? Mueller ut iteratum (vel* ⟨inter⟩ *reliqua).*
³ saevissima dentibus *edd. vet.*

ᵃ As a matter of fact they are more prolific.
ᵇ This statement is erroneous.
ᶜ VII. 68 foll.
ᵈ An emendation gives ' are fiercest with their teeth.'

family likewise looses teeth when two-and-a-half years old, and again six months later; those that have not foaled before they shed their last teeth are sure to be barren.[a] Oxen change their teeth at the age of two. Pigs never shed theirs.[b]

When this indication has come to an end, old age in horses and other beasts of burden is inferred from prominence of the teeth and greyness of the brows and hollows round them, when they are judged to be about sixteen years old.

Human teeth contain a kind of poison, for they *Other facts* dim the brightness of a mirror when bared in front *as to teeth.* of it and also kill the fledglings of pigeons. The rest of the facts about the teeth have been told in the passage [c] dealing with human reproduction. Infants when cutting their teeth are specially liable to illnesses. The animals with serrated teeth have the severest pain in teething.[d]

LXV. Not all species have tongues on the same *The tongue* plan. With snakes the tongue is extremely slender and three-forked, darting, black in colour, and if drawn out to full length extremely long; with lizards it is cleft in two and hairy, and with seals also it is double; but with the species above mentioned it is of the fineness of a hair. With the rest it is available for licking round the jaws, but with fish it adheres through a little less than its whole length, and with crocodiles the whole of it. In aquatic species on the other hand the fleshy palate serves instead of the tongue in tasting. With lions, leopards, and all the species of that genus, even cats, the tongue is rough and corrugated like a file, and can scrape away the human skin by licking, which provokes even those that have been tamed

sanguinem pervenit saliva, invitat ad rabiem. de
173 purpurarum linguis diximus. ranis prima cohaeret,
intuma absoluta a gutture, qua vocem emittunt
mares, cum vocantur ololygones; stato id tempore
evenit, cientibus ad coitum feminas. tum siquidem
inferiore labro demisso ad libramentum aquae modice
receptae in fauces palpitante ibi lingua ululatus
eliditur; tunc extenti buccarum sinus perlucent,
oculi flagrant labore propulsi.[1] quibus in posteriore
parte aculei, his et dentes et lingua, apibus etiam
praelonga, eminens et cicadis; quibus aculeus in ore
fistulosus, his nec lingua nec dentes. quibusdam
insectis intus lingua, ut formicis; ceterum latet et [2]
174 elephanto praecipue. reliquis in suo genere semper
absoluta, homini tantum ita saepe constricta venis [3]
ut intercidi eas necesse sit. Metellum pontificem
adeo inexplanatae fuisse accipimus ut multis mensibus tortus credatur dum meditatur in dedicanda
aede Opi verba [4] dicere; ceteris septumo ferme anno
sermonem exprimit. multis vero talis ars eius contingit ut avium et animalium vocis indiscreta edatur
imitatio.

[1] v.l. perpulsi.
[2] *Mayhoff ex Aristotele*: ceterum lata.
[3] *an* nervis? *Mayhoff.*
[4] *Jan*: opifere.

---

[a] IX. 128.
[b] Perhaps this should be altered to ' sinews.'

to madness when their saliva gets through to the blood. We have spoken [a] of the tongues of the purple-fishes. In frogs the tip of the tongue is attached but the inner part is loose from the throat; it is with this that the males croak, at the time when they are called croakers; this happens at a fixed season, when they are calling the females to mate. In this process they just drop the lower lip and take into the throat a moderate amount of water and let the tongue vibrate in it so as to make it undulate, and a croaking sound is forced out; during this the curves of the cheeks are distended and become transparent, and the eyes stand out blazing with the exertion. Creatures with stings in their hinder part have teeth and a tongue as well, bees even a very long tongue, and cicalas also a projecting one; but those with a tubular sting in the mouth have neither tongue nor teeth. Some insects have a tongue inside the mouth, for instance ants; moreover, the elephant's tongue also is particularly little visible. With the rest of the animals according to their kind the tongue is always quite free, but with man alone it is often so tightly bound by veins [b] that they have to be cut. We find it recorded *Stammering.* that the High Priest Metellus was so tongue-tied that he is believed to have suffered torture for many months while practising the formula to be spoken in dedicating the Temple of Wealth; but in all other cases of stammering the patient usually contrives to speak distinctly after reaching the age of six. Many people on the other hand are endowed with such skill in using the tongue that they can give imitations of the cries of birds and animals that are indistinguishable from the real thing.

Intellectus saporum ceteris in prima lingua, homini et in palato.

175 LXVI. Tonsillae in homine, in sue glandulae. quod inter eas uvae nomine ultumo dependet palato homini tantum est. sub ea minor lingua nulli ova generantium. opera eius gemina duabus interpositae fistulis. interior earum appellatur arteria ad pulmo-

176 nem atque cor pertinens; hanc operit in epulando spiritu et voce illac [1] meante, ne, si potus cibusve in alienum deerraverit tramitem, torqueat. altera exterior appellatur sane gula, qua cibus atque potus devolant; tendit haec ad stomachum, is ad ventrem. hanc per vices operit, cum spiritus tantum aut vox commeat, ne restagnatio intempestiva alvi obstrepat. ex cartilagine et carne arteria, gula e nervo et carne constat.

177 LXVII. Cervix nulli nisi quibus utraque haec; ceteris collum, quibus tantum gula. sed quibus cervix, e multis vertebratisque orbiculatim ossibus flexilis ad circumspectum articulorum nodis iungitur, leoni tantum et lupo et hyaenae singulis rectisque

178 ossibus rigens. cetero spinae adnectitur, spina lumbis, ossea sed tereti structura, per media foramina a cerebro medulla descendente. eandem esse ei naturam quam cerebro colligunt quoniam prae-

---

[1] *Rackham* (in illo *Mayhoff cf.* § 266): illa.

---

[a] *I.e.* the epiglottis.

With all the other species the tip of the tongue *Taste.* is the seat of taste, but with man this is also situated in the palate.

LXVI. Man has tonsils, the pig glands. Man *Tonsils,* alone has what is called the uvula hanging from the *uvula,* back of the palate between the tonsils. No oviparous *windpipe,* species possesses the lesser tongue *a* below the *gullet.* uvula. Its functions are twofold, placed as it is between two tubes. Of these the inner one called the windpipe stretches to the lungs and the heart; this the lesser tongue closes while food is being eaten, as breath and voice passes along it, lest if drink or food should pass into the wrong channel, it might cause pain. The other, the outer tube, is of course called the gullet, down which food and drink fall; this leads to the stomach, and the stomach to the abdomen. This passage the lesser tongue occasionally closes, when only breath or voice is passing, so that an untimely rising of the stomach may not interfere. The windpipe consists of gristle and flesh, the gullet of sinew and flesh.

LXVII. No species except those possessing both *The nape.* windpipe and gullet have a nape; all the others, which have only a gullet, have a neck. But in those possessing a nape it is composed of a number of bones articulated in rings with jointed vertebrae, so as to be capable of bending to look round; only in the lion and wolf and hyena is it a stiff structure of a single straight bone. Moreover it is connected with the spine, and the spine with the loins, in a bony but rounded structure, the marrow passing down from the brain through the orifices in the vertebrae. It is inferred that the spinal cord is of the same substance as the brain for the reason that,

tenui eius membrana modo incisa statim expiretur.
quibus longa crura his longa et colla; item aquaticis
quamvis brevia crura habentibus, simili modo uncos
ungues.

179   LXVIII. Guttur homini tantum et subus intumes-
cit aquarum quae potantur plerumque vitio. summum gulae fauces vocantur, postremum stomachus.
hoc nomine est sub arteria iam carnosa inanitas adnexa
spinae, ad latitudinem ac longitudinem lagoenae
modo fusa. quibus fauces non sunt ne stomachus
quidem est, nec colla nec guttur, ut piscibus, et ora
180 ventribus iunguntur. testudini marinae lingua
nulla est nec dentes, rostri acie comminuit omnia.
postea arteria et stomachus denticulatus callo in
modum rubi ad conficiendos cibos, decrescentibus
rimis¹ quicquid² adpropinquent ventri; novissima
asperitas ut scobinae³ fabrilis.

181   LXIX. Cor animalibus ceteris medio pectore est,
homini tantum infra laevam papillam turbinato
mucrone in priora eminens. piscibus solis ad os
spectat. hoc primum nascentibus formari in utero
tradunt, deinde cerebrum, sicut tardissime oculos,
sed hos primum emori, cor novissime. huic praecipuus çalor. palpitat certe et quasi alterum movetur
intra animal, praemolli firmoque opertum membranae
involucro, munitum costarum et pectoris muro, ut

---

¹ rimis? *Mayhoff*: renis.   ² quacunque? *Hardouin*.
³ *Mayhoff*: scobina.

ᵃ As a matter of fact it has a tongue.

if its extremely slender membrane is merely cut into, death follows immediately. Species with long legs also have long necks; as also have aquatic species even though they have short legs, and similarly if they have hooked claws.

LXVIII. Man and swine alone suffer from swollen *The gullet* throat, usually due to bad drinking water. The top *and the windpipe.* part of the gullet is called the pharynx and the bottom part the stomach. This name denotes the cavity attached to the spine below the fleshy part of the windpipe, bulging out lengthwise and breadthwise like a flagon. Species without a pharynx, for instance fishes, have no stomach either, and no neck nor throat, and the mouth is joined to the abdomen. The sea tortoise has not got a tongue *a* or teeth, but breaks up all its food with the point of its snout. Next comes the windpipe and the stomach, denticulated with ridges of thick skin like bramble-thorns for the purpose of grinding up the food, the interstices growing smaller in proportion as they are nearer to the abdomen : at the bottom it is as rough as a carpenter's rasp.

LXIX. The heart with the other animals is in the *The heart,* middle of the chest, but in man alone it is below the *its func-* left breast, with its conical end projecting forward. *tions.* In fishes only it points towards the mouth. It is stated that at birth the heart is the first organ formed in the womb, and next the brain, just as the eyes develop latest, but that the eyes are the first to die and the heart the last. The heart is the warmest part. It has a definite beat and a motion of its own as if it were a second animal inside the animal; it is wrapped with a very soft and firm covering of membrane, and protected by the wall

182 pariat praecipuam vitae causam et originem. prima
domicilia intra se animo et sanguini praebet sinuoso
specu et in magnis animalibus triplici, in nullo non
gemino; ibi mens habitat. ex hoc fonte duae
grandes venae in priora [1] et terga discurrunt, sparsa-
que ramorum serie per alias minores omnibus membris vitalem sanguinem rigant. solum hoc viscerum
vitiis non maceratur; nec supplicia vitae trahit,
laesumque mortem ilico adfert. ceteris corruptis
vitalitas in corde durat.

183   LXX. Bruta existimantur animalium quibus durum
riget, audacia quibus parvum est, pavida quibus
praegrande; maximum autem est portione muribus,
lepori, asino, cervo, pantherae, mustelis, hyaenis et
omnibus aut [2] timidis aut propter metum maleficis.
in Paphlagonia bina perdicibus corda. in equorum

184 et boum ossa reperiuntur interdum. augeri id per
singulos annos in homine et binas drachmas ponderis
ad quinquagensimum annum accedere, ab eo detrahi
tantundem, et ideo non vivere hominem ultra centen-
simum annum defectu cordis Aegyptii existimant,

185 quibus mos est cadavera adservare medicata. hirto
corde gigni quosdam homines proditur, neque alios
fortioris esse industriae, sicut Aristomenen Messenium

---

[1] v.l. prorsa.   [2] aut add. Rackham.

ᵃ Really it is four-fold.

of the ribs and chest, so that it may give birth to the principle cause and origin of life. It provides the vital principle and the blood with their primary abodes inside it, in a winding recess which in large animals is three-fold[a] and in all others without exception double; this is the dwelling-place of the mind. From this source two large veins run apart to the front and the back of the body, and diffuse the blood of life through other smaller veins with a spreading system of branches to all the limbs. The heart alone is not tortured by the defects of the inner organs; and it does not prolong the torments of life, and when wounded at once brings death. When the rest of the parts have been injured vitality continues in the heart.

LXX. The view is held that dull creatures are those whose heart is stiff and hard, bold ones those whose heart is small, and cowardly ones those in which it is specially large; but it is largest in proportion to their size in mice, the hare, the ass, the stag, the leopard, weasels, hyenas, and all the species that are either timid or rendered dangerous by fear. Partridges in Paphlagonia have two hearts. Bones are occasionally found in the heart of horses and oxen. The people of Egypt, who practise the custom of mummification, have a belief that the human heart grows larger every year and at the age of fifty reaches a weight of a quarter of an ounce, and from that point loses weight at the same rate; and that consequently a man does not live beyond a hundred, owing to heart failure. It is stated that some people are born with a hairy heart, and that they are exceptionally brave and resolute—an example being a Messenian named

Physiology of the heart.

547

qui trecentos occidit Lacedaemonios. ipse convolneratus captus semel per cavernam lautumiarum evasit angustias volpium aditus secutus. iterum captus sopitis custodibus somno ad ignem advolutus lora cum corpore exussit. tertium capto Lacedaemonii pectus dissecuere viventi, hirsutumque cor repertum est.

186 LXXI. In corde summo pinguitudo quaedam est laetis extis. non semper autem in parte extorum habitum est; L. Postumio L. f. Albino rege sacrorum post cxxvi Olympiadem, cum rex Pyrrhus ex Italia decessisset, cor in extis haruspices inspicere coeperunt. Caesari dictatori, quo die primum veste purpurea processit atque in sella aurea sedit, sacrificanti in extis defuit; unde quaestio magna de divinatione argumentantibus, potueritne sine illo viscere hostia

187 vivere an ad tempus amiserit. negatur cremari posse in iis qui cardiaco morbo obierint, negatur et veneno [1] interemptis; certe exstat oratio Vitelli qua Gnaeum Pisonem eius sceleris coarguit hoc usus argumento, palamque testatus non potuisse ob venenum cor Germanici Caesaris cremari. contra genere morbi defensus est Piso.

---

[1] ⟨de⟩ veneno ? *Rackham.*

---

a 275 B.C.   *b* In A.D. 19.

Aristomenes who killed three hundred Spartans. He himself when severely wounded and taken prisoner for the first time escaped through a cave from confinement in the quarries by following the routes by which foxes got in. He was again taken prisoner, but when his guards were fast asleep he rolled to the fire and burnt off his thongs, burning his body in the process. He was taken a third time, and the Spartans cut him open alive and his heart was found to be shaggy.

LXXI. In victims whose organs are propitious there is a certain fatness on the top of the heart. *The heart in divination.* But the heart was not always considered as one of the significant organs; it was after the 126th Olympiad, when Lucius Postumius Albinus, son of Lucius, was King of Sacrifices, after King Pyrrhus had evacuated Italy,[a] that the augurs began to inspect the heart among the organs. On the day when Caesar as dictator first went in procession dressed in purple and took his seat on a golden throne, when he performed a sacrifice the heart was lacking among the organs; and this gave rise to much debate among the students of divination, as to whether the victim had been able to live without that organ or had lost it at the time. It is stated that at the cremation of persons who have died of heart disease the heart cannot be burnt, and the same is said of persons that have been killed by poison; undoubtedly there is extant a speech of Vitellius that employs this argument to prove Gnaeus Piso guilty of poisoning,[b] and explicitly uses the evidence that it had been impossible to cremate the heart of Germanicus Caesar on account of poison. In reply Piso's defence was based on the nature of the disease.

188 LXXII. Sub eo pulmo est spirandique officina, attrahens ac reddens animam, idcirco spongeosus ac fistulis inanibus cavus. pauca eum, ut dictum est, habent aquatilia, cetera ova parientia exiguum spumosumque nec sanguineum; ideo non sitiunt. eadem est causa quare sub aqua diu ranae et phocae urinentur. testudo quoque, quamvis praegrandem et sub toto tegumento habeat, sine sanguine tamen habet. quanto minor hic corporibus tanto velocitas maior. chamaeleoni portione maximus et nihil aliud intus.

189 LXXIII. Iecur in dextera parte est; in eo quod caput extorum vocant, magnae varietatis. M. Marcello circa mortem, cum periit ab Hannibale, defuit in extis; sequenti deinde die geminum repertum est. defuit et C. Mario cum immolaret Uticae, item Gaio principi kal. Ian., cum iniret consulatum quo anno interfectus est, Claudio succes-190 sori eius quo mense interemptus est veneno. divo Augusto Spoleti sacrificanti primo potestatis suae die sex victimarum iocinera replicata intrinsecus ab ima fibra reperta sunt, responsumque duplicaturum intra annum imperium. caput extorum tristis ostenti caesum quoque est, praeterquam in sollicitudine ac

---

^a This is not the case.　　^b 208 B.C.　　^c 107 B.C.
^d Caligula, murdered A.D. 41.　　^e 13 Oct. A.D. 54.

LXXII. Below the heart are situated the lungs, *The lungs.* the breathing apparatus, drawing in and sending back the breath, and consequently spongy in substance and perforated with empty tubes. As has been said, few aquatic species possess lungs, and in the oviparous species they are small and contain froth, not blood; consequently these species do not experience thirst. The same cause makes it possible for frogs and seals to stay long under water. Also the lungs of the tortoise, although very large and spreading under the whole of its shell, are nevertheless devoid of blood. The speed of a creature's movement varies inversely with the size of its lungs. The chamaeleon's lungs are extremely large in proportion to its size,[a] and it has no other internal organ.

LXXIII. The liver is on the right hand side; it *The liver in* contains what is called the head of the internal *divination.* organs, which varies a great deal. Marcus Marcellus, near the time of his death,[b] when he was killed by Hannibal, found the liver missing among the organs, but on the following day a double liver was discovered. The liver was also missing with Gaius Marius when he offered sacrifice [c] at Utica, and also with the Emperor Gaius [d] on January 1 at the commencement of his consulship in the year of his murder, and with his successor Claudius in the month in which he was poisoned.[e] When the late lamented Augustus was sacrificing at Spoleto on the first day he was in power the livers of six victims were found with the bottom of their tissue folded back inward, and this was interpreted to mean that he would double his power within a year. It is also of gloomy omen when the head of the liver is accidentally cut— except at a period of trouble and alarm, when it

metu; tunc enim perimit curas. bina iocinera
leporibus circa Briletum et Tharnem et in Cherroneso
ad Propontidem, mirumque, tralatis alio interit
alterum.

191   LXXIV. In eodem est fel, non omnibus datum
animalibus. in Euboeae Chalcide nullum pecori, in
Naxo praegrande geminumque, ut sit [1] prodigii loco
utrumque advenae. equi, muli, asini, cervi, capreae,
apri, cameli, delphini non habent; murium aliqui
habent. hominum paucis non est, quorum valitudo
192 firmior et vita longior. sunt qui equo non quidem
in iecore esse sed in alvo putent et cervo in cauda aut
intestinis, ideo tantam amaritudinem ut a canibus non
attingantur. est autem nihil aliud quam purga-
mentum, pessimumque sanguinis ideo et [2] in materia
eius. certe iecur nulli est nisi sanguinem habentibus.
accipit hoc a corde cui iungitur, funditque in venas.

193   LXXV. Sed in felle nigro insaniae causa homini,
morsque toto reddito. hinc et in mores crimen
bilis nomine: adeo magnum est in hac parte
virus cum se fundit in animum. quin et toto vagum
corpore colorem oculis quoque aufert, illud [3] quidem
redditum etiam aenis, nigrescuntque contacta eo,
ne quis miretur id venenum esse serpentium.

---

[1] sit add. *Mayhoff.*   [2] *Mayhoff* : et ideo.
[3] illum ? *Mayhoff.*

---

[a] *I.e.* any visitor to either place who has occasion to offer
a sacrifice there.

[b] *I.e.* into which the fluid is passed.

removes anxieties. Hares with two livers are found in the district of Briletum and Tharnes and in the Chersonese on the Sea of Marmara, and surprising to say, when the animals are moved to another place one of the two livers disappears.

LXXIV. The liver also contains the gall-bladder, *The gall-bladder.* but not all animals possess one. At Chalcis in Euboea the cattle have none, while at Naxos they have a very large double one, so that both facts seem portentous to a stranger.[a] Horses, mules, asses, stags, wild goats, boars, camels and dolphins have not got one; some mice have. Among human beings few lack one; those who do are exceptionally strong in health and long-lived. Some think that the horse has a gall-bladder not indeed in the liver but in the belly, and that the stag has one in the tail or in the bowels, and that consequently they have such a bitter flavour that dogs will not touch them. But as a matter of fact it is only excrement, and because of this the substance of this part also contains the worst portion of the blood. Unquestionably only sanguineous animals possess a liver. The liver receives the blood from the heart with which it is connected, and passes it into the veins.

LXXV. But with a human being black gall contains *Psycho-logical effect of gall.* the cause of insanity, and when it is all excreted death follows. Hence the reproach made against a man's character under the term 'bile': so powerful a poison is contained in this part when it spreads to the mind. Moreover when it is diffused all over the body it takes away the colour even of the eyes, and indeed, when excreted, even from bronze vessels,[b] which turn black when touched by it—so that nobody need be surprised that snakes' gall is poison.

194 carent eo quae apsinthio vescuntur in Ponto. sed
renibus et parte tantum[1] altera intestino iungitur
in corvis, coturnicibus, phasianis, quibusdam intestino
tantum, ut in columbis, accipitre, murenis; paucis
avium in iecore. serpentibus portione maxime
195 copiosum et piscibus. avibus[2] autem est toto plerisque intestino, sicut accipitri, milvo; praeterea et in
iecore est, ut cetis omnibus.[3] vitulis quidem marinis
ad multa quoque nobile. taurorum felle aureus
ducitur color; haruspices id Neptuno et umoris
potentiae dicavere, geminumque fuit divo Augusto
quo die apud Actium vicit.

196   LXXVI. Murium iocusculis fibrae ad numerum
lunae in mense congruere dicuntur, totidemque
inveniri quotum lumen eius sit; praeterea bruma
increscere. cuniculorum exta in Baetica gemina
saepe reperiuntur. ranarum rubetarum altera fibra
a formicis non attingitur propter venenum, ut
arbitrantur. iecur maxime vetustatis patiens centenis durare annis obsidionum exempla[4] prodidere.

197   LXXVII. Exta serpentibus et lacertis longa.
Caecinae Volaterrano dracones emicuisse de extis
laeto prodigio traditur; et profecto nihil incredibile

---

[1] tamen *Mayhoff.*
[2] avibus *add. Sillig.*
[3] *sic edd.* : praeterea et in pectore est et ceteris avibus.
[4] *nomina auctorum in his latere videntur: Mayhoff.*

---

[a] Defeat of Antony, 31 B.C.
[b] Probably the Latin is corrupt and conceals the names of
authorities for the statement.

(Animals in the Pontus that eat wormwood are free from bile.) Again the gall-bladder is connected with the kidneys and only on one side with the intestine in ravens, quails and pheasants, and in some only with the intestine, as in pigeons, the hawk, lampreys; and with a few birds it is in the liver. With snakes it is proportionally extremely copious, and so with fishes. But with birds it usually fills the whole intestine, as with the hawk and kite; moreover it is also in the liver, as in the case of all the large marine animals. Indeed in the case of seals it is in high repute for many purposes as well. From bulls' gall a golden colour is extracted. The augurs have consecrated the gall to Neptune and the power of the watery element, and the late lamented Augustus found a double gall-bladder on the day on which he won the battle of Actium.[a]

LXXVI. It is said that the filaments in the tiny *The liver.* livers of mice correspond with the number of the days of the moon in the month, and are found to correspond with its degree of light; and also that they grow larger with winter. Rabbits are often found in Southern Spain with a double set of internal organs. One of the two filaments of toads ants do not touch, because of their poison, as is believed. The liver is extremely capable of enduring age, and has been proved by instances of sieges [b] to last a hundred years.

LXXVII. Snakes and lizards have long internal *Other internal organs;* organs. There is a record that when a person at Volterra named Caecina was performing a sacrifice, *psycho-physiology.* some snakes darted out from the internal organs of the victim—a joyful portent; and indeed it would seem nothing incredible to those considering that on

sit aestimantibus Pyrrho regi quo die periit praecisa
hostiarum capita repsisse sanguinem suum lambentia.
exta homini ab inferiore viscerum parte separantur
membrana, quam praecordia appellant quia cordi
praetenditur: quod Graeci appellaverunt φρένας.
198 omnia quidem principalia viscera membranis propriis
ac velut vaginis inclusit providens natura; in hac
fuit et peculiaris causa vicinitas alvi, ne cibo suppri-
meretur animus. huic certe refertur accepta subtilitas mentis; ideo nulla est ei caro, sed nervosa
exilitas. in eadem praecipua hilaritatis sedes, quod
titillatu maxime intellegitur alarum ad quas subit,
non aliubi tenuiore humana cute ideoque scabendi
dulcedine ibi proxima. ob hoc in praeliis gladiator-
umque spectaculis mortem cum risu traiecta praecordia attulerunt.

199   LXXVIII. Subest venter stomachum habentibus,
ceteris simplex, ruminantibus geminus, sanguine
carentibus nullus; intestinum enim ab ore incipiens
quibusdam eodem reflectitur, ut saepiae et polypo.
in homine adnexus infimo stomacho similis canino.
his solis animalium inferiore parte angustior, itaque
et sola vomunt, quia repleto propter angustias
supprimitur cibus, quod accidere non potest iis

---

^a 272 B.O.   ^b The octopus.

a 272 B.O.   b The octopus.

the day on which King Pyrrhus died[a] the heads of his victims when cut off crawled about licking up their own blood. In man the chief internal organs are separated from the lower part of the viscera by a membrane which is called the *praecordia* (diaphragm), because it is stretched *prae* (in front of) the *cor* (heart): the Greek word for it is *phrenes*. Indeed provident Nature has enclosed all the principal internal organs with special membranes serving as sheaths; but in the case of this membrane a special cause also was the proximity of the bowels, to prevent the food from pressing down on the vital principle. To this membrane unquestionably is due the subtilty of the intellect; it consequently has no flesh, but is of a spare sinewy substance. In it also is the chief seat of merriment, a fact that is gathered chiefly from tickling the arm-pits to which it rises, as nowhere else is the human skin thinner, and consequently the pleasure of scratching is closest there. On this account there have been cases in battle and in gladiatorial shows of death caused by piercing the diaphragm that has been accompanied by laughter.

LXXVIII. In creatures possessing a stomach the abdomen is below it; it is single in the other species but double in the ruminants. Species without blood have no stomach, because in some, for instance the cuttle-fish and the polyp,[b] the intestine beginning at the mouth bends back to the same point. In man the abdomen is connected with the bottom of the stomach, like the dog's. These are the only animals in which it is narrower at the lower part, and consequently they are the only ones that vomit, because when the abdomen is full this narrowness prevents the food from passing, which cannot happen to those

The stomach and abdomen.

quorum spatiosa laxitas eum in inferiora trans-
mittit.

200 LXXIX. Ab hoc ventriculo lactes in ove et homine
per quas labitur cibus, in ceteris hillae a quibus
capaciora intestina ad alvum, hominique flexuosissimis
orbibus. idcirco magis avidi ciborum quibus ab alvo
longius spatium; item minus sollertes quibus obesis-
simus venter. aves quoque geminos sinus habent
quaedam, unum quo merguntur recentia ad [1] guttur,
alterum in quem ex eo dimittunt concoctione ma-
turata, ut gallinae, palumbes, columbae, perdices.
201 ceterae fere carent eo, sed gula patentiore utuntur,
ut graculi, corvi, cornices. quaedam neutro modo,
sed ventrem proximum habent, quibus praelonga colla
et angusta, ut porphyrioni. venter solidipedum
asper et durus. terrestrium aliis denticulatae asperitatis, aliis cancellatim mordacis. quibus neque
dentes utrimque nec ruminatio, hic conficiuntur
202 cibi, hinc in alvum delabuntur. media haec umbilico
adnexa in [2] omnibus, in homine suillae infima parte
similis, a Graecis appellatur colon, ubi dolorum magna
causa. angustissima canibus, qua de causa vehementi
nisu nec sine cruciatu levant eam. insatiabilia
animalium quibus a ventre protinus recto intestino

---

[1] *Detlefsen* : ut *vel* aut.   [2] in *add. Gelen.*

in which the roomy laxity of the abdomen passes
the food on to the lower parts.

LXXIX. From this abdomen start in the sheep *The intes-*
and in man the smaller intestines through which the *tines. The physiology*
food passes, and in the other species the entrails, *of digestion.*
from which the roomier intestines pass to the belly,
and in the case of man in extremely winding coils.
On this account species in which the distance from
the belly is longer are greedier for food; moreover
those with a very fat abdomen are less clever.
Birds also in some cases have two receptacles, one
down which food just eaten passes to the throat, the
other into which they pass the food from the throat
when digested—*e.g.* hens, ring-doves, pigeons and
partridges. Almost all the other species in most
cases have not got this, but make use of a more
widely opened gullet, for instance jays, ravens
and crows. Some species treat the food in neither
manner, but have the abdomen very near; these are
species that have specially long and narrow necks,
for instance the sultana-hen. The abdomen of
whole-hoofed animals is rough and hard. In that of
some land animals the roughness is denticulated,
and in that of others it has a latticed bite. Species
that are without teeth in both jaws and that do not
ruminate digest their food here and pass it down
from here into the belly. This in all species is
attached at its middle to the navel; in man at its
lower part it resembles the belly of a pig; the
Greeks call it the colon; it is the seat of a great
cause of pain. In dogs it is extremely narrow, and
for this reason they can only relieve it with a violent
effort and not without severe pain. The most
ravenous animals are those in whom the food passes

transeunt cibi, ut lupis cervariis et inter aves mergis.
203 ventres elephanto quattuor, cetera subus similia,
pulmo quadruplo maior bubulo. avibus venter
carnosus callosusque. in ventre hirundinum pullis
lapilli candido aut rubenti colore, qui chelidonii
vocantur, magicis narrati artibus, reperiuntur. et in
iuvencarum secundo ventre pilae rotunditate nigricans tophus, nullo pondere, singulare, ut putant,
remedium aegre parientibus si tellurem non attigerit.
204   LXXX. Ventriculus atque intestina pingui ac
tenui omento integuntur praeterquam ova gignenti
bus. huic adnectitur lien in sinistra parte adversus
iecori, cum quo locum aliquando permutat, sed
prodigiose. quidam eum putant inesse ova parientibus, item serpentibus admodum exiguum ; ita certe
apparet in testudine et crocodilo et lacertis et ranis.
aegocephalo avi non inesse constat, neque iis quae
205 careant sanguine. peculiare cursus inpedimentum
aliquando in eo, quamobrem minuitur cursorum
laborantibus. et per vulnus etiam exempto vivere
animalia tradunt. sunt qui putent adimi simul risum
homini intemperantiamque eius constare lienis
magnitudine. Asiae regio Scepsis appellatur in qua
minimos esse pecori tradunt, et inde ad lienem
invecta[1] remedia.

---

[1] *Chiffl.*: inventa.

---

[a] Really five.
[b] Really of hair that they have swallowed.

directly from the abdomen right down the gut; this is the case with lynxes, and among birds cormorants. The elephant has four [a] abdomens, but its other parts resemble those of pigs; its lungs are four times as large as those of an ox. Birds have a fleshy and hard abdomen. In the abdomen of swallow chicks there are found white or red coloured pebbles, called swallow-stones; there are accounts of these in the treatises on magic. Also in the second abdomen of heifers is found a round ball [b] of blackish tufa that weighs nothing; this is thought to be a sovereign remedy for difficulty in child-birth if it has never been allowed to touch the ground.

LXXX. The abdomen and bowels except in the *The spleen.* oviparous species are wrapped in a fat thin caul. To this is attached the spleen on the left side opposite the liver, with which it occasionally changes place, but this constitutes a portent. Some think that oviparous species contain a spleen, and also snakes a rather small one; this undoubtedly appears to be so in the case of the tortoise, the crocodile, lizards and frogs. It is certain that the goat's-head bird has not got a spleen, nor have the bloodless species. Sometimes it causes a peculiar impediment in running, owing to which runners who have trouble have an operation to reduce it. Also cases are reported of animals living after it has been removed by an incision. There are some who think that this operation deprives a man of the power of laughing, and that inability to control one's laughter is caused by enlargement of the spleen. It is said that in a district in Asia called Scepsis the cattle have extremely small spleens, and that remedies for the spleen have been imported from there.

206 LXXXI. Renes[1] habent omnia quadripedum quae animal generant, ova parientium testudo sola, quae et alia omnia viscera, sed ut homo bubulis similes velut e multis renibus compositos. at in Brileto et Tharne quaterni renes cervis, contra pinnatis squamosisque nulli. de cetero summis adhaerent lumbis. dexter omnibus elatior et minus pinguis sicciorque; utrique autem pinguitudo e medio exit praeterquam in vitulo marino. animalia in renibus pinguissima, oves quidem letaliter circum eos concreto pingui. aliquando in iis inveniuntur lapilli.

207 LXXXII. Pectus, hoc est ossa, praecordiis et vitalibus natura circumdedit, at ventri, quem necesse erat increscere, ademit; nulli animalium circa ventrem ossa. pectus homini tantum latum, reliquis carinatum, volucribus magis et inter eas aquaticis maxime. costae homini octonae, subus denae, cornigeris XIII, serpentibus XXX.

208 LXXXIII. Infra alvum est a priore parte vesica, quae nulli ova gignentium praeter testudinem, nulli nisi sanguineum pulmonem habenti, nulli pedibus carentium. inter eam et alvom arteriae ad pubem tendentes quae ilia appellantur. in vesica lupi lapillus qui syrites vocatur; sed in hominum quibusdam diro cruciatu subinde nascentes calculi et saetarum capillamenta. vesica membrana constat quae volnerata cicatrice non solidescit, nec qua

[1] Renes . . . compositos *hic*? *Mayhoff*: *infra post* lapilli.

---

[a] This sentence belongs here, but in the MSS. it comes at the end of the section.

[b] This is not the case.

LXXXI. All viviparous quadrupeds [a] have kidneys, *The kidneys.* but among oviparous ones only the tortoise, which has all the other internal organs also, but, as with man, its kidneys resemble those of the ox, and look like a cluster of several kidneys. But at Briletum and Tharne stags have four kidneys while the species possessing feathers and scales have none.[b] For the rest, they are attached to the top of the loins. In all cases the right kidney is higher, and not so fat, and drier; but with both the fat is discharged out of the middle, except in the seal. Animals accumulate fat most in the kidneys, sheep indeed with fatal results, because the fat solidifies round them. Occasionally stones are found in the kidneys.

LXXXII. Nature has surrounded the heart and *The ribs.* the vital parts with the chest, a bony structure, but has made it stop at the abdomen which had to be allowed room to increase in size; no animal has bones round the abdomen. Man alone has a broad chest; with all the other animals it is keel-shaped, more so with birds, and among them most of all with the aquatic species. Man has eight ribs, pigs ten, horned animals thirteen and serpents thirty.

LXXXIII. Below the belly in front is the bladder, *The bladder.* which occurs in none of the oviparous kinds except the tortoise, in none devoid of lungs filled with blood, and in none without feet. Between the bladder and the belly are the tubes called the groin, stretching to the private parts. The bladder of the wolf contains a stone named syrites; but in some human beings there continually form terribly painful stones and bristly fibres. The bladder consists of a membrane that when wounded does not form a solid scar; it is not the same as the one that enfolds the

cerebrum aut cor involvitur, plura enim membra-
narum genera.

209   LXXXIV. Feminis eadem omnia praeterque vesicae iunctus utriculus, unde dictus uterus; quod alio
nomine locos appellant, hoc in reliquis animalibus
volvam. haec viperae et intra se parientibus
duplex, ova generantium adnexa praecordiis; et in
muliere geminos sinus ab utraque parte laterum habet,
210 funebris quotiens versa spiritum inclusit. boves
gravidas negant praeterquam dextero vulvae sinu
ferre, etiam cum geminos ferant. vulva eiecto
partu melior quam edito; eiecticia vocatur illa, haec
porcaria. primiparae suis optima, contra effetis. a
partu, praeterquam eodem die suis occisae, livida
211 ac macra; nec novellarum suum praeter primiparas
probatur, potiusque veterum, dum ne effetarum, nec
biduo ante partum aut post partum aut quo eiecerint
die. proxima ab eiecticia est occisae uno die post
partum; huius et sumen optimum, si modo fetus
non hauserit; eiecticiae deterrimum. antiqui abdomen vocabant priusquam calleret, incientes
occidere non adsueti.

212   LXXXV. Cornigera una parte dentata et quae in

brain or the heart, as there are several kinds of membrane.

LXXXIV. Women have all the same organs, and in addition, joined to the bladder, a small sac, called from its shape the uterus or womb; another name for it is 'the parts,' and in the rest of the animals it is called the matrix. This in the viper and the viviparous species is double; in the oviparous ones it is attached to the diaphragm; and in women it has two recesses on either side of the flanks, and it causes death whenever it is displaced and interferes with the breathing. It is said that cows when pregnant only carry in the right cavity of the womb, even when carrying twins. Sow's paunch is a better dish after a miscarriage than after a successful delivery; in the former case it is called 'miscarryings' and in the latter 'farrowings.' That of a sow farrowing for the first time is best, and the contrary with those exhausted with breeding. After farrowing the paunch is a bad colour and lacking in fat, unless the sow was killed the same day; nor is that of young sows thought much of, except from those farrowing for the first time, and the paunch of old sows is preferable provided they are not quite worn out, and not killed on the actual day of farrowing or the day before or the day after. The paunch next best to miscarryings is that of a sow slaughtered the day after farrowing; also its paps are the best, provided it has not yet suckled the litter; the paps of a sow that has had a miscarriage are the worst. In old days people called it sow's abdomen before it got hard, as they used not to slaughter sows when they were with young.

LXXXV. Horned animals with teeth in one jaw

The female organs.

Varieties of fat.

pedibus talos habent sebo pinguescunt, bisulca scissisve in digitos pedibus et non cornigera adipe. concretus hic et, cum refrixit, fragilis, semperque in fine carnis, contra pingue inter carnem cutemque suco liquidum. quaedam non pinguescunt, ut lepus, perdix. steriliora cuncta pinguia et in maribus et in feminis; senescunt quoque celerius praepinguia.

213 omnibus animalibus est quoddam in oculis pingue. adips cunctis sine sensu, quia nec arterias habet nec venas; plerisque animalium et pinguitudo sine sensu, quam ob causam sues spirantes a muribus tradunt adrosos. quin et L. Aproni consularis viri filio detractos adipes levatumque corpus inmobili onere.

214   LXXXVI. Et medulla ex eodem videtur esse, in iuventa rubens et in senecta albescens. non nisi cavis haec ossibus, nec cruribus iumentorum aut canum, quare fracta non ferruminantur, quod defluente evenit medulla. est autem pinguis his quibus adips, sebosa cornigeris, nervosa et in spina tantum dorsi ossa non habentibus, ut piscium generi, ursis nulla, leoni in feminum et bracchiorum ossibus paucis exigua admodum, cetera sunt tanta duritia ut ignis

215 elidatur velut e silice. LXXXVII. Et iis dura quae

and those that have pastern-bones in the feet put
on fat in the form of suet, but in those with cloven
hooves or feet divided into toes, and without horns,
it forms grease. This is of a solid substance and
when it has cooled off can be broken up, and it is
always where the flesh ends; whereas fat is between
the flesh and the skin, and is moist and fluid. Some
animals, for instance the hare and the partridge, do
not grow fat. All fat animals are more liable to
barrenness, in the case of both males and females;
also excessively fat ones get old more quickly. All
animals have some fat in the eyes. In all cases the
greasy fat has no sensation, because it does not possess
arteries or veins; and in most animals also fatness of
condition causes insensitiveness, and it is recorded
that because of this pigs have been gnawed by mice
while still alive. It is also on record that the son of
the consular Lucius Apronius had his fat removed
by an operation and relieved his body of unmanageable weight.

LXXXVI. Marrow also appears to consist of the *Marrow.*
same substance, being of a red colour in youth and
turning white in old age. It is only found in hollow
bones, and there is none in the legs of oxen or dogs,
in consequence of which when they are fractured the
bone does not join again, this being caused by the
flow of marrow from a fracture. But the marrow
is fat in the animals that contain lard, suety in those
with horns, sinewy and only present in the spine
in those without bones, like the fish kind; and bears
have none, and the lion a rather small amount
in a few of the bones of the thighs, and forelegs,
while the other bones are so hard that fire can be
struck from them as from a flint. LXXXVII. Also *The bones.*

non pinguescunt; asinorum ad tibias canora. delphinis ossa, non spinae, animal enim pariunt, serpentibus spinae. aquatilium mollibus nulla, sed corpus circulis carnis vinctum, ut sepiae atque loligini. et insectis negatur aeque esse ulla. cartilaginea aquatilium habent medullam in spina, vituli 216 marini cartilaginem, non ossa. Item omnium auriculae ac nares quae modo eminent flexili mollitia, naturae providentia ne frangerentur. cartilago rupta non solidescit, nec praecisa ossa recrescunt praeterquam veterinis ab ungula ad suffraginem. homo crescit [1] in longitudinem usque ad ter septenos annos, tum deinde ad plenitudinem; maxime autem pubescens nodum quendam solvere, et praecipue aegritudine, sentitur.

217 LXXXVIII. Nervi orsi a corde, bubuloque etiam circumvoluti, similem naturam et causam habent, in omnibus lubricis applicati ossibus, nodosque corporum qui vocantur articuli aliubi interventu, aliubi ambitu, aliubi transitu ligantes, hic teretes, illic 218 lati ut in unoquoque poscit figuratio. nec hi solidantur incisi, mirumque vulneratis summus dolor, praesectis nullus. sine nervis sunt quaedam animalia ut pisces, arteriis enim constant; sed neque his

---

[1] crescit *add. edd.* (⟨celeriter crescunt cetera animalia⟩, homo? *Mayhoff*).

---

[a] *I.e.* molluscs, shell-fish.

the animals that do not get fat have hard bones; those of asses are resonant enough to use as flutes. Dolphins being viviparous have bones and not spines, but snakes have spines. Soft aquatic species have no bones, but rings of flesh bound round the body, for instance the two kinds of cuttle-fish. Insects also are said to be equally devoid of bones. The gristly aquatic species have marrow in the spine, and seals have gristle, not bones. Similarly with all that have ears and nostrils that just project these are soft and flexible, nature thus insuring them against fracture. When gristle is burst it does not join up, and when bones are amputated they do not grow again, except the bone between the hoof and the hock in beasts of burden. Human beings grow taller to the age of twenty-one and from then onward fill out; but more particularly at the period of puberty they are noticed to get free from a sort of impediment to their growth, and especially so in sickness.

LXXXVIII. The sinews starting from the heart, *The sinews.* and in the ox actually wrapped round the heart, have a similar nature and explanation, being in all animals attached to the slippery bones and binding together the links of the bodily frame called joints, in some cases by coming between them, in others by surrounding them and in others by passing from one to another, being at one point rounded and at another flattened as the conformation of the joint requires in each case. The sinews also do not join again if cut, and, what is surprising, though extremely painful if wounded cause no pain at all if cut through. Some animals, for instance fishes, have no sinews, as they are held together by their arteries; although the soft species [a] of the fish genus lack arteries as well.

molles piscium generis. ubi sunt nervi, interiores
conducunt membra, superiores revocant.

219 LXXXIX. Inter hos latent arteriae, id est spiritus
semitae; his innatant venae, id est sanguinis rivi.
arteriarum pulsus in cacumine maxime membrorum
evidens index fere morborum, in modulos certos
legesque metricas per aetates—stabilis aut citatus
aut tardus—discriptus ab Herophilo medicinae vate
miranda arte; nimiam propter suptilitatem desertus,
observatione tamen crebri aut languidi ictus guber-
220 nacula vitae temperat.[1] arteriae carent sensu, nam
et sanguine, nec omnes vitalem continent spiritum;
praecisisque torpescit tantum pars ea corporis. aves
nec venas nec arterias habent, item serpentes, testudines, lacertae, minimumque sanguinis.

Venae in praetenues postremo fimbrias supter
totam cutem dispersae adeo in angustam suptilitatem
tenuantur ut penetrare sanguis non possit aliudve
quam excitus[2] umor ab illo cacuminibus innumeris
qui[3] sudor appellatur. venarum in umbilico nodus
ac coitus.

221 XC. Sanguis quibus multus et pinguis iracundi.
maribus quam feminis nigrior et iuventae quam
senio; et inferiore parte pinguior. magna et in eo

---

[1] *v.l.* temperant: temperavit (*sc.* Herophilus)? *Rackham.*
[2] *Mayhoff*: exitus *aut* exilis.
[3] qui *ante* cacuminibus *codd.*: exilis umor ab . . . illo cac
innum. ⟨stillans⟩ qui, *et alia edd. vet.*

---

[a] Or possibly 'He . . . his . . . he supplied'.

Where there are sinews, the inner ones contract the limbs and the ones on the surface reverse the movement.

LXXXIX. Between the sinews lie the arteries, *The arteries and veins.* which are the passages for the breath, and on these float the veins, which are the channels for the blood. The pulse of the arteries being particularly evident at the extremity of the limbs is usually a sign of diseases; with remarkable scientific skill it has been reduced by that high priest of medicine, Herophilus, to definite rhythms and metrical rules throughout the periods of life—steady or hurried or slow. This sign[a] has been neglected because of its excessive subtlety, but yet really it[a] supplies[a] a rule for the guidance of life by observation of the pulse-beat, rapid or languid. The arteries have no sensation, for they even are without blood, nor do they all contain the breath of life; and when they are cut only the part of the body concerned is paralysed. Birds have not got either veins or arteries, nor yet have snakes, tortoises and lizards, and they have only a very small amount of blood.

The veins spread underneath the whole skin, finally ending in very thin threads, and they narrow down into such an extremely minute size that the blood cannot pass through them nor can anything else but the moisture passing out from the blood in innumerable small drops which is called sweat. The junction and meeting point of the veins is at the navel.

XC. Creatures whose blood is copious and thick *The blood.* are hot-tempered. The blood of males is darker than that of females, and that of youth than that of old age; and it is thicker in the lower part of the body. The blood also contains a large proportion of vitality,

vitalitatis portio, emissus spiritum secum trahit;
tactum tamen non sentit. animalium fortiora
quibus crassior sanguis, sapientiora quibus tenuior,
222 timidiora quibus minimus aut nullus. taurorum
celerrime coit atque durescit—ideo pestifer potu—,
proxime[1] aprorum, at[2] cervorum caprearumque et
bubalorum omnino[3] non spissatur. pinguissimus
asinis, homini tenuissimus. iis quibus plus quaterni
pedes nullus. obesis minus copiosus, quoniam
223 absumitur pingui. profluvium eius uni fit in maribus
homini, aliis nare alterutra, aliis utraque, quibusdam
per inferna, multis per ora, stato tempore, ut nuper
Marcrino Visco praetorio viro et omnibus annis
Volusio Saturnino urbis praefecto, qui nonagen-
simum etiam excessit annum. solum hoc in corpore
temporarium sentit incrementum, siquidem hostiae
abundantiorem fundunt si prius bibere.
224 XCI. Quae animalium latere certis temporibus
diximus non habent tunc sanguinem praeter exiguas
admodum circa corda guttas, miro opere naturae,
sicut in homine vim eius ad minima momenta mutari,
non somno[4] tantum minore materia suffusi verum
ad singulos animi habitus, pudore, ira, metu, palloris
pluribus modis, item ruboris: alius enim irae est[5]
225 alius verecundiae. nam in metu refugere et nus-

---

[1] *v.l.* maxime.   [2] *Mayhoff:* ac.
[3] *Mayhoff:* omnium.   [4] *Mayhoff ex Ar.:* modo.
[5] *Detlefsen:* et *aut om.*

---

^a VIII 122, IX 87.

and when shed it draws the breath with it; but it has no sense of touch. The animals with denser blood are braver, those with thinner blood wiser, and those with very little blood, or none at all, more timid. The blood of bulls coagulates and hardens most quickly (and consequently is noxious to drink); that of boars next quickly, but that of stags and goats and antelopes does not thicken at all. Asses have the thickest blood and man the thinnest. Species with more than four feet have no blood. Fat animals have a smaller supply of blood, because it is used up in the fat. In the human race alone a flux of blood occurs in the males, in some cases at one of the nostrils, in others at both, with some people through the lower organs, with many through the mouth; it may occur at a fixed period, as recently with a man of praetorian rank named Macrinus Viscus, and every year with the City Prefect Volusius Saturninus, who actually lived to be over 90. This alone of the bodily affections experiences an occasional increase, inasmuch as sacrificial victims bleed more copiously if they have previously drunk.

XCI. Those animals which we have specified *a* as *Variations of the blood-supply.* going into hiding at fixed seasons have not any blood at those periods except quite scanty drops in the neighbourhood of the heart, by a marvellous contrivance of nature, just as in man she causes the blood-supply to alter at the smallest impulses, the blood not only being suffused with less matter by sleep but at each separate state of mind, by shame, anger, and fear, there being various ways of turning pale, and also of blushing—as the blush of anger is different from that of modesty. For it is certain that in fear the

quam esse certum est, multisque non profluere transfossis, quod homini tantum evenit. nam quae mutare diximus colorem alienum accipiunt quodam repercussu, homo solus in se mutat. morbi omnes morsque sanguinem absumunt.

226 XCII. Sunt qui suptilitatem animi constare non tenuitate sanguinis putent, sed cute operimentisque corporum magis aut minus bruta esse, ut ostreas et testudines; boum terga, saetas suum obstare tenuitati immeantis spiritus, nec purum liquidumque tramitti; sic et in homine, cum crassior callosiorve excludat cutis—ceu vero non crocodilis et duritia

227 tergoris tribuatur et sollertia. XCIII. hippopotami corio crassitudo talis ut inde tornentur hastae et tamen quaedam ingenio medica diligentia. elephantorum quoque tergora inpenetrabiles cetras praebent [1] (cum tamen omnium quadripedum suptilitas animi praecipua perhibetur [2] illis); ergo cutis ipsa sensu caret, maxume in capite. ubicumque per se ac sine carne est volnerata non coit, ut in bucca cilioque.

228 XCIV. Quae animal pariunt pilos habent, quae ova pinnas aut squamas aut corticem ut testudines aut cutem puram ut serpentes. pinnarum caules omnium cavi; praecisae non crescunt, evulsae renascuntur. membranis volant fragilibus insecta, umentibus

---

[1] *Rackham* : habent.　　　　[2] perhibeatur *edd.*

---

[a] VIII. 122, IX. 87.　　　　[b] See VIII. 96.

blood retreats and is nowhere to be found, and that many creatures do not shed blood when stabbed, which happens only to a human being. For those which we have spoken of [a] as changing their colour really assume the colour of some other object by a sort of reflexion; only man actually changes colour in himself. All diseases and death reduce the amount of blood.

XCII. There are persons who think that subtlety of mind is not due to thinness of the blood, but that animals are more or less brutish owing to their skin and bodily coverings, as for instance molluscs and tortoises; and that the hides of oxen and bristles of pigs obstruct the thinness of the air when being inhaled, and it is not transmitted pure and liquid; so also in man, when his skin being thicker or more callous shuts it out—just as if crocodiles did not possess both a hard hide and cunning. XCIII. The skin of the hippopotamus is so thick that it is used for the points of spears, and yet its mind possesses a certain medical ability.[b] The hides of elephants also supply impenetrable bucklers (though nevertheless they are credited with the most outstanding mental subtlety of all quadrupeds); and consequently their skin itself is devoid of sensation, especially in the head. It does not heal up when wounded in any place where there is only skin and no flesh, as in the cheek and eyelid.

XCIV. Viviparous species have bristles, but oviparous ones have feathers or scales, or shells like tortoises, or bare skin like snakes. Feathers in all cases have hollow stalks; when cut off they do not grow again, but when plucked out others grow in their place. Insects use fragile membranes to fly

Psycho-physiology.

Bristles, feathers and scales.

575

hirundines in mari, siccis inter tecta vespertiliones; horum[1] alae quoque articulos habent.

229 Pili e cute exeunt crassa hirti, feminis tenuiores; quis in iuba largi, in armis leoni, dasypodi et in buccis intus et sub pedibus; quae utraque Trogus et in lepore tradidit, hoc exemplo libidinosiores esse[2] hominum quoque hirtos colligens: villosissimus

230 animalium lepus. pubescit homo solus, quod nisi contigit, sterilis in gignendo est, seu masculus seu femina. pili in homine partim simul partim postea gignuntur; hi castratis non nascuntur, congeniti autem non desinunt; sicut nec feminis magno opere, inventae tamen quaedam defluvio capitis invalidae, ut et lanugine oris, cum menstrui cursus stetere. quibusdam post geniti[3] viris sponte non gignuntur. quadripedibus pilum cadere atque sub-

231 nasci annuum est. viris crescunt maxime in capillo, mox in barba. recisi non ut herbae ac cetera ab incisura augentur, sed ab radice exeunt. crescunt et in quibusdam morbis, maxime phthisi, et in senecta, defunctis quoque corporibus. libidinosis congeniti maturius defluunt, agnati celerius crescunt. quadripedibus senectute crassescunt lanaeque rarescunt. quadripedum dorsa pilosa, ventres glabri.

---

[1] *Rackham*: vespertilio horum *aut* vespertilionum.
[2] esse *add. Rackham.*
[3] *Barb.*: genitis (post genituri sponte *Mayhoff*).

with, flying-fish fly over the sea with damp membranes and bats among houses with dry ones; the wings of bats also have joints.

Shaggy hair grows out of a thick skin, whereas *Hair.* women have finer hair; horses have abundant hair in the mane, lions on the shoulders, rabbits on the cheeks inside and also under the feet, hair in both places being also recorded in the case of the hare by Trogus, who infers from this example that among human beings also the hairy ones are more licentious: the hare is the shaggiest animal there is. Man alone grows hair on the private parts, and if this does not occur is sterile, this applying to both sexes. Human beings have some hair at birth and grow some later; the latter does not grow with men who have been castrated, though the hair they had at birth does not fall off; just as women also do not much lose their hair, although there have been cases of women afflicted with baldness, and also with down on the face, when menstruation has ceased. With some men the hair that comes after birth does not grow readily. Four-footed animals shed their hair and grow it again every year. With men the hair of the head grows fastest and next that of the beard. When the hair is cut it does not grow again from the incision, as plants and all other things do, but continues growing from the root. The hair grows longer in some diseases, especially consumption, and in old age too, and also on the bodies of the dead. Licentious people loose the hair they had at birth earlier and grow fresh hair more quickly. With four-footed animals the hair gets thicker with age and the wool thinner. Four-footed animals have shaggy backs and bare bellies.

Boum coriis glutinum excoquitur, taurorumque praecipuum.

232   XCV. Mammas homo solus e maribus habet, cetera animalia mammarum notas tantum. sed ne feminae quidem in pectore nisi quae possunt partus suos attollere. ova gignentium nulli; nec lac[1] nisi animal parienti. volucrum vespertilioni tantum; fabulosum enim arbitror de strigibus ubera eas infantium labris inmulgere. esse in maledictis iam antiquis strigem convenit, sed quae sit avium constare non arbitror.

233   Asinis a fetu dolent, ideo sexto mense arcent partus, cum equae anno prope toto praebeant. quibus solida ungula nec supra geminos fetus, haec omnia binas habent mammas, nec aliubi quam in feminibus. eodem loci bisulca et cornigera, boves quaternas, oves et caprae binas; quae numeroso fecunda partu et quibus digiti in pedibus, haec plures habent et toto ventre duplici ordine, ut sues, generosae duodenas, volgares binis minus; similiter canes. alia ventre medio quaternas, ut pantherae, alia binas, ut leaenae. elephans tantum sub armis duas, nec in pectore sed iuxta[2] in alis occultas. nulli in
234 feminibus digitos habentium. primis genitis in

----

[1] v.l. hic et infra lact.
[2] an circa (vel iuxta)? Mayhoff: citra.

Boiling oxhide produces glue; bull's hide makes the best.

XCV. Man is the only species in which the male *The lacti-ferous organs.* has teats; with the rest of the animals there are only the marks of teats. But with the females also only those have teats on the breast that are able to lift their offspring up to them. No oviparous species has teats; and only the viviparous have milk. Among flying species only the bat has milk, as I think the story about screech-owls, that they drop milk from their teats into the mouths of babies, is a fabrication. It is an ackowledged fact that even in old days the screech-owl was one of the creatures under a curse, but what particular bird is meant I believe to be uncertain.

With asses the teats are painful after foaling, and consequently they refuse to suckle their foals after five months, whereas mares give suck almost a whole year. Whole-hooved species that never have more than two foals all have two dugs, and these always between the thighs. Animals with cloven feet and horns have the dugs in the same place, cows having four and sheep and goats two. Those that bear large litters and that have toes on the feet have more dugs, and these in a double row the whole length of the belly—for instance swine, of which the good breeds have twelve dugs and the common ones two less; similarly with dogs. Some species have four dugs in the middle of the belly, for instance leopards, others two, for instance lionesses. The elephant has only two dugs beneath the shoulders and not on the breast but close to it, concealed under the shoulder-blades. None of the species with toes have dugs beneath the thighs.

quoque partu sues primas praebent, eae sunt
faucibus proximae, et suam quisque novit in fetu
quo genitus est ordine eaque alitur nec alia. detracto illa alumno suo sterilescit ilico ac resilit, uno
vero ex omni turba relicto sola munifex quae genito
235 fuerat adtributa dependet. ursae mammas quaternas gerunt. delphini binas in ima alvo papillas
tantum, nec evidentes et paulum in oblicum por-
rectas; neque aliud animal in cursu lambitur. et
ballaenae autem vitulique marini [1] mammis nutriunt
fetus.

236 XCVI. Mulieri ante septimum mensem profusum
lac inutile, ab eo mense, quo vitalis est [2] partus,
salubre. plerisque autem totis mammis atque
etiam alarum sinu fluit. cameli lac habent donec
iterum gravescant; suavissimum id existimatur ad
unam mensuram tribus aquae additis. bos ante
partum non habet; et primo semper a partu colostrae
fiunt, ni admisceatur aqua in spumae [3] modum
237 coeunte duritia. asinae praegnates continuo lactes-
cunt. pullos earum, ubi pingue pabulum, biduo a
partu maternum lac gustasse letale est; genus mali
vocatur colostratio. caseus non fit ex utrimque
dentatis, quoniam eorum lac non coit. tenuissimum
camelis, mox equis, crassissimum asinae, ut quo
238 coaguli vice utantur. conferre aliquid et candori

[1] marini *add. Dalec.*   [2] *vulg.* vitales.
[3] *Detlefsen*: in pumicis.

---

[a] The MSS. give 'which harden into a sort of pumice-stone.'

Sows give their first dugs to the pigs born first in each litter, these being the dugs nearest to their throats, and each pig in the litter knows its own dug in the order in which it was born, and gets its food from that one and not at another. If its nurseling is taken away from it the dug at once goes dry and shrivels up, whereas if one out of the whole litter is left the dug that had been assigned to it at birth alone hangs down and does service. She-bears carry four dugs. Dolphins only have two nipples at the bottom of the belly, which are not prominent and project slightly sideways; and the dolphin is the only animal that gives suck while in motion. But whales and seals also suckle their young.

XCVI. A woman's milk produced before the seventh month is of no use, but from that month, when the embryo is alive, it is healthy. With the females of most species milk flows from the whole of the dugs and even from the fold of the shoulder-blades. Camels have milk until they are in foal again; camel's milk is thought to be most agreeable if three parts of water are added to one of milk. A cow does not have milk before calving; and after the first calving there are always biestings, which condense into a sort of foam [a] unless water is mixed with them. Asses in foal begin to give milk at once. Where the pasture is rich it is fatal for their foals to have tasted their mothers' milk in the two days after birth; the name for the illness is biestings-fever. Cheese is not made from species with teeth in both jaws, as their milk does not curdle. Camel's milk is the thinnest and mares' milk the next thin; asses' milk is thickest, so that it is used as a substitute for rennet. Asses' milk is actually thought

Lactation. Uses of milk.

in mulierum cute existimatur; Poppaea certe Domiti
Neronis coniunx quingentas per omnia secum fetas
trahens balnearum etiam solio totum corpus illo
lacte macerabat, extendi quoque cutem credens.
omne autem igne spissatur, frigore serescit.[1] bubu-
lum caseo fertilius quam caprinum, ex eadem mensura
paene altero tanto. quae plures quaternis mammas
habent caseo inutilia, et meliora quae binas.

239 Coagulum hinnulei,[2] leporis, haedi laudatum,
praecipuum tamen dasypodis, quod et profluvio alvi
medetur, unius utrimque dentatorum. mirum bar-
baras gentes quae lacte vivant ignorare aut spernere
tot saeculis casei dotem, densantes id alioqui in
acorem iucundum et pingue butyrum. spuma id
est lactis [3] concretior lentiorque quam quod serum
vocatur; non omittendum in eo olei vim esse et
barbaros omnes infantesque nostros ita ungui.

240 XCVII. Laus caseo Romae, ubi omnium gentium
bona comminus iudicantur, e provinciis Nemausensi
praecipua, e[4] Lesure Gabalicoque pagis; sed brevis ac
musteo tantum commendatio. duobus Alpes generibus pabula sua adprobant: Dalmaticae Docleatem

241 mittunt, Centronicae Vatusicum. numerosior Appennino: Coebanum hic e Liguria mittit, ovium maxime

---

[1] *Hermolaus*: umore fervescit.   [2] *v.l.* inutile.
     [3] *v.l.* lacte.   [4] e *add. Rackham.*

to contribute something to the whiteness in women's skin; at all events Domitius Nero's wife Poppaea used to drag five hundred she-asses with foals about with her everywhere and actually soaked her whole body in a bath-tub with ass's milk, believing that it also smoothed out wrinkles. All milk is made thicker by fire and turned into whey by cold. Cow's milk makes more cheese than goat's milk, almost as much again from the same quantity. Animals with more than four dugs are not serviceable for cheese, and those with two are better.

The curds of the roebuck, hare and goat are praised, but that of the rabbit is the best, and is even a cure for diarrhoea—the rabbit is the only animal with teeth in both jaws that has this property. It is remarkable that the foreign races that live on milk for so many centuries have not known or have despised the blessing of cheese, at most condensing their milk into agreeable sour curds and fat butter. Butter is a foam of milk of thicker and stickier substance than what is called whey; it must be added that it possesses the quality of oil and is used for anointing by all foreigners and by ourselves in the case of children.

XCVII. Of cheese from the provinces the most ^{Cheese} highly praised at Rome, where the good things of all nations are estimated at first hand, is that of the district of Nîmes, coming from the villages of La Lozère and Gévaudan; but it only wins approval for a short time and when fresh. The Alps prove the value of their pastures by two kinds of cheese: the Dalmatian Mountains send the Docleate and the Tarentaise the Vatusic. A larger number belong to the Apennines: these send Coebanum cheese

e [1] lacte, Sarsinatem ex Umbria, mixtoque Etruriae
atque Liguriae confinio Luniensem magnitudine
conspicuum, quippe et ad singula milia pondo premitur; proximum autem urbi Vestinum, eumque e
Caedicio campo laudatissimum. et caprarum gregibus sua laus est, in recenti maxime augente gratiam
fumo, qualis in ipsa urbe conficitur cunctis praefer-
endus. nam Gallicarum [2] sapor medicamenti vim
optinet. trans maria vero Bithynus fere in gloria est.

242 inesse pabulis salem, etiam ubi non videtur, ita
maxime intellegitur, omni in salem caseo senescente,
quales redire in museteum saporem aceto et thymo
maceratos certum est. tradunt Zoroastren in
desertis caseo vixisse annis xx ita temperato ut
vetustatem non sentiret.

243 XCVIII. Terrestrium solus homo bipes; uni
iugulum, umeri (ceteris armi), uni ulnae. quibus
animalium manus sunt, intus tantum carnosae, extra
nervis et cute constant.

244 XCIX. Digiti quibusdam in manibus seni. M.
Coranii ex patricia gente filias duas ob id Sedigitas
accipimus appellatas, et Volcatium Sedigitum inlus-
trem in poetica. hominis digiti ternos articulos
habent, pollex binos, et digitis adversus universis
flectitur, per se vero in oblicum porrigitur, crassior

---

[1] *add. Jan.*   [2] *Rackham* : Galliarum.

from Liguria, chiefly made of sheep's milk, Sarsina cheese from Umbria, and Luni cheese from the borderland of Tuscany and Liguria—this cheese is remarkable for its size, in fact it is actually made up to the weight of 1000 pounds the cheese; but nearest to Rome is the Vestinian, and the kind from the Caedician Plain is the most approved. Herds of goats also have their special reputation for cheese, in the case of fresh cheese especially when smoke increases its flavour, as with the supremely desirable cheese made in the city itself; for the cheese of the Gallic goats always has a strong medicinal taste. But of cheeses from over seas the Bithynian is quite famous. That pastures contain salt, even where it is not visible, is chiefly detected from the fact that all cheese as it gets old turns saltish, just as cheeses steeped in vinegar and thyme undoubtedly return to their original fresh flavour. It is recorded that Zoroaster in the desert lived for twenty years on cheese that had been so treated as not to be affected by age.

XCVIII. Man is the only land two-footed animal, *Peculiarities* and the only one that has a throat, shoulders instead *of structure* of forequarters like the others, and elbows. In *in man.* animals possessing hands, the hands only have flesh inside, the outside consisting of sinews and skin.

XCIX. Some people have six fingers on each *The fingers* hand. It has come down to us that the two daughters *and toes.* of a man of patrician family named Marcus Coranius were called the Miss Six-Fingers on this account, and that Volcatius Sedigitus was distinguished in poetry. The human fingers have three joints and the thumb two, and it bends in the opposite direction to all the fingers, stretching out by itself on a slant,

ceteris. huic minimus mensura par, ac duo reliqui sibi, inter quos medius longissime protenditur. quibus ex rapina victus quadripedum quini digiti in 245 prioribus pedibus, in reliquis quaterni. leones, lupi, canes, panthera[1] in posterioribus quoque quinos unguis habent, uno iuxta cruris articulum dependente; reliqua, quae sunt minora, et digitos quinos.

Bracchia non omnibus paria secum; Studioso Threci in C. Caesaris ludo notum est dexteram fuisse proceriorem.

Animalium quaedam ut manibus utuntur priorum ministerio pedum sedentque ad os illis admoventia 246 cibos, ut sciuri. C. Nam simiarum genera perfectam hominis imitationem continent facie, naribus, auribus, palpebris, quas solae quadripedum et in inferiore habent gena, iam mammas in pectore et bracchia et crura in contrarium similiter flexa, in manibus ungues, digitos longioremque medium. pedibus paulum differunt; sunt enim ut manus praelongae, sed vestigium palmae simile faciunt. pollex quoque iis et articuli ut homini; ac praeter genitale, et hoc in maribus tantum, viscera etiam interiora omnia ad exemplar.

247 CI. Ungues clausulae nervorum summae existimantur. omnibus hi quibus et digiti, sed simiae imbricati, hominibus lati, (et defuncto crescunt),

---

[1] *Mayhoff ex Aristotele*: canes et pauca.

and it is thicker than the others. The thumb is equal to the smallest finger in length, and two of the rest are equal to one another, between them the middle finger extending longest. The four-footed animals that live by plunder have five toes on the front feet and four on the others. Lions, wolves, dogs and the leopard have five claws on the hind feet as well, with the one next the joint of the leg hanging down; the other species, which are smaller, have five toes also.

Not all people's arms are a pair; it is known that a Thracian gladiator named Studiosus in Gaius Caesar's training-school had his right arm longer than his left.

Some animals use the service of their front feet as hands, and sit moving their food to their mouth with them, for instance squirrels. C. In fact the monkey tribes have a perfect imitation of a human being in their face, nostrils, ears and eyelashes—they are the only four-footed animals with eyelashes—on the lower lid as well, also paps on the breast, and arms and legs bending similarly in opposite directions, and nails on their hands, and fingers, and a longer middle finger. They differ a little from human beings in their feet, for these are very long like their hands, but make a foot-print like the palm of a hand. They also have a thumb and knuckles like a human being; and besides a genital organ, and this in the males only, they also have all internal organs to pattern. *Anthropoid apes.*

CI. It is believed that nails are the extremities at the end of sinews. All creatures have nails that also have fingers, but in the monkey they overlap like tiles, whereas in man they are broad (and they continue to grow after a man is dead); and they *Fingernails and toenails.*

587

rapacibus unci, ceteris recti, ut canibus, praeter eum
248 qui a crure plerisque dependet. omnia digitos
habent quae pedes, excepto elephanto; huic enim
informes, numero quidem quinque, sed indivisi ac
leviter discreti, ungulisque, non unguibus, similes,
et pedes maiores priores, in posterioribus articuli
breves, idem poplites intus flectit hominis modo,
cetera animalia in diversum posterioribus pedibus
quam prioribus; nam quae animal generant genua
ante se flectunt et suffraginum artus in aversum.

249 CII. Homini genua et cubita contraria; item ursis
et simiarum generi, ob id minime pernicibus. ova
parientibus quadripedum, crocodilo, lacertis, priora
genua post curvantur, posteriora in priorem partem,
sunt autem crura his obliqua humani pollicis[1] modo;
sic et multipedibus praeterquam novissima salienti-
bus. aves ut quadripedes alas in priora curvant,
suffraginem in posteriora.

250 CIII. Hominis genibus quaedam et religio inest
observatione gentium. haec supplices attingunt, ad
haec manus tendunt, haec ut aras adorant, fortassis
quia inest iis vitalitas. namque in ipsa genus
utriusque commissura, dextra laevaque, a priore
parte gemina quaedam buccarum inanitas inest, qua
perfossa ceu iugulo spiritus fluit. inest et aliis

---

[1] poplitis *Hermolaus.*

are crooked in beasts of prey but straight in the other animals, for instance dogs, excepting the nail that in most species hangs downward from the leg. All animals with feet have toes, except the elephant; for the elephant's toes are unshaped and though five in number yet undivided and only slightly separated, and resembling hooves, not nails, and the fore feet are larger, the joints of the hind feet being short, and also an elephant's knees bend inward like a man's, whereas the other animals bend the knees of the hind legs in the opposite direction to those of the forelegs; for viviparous animals bend their knees in front of them and the joints of the hocks backward.

CII. In man the knees and elbows bend in opposite directions, and the same is the case with bears and the monkey tribe, which are consequently not at all swift. In the oviparous quadrupeds, the crocodile and the lizards, the front knees curve backward and the hind knees forward, but these species have legs that bend like the human thumb; and so also have the multipedes, except the hindermost legs of the species that jump. Birds curve their wings forward like the front legs of quadrupeds but their thigh backward. *Knees and elbows.*

CIII. The knees of a human being also possess a sort of religious sanctity in the usage of the nations. Suppliants touch the knees and stretch out their hands towards them and pray at them as at altars, perhaps because they contain a certain vital principle. For in the actual joint of each knee, right and left, on the front side there is a sort of twin hollow cavity, the piercing of which, as of the throat, causes the breath to flow away. There is a religious sanctity *Psychological associations of parts of the body.*

partibus quaedam religio, sicut in dextera: osculis
251 aversa adpetitur, in fide porrigitur. antiquis Graeciae
in supplicando mentum attingere mos erat. est in
aure ima memoriae locus, quem tangentes antesta-
mur[1]; est post aurem aeque dexteram Nemeseos
(quae dea Latinum nomen ne in Capitolio quidem
invenit), quo referimus tactum ore proximum a
minimo digitum, veniam sermonis a dis ibi recon-
dentes.[2]

252   CIV. Varices in cruribus viro tantum, mulieri raro.
C. Marium qui VII cos. fuit stanti sibi extrahi
passum unum hominum Oppius auctor est.

253   CV. Omnia animalia a dextris partibus incedunt,
sinistris incubant. reliqua ut libitum est gradiuntur, leo tantum et camelus pedatim, hoc est ut
sinister pes non transeat dextrum sed subsequatur.
pedes homini maximi; feminis tenuiores in omni
genere; surae homini tantum et crura carnosa.
reperitur apud auctores quendam in Aegypto non
habuisse suras. vola homini tantum (exceptis
254 quibusdam: namque et hinc cognomina inventa
Planci, Plauti, Pansae, Scauri, sicut a cruribus Vari,
Vatiae, Vatini, quae vitia et in quadripedibus).
solidas habent ungulas quae non sunt cornigera:
igitur pro his telum ungulae ictus est illis. nec

---

[1] *Lipsius*: attestamur.   [2] *v.l.* a dis exposcentes.

belonging to other parts also, for instance in the right hand: kisses are imprinted on the back of it, and it is stretched out in giving a pledge. It was a custom with the Greeks in early days to touch the chin in entreaty. The memory is seated in the lobe of the ear, the place that we touch in calling a person to witness; similarly behind the right ear is the seat of Nemesis (a goddess that even on the Capitol has not found a Latin name), and to it we apply the third finger after touching our mouths, the mouth being the place where we locate pardon from the gods for our utterances.

CIV. Varicose veins in the legs occur only in a *Varicosity.* man but rarely in a woman. Oppius records that Gaius Marius who was seven times consul was the only man who underwent an operation for the removal of varicose veins without lying down.

CV. All animals start walking with the right *Modes of walking.* foot and lie down on the left side. Whereas the *Structure of feet and legs.* other animals walk as they like, only the lion and the camel pace with one foot after the other, that is with the left foot not passing but following the right foot. Human beings have the largest feet; the females of all species have more slender feet; man alone has calves and legs that are fleshy. We find it stated in the authorities that a certain person in Egypt had no calves. Man alone has an arched sole to the foot (with some exceptions—a deformity that is the origin of the surnames Flatfoot, Broadfoot, Splayfoot, Swellfoot, just as from the legs come the names Knock-knee, Bowleg, Bandyleg, deformities that also occur in animals). Some animals without horns have solid hooves: consequently in place of horns a kick of the hoof is their weapon. And the

talos habent eadem, at quae bisulca sunt habent.
iidem digitos habentibus non sunt, neque in prioribus
omnino pedibus ulli. camelo tali similes bubulis
sed minores paulo; est enim bisulcus discrimine
exiguo pes, in vestigio carnosus ut ursi, qua de
causa in longiore itinere sine calciatu fatiscunt.

255 CVI. Ungulae veterino tantum generi renascuntur.
sues in Illyrico quibusdam locis solidas habent
ungulas. cornigera fere bisulca. solida ungula et
bicorne nullum, unicorne asinus tantum Indicus,
unicorne et bisulcum oryx. talos asinus Indicus unus
solidipedum habet, nam sues ex utroque genere
existimantur, ideo foedi earum. hominem qui
existimarunt habere facile convicti. lynx tantum
digitos habentium simile quiddam talo habet, leo
etiamnum tortuosius. talus autem rectus est in
articulo pedis, ventre eminens concavo,[1] in vertebra
ligatus.

256 CVII. Avium aliae digitatae, aliae palmipedes,
aliae inter utrumque divisis digitis adiecta latitudine;
sed omnibus quaterni digiti, tres in priore parte,
unus a calce: hic deest quibusdam longa crura
habentibus; iynx sola utrimque binos habet.
eadem linguam serpentium similem in magnam
longitudinem porrigit, collum circumagit in aversam

---

[1] concava *cum seqq. iunctum edd.*

same animals have no pastern-bone, but those with cloven hooves have one. Pastern-bones are also lacking in animals having toes, and no animal has them in the forefeet. The camel's pastern-bones resemble those of the ox but are a little smaller; for the camel's foot is divided in two by a very small cleft, and is fleshy at the tread like a bear's, for which reason a camel's feet are liable to split on too long a journey without shoeing.

CVI. Only with animals of the draught kind do the hooves grow again. In some places in Illyria pigs have solid hooves. Horned animals mostly have cloven hooves. No species has both solid hooves and two horns; the only animal with one horn is the rhinoceros, and the only one with one horn and cloven hooves the antelope. The rhinoceros is the only solid-hooved animal that has pastern-bones, for pigs are thought to belong to both classes, and consequently their pastern-bones are mis-shapen. Persons who have thought that a human being has pastern-bones have been easily refuted. Of the animals with toes only the lynx has something resembling a pastern-bone, and the lion a still more twisted one. But the true pastern-bone is at the ankle-joint, projecting with a hollow bulge and attached with a ligature onto the joint.

Hooves and pasterns.

CVII. Some birds have toes, others are web-footed, and others intermediate, with separate toes but also broad feet; but all have four toes, three in front and one at the heel—the latter however absent in some long-legged species; the wry-neck alone has two toes on either side of the foot. The same bird has a tongue like a snake's which it stretches out a long way, and it turns its neck round towards

Birds' feet.

257 se; ungues ei grandes ceu graculis. avium quibusdam gravioribus in cruribus additi radii, nulli uncos habentium ungues. longipedes porrectis ad caudam cruribus volant, quibus breves, contractis ad medium. qui negant volucrem ullam sine pedibus esse confirmant et apodas habere breviores et drepanin, quae[1] rarissime apparet. visae iam et serpentes anserinis pedibus.

258 CVIII. Insectorum pedes primi longiores duros habentibus oculos, ut subinde pedibus eos tergeant, ceu notamus in muscis. quae ex his novissimos habent longos saliunt, ut locustae. omnibus autem his seni pedes. araneis quibusdam praelongi accedunt bini. internodia singulis terna. octonos et marinis esse diximus, polypis, sepiis, lolliginibus, cancris, qui bracchia in contrarium movent, pedes in orbem aut in oblicum; isdem solis animalium

259 rotundi. cetera binos pedes duces habent, cancri tantum quaternos. quae hunc numerum pedum excessere terrestria, ut plerique vermes, non infra duodenos habent, aliqua vero et centenos. numerus pedum impar nulli est.

260 Solidipedum crura statim iusta nascuntur mensura, postea exporrigentia se verius quam crescentia, itaque in infantia scabunt aures posterioribus pedibus, quod addita aetate non queunt, quia longitudo superficiem corporum solam ampliat. hac de causa

---

[1] habere, docent et drepanin, quare ex his *Mueller (codd. corruptissima).*

its back; it has large claws like a jay's. Some of the heavier birds, though none of those with crooked talons, have spurs added on the legs. The long-legged birds fly with their legs extended towards their tail, but the short-legged ones draw them into their middle. Those who say that there is no bird without feet assert that black martins have specially short feet, and also the Alpine swift, a bird that is very rarely seen. Even snakes with the feet of geese have been seen before now.

CVIII. The insects with hard eyes have the front feet longer, so that they may occasionally rub their eyes with their feet, as we observe in house-flies. Insects with long hind feet leap, for instance locusts. But all these have six feet. Some*a* spiders have two very long feet in addition. Each foot has two joints. We have said *b* that some marine species also have eight feet, octopuses, cuttle-fish of both varieties, and crabs, which move their fore-feet in the opposite direction to the others and their hind-feet in a circle or slantwise; they are also the only animals with feet of a rounded shape. All the other species have two guiding feet, only crabs have four. Land species that exceed this number of feet, as most worms, have not less than twelve, and some as many as a hundred. No kind has an odd number of feet.

Insects feet.

In the species with solid feet the legs are of the proper size at birth, afterwards more truly stretching out than growing. Consequently in infancy they scratch their ears with their hind feet, which when older they are unable to do, because length of time increases the size of only the surface of their bodies.

Growth of hooves.

---

a All, as a matter of fact.　　　*b* IX 83

inter initia pasci nisi summissis genibus non possunt,
nec usque dum cervix ad iusta incrementa perveniat.

Pumilionum genus in omnibus animalibus est,
atque etiam inter volucres.

261 CIX. Genitalia maribus quibus essent retrorsa
diximus. ossea sunt lupis, vulpibus, mustelis,
viverris, unde etiam calculo humano remedia praecipua. urso quoque simul atque expiraverit cornescere
aiunt. camelino arcus intendere orientis populis
fidissimum. nec non aliqua gentium quoque in
hoc discrimina et sacrorum etiam, citra perniciem
262 amputantibus Matris Deum Gallis. contra mulierum
paucis prodigiosa adsimilatio, sicut hermaphroditis
utriusque sexus, quod etiam quadripedum generi
accidisse Neronis principatu primum arbitror: osten-
tabat certe hermaphroditas subiunctas carpento suo
equas, in Treverico Galliae agro repertas—ceu plane
visenda res esset principem terrarum insidere
portentis.

263 CX. Testes pecori armentoque ad crura decidui,
subus adnexi. delphino praelongi ultuma conduntur
alvo, et elephanto occulti. ova parientium lumbis
intus adhaerent, qualia ocissima in venere. piscibus
serpentibusque nulli, sed eorum vice binae ad

For this reason at the early stages they can only feed by bending their knees, and this goes on till their neck reaches full growth.

There is a dwarf kind in all species of animals, and even among birds.

CIX. We have already specified[a] the species of which the males have genital organs behind them. These organs are bony in wolves, foxes, weasels and ferrets, which also furnish sovereign remedies for stone in man. In the bear too it is said, these organs become horny as soon as the animal dies. The eastern peoples think that this organ in the camel makes a most reliable bowstring. There are also certain racial distinctions in connexion with it, and even varieties of ritual, the Galli, priests of the Mother of the Gods, practising amputation within the limits of injury. On the other hand in a few women there is a curious resemblance to the male organ, as there is in hermaphrodites of either sex, a thing that I believe first occurred with the class of quadrupeds also in the principate of Nero: at all events Nero used to show off a team of hermaphrodite mares, that he had found in the Trier district in Gaul, harnessed to his chariot, apparently deeming it a very remarkable spectacle to see the Emperor of the World riding in a miraculous carriage.

The genital organs.

CX. The testicles in sheep and oxen hang down against the legs, but in pigs they are closely knit to the body. In the dolphin they are very long, and stowed away in the lower part of the belly, and in the elephant also they are concealed. In oviparous creatures they are attached to the loins on the inside, these animals being very rapid in copulation. Fishes and snakes have no testicles, but instead of them

The testicles.

genitalia a renibus venae. buteonibus terni. homini
tantum iniuria aut sponte naturae franguntur, idque
tertium ab hermaphroditis et spadonibus semiviri
genus habent. mares in omni genere fortiores
sunt praeterquam pantheris et ursis.

264 CXI. Caudae praeter hominem ac simias omnibus
fere et animal et ova gignentibus pro desiderio
corporum, nudae hirtis, ut apris, parvae villosis, ut
ursis, praelongae saetosis, ut equis. amputatae
lacertis et serpentibus renascuntur. piscium meatus
gubernaculi modo regunt, atque etiam in dexteram
ac laevam motae ut remigio quodam impellunt.

265 lacertis inveniuntur et geminae. boum caudis
longissimus caulis atque in ima parte hirtus; idem
asinis longior quam equis, sed saetosus veterinis.
leoni in prima parte ut bubus et soricibus,[1] pantheris
non item; vulpibus et lupis villosus ut ovibus, quibus
procerior. sues intorquent, canum degeneres sub
alvom reflectunt.

266 CXII. Vocem non habere nisi quae pulmonem et
arteriam[2] habeant, hoc est nisi quae spirent, Aristoteles putat; idcirco et insectis sonum esse, non
vocem, intus inmeante spiritu et incluso sonante,
alia murmur edere, ut apes, alia contractum[3] stridorem, ut cicadas, receptum enim duobus sub
pectore cavis spiritum, mobili occursante membrana

---

[1] *Rackham*: sorici.
[2] *Mayhoff*: arterias.
[3] *Mayhoff* (contractu *Detlefsen*): cum tractu.

---

[a] *I.e.* ante-natal disease.
[b] The sounds referred to are really caused by the wings
vibrating.

two passages from the kidneys to the genitals. Buzzards have three. In man only they may be crushed owing to an injury or from natural causes,[a] and this forms a third class, in distinction from hermaphrodites and eunuchs, the impotent. In every species except leopards and bears the mares are the stronger.

CXI. Almost all species except man and monkeys, *The tail.* both the viviparous and the oviparous, have tails corresponding to the requirements of their bodies, bare with the hairy species, like boars, small with the shaggy ones, like bears, very long with the bristly, like horses. With lizards and snakes when cut off they grow again. The tails of fishes steer their winding courses after the manner of a rudder, and even serve to propel them like a sort of oar by being moved to the right and left. Actual cases of two tails are found in lizards. Oxen's tails have a very long stem, with a tuft at the end, and in asses it is longer than in horses, but it is bristly in beasts of burden. A lion's tail is shaggy at the end, as with oxen and shrew-mice, but not so with leopards; foxes and wolves have a hairy tail, as have sheep, with which it is longer. Pigs curl the tail, dogs of low breeds keep it between their legs.

CXII. Aristotle thinks that only animals with *The voice.* lungs and windpipe, that is those that breathe, possess a voice; and that consequently even insects make a sound,[b] but have not a voice, the breath passing inside them and making a sound when shut up there, and that some, as bees, give out a buzz, others, as grasshoppers, a brief hiss, because the breath is received in two hollows under the chest and encountering a movable membrane inside makes

intus, attritu eius sonare. muscas, apes, cetera
similia cum volatu et incipere audiri et desinere,
sonum enim attritu et interiore aura, non anima,
reddi; locustas pinnarum et feminum attritu sonare.
267 creditur sane item aquatilium pectines stridere cum
volant, mollia et crusta intecta nec vocem nec sonum
ullum habere. sed ceteri pisces, quamvis pulmone
et arteria careant, non in totum sine ullo sono sunt—
stridorem eum dentibus fieri cavillantur—et is
qui aper[1] vocatur in Acheloo amne grunnitum habet,
et alii de quibus diximus. ova parientibus sibilus,
serpentibus longus, testudinibus[2] abruptus. ranis
sui generis vox,[3] ut dictum est—nisi si et in his
ferenda dubitatio est, quia vox in ore concipitur,
non in pectore. multum tamen in his refert et
locorum natura: mutae in Macedonia traduntur,
268 muti et apri. avium loquaciores quae minores et
circa coitus maxume. aliis in pugna vox, ut coturnicibus, aliis ante pugnam, ut perdicibus, aliis cum
vicere, ut gallinaceis. iisdem sua maribus, aliis
eadem et feminis, ut lusciniarum generi. quaedam
toto anno canunt, quaedam certis temporibus, ut
269 in singulis dictum est. elephans citra nares ore
ipso sternumento similem elidit sonum, per nares

---

[1] *Rackham ex Ar. Hist. An.* 535 b 18: caper.
[2] *Rackham*: testudini.
[3] vox *add ? Mayhoff.*

---

[a] Perhaps one of the blennies.   [b] IX. 70.
[c] XI. 172.

a sound by rubbing against it. He thinks that flies, bees and other similar creatures begin and cease to give an audible sound when they begin and cease to fly, as the sound is caused by friction and by the air inside them, not by breathing; and that locusts make a sound by rubbing their wings against their thighs. It is indeed believed that among aquatic creatures scallops similarly make a rushing sound when they fly, but that shell-fish and crustaceans have no voice nor sound of any kind. But the other fishes, although they lack lungs and windpipe, are not entirely devoid of any sound at all—people advance the quibble that their hiss is made with the teeth—and the fish in the river Achelous called the boar-fish *a* has a grunt, and so have others about which we have spoken.*b* Oviparous species have a hiss—snakes a long one, tortoises an abrupt one. Frogs have a special kind of voice, as has been said,*c* unless in their case also we are to allow some uncertainty, because ' voice ' means a sound formed in the mouth, not in the chest. Still in the case of frogs the nature of the localities also makes a great deal of difference: the frogs in Macedonia are reported to be dumb, and also the boars. Among birds the smaller ones are more talkative, and particularly at the mating season. Some birds, e.g. quails, give a cry when fighting, others, e.g. partridges, before a fight, others, e.g. domestic fowls, when they have won. With the latter the cocks have a crow of their own, but with other birds, for instance the nightingale class, the hens also have the same note. Some birds sing all the year, some at certain seasons, as has been said in dealing with the species separately. The elephant squeezes out a sound like a sneeze from its actual mouth, not through

autem tubarum raucitati. bubus tantum feminis
vox gravior, in alio omni genere exilior quam mari-
270 bus, in homine etiam castratis. infantis in nas-
cendo nulla auditur ante quam totus emergat utero.
primus sermo anniculo; set semenstris locutus est
Croesi filius et in crepundiis prodigio quo totum id
concidit regnum. qui celerius fari ceopere tardius
ingredi incipiunt. vox roboratur a xiv annis, eadem
in senecta exilior; neque in alio animalium saepius
mutatur.

Mira praeterea sunt de voce digna dictu; theatro-
rum in orchestris scobe aut harena superiacta devora-
tur, item [1] in rudi parietum circumiectu, doliis etiam
inanibus. currit eadem recto vel conchato parietum
spatio, quamvis levi sono dicta verba ad alterum
caput perferens, si nulla inaequalitas impediat.
271 vox in homine magnam voltus habet partem:
adgnoscimus ea prius quam cernamus non aliter
quam oculis; totidemque sunt hae quot in rerum
natura mortales, et sua cuique sicutfa cies. hinc illa
tot [2] gentium totque linguarum toto orbe diversitas,
hinc tot cantus et moduli flexionesque, sed ante omnia
explanatio animi quae nos distinxit a feris, et inter

---

[1] *Mayhoff*: et.   [2] tot *add. Rackham.*

ᵃ At Rome senators sat here.

the nostrils, but through the nostrils it emits a harsh trumpet sound. In oxen alone the lowing of the females is louder, but in every other kind of animal the females' voice is not so loud as that of the males, even (in the case of the human race) those that have been castrated. The infant gives no sound at birth until it emerges entirely from the womb. It begins to talk when a year old; but Croesus had a son who spoke at six months and while still at the rattle stage, a portent that brought the whole of that realm to downfall. Infants that began to speak quicker are slower in starting to walk. The voice gets stronger at fourteen, but it gets weaker in old age; and it does not alter more often in any other animal.

There are other facts besides about the voice that *Acoustics.* deserve mention. It is absorbed by the sawdust or sand that is thrown down on the floor in the theatre orchestras,[a] and similarly in a place surrounded by rough walls, and it is also deadened by empty casks. Also it runs along a straight or concave surface of wall and carries words although spoken in a low tone to the other end, if no unevenness of the surface hinders it. In a human being the voice *Character* constitutes a large part of the external personality: *of voices.* we recognise a man by it before we see him just in the same way as we recognise him with our eyes; and there are as many varieties of voices as there are mortals in the world, and a person's voice is as distinctive as his face. This is the source of the difference between all the races and all the languages all over the world, and of all the tunes and modulations and inflexions, but before all things of the power of expressing the thoughts that has made us different from the beasts, and has also caused another dis-

ipsos quoque homines discrimen alterum aeque grande quam a beluis fecit.

272 CXIII. Membra animalibus agnata inutilia sunt, sicut sextus homini semper digitus. placuit in Aegypto nutrire portentum, binis et in aversa capitis parte oculis hominem, sed iis non cernentem.

273 CXIV. Miror equidem Aristotelem non modo credidisse praescita vitae esse aliqua in corporibus ipsis verum etiam prodidisse. quae quamquam vana existimo, nec sine cunctatione proferenda ne in se quisque ea auguria anxie quaerat, attingam tamen,

274 quia tantus vir in doctrinis non sprevit. igitur vitae brevis signa ponit raros dentes, praelongos digitos, plumbeum colorem pluresque in manu incisuras nec perpetuas; contra longae esse vitae incurvos umeris et in manu unam aut duas incisuras longas habentis et plures quam xxxii dentes, auribus amplis. nec universa haec, ut arbitror, sed singula observat, frivola, ut reor, et volgo tamen narrata. addidit morum quoque spectus simili modo apud nos Trogus et ipse auctor e severissimis, quos

275 verbis eius subiciam: ' Frons ubi est magna segnem animum subesse significat, quibus parva mobilem,

tinction between human beings themselves that is as wide as that which separates them from the lower animals.

CXIII. When animals are born with extra limbs *Monstrosities.* these are useless, as is always the case when a human being is born with a sixth finger. In Egypt it was decided to rear a monstrosity, a human being with another pair of eyes at the back of the head, though he could not see with these.

CXIV. For my own part I am surprised that *Prognostication from physiological conformation.* Aristotle not only believed but also published his belief that our bodies contain premonitory signs of our career. But although I think this view unfounded, and not proper to be brought forward without hesitation lest everybody should anxiously seek to find these auguries in himself, nevertheless I will touch upon it, because so great a master of the sciences as Aristotle has not despised it. Well then, he puts down as signs of a short life few teeth, very long fingers, a leaden complexion and an exceptional number of broken creases in the hand; and on the other side he says that those people are long-lived who have sloping shoulders, one or two long creases in the hand, more than thirty-two teeth, and large ears. Yet he does not, I imagine, note all these attributes present in one person, but separately, trifling things, as I consider them, though nevertheless commonly talked about. In a similar manner among ourselves Trogus, himself also one of the most critical authorities, has added some outward signs of character which I will append in his own words: ' When the forehead is large it indicates that the mind beneath it is sluggish; people with a small forehead have a nimble mind, those with a round fore-

quibus rotunda iracundum '—velut hoc vestigio
tumoris apparente. ' supercilia quibus porriguntur
in rectum molles significant, quibus iuxta nasum
flexa sunt austeros, quibus iuxta tempora inflexa
derisores, quibus in totum demissa malivolos et
276 invidos. oculi quibus utrimque[1] sunt longi malificos
moribus esse indicant; qui carnosos a naribus
angulos habent malitiae notam praebent; candida
pars extenta notam inpudentiae habet: qui identi-
dem operiri solent inconstantiae. oricularum magnitudo loquacitatis et stultitiae nota est,' hactenus
Trogus.

277   CXV. Animae leonis virus grave, ursi pestilens :
contacta halitu eius nulla fera attingit, ociusque
putrescunt adflata. e reliquis[2] hominis[3] tantum
infici natura voluit plurimis modis, et ciborum ac
dentium vitiis sed maxime senio. dolorem sentire
non potest,[4] tactu esuque[5] omni caret[6] sine quibus[7]
nihil sentitur; eadem commeat ab eo[8] recedens[9]
278 assidue, exitura supremo et sola ex homine superfu-
tura denique. haec trahebatur e caelo: huius quoque tamen reperta poena est, ut neque id ipsum
quo vivitur in vita iuvaret. Parthorum populis haec
praecipue et a iuventa propter indiscretos cibos,
namque et vino fetent ora nimio. sed sibi proceres

<hr>

[1] *Mayhoff ex Aristotele*: quibuscunque.
[2] *sic Mueller*: adflatae (adflatu *Caesarius*) reliquis.
[3] *v.l.* homini.   [4] *Dalec.*: poterat.
[5] *v.l.* sensuque.   [6] *Dalec.*: carebat.
[7] *v.l.* sine qua.   [8] *v.l.* commeabat.
[9] *v.l.* recens.

<hr>

[a] This clause seems to be a comment of Pliny's.

head an irascible mind'—as if this were a visible indication of a swollen temper!^a 'When people's eyebrows are level this signifies that they are gentle, when they are curved at the side of the nose, that they are stern, when bent down at the temples, that they are mockers, when entirely drooping, that they are malevolent and spiteful. If people's eyes are narrow on both sides, this shows them to be malicious in character; eyes that have fleshy corners on the side of the nostrils show a mark of maliciousness; when the white part of the eyes is extensive it conveys an indication of impudence; eyes that have a habit of repeatedly closing indicate unreliability. Large ears are a sign of talkativeness and silliness,' Thus far Trogus.

CXV. The lion's breath contains a severe poison *The breath.* and the bear's is pestilential: no wild animal will touch things that have come in contact with its vapour, and things that it has breathed upon go bad more quickly. Of the remaining species nature has willed that in man alone the breath shall be corrupted in a great many ways, even by bad food and bad teeth, but most of all by old age. The old man cannot feel pain, he lacks all touch and taste, without which there is no sensation at all; his breath comes and goes, constantly retiring from him, ultimately to depart from him and thereafter to be all that remains out of a human being. The breath was a draught drawn from heaven; yet for it also a penalty has been invented, so that even that which is the very means of living may not give us joy in life. This applies specially to the Parthian races, even from youth up, because of their lack of discrimination in diet, for even their mouths smell from too much wine. But their

medentur grano Assyrii mali, cuius est suavitas
praecipua, in esculenta addito.

279   Elephantorum anima serpentes extrahit, cervorum
urit. diximus hominum genera qui venena serpentium suctu corporibus eximerent. quin et subus
serpentes in pabulo sunt, et aliis[1] venenum est.
quae insecta appellavimus, omnia olei aspersu
necantur, vultures unguento (qui fugat alios appetunt
odorem), scarabaei rosa. quasdam serpentes scorpio
occidit. Scythae sagittas tingunt viperina sanie et
humano sanguine; inremediabile id scelus : mortem
ilico affert levi tactu.

280   CXVI. Quae animalium pascerentur veneno diximus. quaedam innocua alioqui venenatis pasta
noxia fiunt et ipsa. apros in Pamphylia et Ciliciae
montuosis salamandra ab his devorata qui edere
moriuntur, neque enim est intellectus ullus in odore
vel sapore; et aqua vinumque interimit[2] salamandra
ibi inmortua, vel si omnino unde biberit[3] potetur;
item rana quam rubetam vocant :   tantum
281   insidiarum est vitae! vespae serpente avide vescuntur, quo alimento mortiferos ictus faciunt.
adeoque magna differentia est victus ut in tractu
pisce viventium Theophrastus prodat boves quoque
pisce vesci, sed non nisi vivente.

282   CXVII. Homini cibus utilissimus simplex, acer-
vatio saporum pestifera et condimento perniciosior.

---

¹ et aliis *corruptum* : nec alvo ? *Mayhoff.*
² *v.l.* interemit.   ³ *Dalec.* : biberit unde.

ᵃ VII. 13 sq.
ᵇ Perhaps the text should be altered to give ' and to their
stomach it is not poisonous.'
ᶜ X. 69.

upper classes use as a remedy the seed of the citron-tree, which has a remarkably sweet aroma, adding it to their food.

The breath of elephants attracts snakes out of *Poisons.* their holes, that of stags scorches them. We have mentioned *a* the races of men that rid their bodies of snakes' poison by sucking it out. Moreover swine will eat snakes, and to other animals it is poison.*b* The creatures we have designated insects can all be killed by sprinkling with oil; vultures are killed by ointment (they are attracted by the scent, which repels other birds), and beetles by a rose. A scorpion kills some snakes. In Scythia the natives poison their arrows with vipers' venom and human blood; this nefarious practice makes a wound incurable—by a light touch it causes instant death.

CXVI. We have said *c* which animals feed on poison. *Transmission of poison.* Some otherwise harmless species after feeding on poisonous things become harmful themselves also. In Pamphylia and the mountain regions of Cilicia people who eat boars when these have devoured a salamander die, for there is no indication in the smell or taste; also water or wine when a salamander has died in it is fatal, and so is even drinking from a vessel out of which one has drunk; and similarly with the kind of frog called a toad! so full of traps is life! Wasps devour a snake greedily, and by so doing make their sting fatal. And so widely does diet vary that according to Theophrastus in a district where people live on fish the cattle also eat fish, but only live fish.

CXVII. Simple food is the most serviceable for a *Gastronomy.* human being—an accumulation of flavours is unwholesome, and more harmful than sauces. But it is

difficulter autem perficiuntur omnia in cibis acria, aspera, inconsueta, varia, nimia et avide hausta, et aestate quam hieme difficilius, et in senecta quam iuventa. vomitiones homini ad haec in remedium excogitatae frigidiora corpora faciunt, inimicae oculis maxime ac dentibus.

283 Somno concoquere corpulentiae quam firmitati utilius; ideo athletas ambulatione malunt cibos perficere: pervigilio quidem praecipue vincuntur cibi. CXVIII. augescunt corpora dulcibus atque pinguibus et potis, minuuntur siccis et aridis frigidisque ac siti. quaedam animalia et pecudes quoque in Africa quarto die bibunt. homini non utique septimo letalis inedia; durasse et ultra undecimum plerosque certum est. morbus esuriendi semper inexplebili aviditate uni animalium homini.

284 CXIX. Quaedam rursus exiguo gustu famem ac vitim sedant conservantque vires, ut batyrum, hippace, glycyrrhiza. perniciosissimum autem et in omni quidem vita quod nimium, praecipue tamen corpori, minimeque quod gravet quolibet modo utilius.

Verum ad reliqua naturae transeamus.

---

a It must be remembered that in the Latin idiom Wednesday would be called ' the fourth day ' after Sunday, Monday being *secundus*, ' the following day,' and Tuesday *tertius*.

difficult completely to digest all the components contained in articles of food, all that is sharp or rough or unusual or varied, or excessive in quantity and swallowed greedily; and it is more difficult in summer than in winter, and in old age than in youth. The emetics that have been devised for digestive troubles have a chilling effect on the body, and are extremely bad for the eyes and the teeth.

To digest one's food while asleep is more con- *Digestion.* ducive to corpulence than to strength, and conse- *Abstinence* *and* quently it is thought preferable for men in training *moderation.* to assist their digestion by taking a walk; at all events food is most thoroughly assimilated while keeping awake. CXVIII. Sweet and fat foods and drinking add bulk, whereas dry and lean and cold foods and thirst reduce it. Some animals and also domestic cattle in Africa only drink once in three *a* days. Starvation is not fatal to a human being after even five days; it is certain that a good many people have actually endured it more than ten days. Man is the only animal liable to the disease of a continuously insatiable appetite.

CXIX. Again some things tasted in a very small quantity allay hunger and thirst and conserve the strength, for instance butter, mare's milk cheese, liquorice root. But anything in excess is exceedingly detrimental, even in all departments of life, but particularly to the body, and it pays better to reduce the quantity of what is in any manner burdensome.

But let us pass on to the remaining branches of Natural Science.

INDEX

PERSONS

A few biographical details are given to supplement those in the text

613

INDEX

INDEX

INDEX